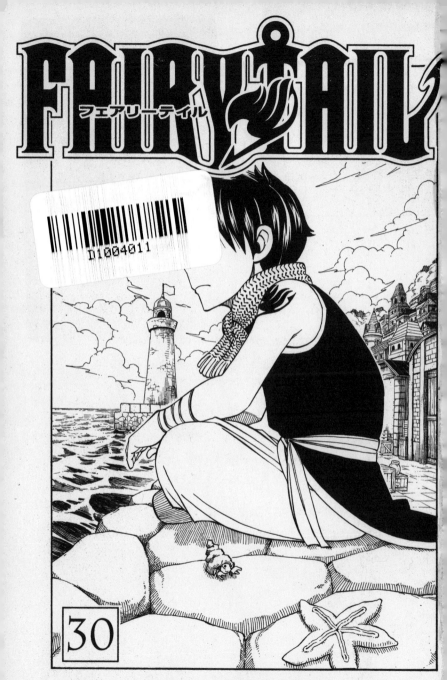

FAIRY TAIL
フェアリーテイル

30

HIRO MASHIMA

FAIRY TAIL 30 CONTENTS

FAIRY TAIL

フェアリーテイル

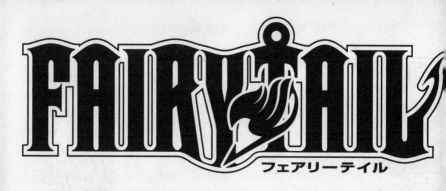

Chapter 249: Magic Is Alive

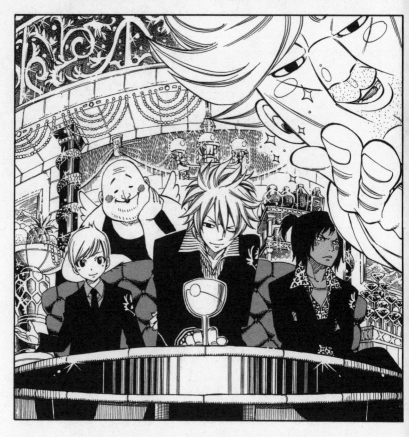

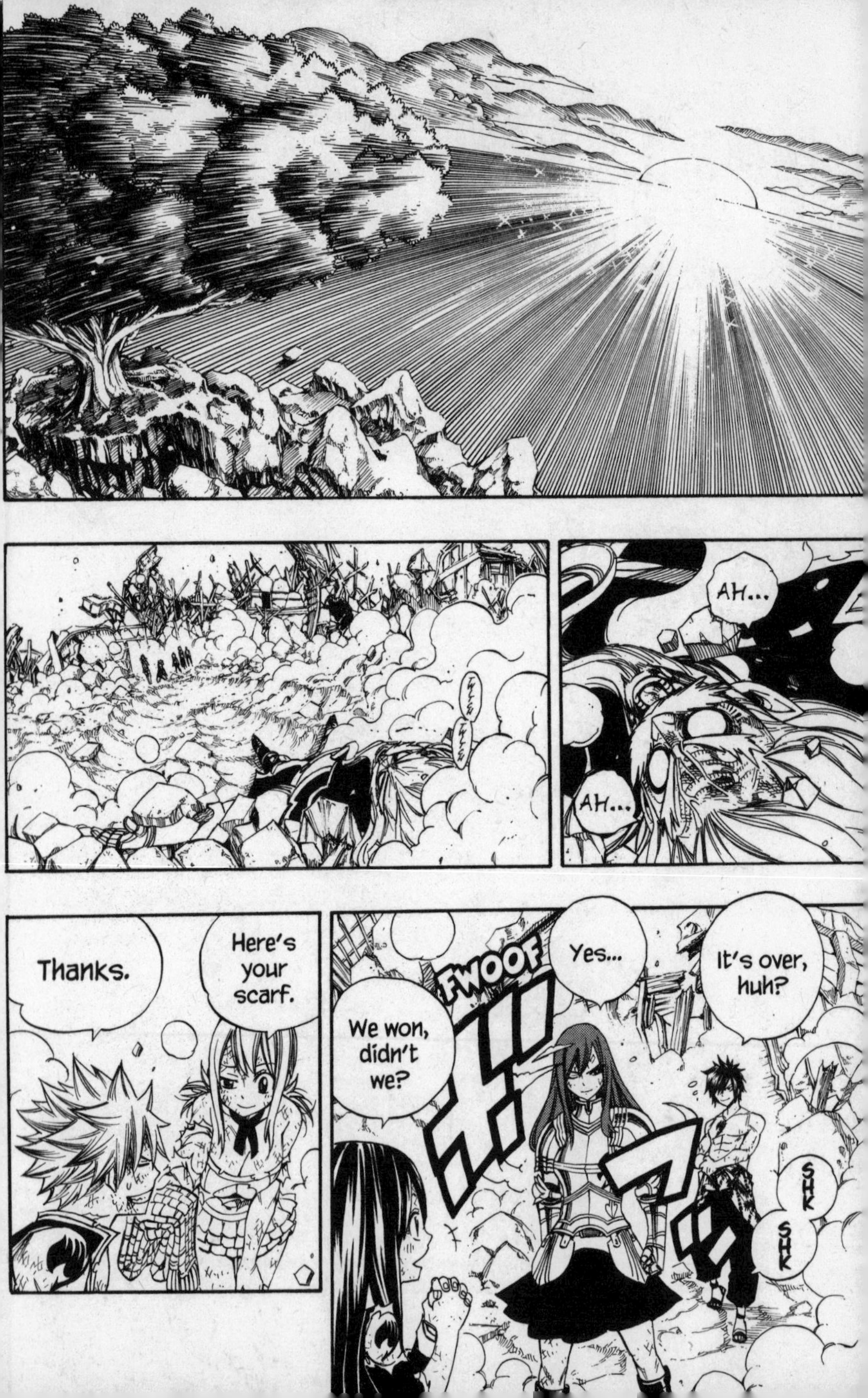
AH...
AH...
It's over, huh?
Yes...
FWOOF
We won, didn't we?
SHK
SHK
Here's your scarf.
Thanks.

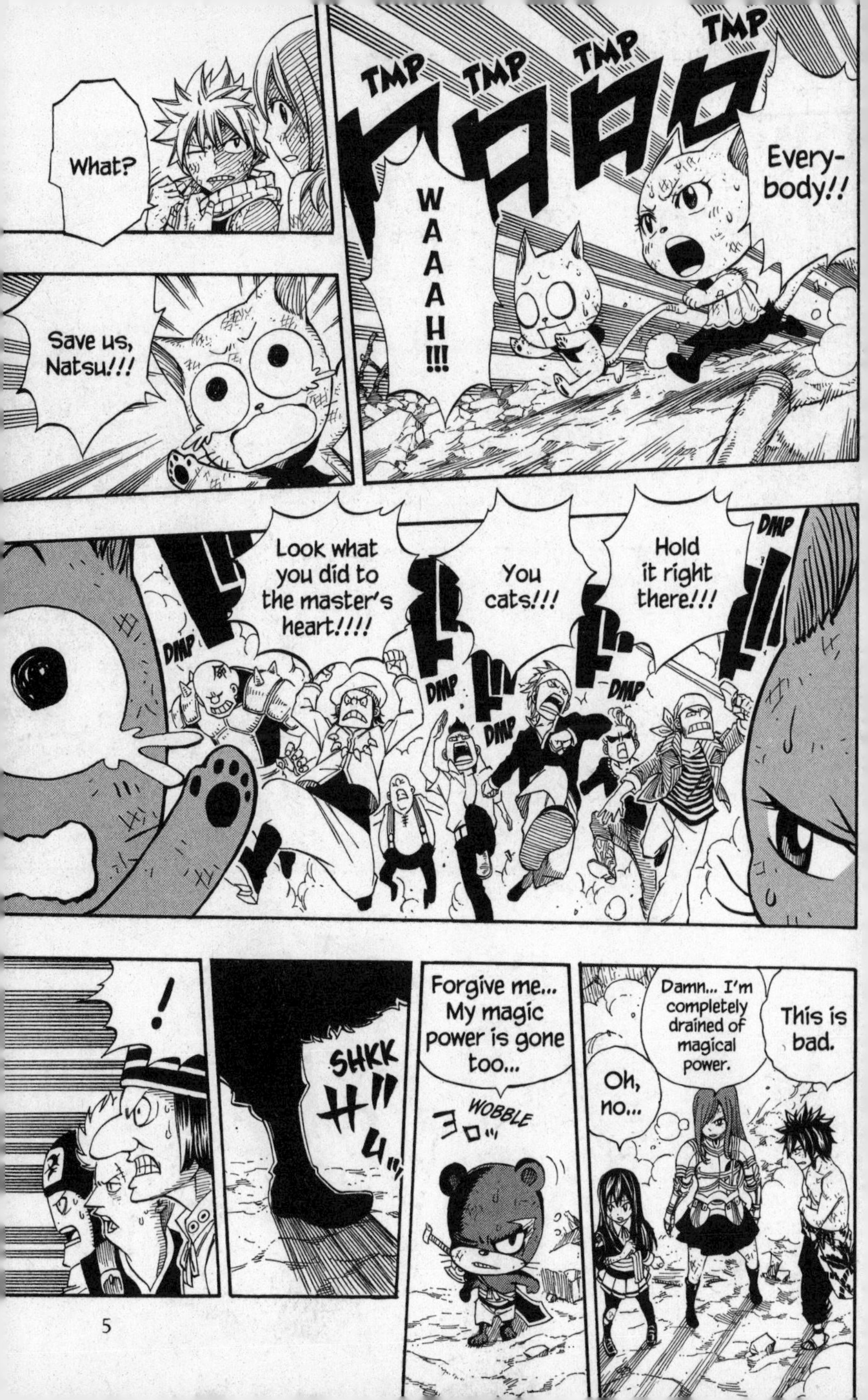
TMP TMP TMP TMP
Every-body!!
WAAAAH!!!
What?
Save us, Natsu!!!
DMP
Hold it right there!!!
You cats!!!
Look what you did to the master's heart!!!!
DMP
DMP
DMP
DMP
This is bad.
Damn... I'm completely drained of magical power.
Oh, no...
Forgive me... My magic power is gone too...
WOBBLE
ヨロッ
SHKK
!

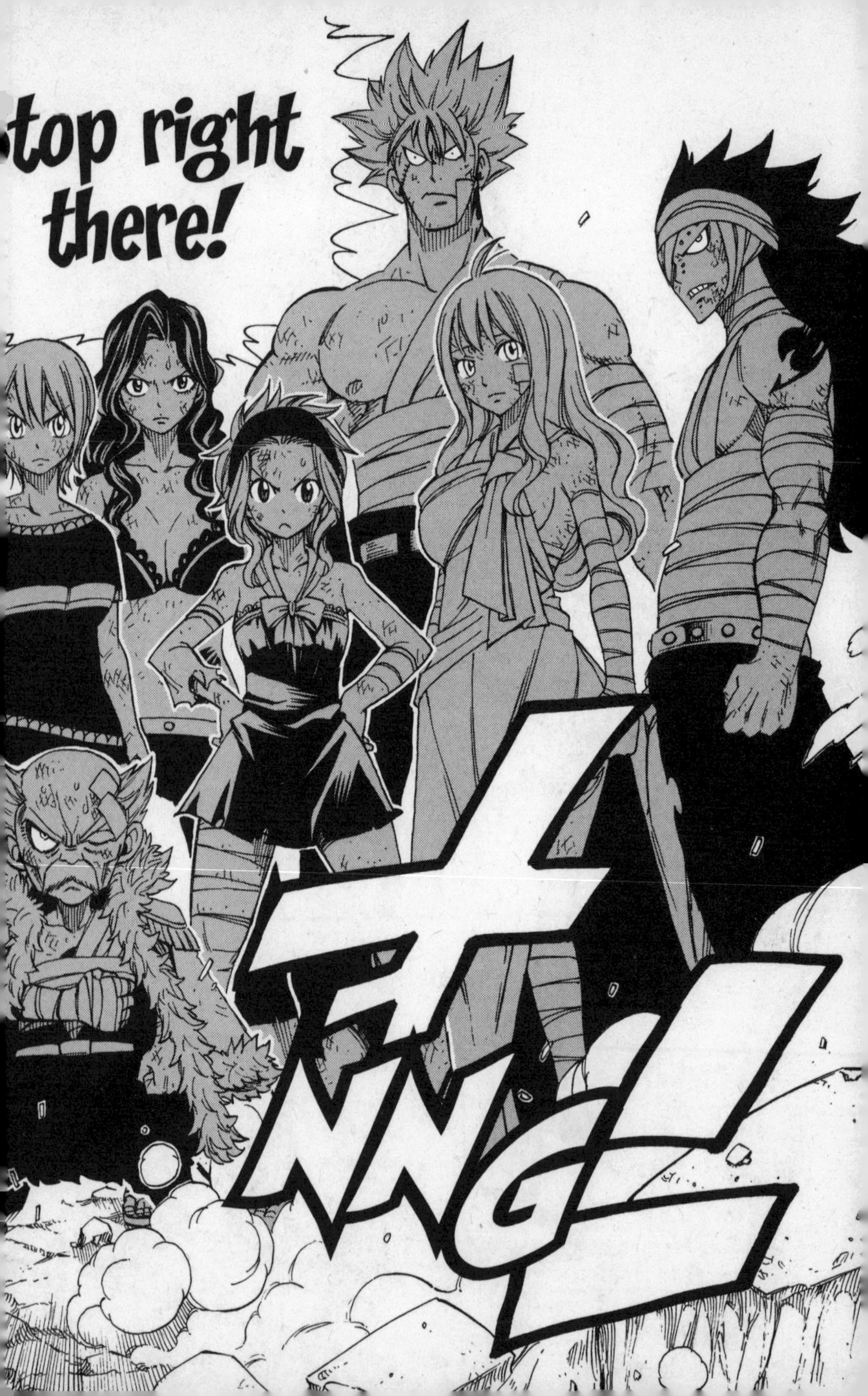

Stop right there!
FA-WNG!

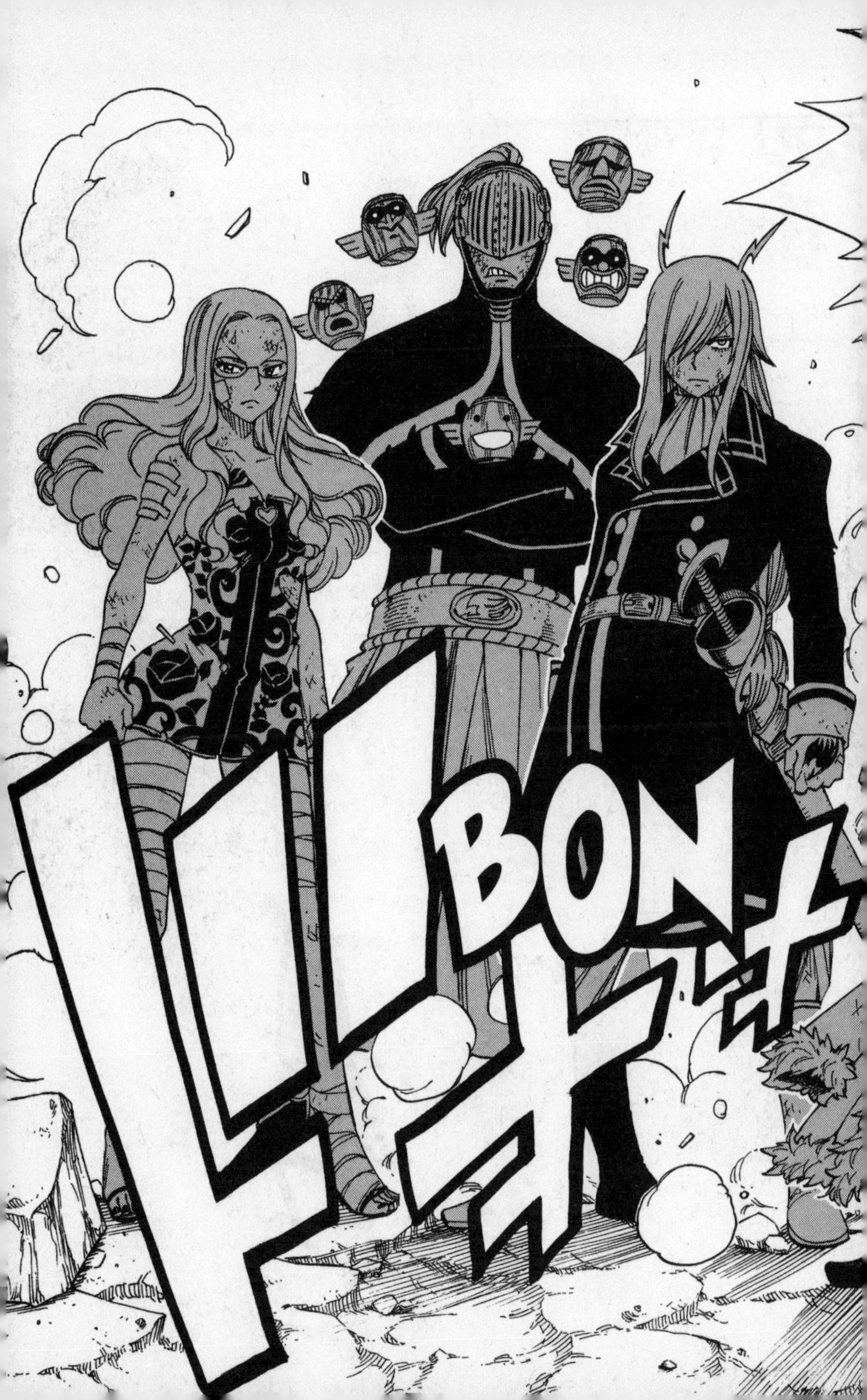
BON

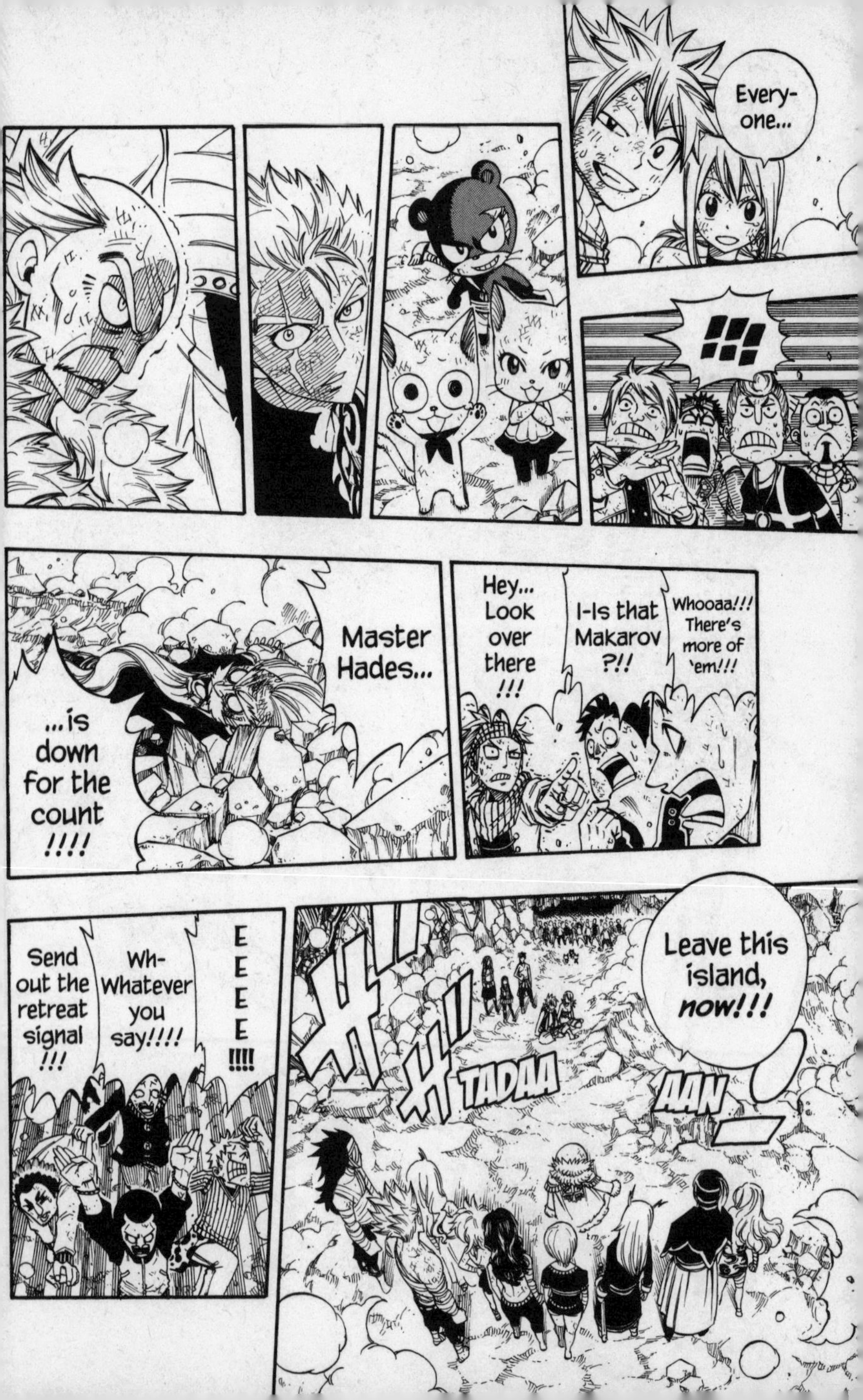
Every-one...
Whooaa!!! There's more of 'em!!!
I-Is that Makarov ?!!
Hey... Look over there !!!
Master Hades...
...is down for the count !!!!
Leave this island, now!!!
TADAA
AAN
EEEE !!!!
Wh- Whatever you say!!!!
Send out the retreat signal !!!

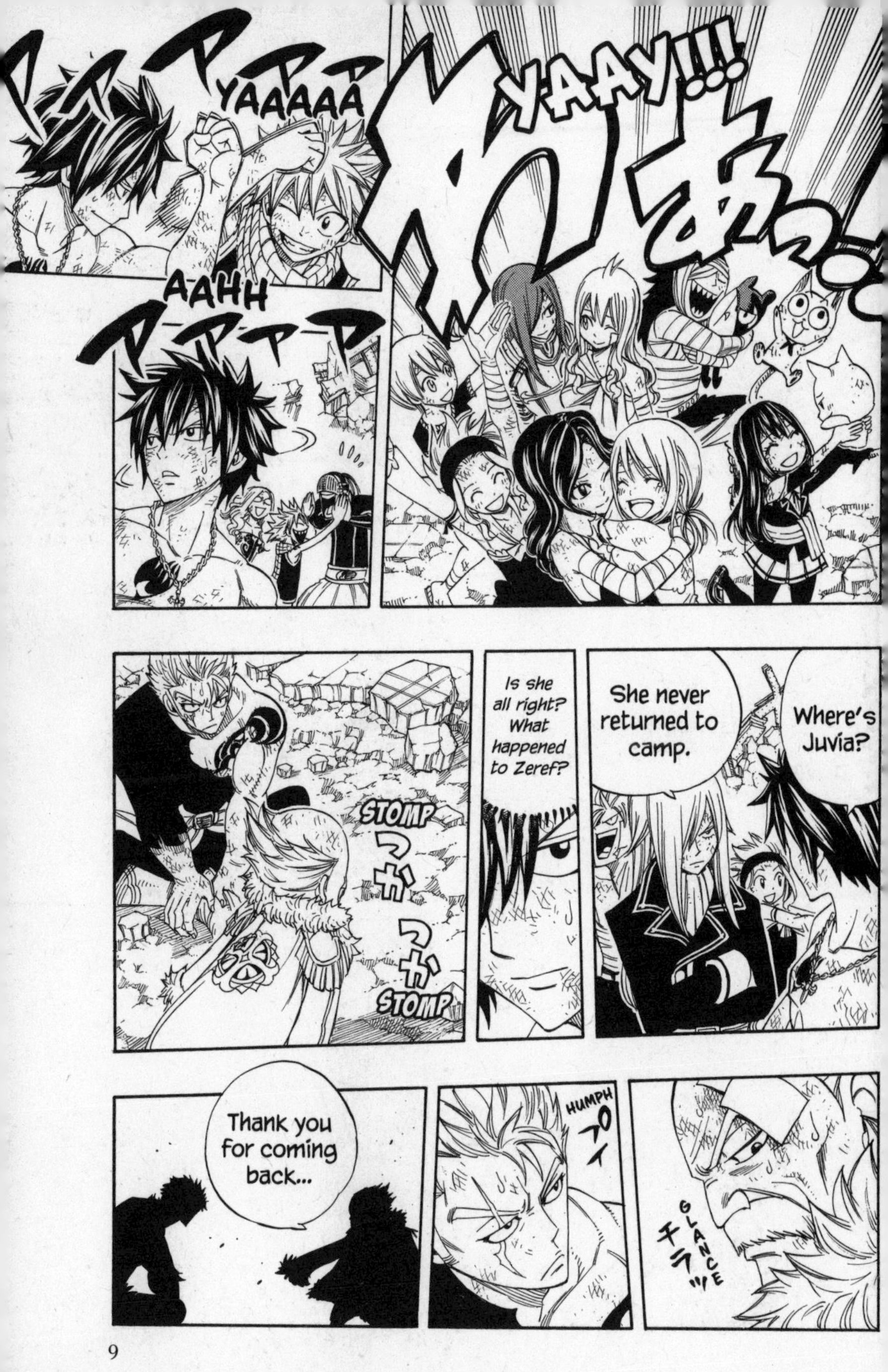
YAAY!!!
YAAAAA
AAHH
Where's Juvia?
She never returned to camp.
Is she all right? What happened to Zeref?
STOMP
STOMP
GLANCE
HUMPH
Thank you for coming back...

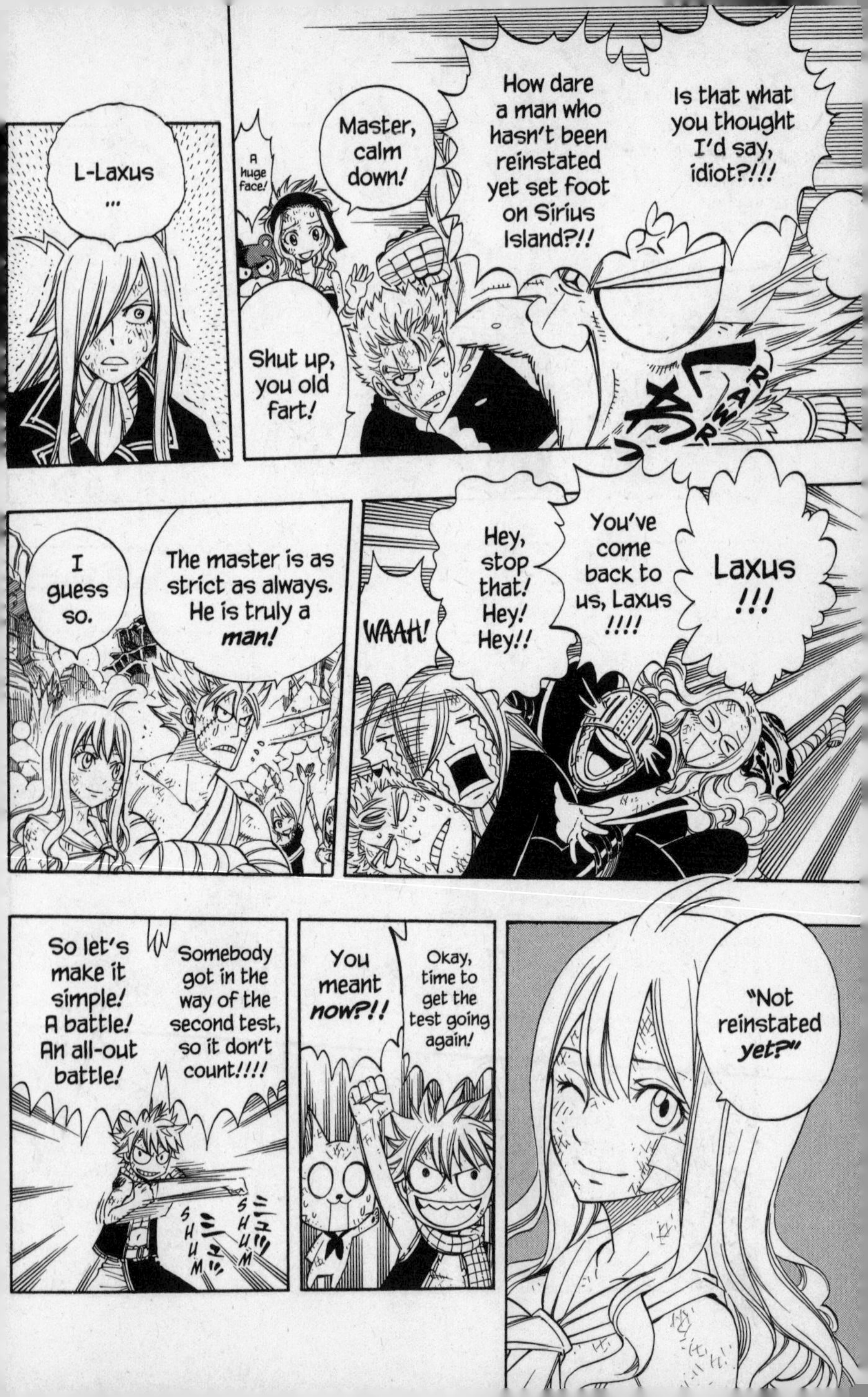
Is that what you thought I'd say, idiot?!!!
How dare a man who hasn't been reinstated yet set foot on Sirius Island?!!
RAWR
Master, calm down!
A huge face!
Shut up, you old fart!
L-Laxus ...
Laxus !!!
You've come back to us, Laxus !!!!
Hey, stop that! Hey! Hey!!
WAAH!
The master is as strict as always. He is truly a *man!*
I guess so.
"Not reinstated *yet?*"
Okay, time to get the test going again!
You meant *now?!!*
Somebody got in the way of the second test, so it don't count!!!!
So let's make it simple! A battle! An all-out battle!
SHUM
SHUM

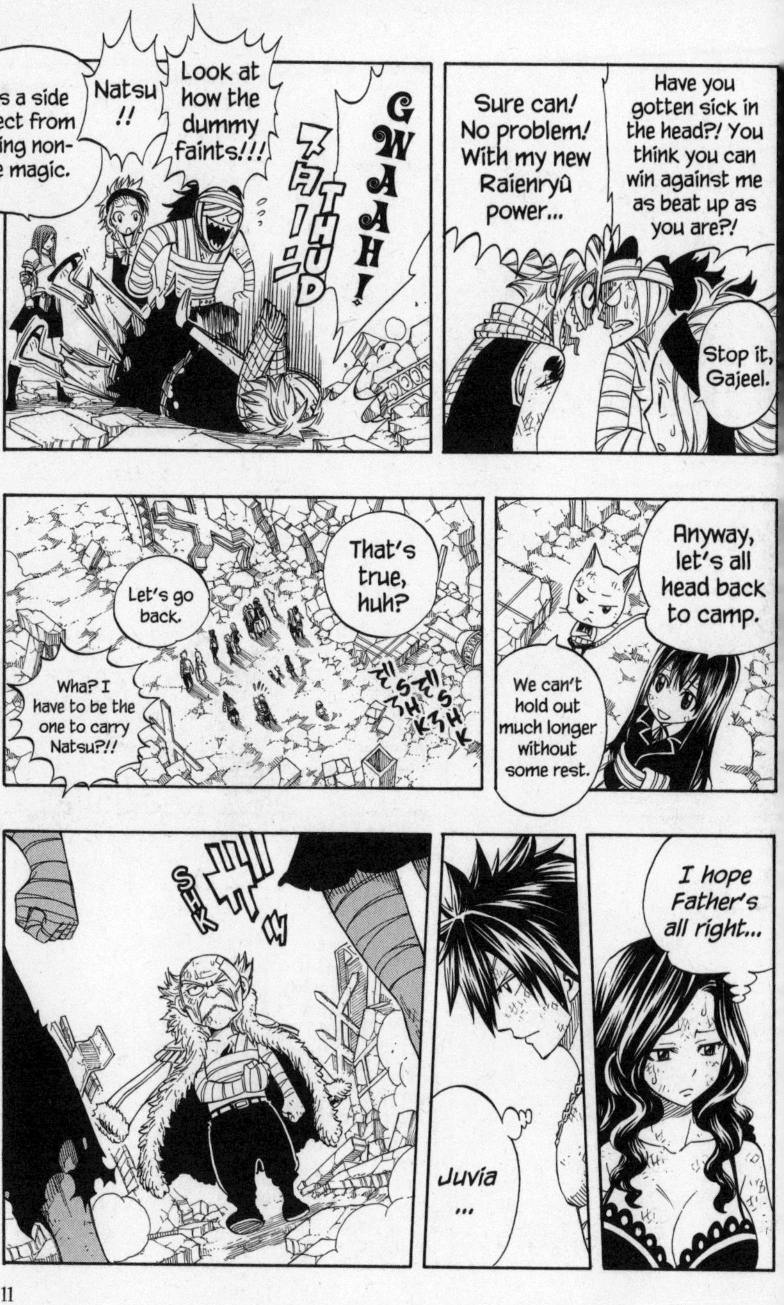
Have you gotten sick in the head?! You think you can win against me as beat up as you are?!
Sure can! No problem! With my new Raienryû power...
Stop it, Gajeel.
GWAAH!
THUD
Look at how the dummy faints!!!
Natsu !!
It is a side effect from eating non-fire magic.
Anyway, let's all head back to camp.
We can't hold out much longer without some rest.
That's true, huh?
SHK SHK
Let's go back.
Wha? I have to be the one to carry Natsu?!!
I hope Father's all right...
Juvia ...
SHK

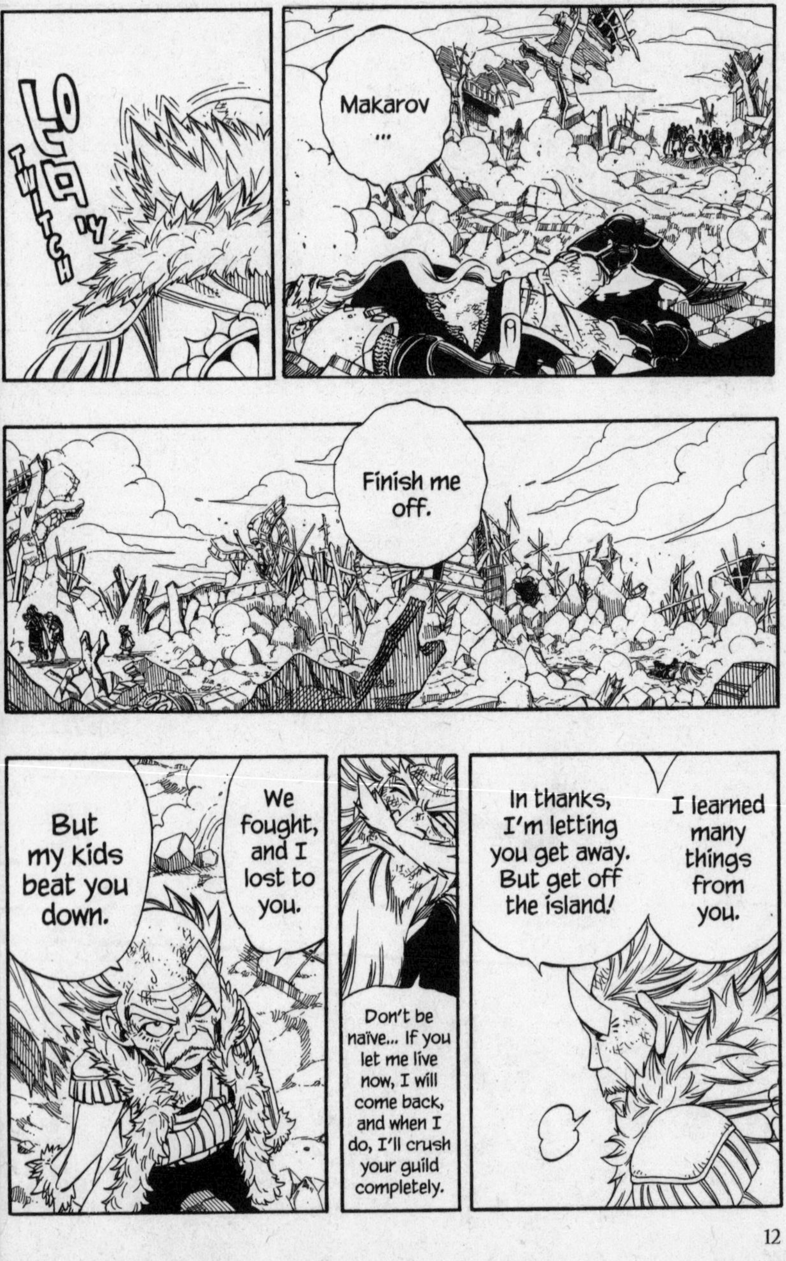
Makarov ...
TWITCH
Finish me off.
I learned many things from you.
In thanks, I'm letting you get away. But get off the island!
Don't be naïve... If you let me live now, I will come back, and when I do, I'll crush your guild completely.
We fought, and I lost to you.
But my kids beat you down.

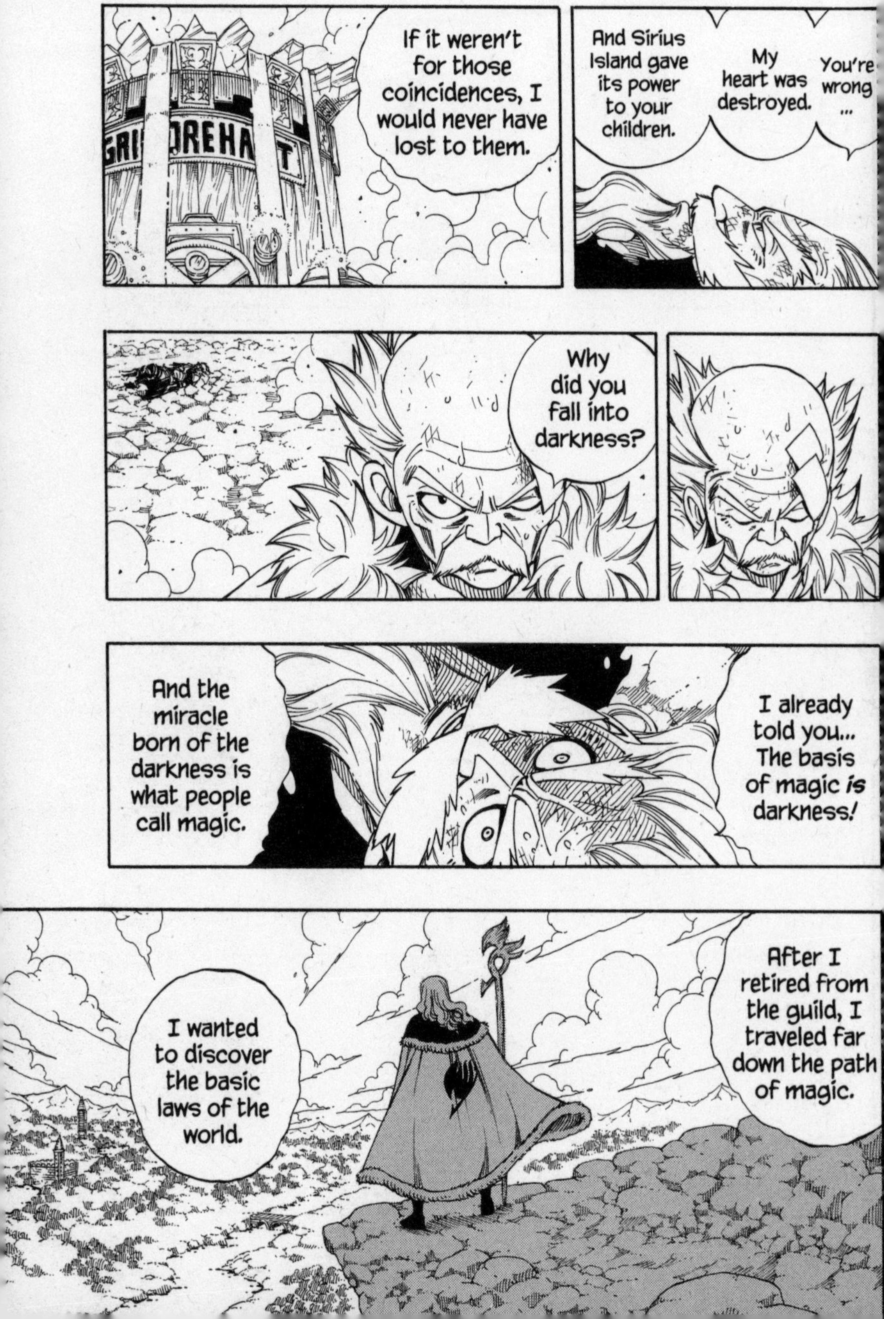
You're wrong ...
My heart was destroyed.
And Sirius Island gave its power to your children.
If it weren't for those coincidences, I would never have lost to them.
Why did you fall into darkness?
I already told you... The basis of magic *is* darkness!
And the miracle born of the darkness is what people call magic.
After I retired from the guild, I traveled far down the path of magic.
I wanted to discover the basic laws of the world.

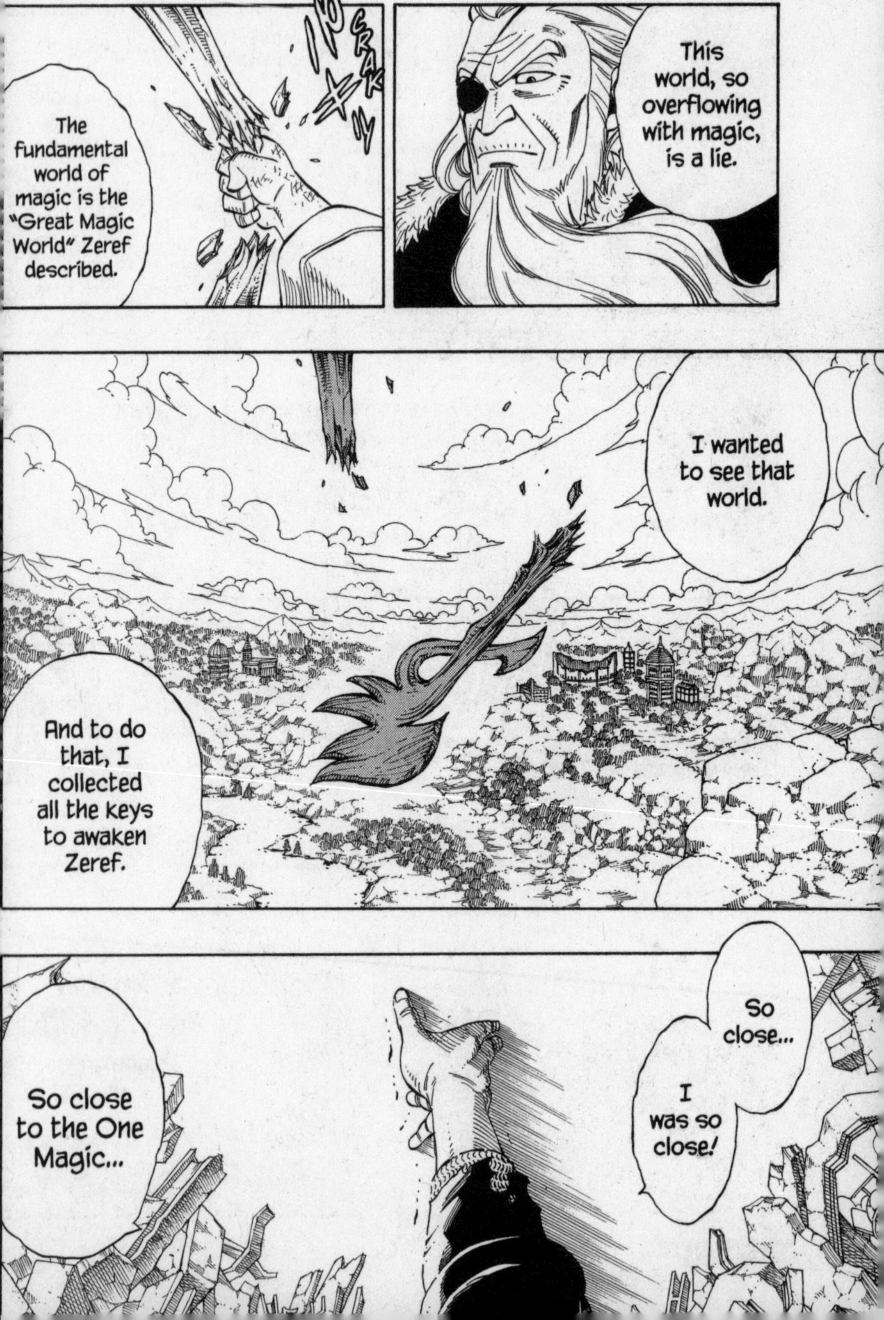
This world, so overflowing with magic, is a lie.
CRAK
The fundamental world of magic is the "Great Magic World" Zeref described.
I wanted to see that world.
And to do that, I collected all the keys to awaken Zeref.
So close...
I was so close!
So close to the One Magic...

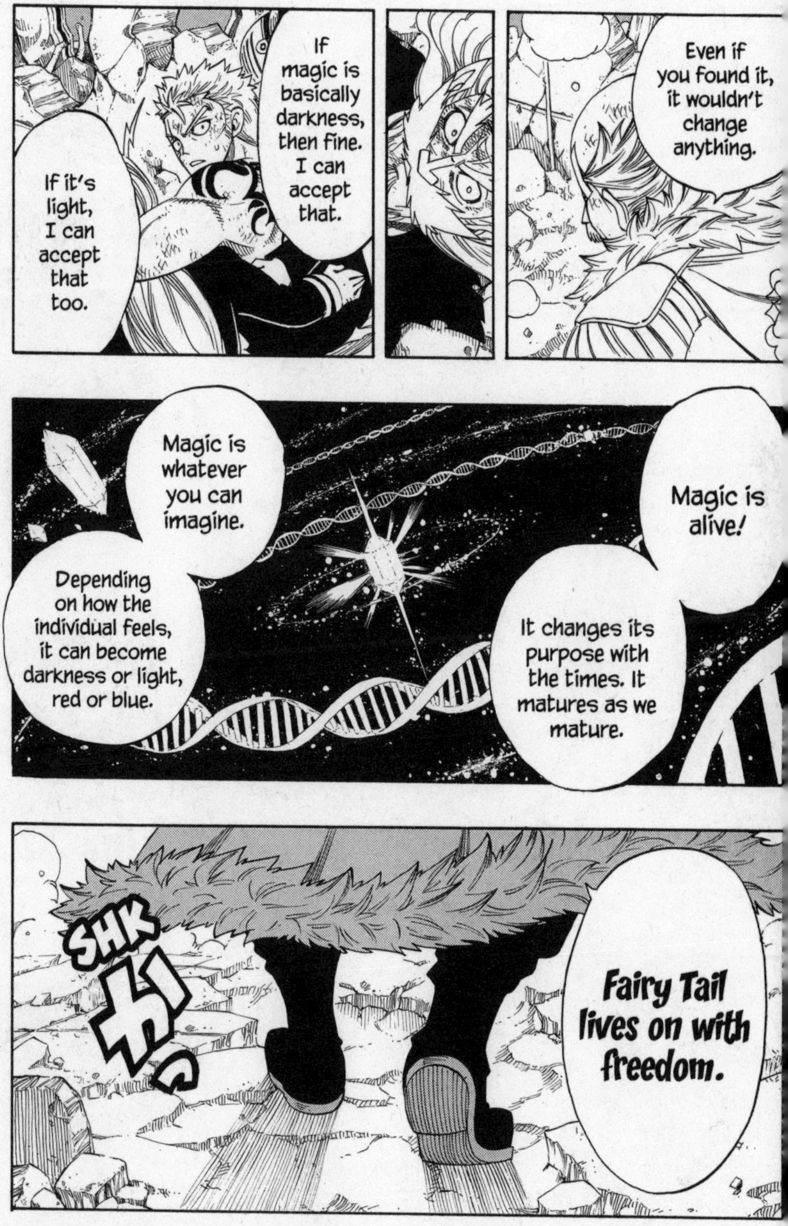
Even if you found it, it wouldn't change anything.
If magic is basically darkness, then fine. I can accept that.
If it's light, I can accept that too.
Magic is alive!
It changes its purpose with the times. It matures as we mature.
Magic is whatever you can imagine.
Depending on how the individual feels, it can become darkness or light, red or blue.
Fairy Tail lives on with freedom.
SHK

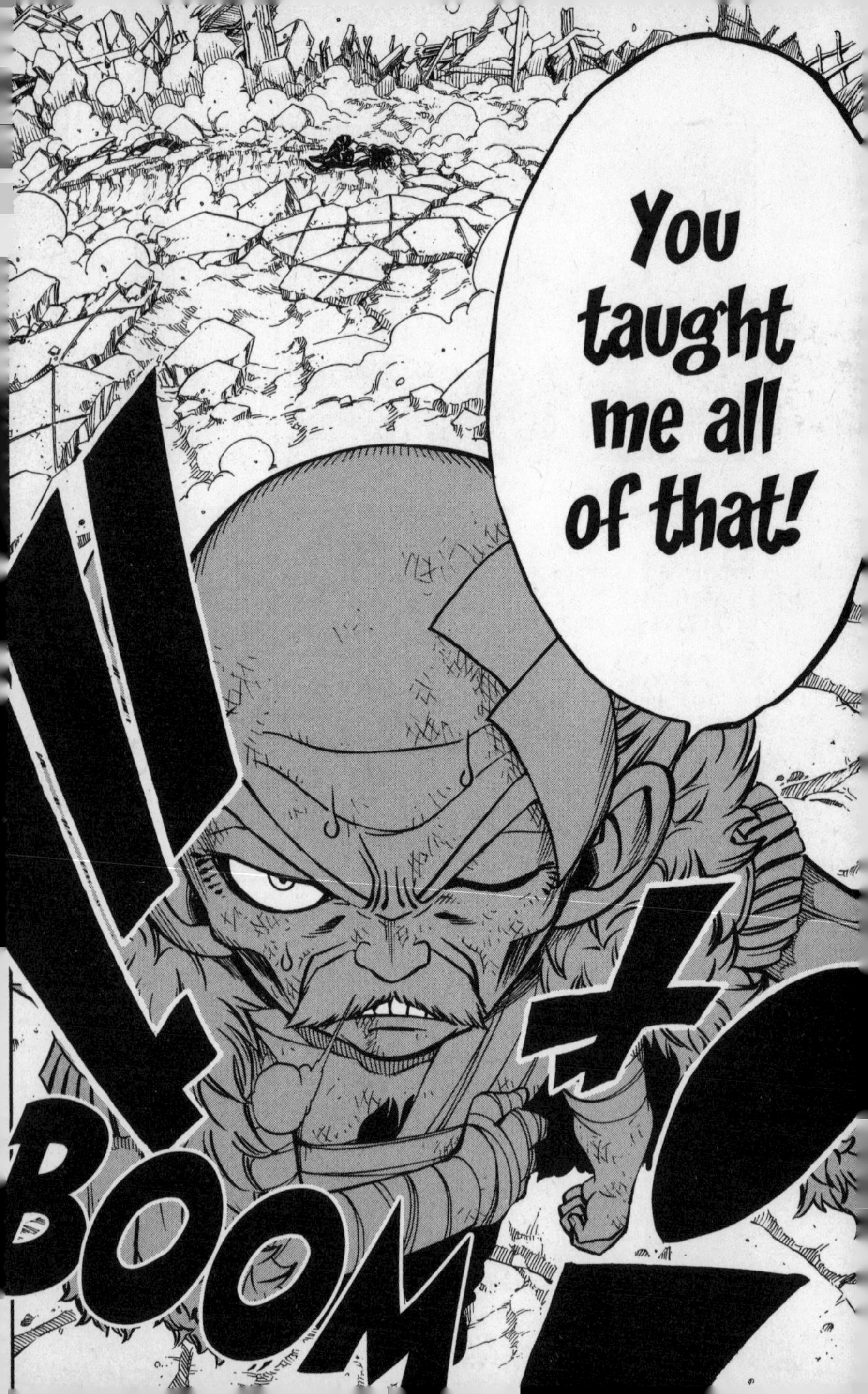
You taught me all of that!
BOOM

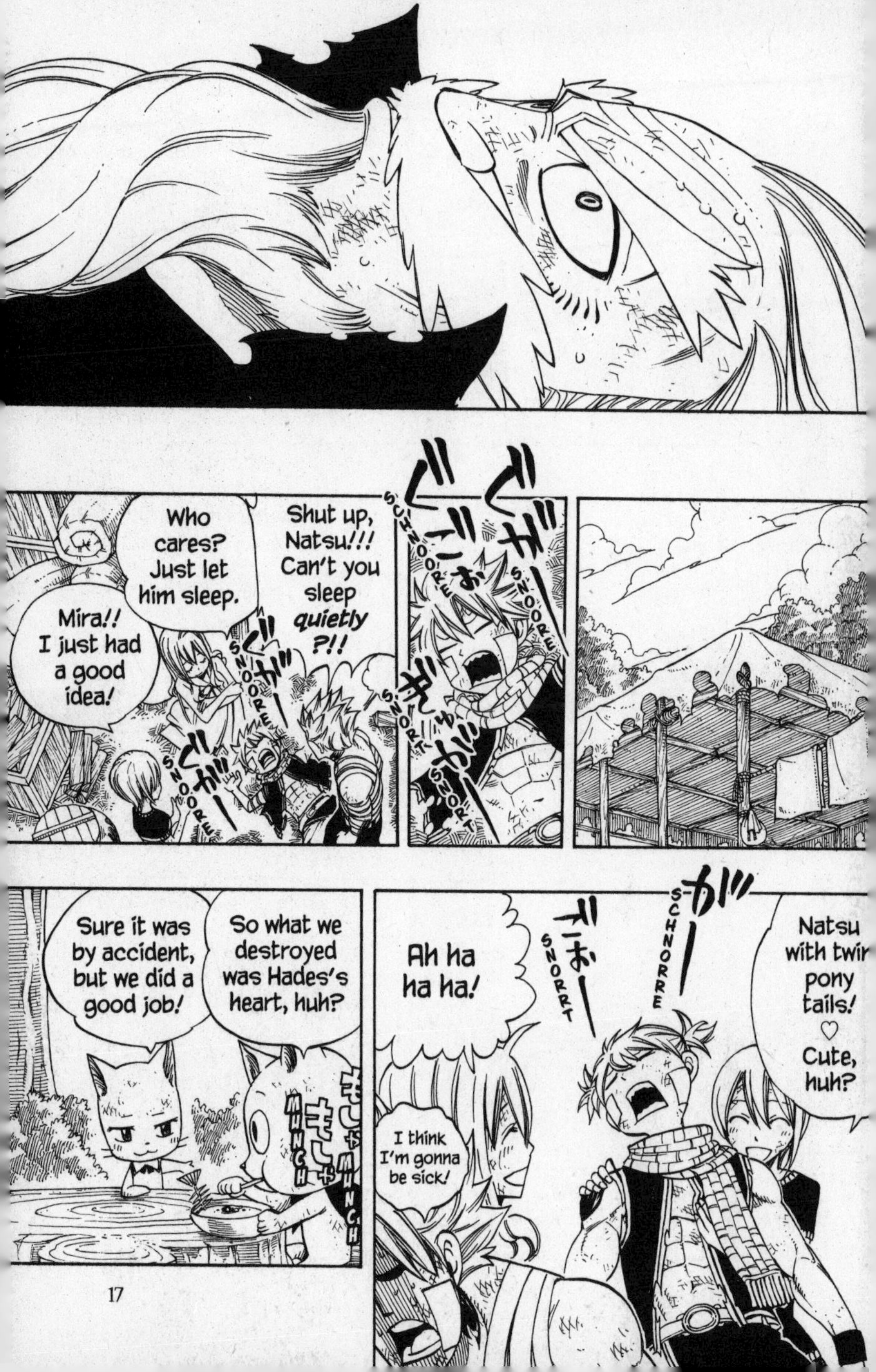
SCHNOORE
SNOORE
SNORT
SNORT
Shut up, Natsu!!! Can't you sleep quietly?!!
Who cares? Just let him sleep.
Mira!! I just had a good idea!
SNOORE
SNOORE
Natsu with twin pony tails! ♡ Cute, huh?
SCHNORRE
SNORRT
Ah ha ha ha!
I think I'm gonna be sick!
So what we destroyed was Hades's heart, huh?
Sure it was by accident, but we did a good job!
MUNCH
MUNCH

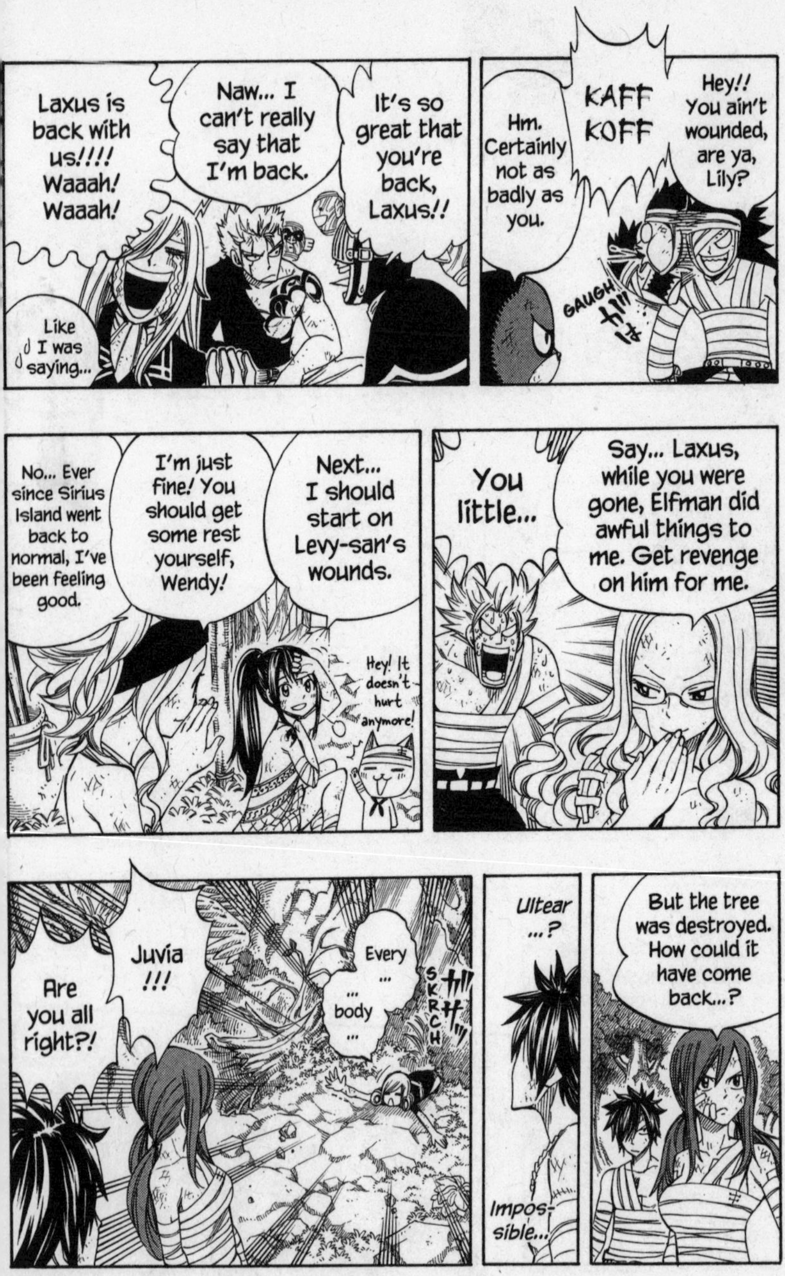
Hey!! You ain't wounded, are ya, Lily?
KAFF KOFF
Hm. Certainly not as badly as you.
GAUGH
It's so great that you're back, Laxus!!
Naw... I can't really say that I'm back.
Laxus is back with us!!!! Waaah! Waaah!
Like I was saying...
Say... Laxus, while you were gone, Elfman did awful things to me. Get revenge on him for me.
You little...
Next... I should start on Levy-san's wounds.
Hey! It doesn't hurt anymore!
I'm just fine! You should get some rest yourself, Wendy!
No... Ever since Sirius Island went back to normal, I've been feeling good.
But the tree was destroyed. How could it have come back...?
Ultear ...?
Impossible...
SKRCH
Every ... ... body ...
Juvia !!!
Are you all right?!

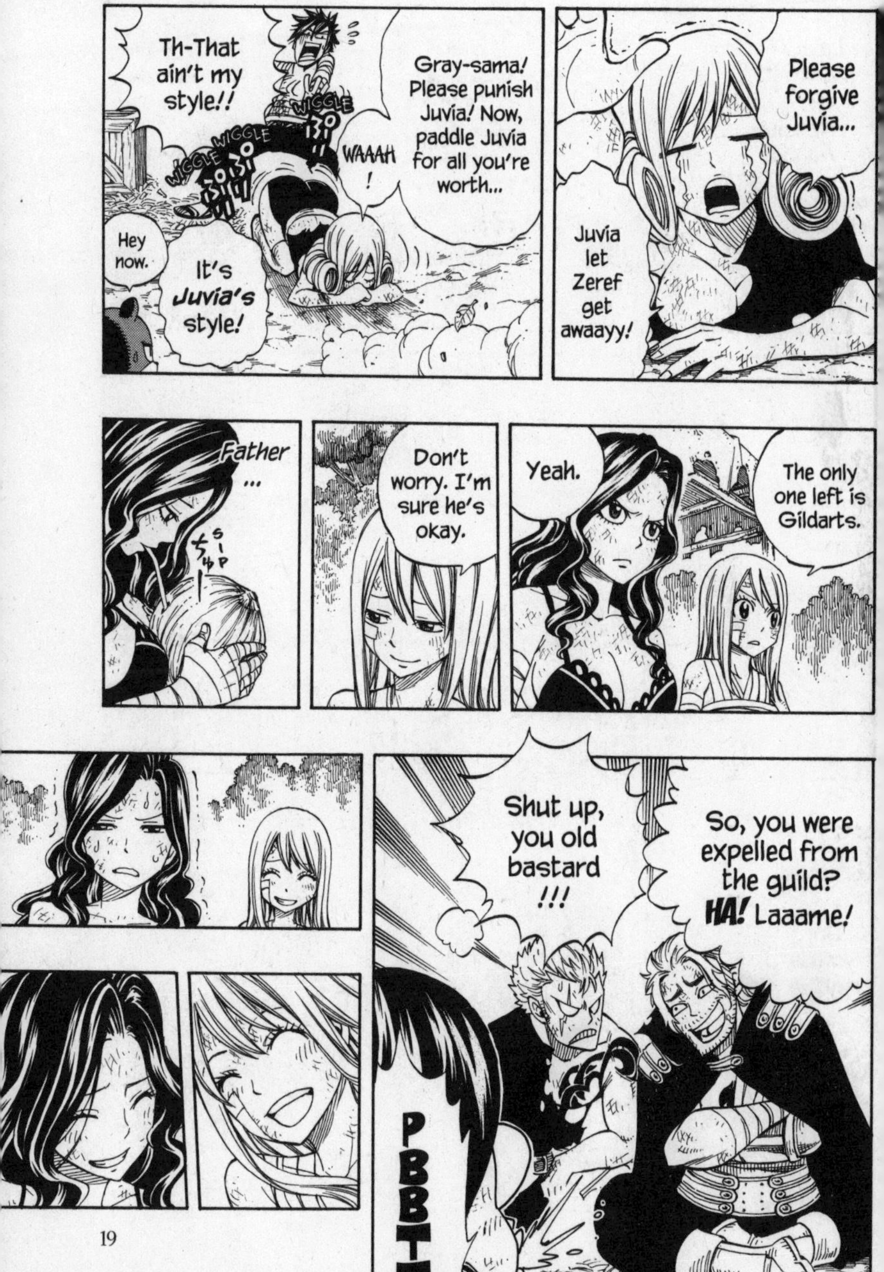
Please forgive Juvia...
Juvia let Zeref get awaaayy!
Gray-sama! Please punish Juvia! Now, paddle Juvia for all you're worth...
WAAAH!
WIGGLE
WIGGLE
WIGGLE
Th-That ain't my style!!
It's Juvia's style!
Hey now.
The only one left is Gildarts.
Yeah.
Don't worry. I'm sure he's okay.
Father ...
SIP
So, you were expelled from the guild? HA! Laaame!
Shut up, you old bastard!!!
PBBTT

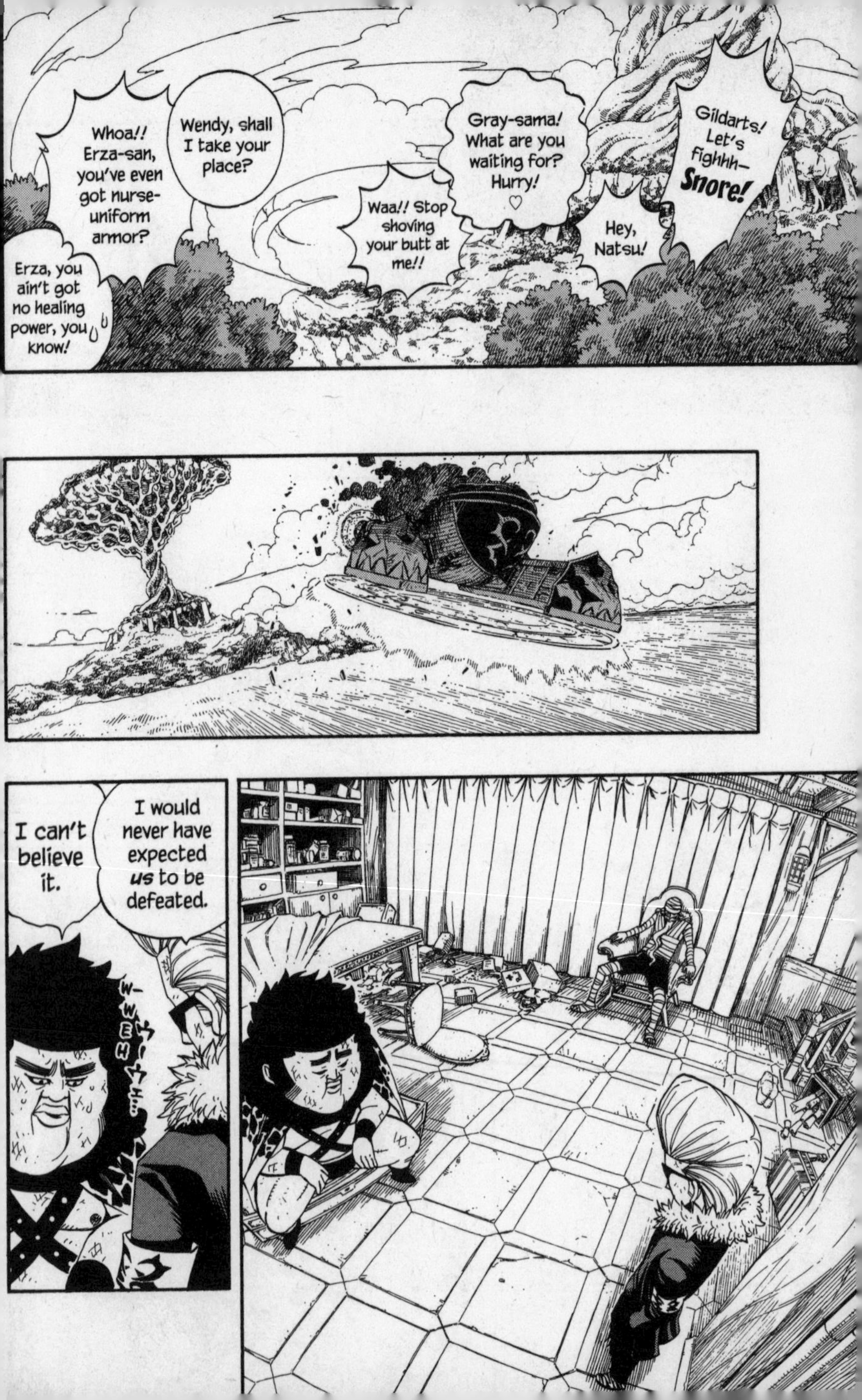

Gildarts! Let's fighhh— Snore!
Hey, Natsu!
Gray-sama! What are you waiting for? Hurry! ♡
Waa!! Stop shoving your butt at me!!
Wendy, shall I take your place?
Whoa!! Erza-san, you've even got nurse-uniform armor?
Erza, you ain't got no healing power, you know!
I would never have expected us to be defeated.
I can't believe it.
W-WEH...

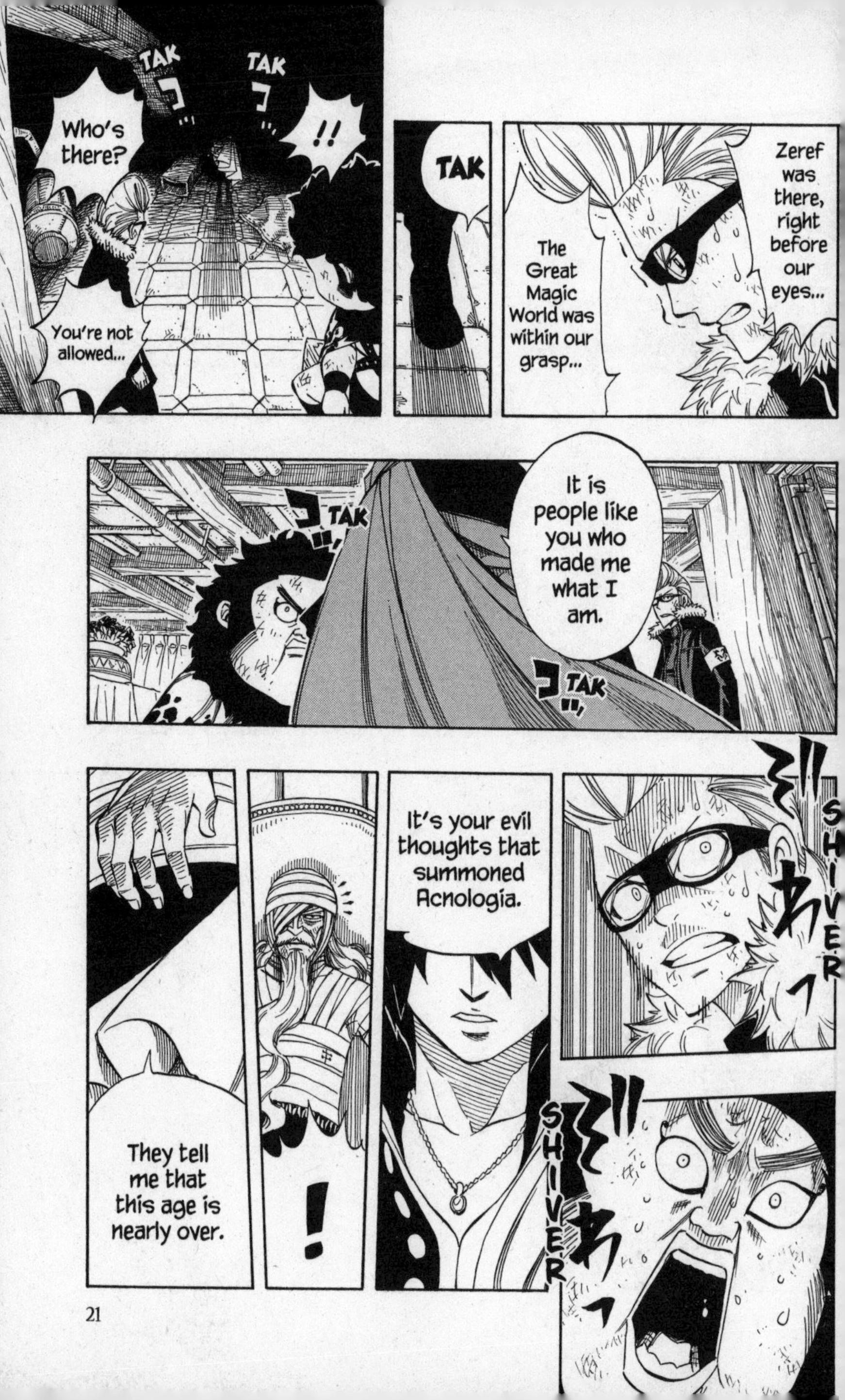
Zeref was there, right before our eyes...
The Great Magic World was within our grasp...
TAK
TAK
TAK
!!
Who's there?
You're not allowed...
TAK
It is people like you who made me what I am.
TAK
SHIVER
It's your evil thoughts that summoned Acnologia.
SHIVER
!
They tell me that this age is nearly over.

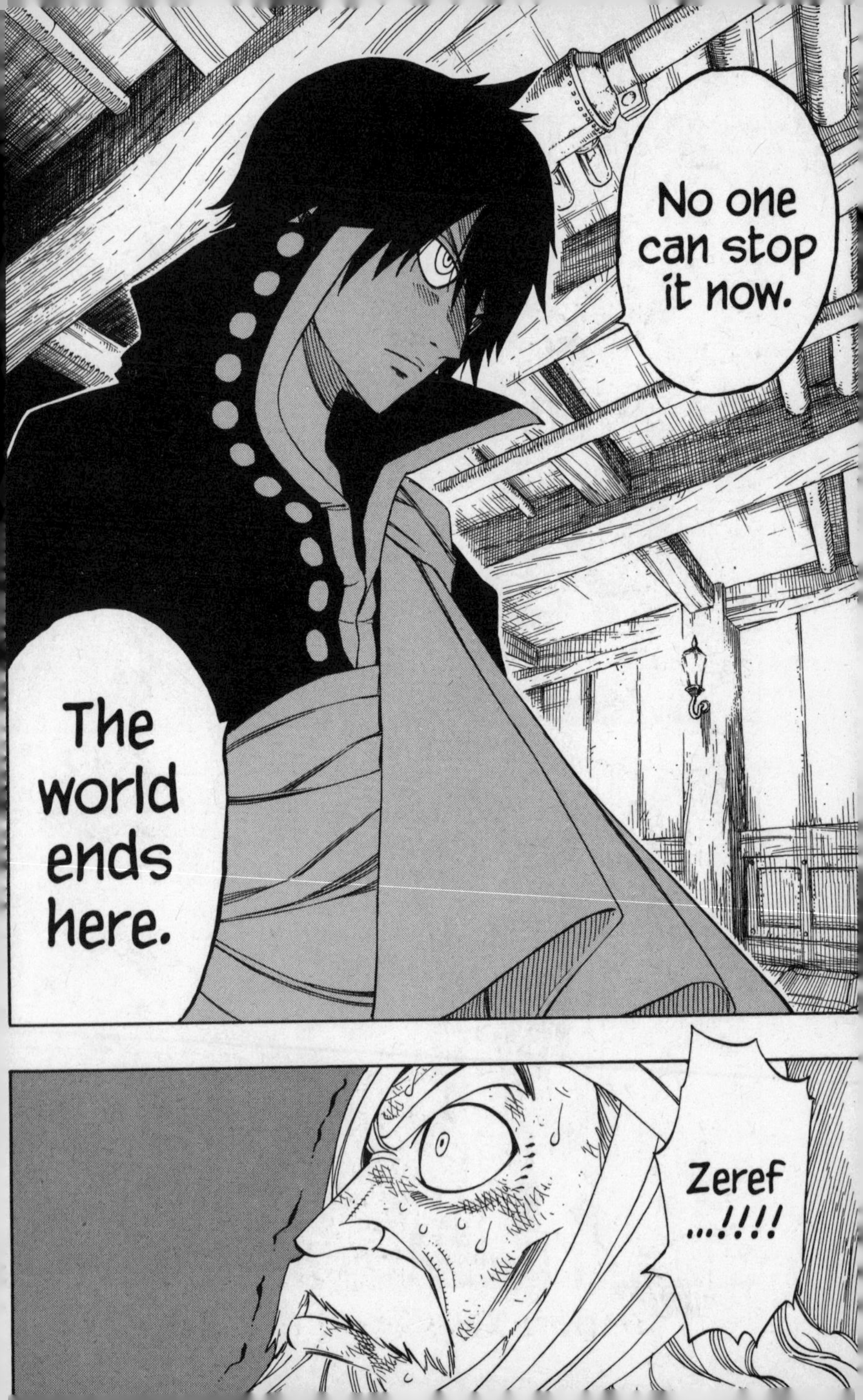
No one can stop it now.
The world ends here.
Zeref ...!!!!

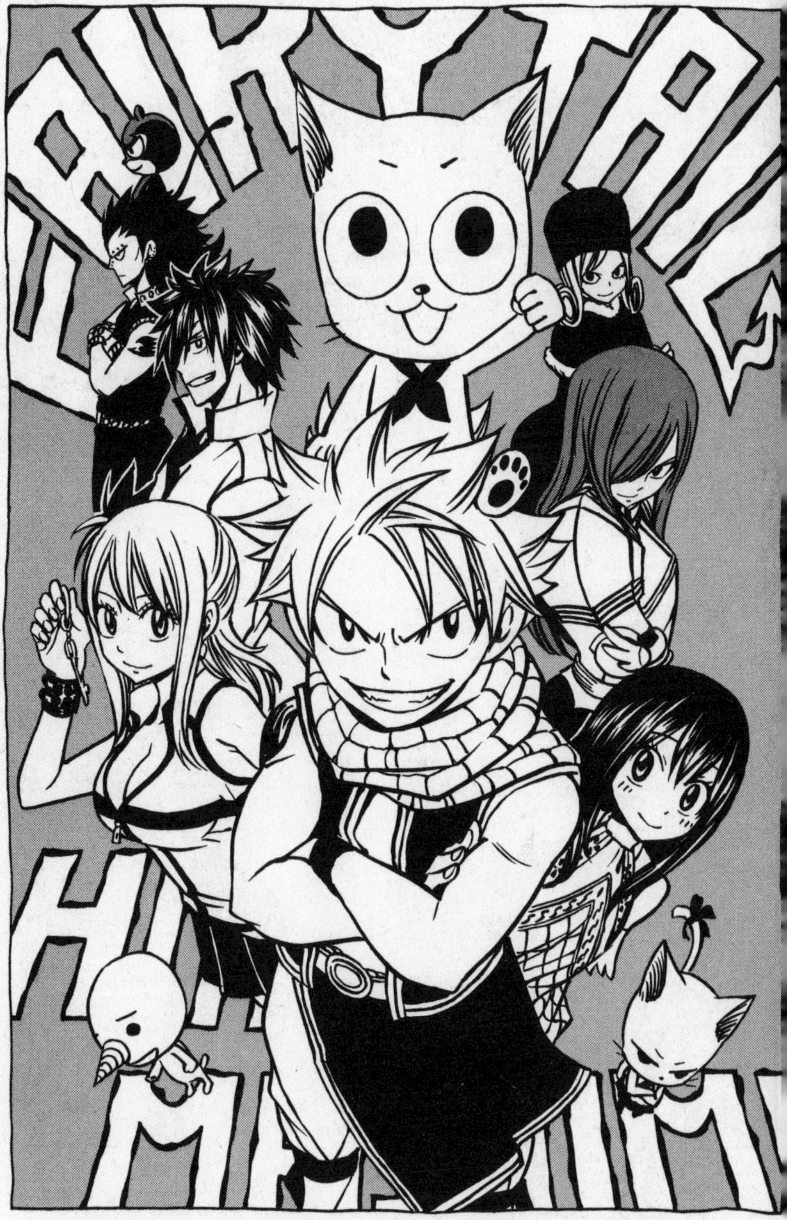

Chapter 250: Zeref Awakened

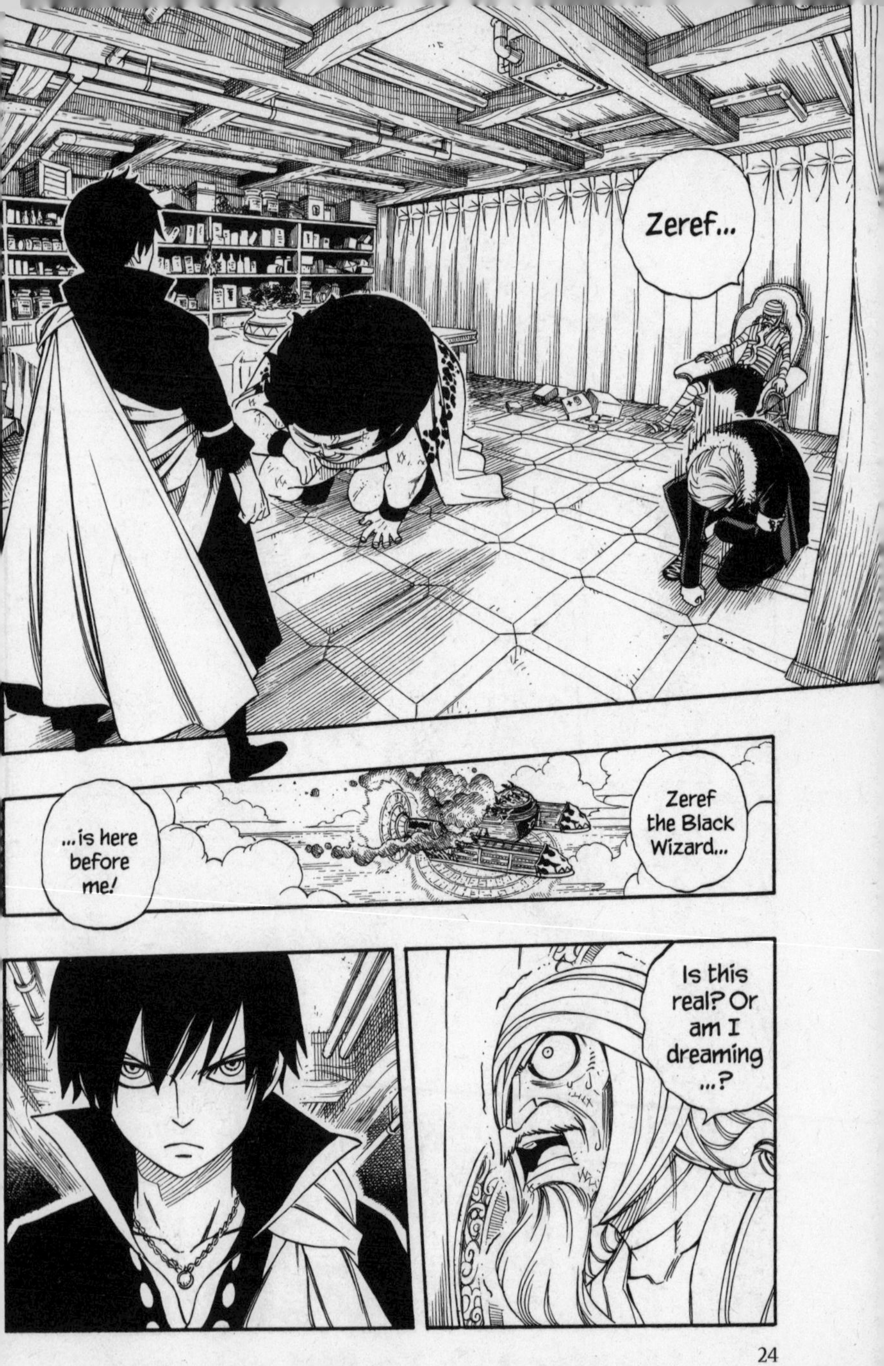
Zeref...
Zeref the Black Wizard...
...is here before me!
Is this real? Or am I dreaming ...?

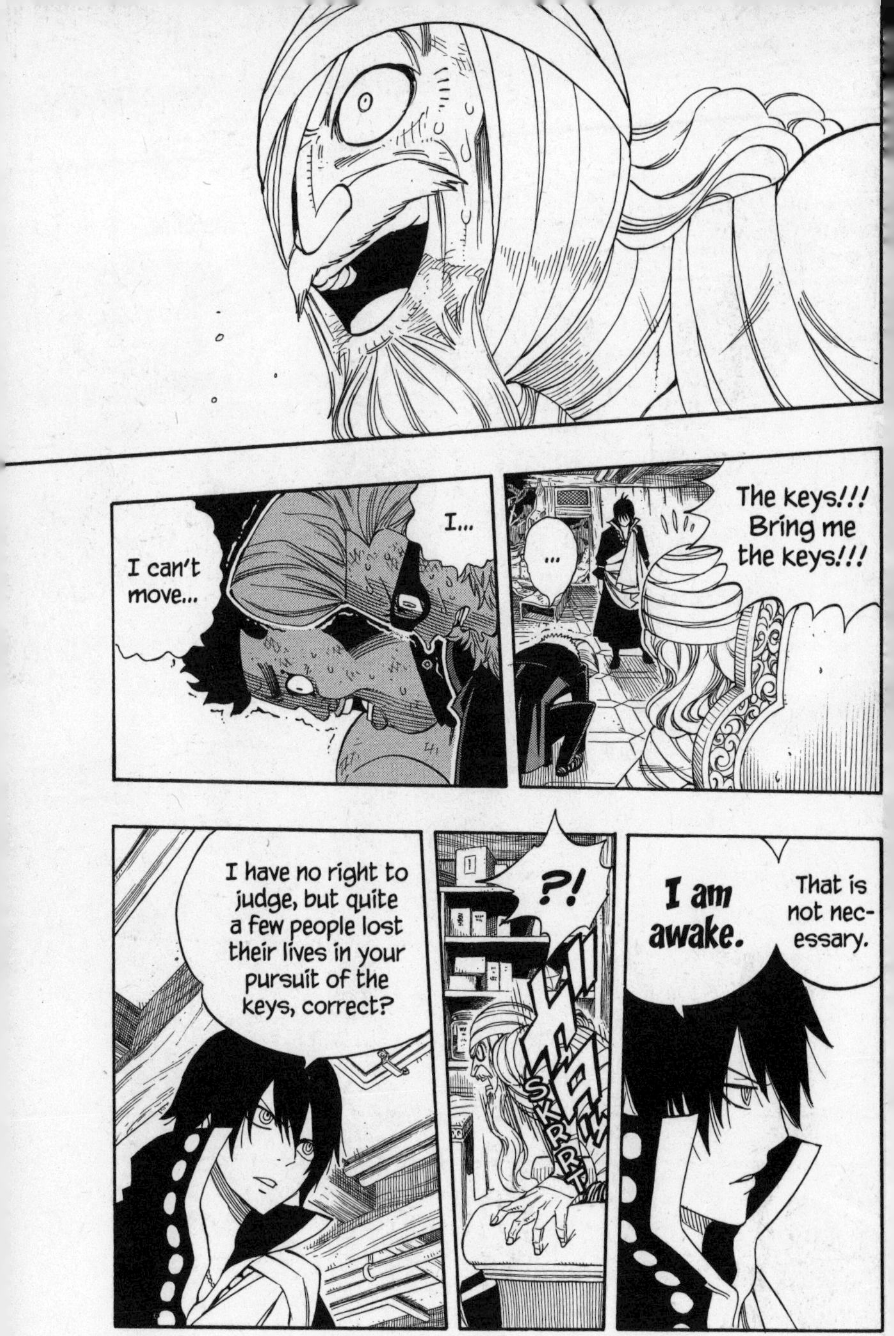
The keys!!! Bring me the keys!!!
...
I...
I can't move...
That is not nec-essary.
I am awake.
?!
SKRRT
I have no right to judge, but quite a few people lost their lives in your pursuit of the keys, correct?

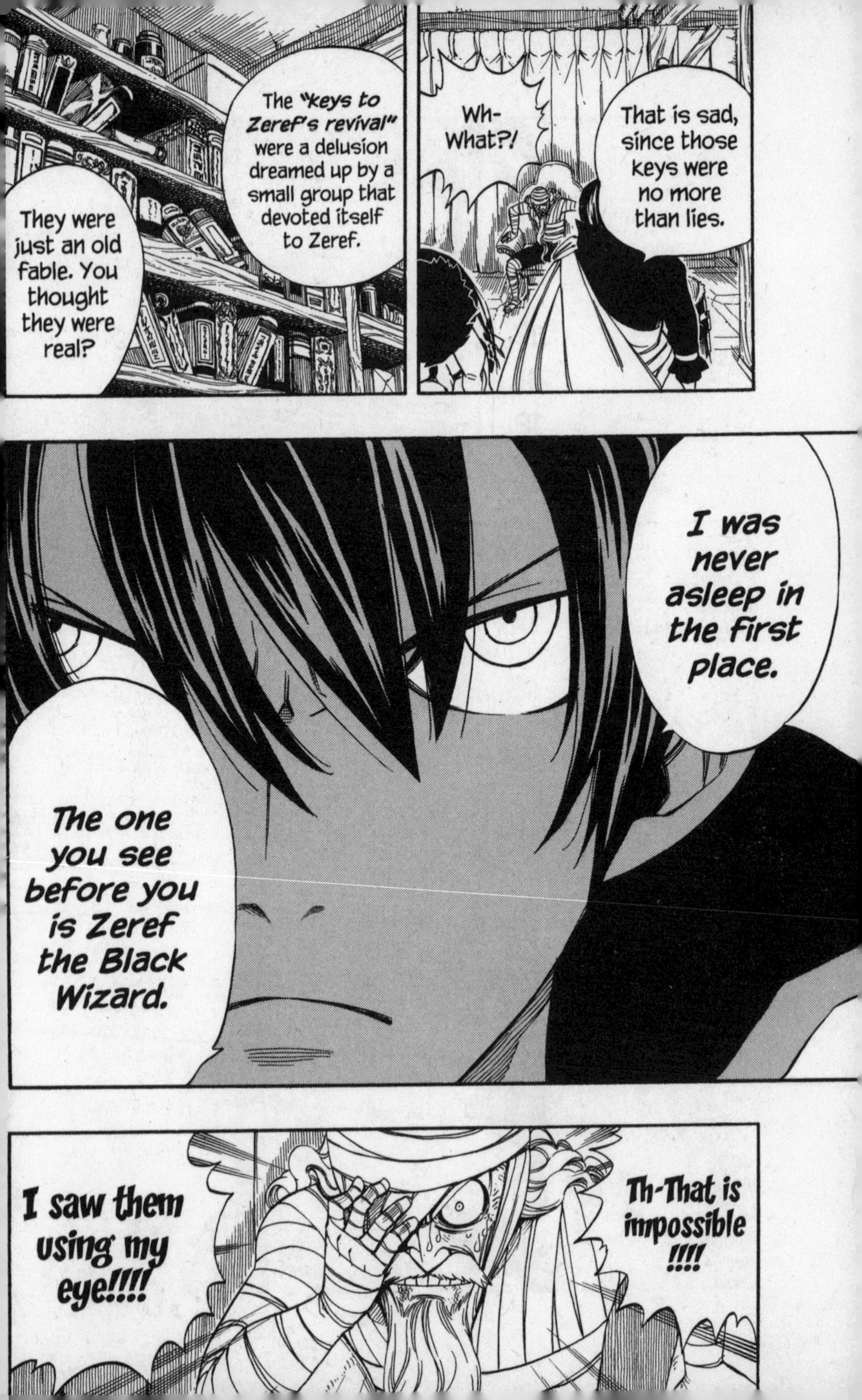
That is sad, since those keys were no more than lies.
Wh-What?!
The "keys to Zeref's revival" were a delusion dreamed up by a small group that devoted itself to Zeref.
They were just an old fable. You thought they were real?
I was never asleep in the first place.
The one you see before you is Zeref the Black Wizard.
Th-That is impossible!!!!
I saw them using my eye!!!!

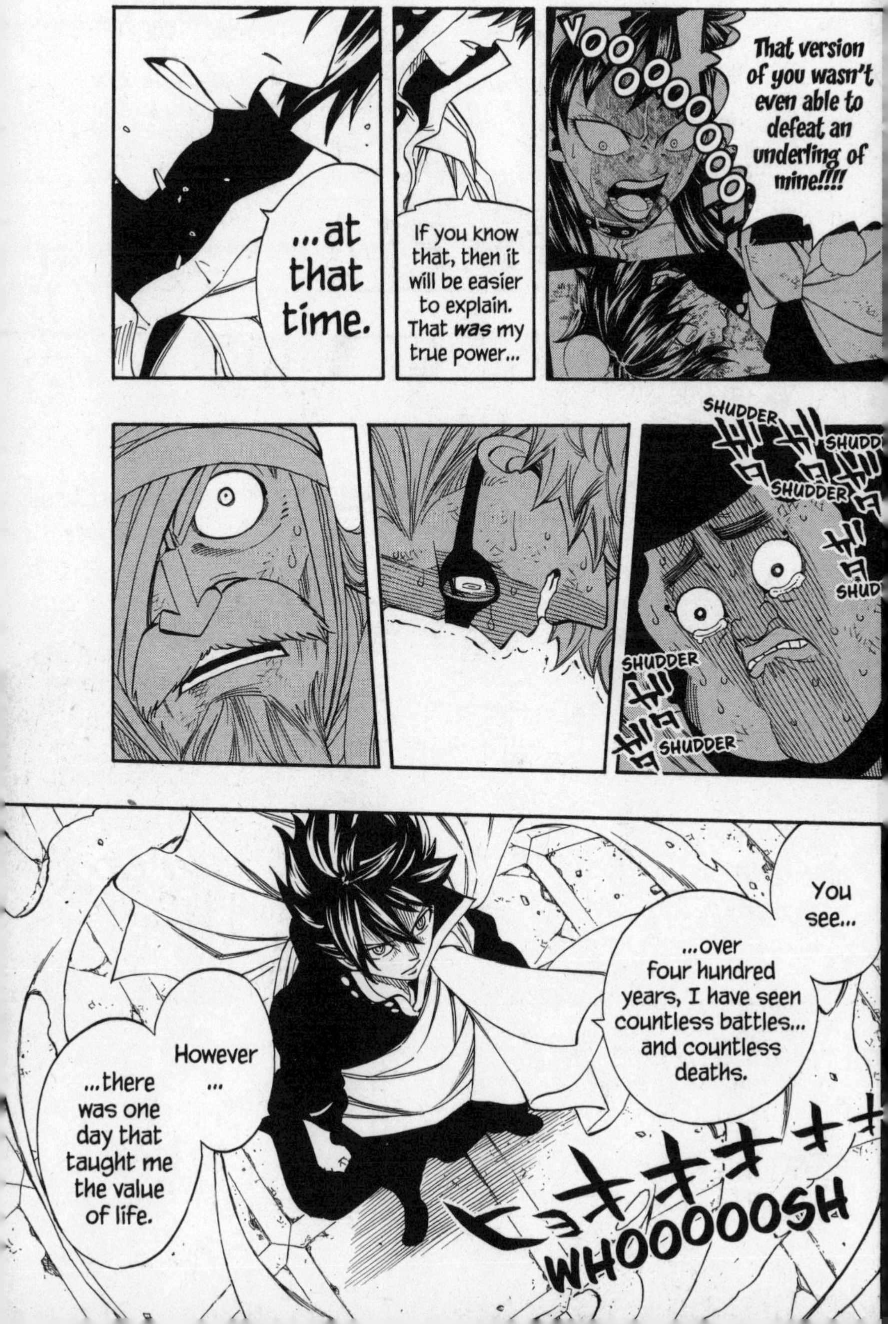
VOOOOOOOOO
That version of you wasn't even able to defeat an underling of mine!!!!
If you know that, then it will be easier to explain. That *was* my true power...
...at that time.
SHUDDER
SHUDD
SHUDDER
SHUD
SHUDDER
SHUDDER
You see...
...over four hundred years, I have seen countless battles... and countless deaths.
However...
...there was one day that taught me the value of life.
WHOOOOOOSH

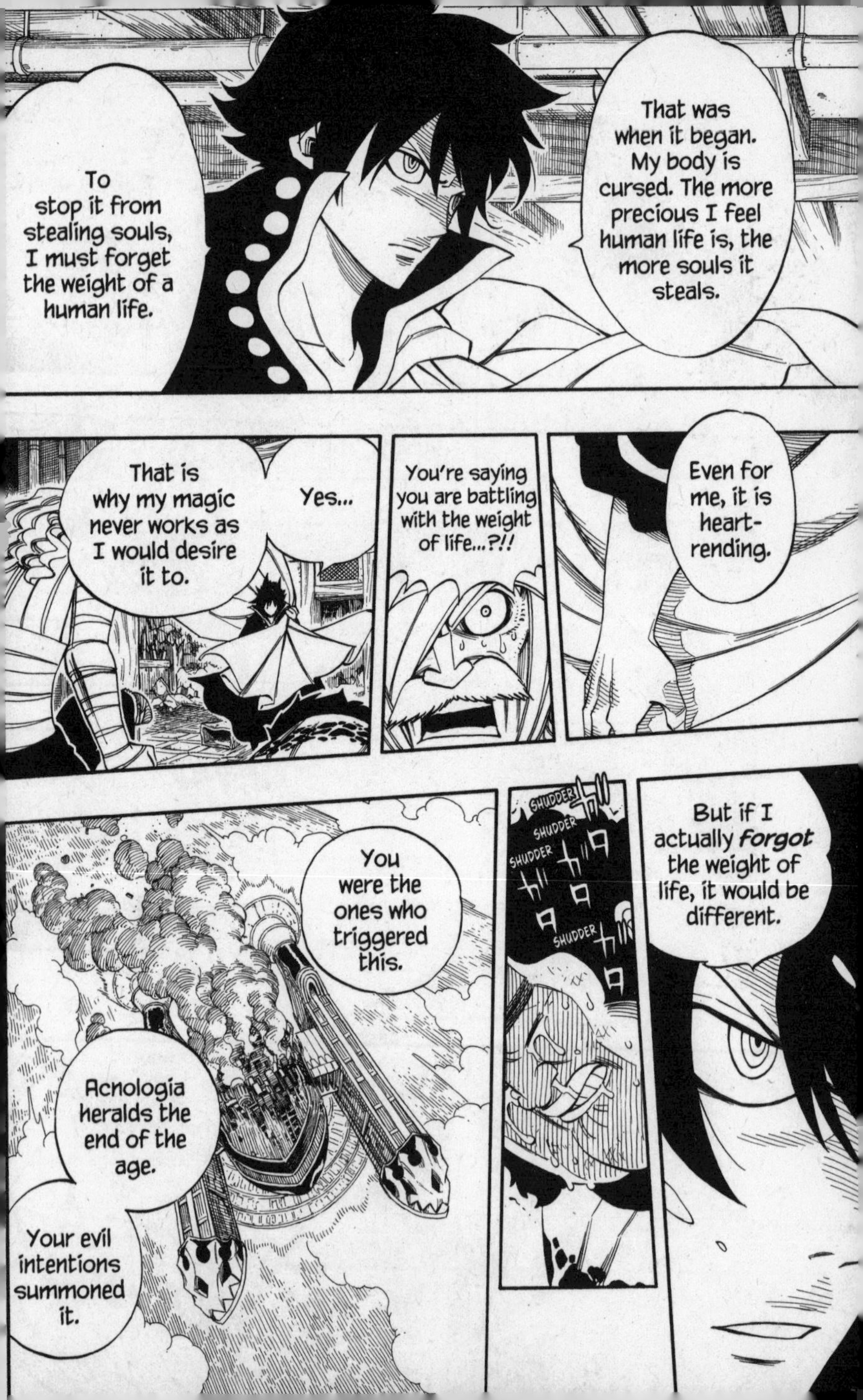
That was when it began. My body is cursed. The more precious I feel human life is, the more souls it steals.
To stop it from stealing souls, I must forget the weight of a human life.
Even for me, it is heart-rending.
You're saying you are battling with the weight of life...?!!
Yes...
That is why my magic never works as I would desire it to.
But if I actually *forgot* the weight of life, it would be different.
SHUDDER
SHUDDER
SHUDDER
SHUDDER
You were the ones who triggered this.
Acnologia heralds the end of the age.
Your evil intentions summoned it.

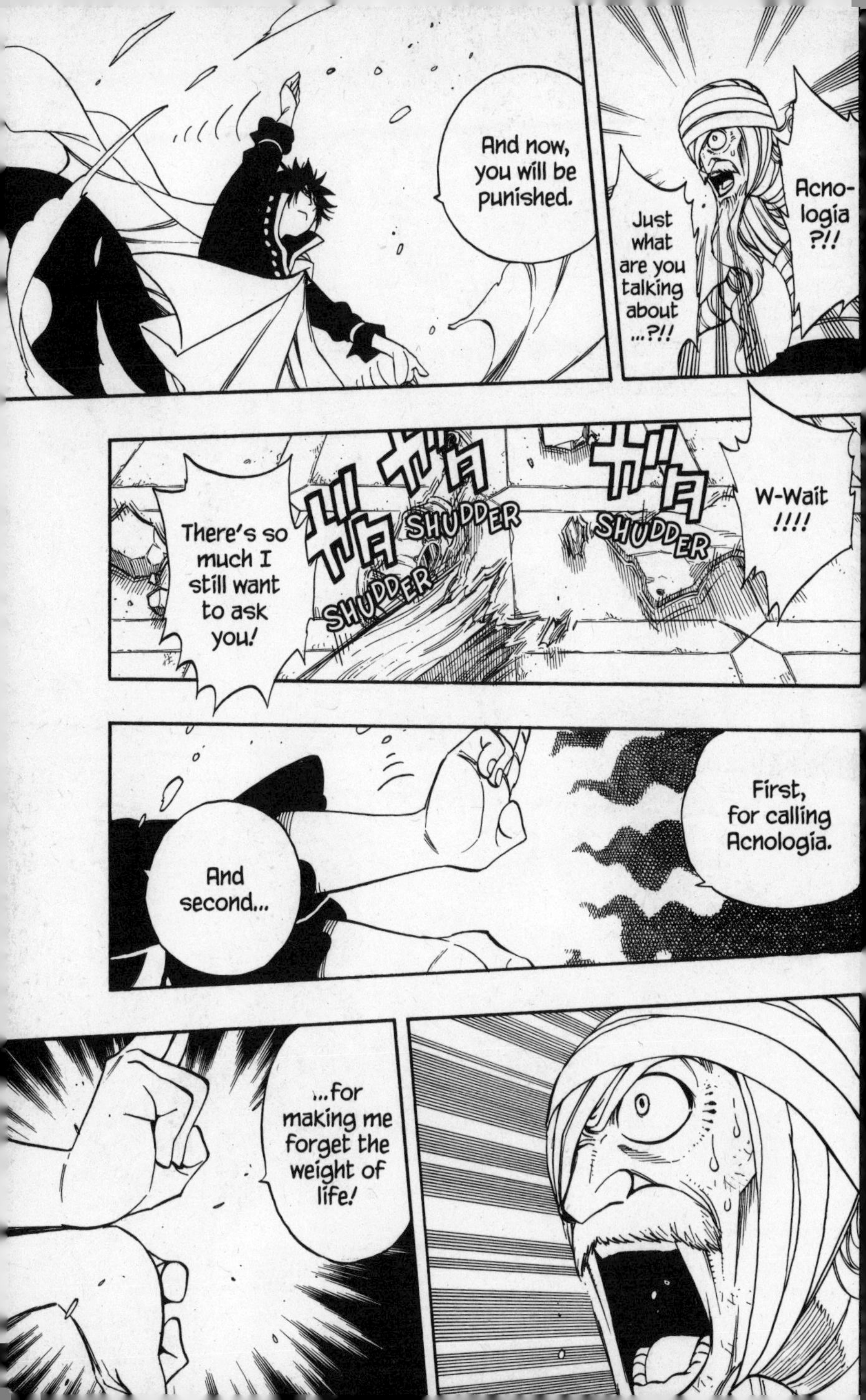
Acnologia?!!
Just what are you talking about...?!!
And now, you will be punished.
W-Wait!!!!
ガタ
SHUDDER
ガタ
SHUDDER
SHUDDER
There's so much I still want to ask you!
First, for calling Acnologia.
And second...
...for making me forget the weight of life!

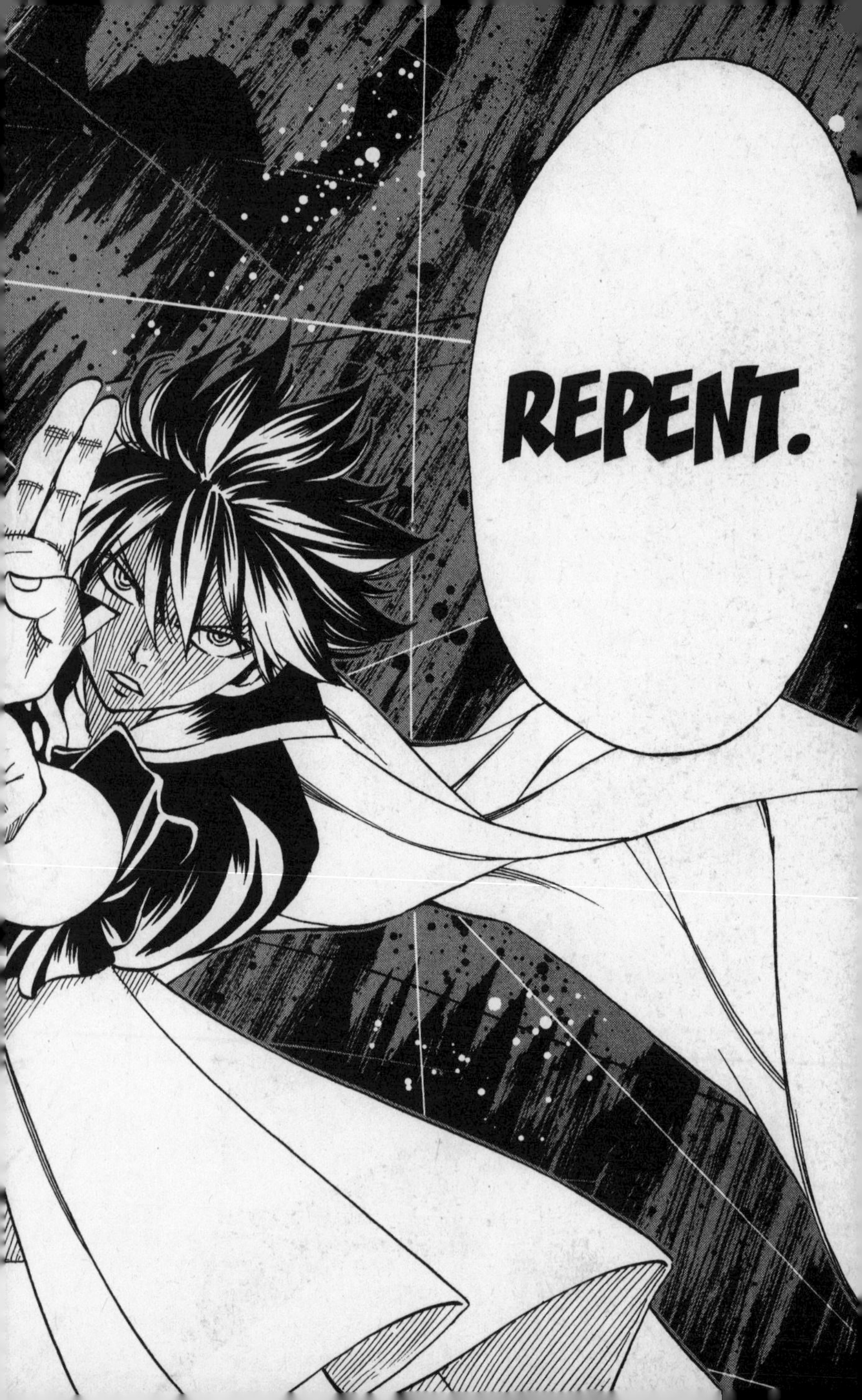
REPENT.

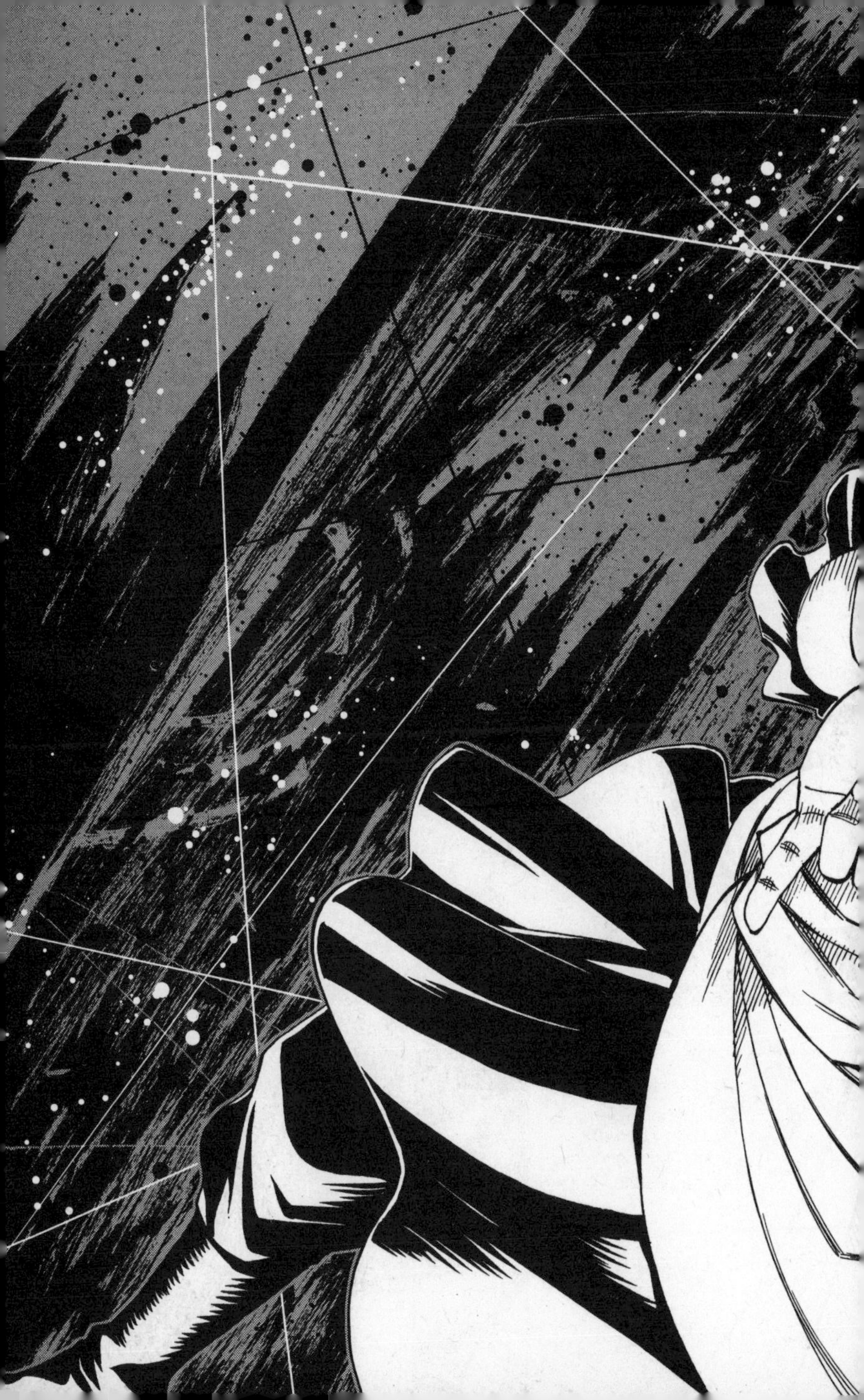

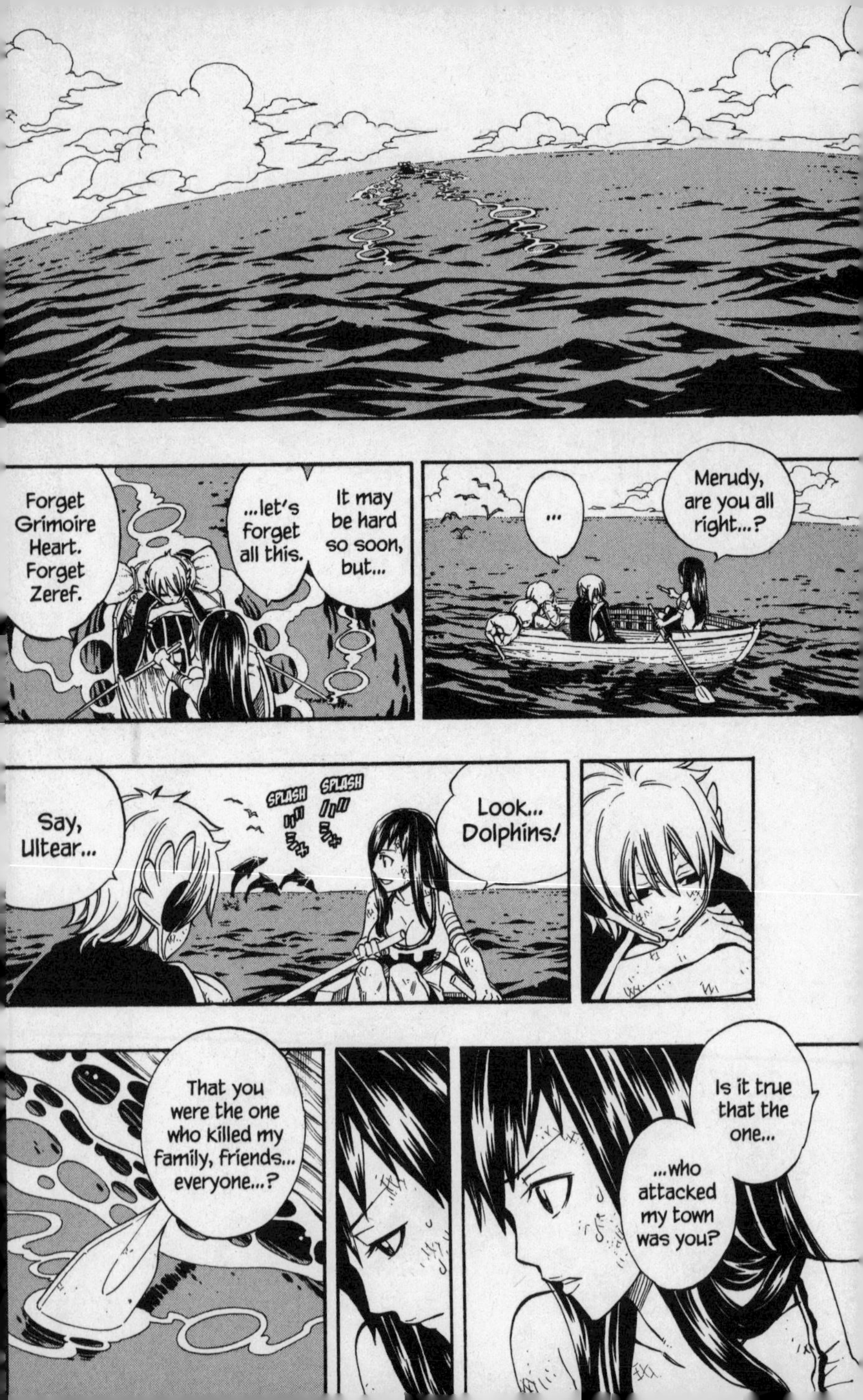
Merudy, are you all right...?
...
It may be hard so soon, but...
...let's forget all this.
Forget Grimoire Heart. Forget Zeref.
Look... Dolphins!
SPLASH
SPLASH
Say, Ultear...
Is it true that the one...
...who attacked my town was you?
That you were the one who killed my family, friends... everyone...?

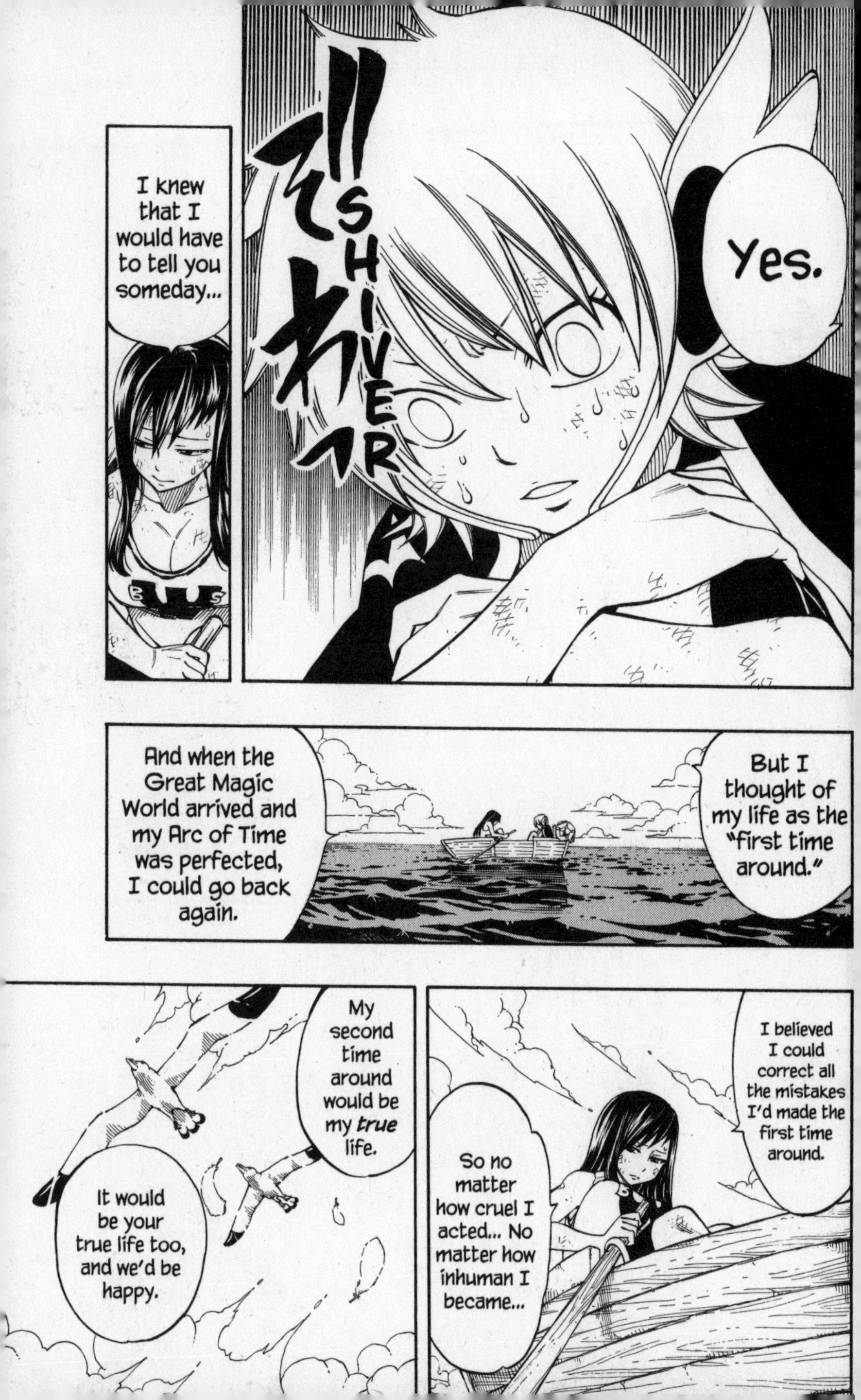
Yes.
SHIVER
I knew that I would have to tell you someday...
But I thought of my life as the "first time around."
And when the Great Magic World arrived and my Arc of Time was perfected, I could go back again.
I believed I could correct all the mistakes I'd made the first time around.
So no matter how cruel I acted... No matter how inhuman I became...
My second time around would be my *true* life.
It would be your true life too, and we'd be happy.

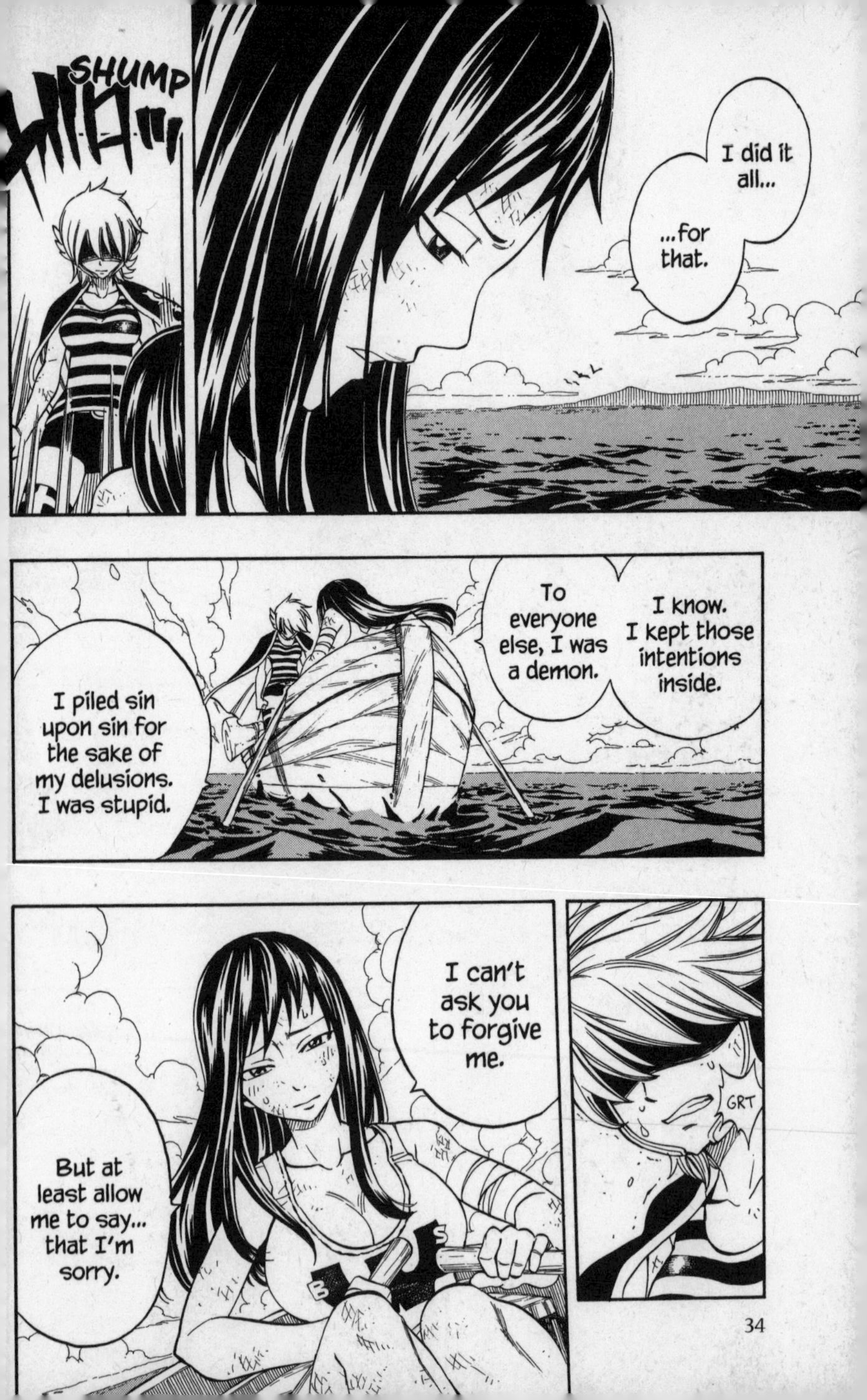
I did it all...
...for that.
SHUMP
I know. I kept those intentions inside.
To everyone else, I was a demon.
I piled sin upon sin for the sake of my delusions. I was stupid.
GRT
I can't ask you to forgive me.
But at least allow me to say... that I'm sorry.

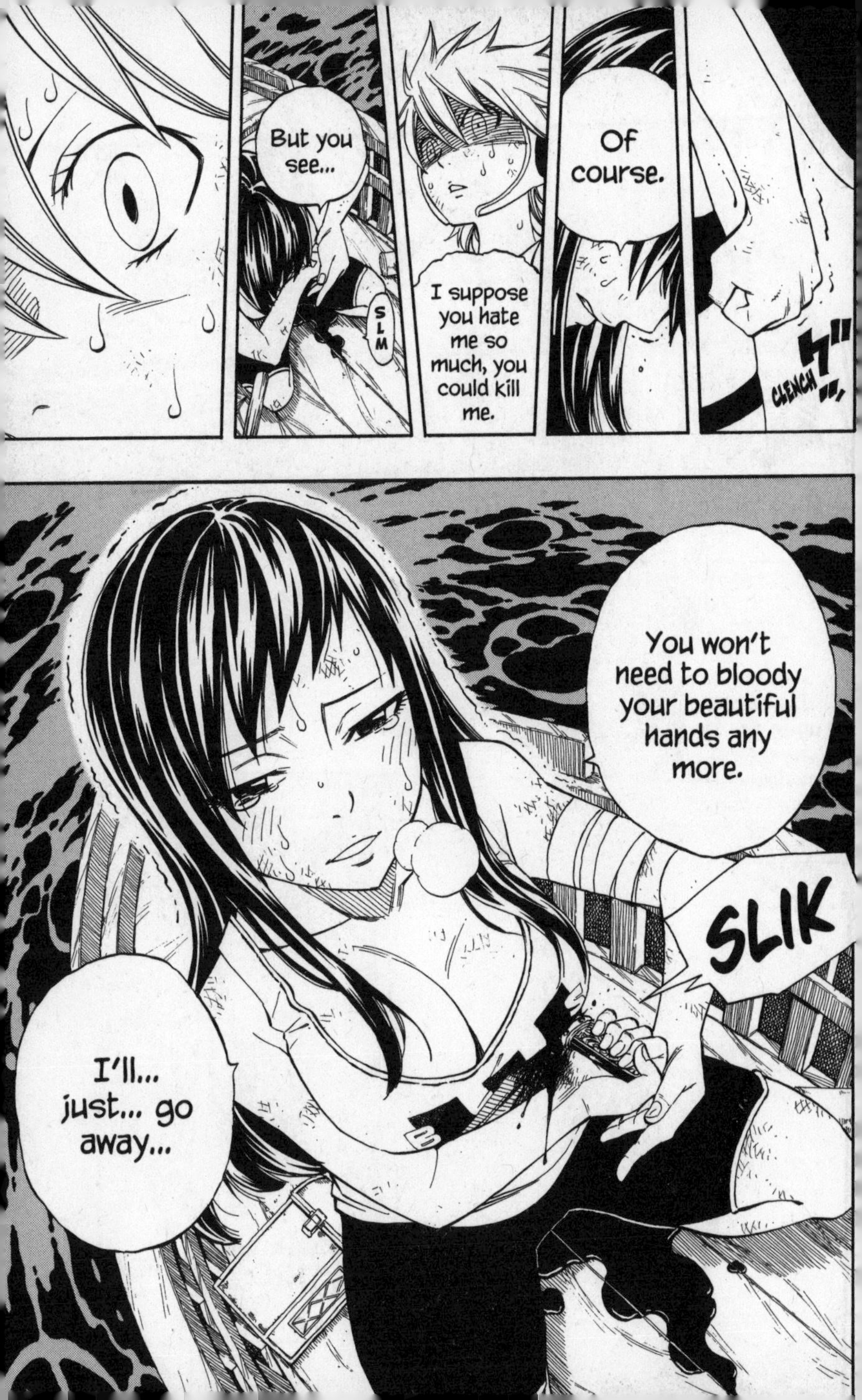
CLENCH
Of course.
I suppose you hate me so much, you could kill me.
But you see...
SLM
You won't need to bloody your beautiful hands any more.
SLIK
I'll... just... go away...

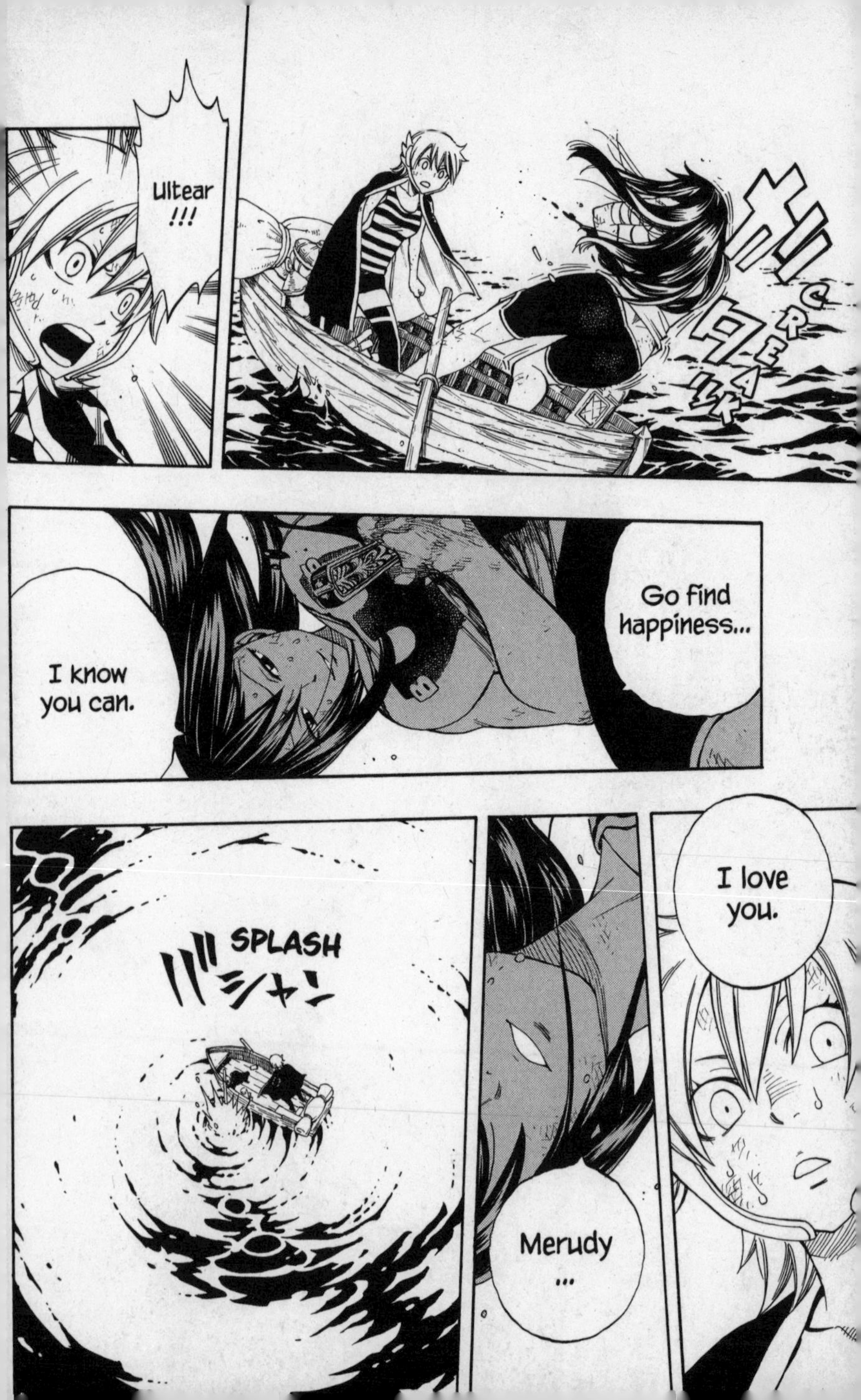
CREAK
Ultear!!!
Go find happiness...
I know you can.
I love you.
Merudy ...
SPLASH

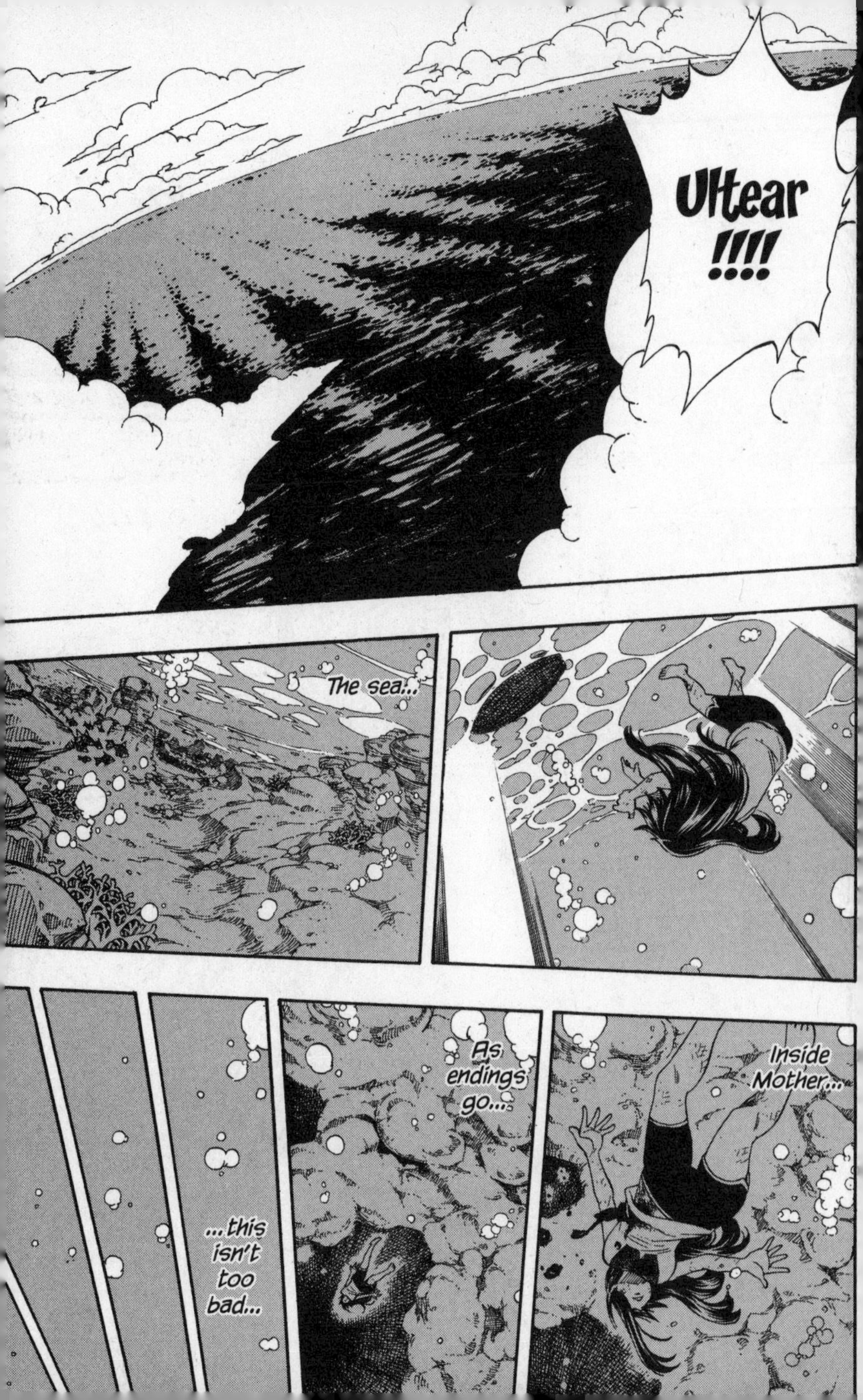
Ultear !!!!
The sea...
Inside Mother...
As endings go...
...this isn't too bad...

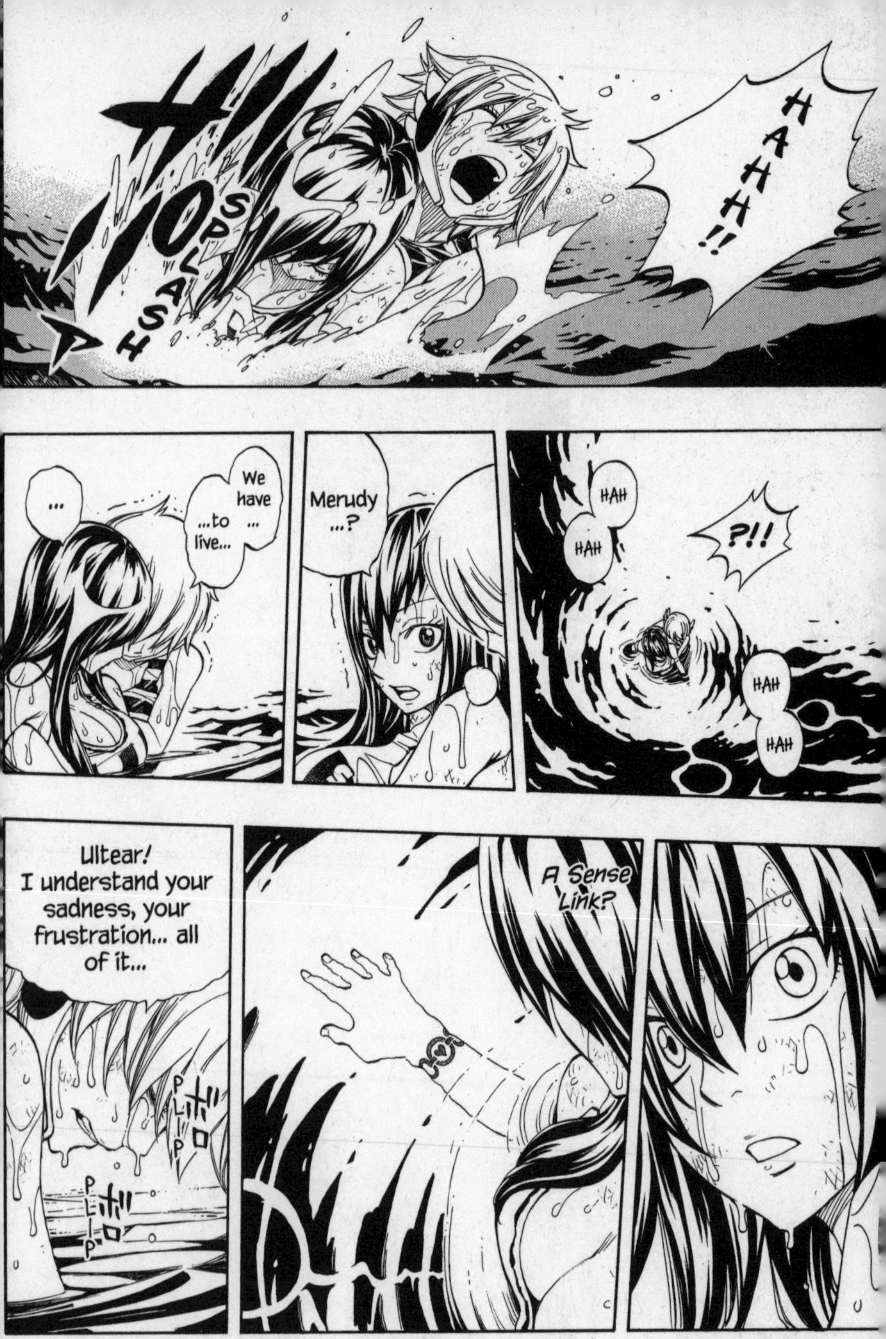
HAHHH!!
SPLASH
HAH
HAH
?!!
HAH
HAH
Merudy ...?
We have ...to live...
...
A Sense Link?
Ultear! I understand your sadness, your frustration... all of it...
PLIP
PLIP

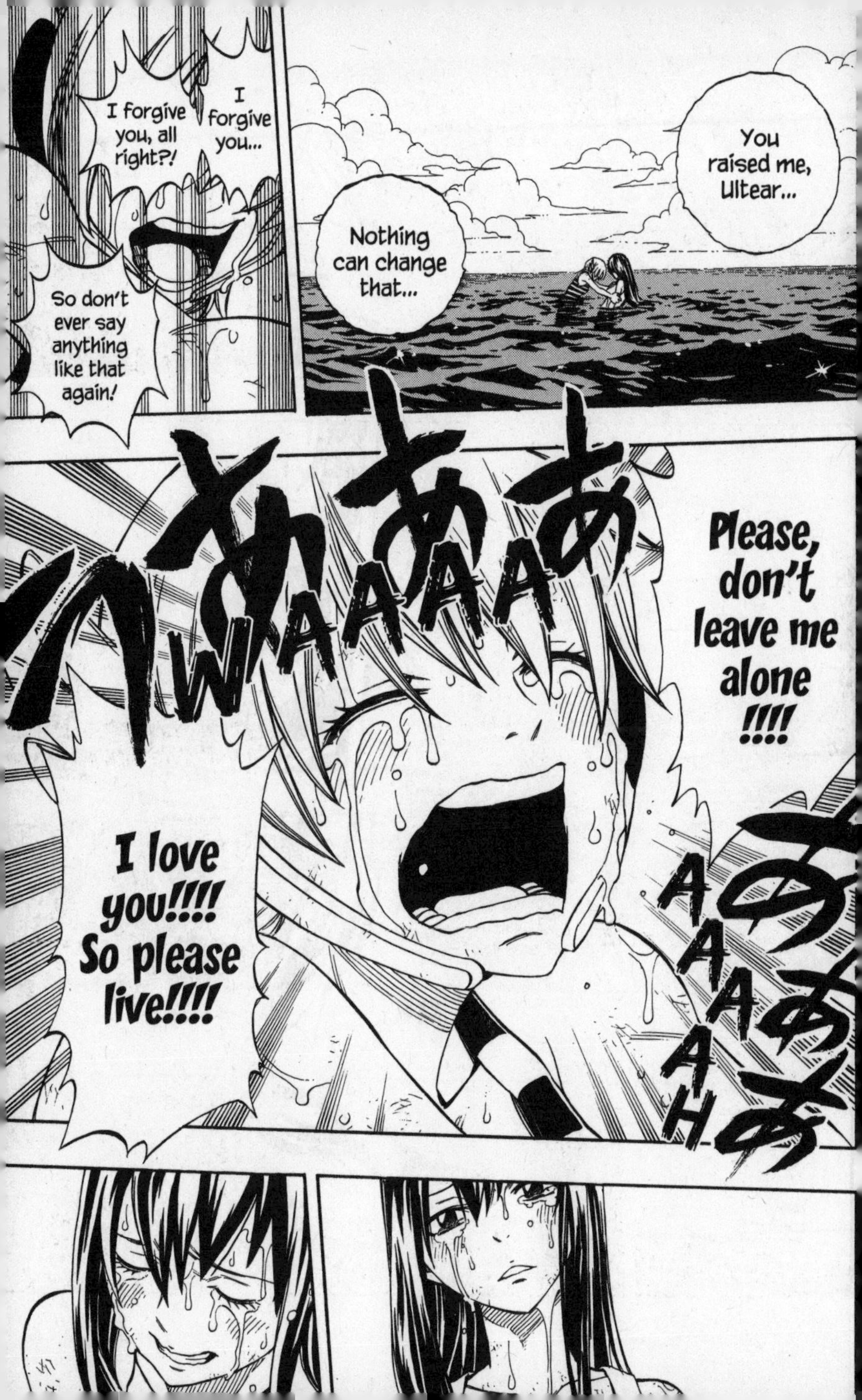
You raised me, Ultear...
Nothing can change that...
I forgive you...
I forgive you, all right?!
So don't ever say anything like that again!
Please, don't leave me alone!!!!
AAAAH
WAAAAAA
I love you!!!! So please live!!!!

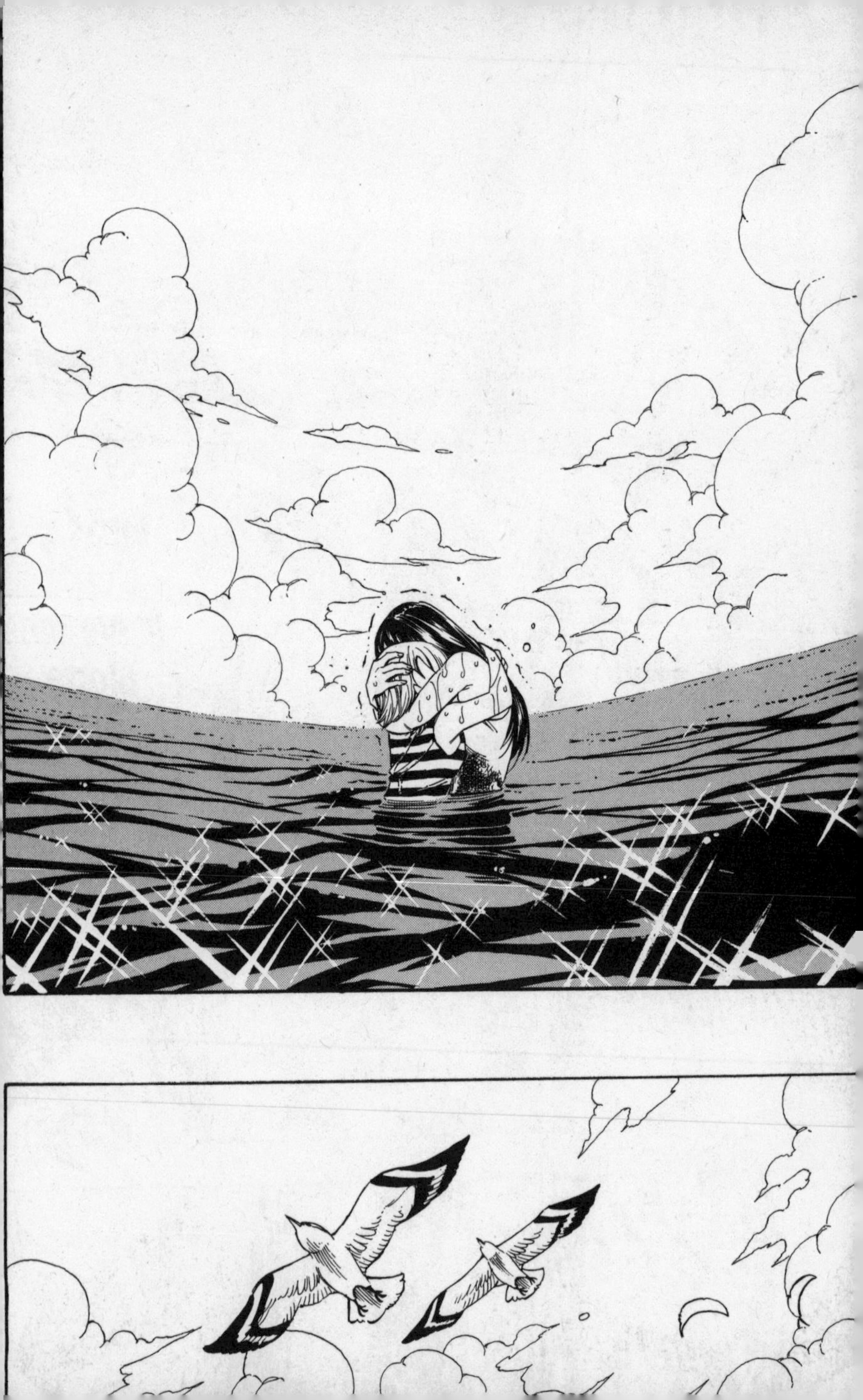

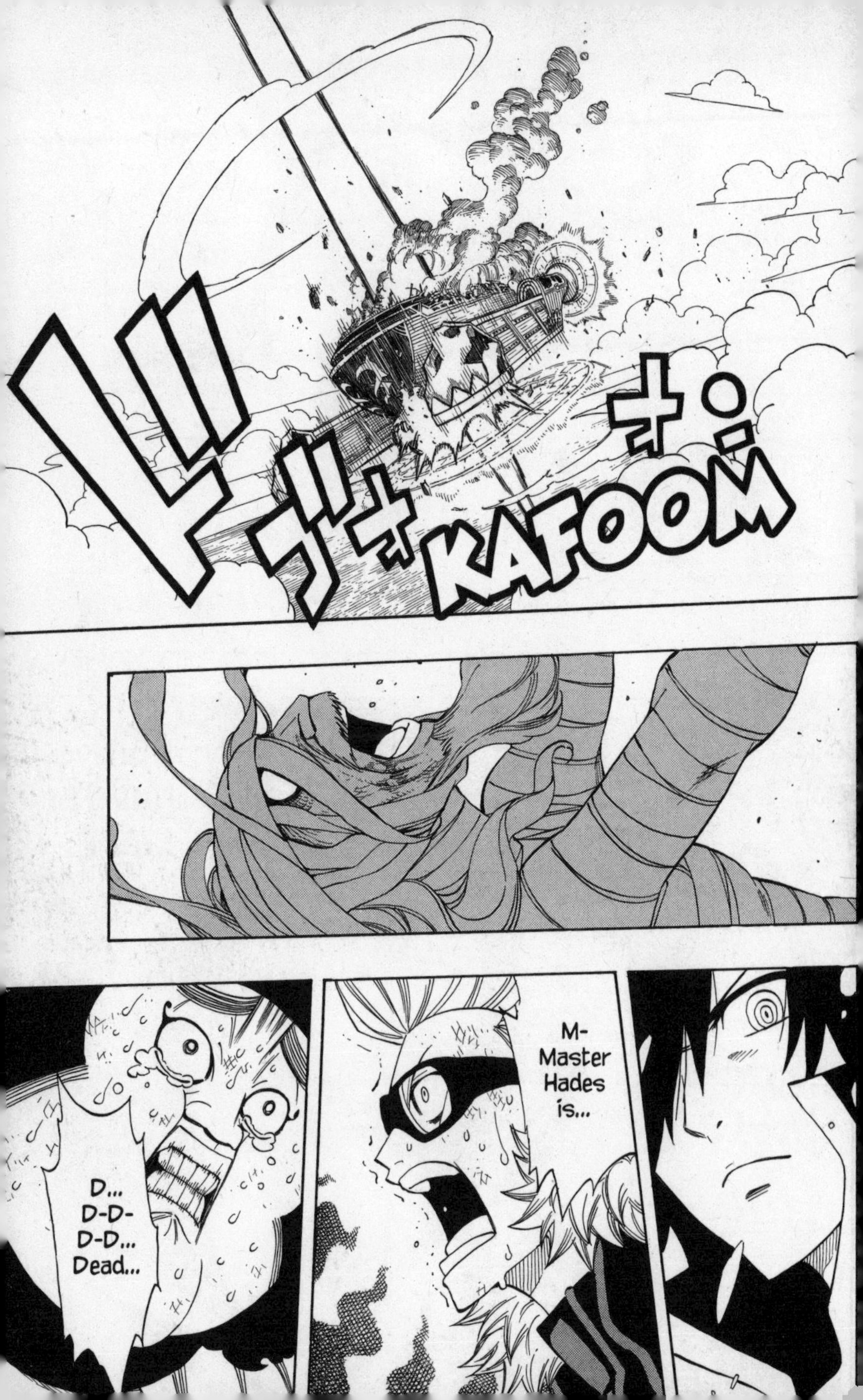
KAFOOM
M- Master Hades is...
D... D-D- D-D... Dead...

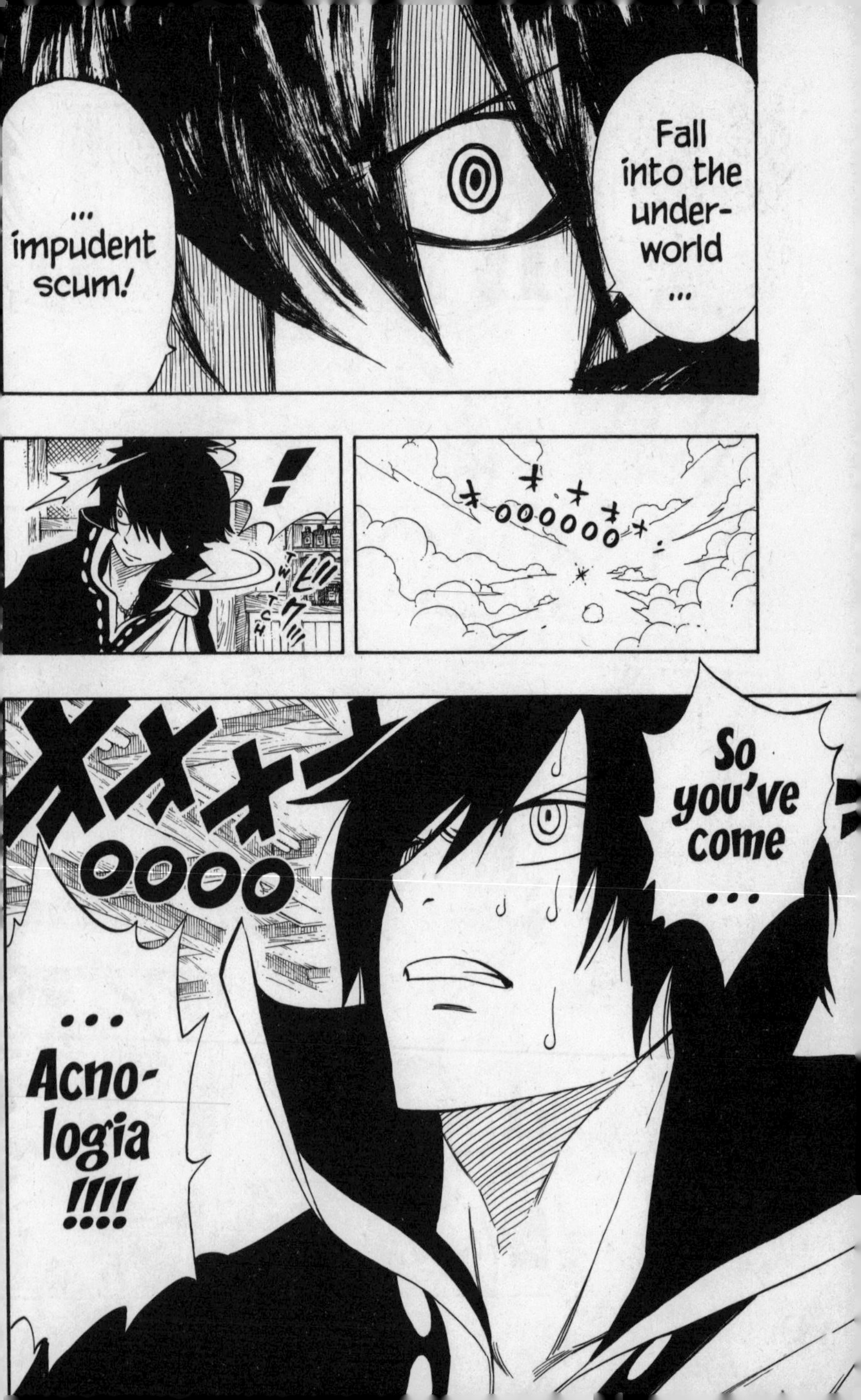
Fall into the under-world ...
... impudent scum!
!
TWITCH
So you've come ...
... Acno-logia !!!!

FAIRY TAIL

フェアリーテイル

Chapter 251: The Right to Love

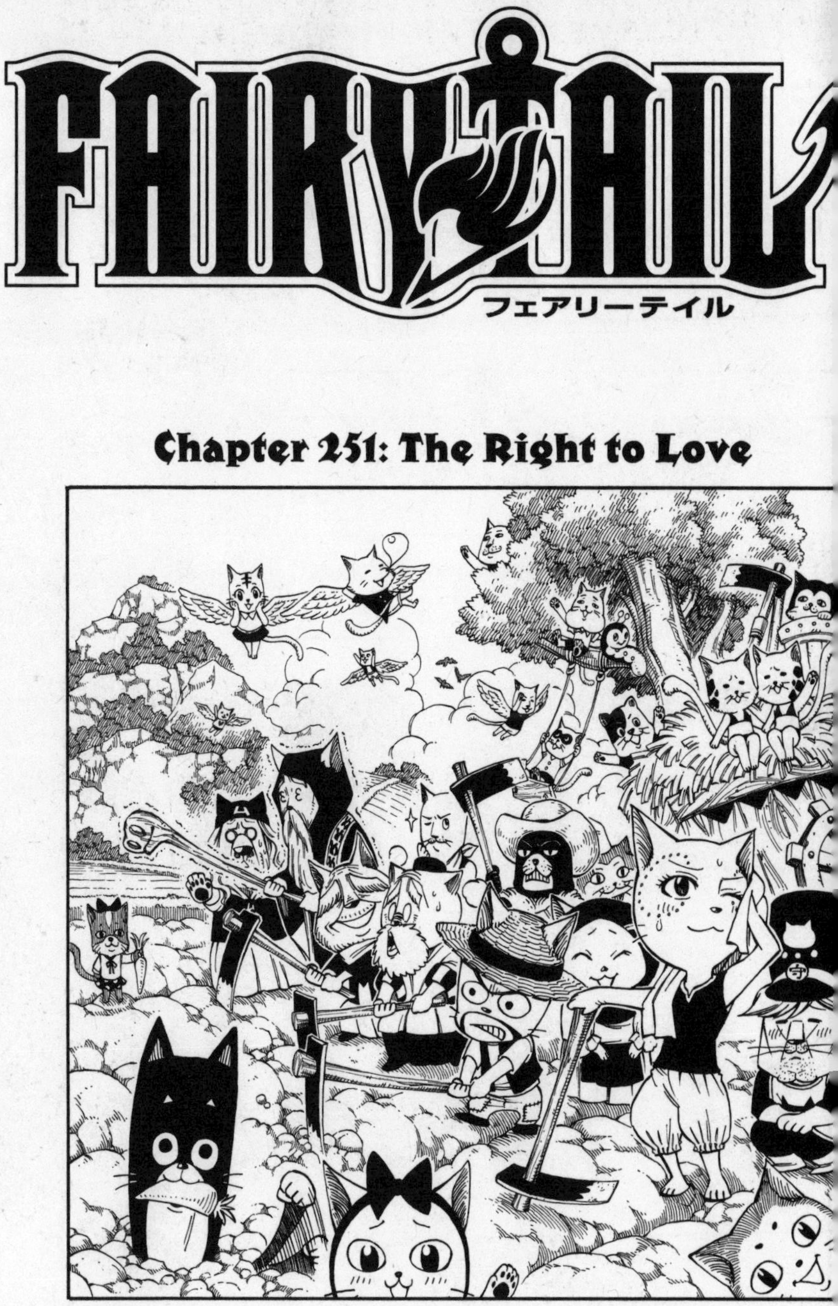

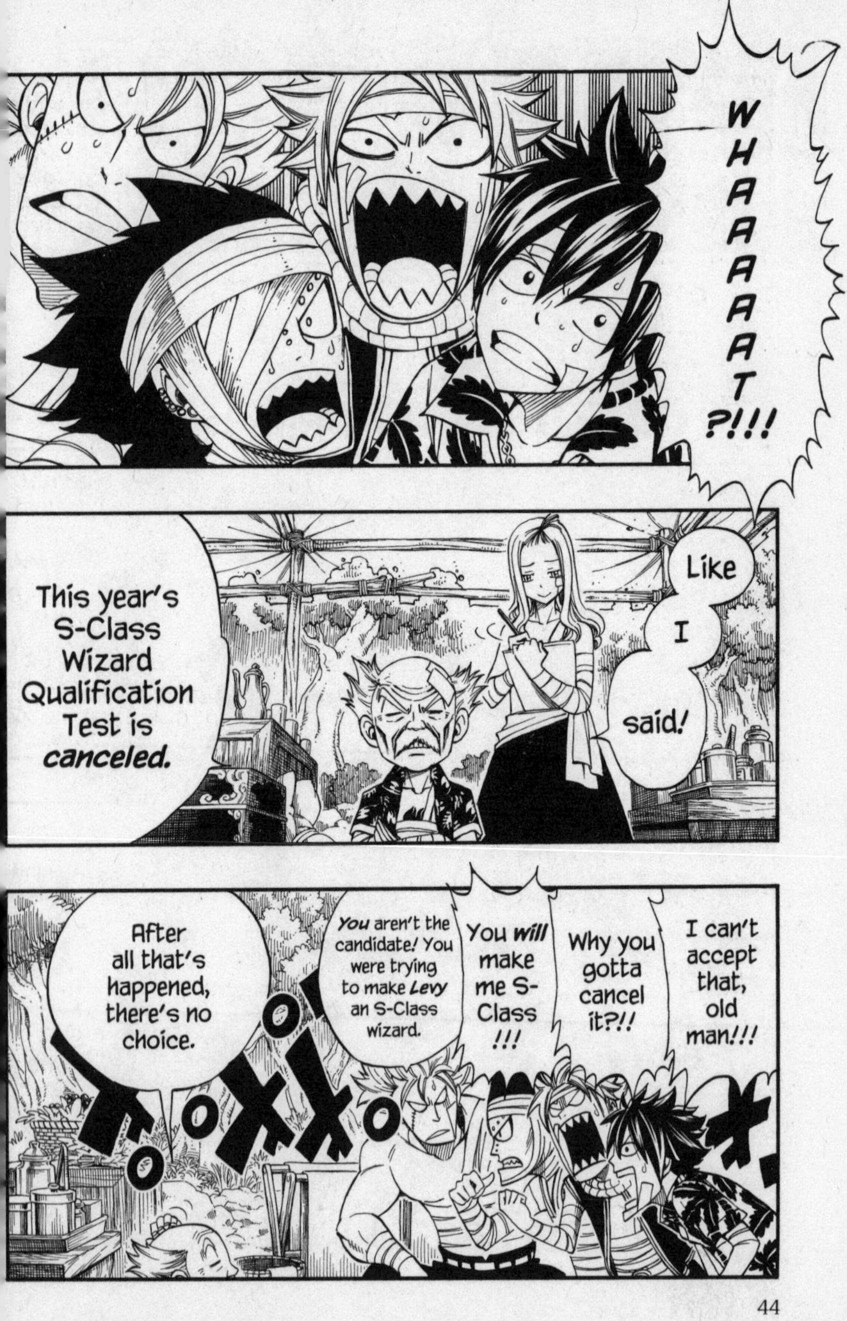

WHAAAAAT?!!!
Like I said!
This year's S-Class Wizard Qualification Test is *canceled.*
I can't accept that, old man!!!
Why you gotta cancel it?!!
You *will* make me S-Class!!!
You aren't the candidate! You were trying to make *Levy* an S-Class wizard.
After all that's happened, there's no choice.

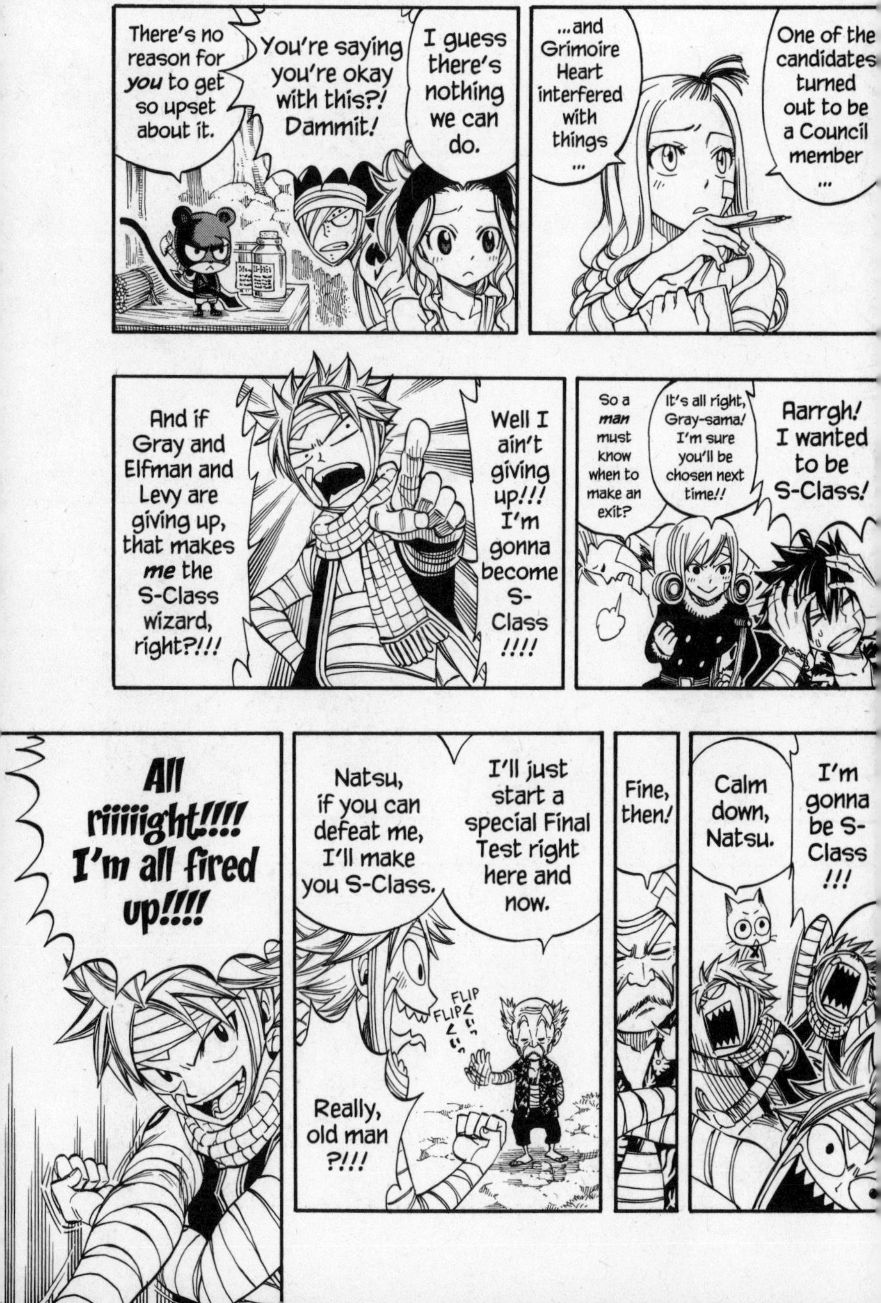
One of the candidates turned out to be a Council member ...
...and Grimoire Heart interfered with things ...
I guess there's nothing we can do.
You're saying you're okay with this?! Dammit!
There's no reason for *you* to get so upset about it.
Aarrgh! I wanted to be S-Class!
It's all right, Gray-sama! I'm sure you'll be chosen next time!!
So a *man* must know when to make an exit?
Well I ain't giving up!!! I'm gonna become S-Class!!!!
And if Gray and Elfman and Levy are giving up, that makes *me* the S-Class wizard, right?!!!
I'm gonna be S-Class!!!
Calm down, Natsu.
Fine, then!
I'll just start a special Final Test right here and now.
Natsu, if you can defeat me, I'll make you S-Class.
FLIP FLIP
Really, old man?!!!
All riiiiight!!!! I'm all fired up!!!!

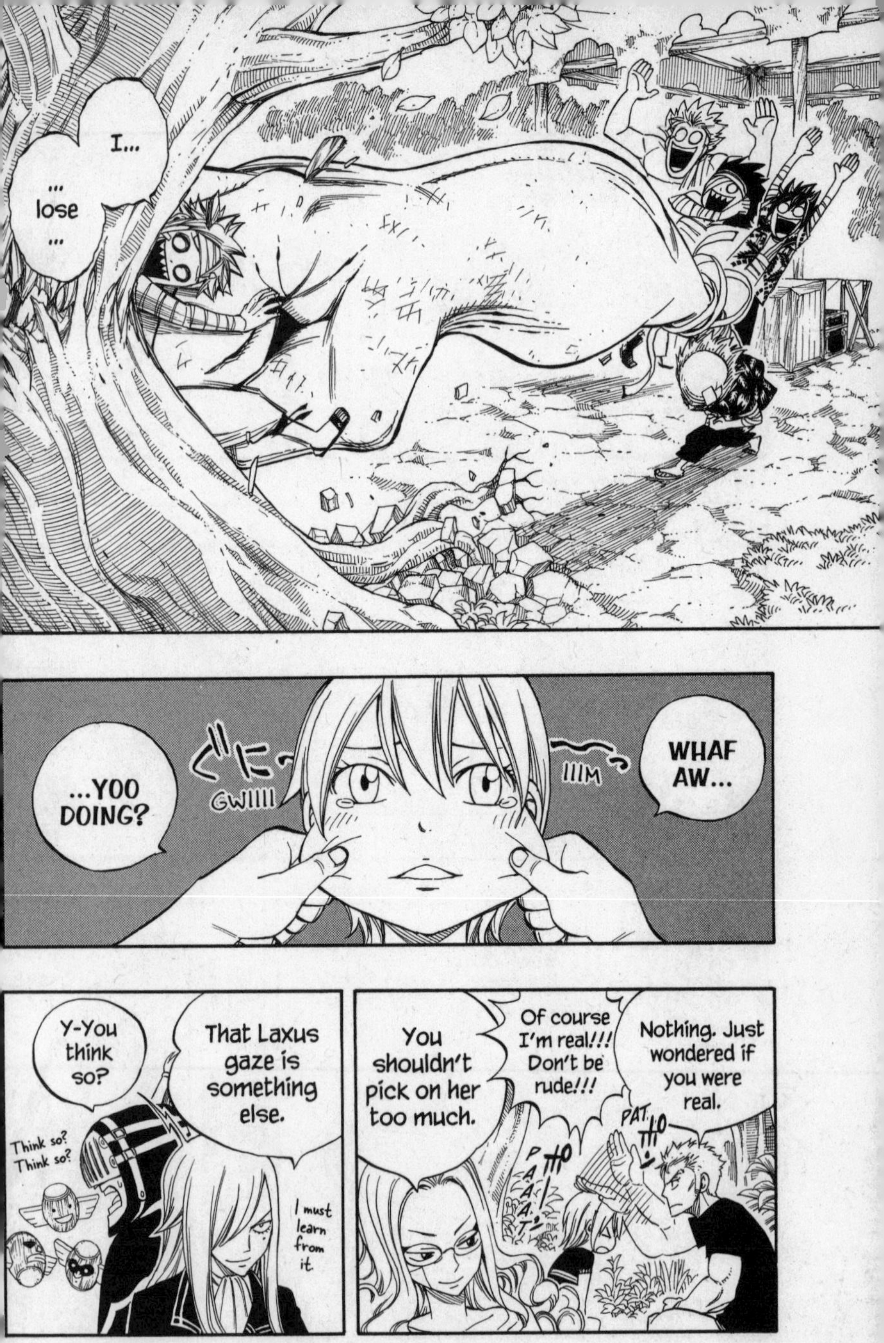
I...
... lose ...
WHAF AW...
IIIM
ぐに〜
GWIIIII
...YOO DOING?
Nothing. Just wondered if you were real.
PAT
Of course I'm real!!! Don't be rude!!!
You shouldn't pick on her too much.
That Laxus gaze is something else.
Y-You think so?
I must learn from it.
Think so? Think so?

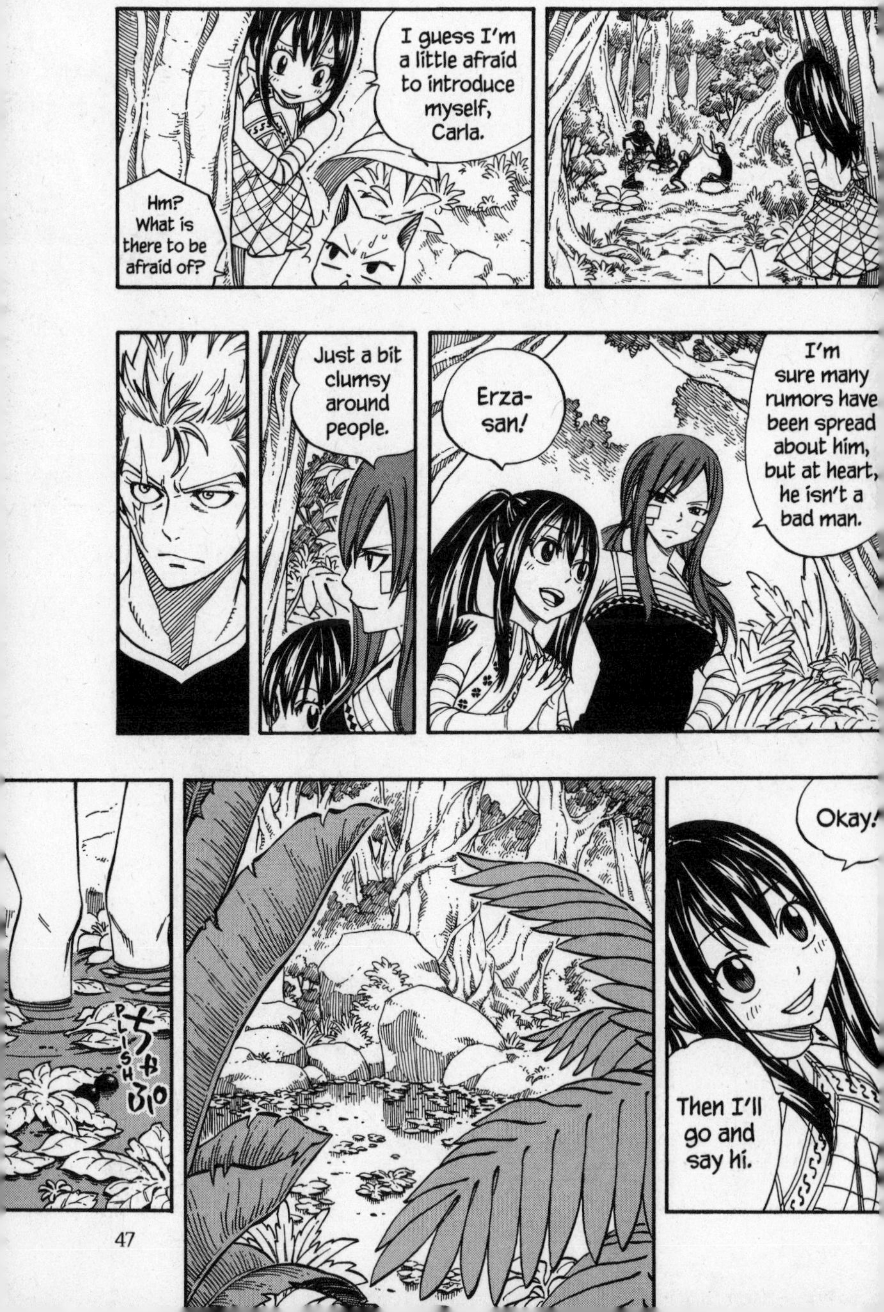
I guess I'm a little afraid to introduce myself, Carla.
Hm? What is there to be afraid of?
I'm sure many rumors have been spread about him, but at heart, he isn't a bad man.
Erza-san!
Just a bit clumsy around people.
Okay!
Then I'll go and say hi.
PLISH

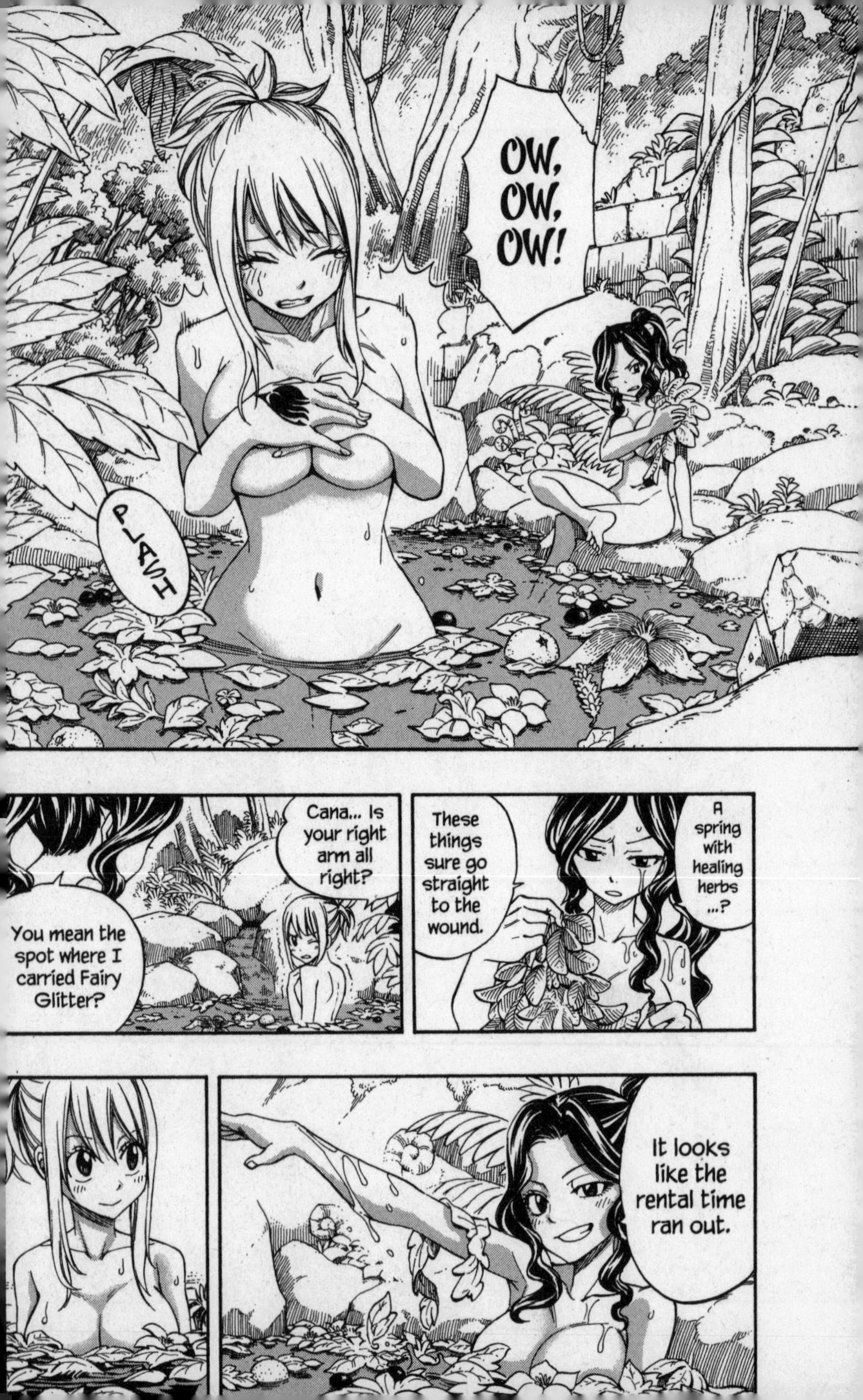
OW, OW, OW!
PLASH
A spring with healing herbs ...?
These things sure go straight to the wound.
Cana... Is your right arm all right?
You mean the spot where I carried Fairy Glitter?
It looks like the rental time ran out.

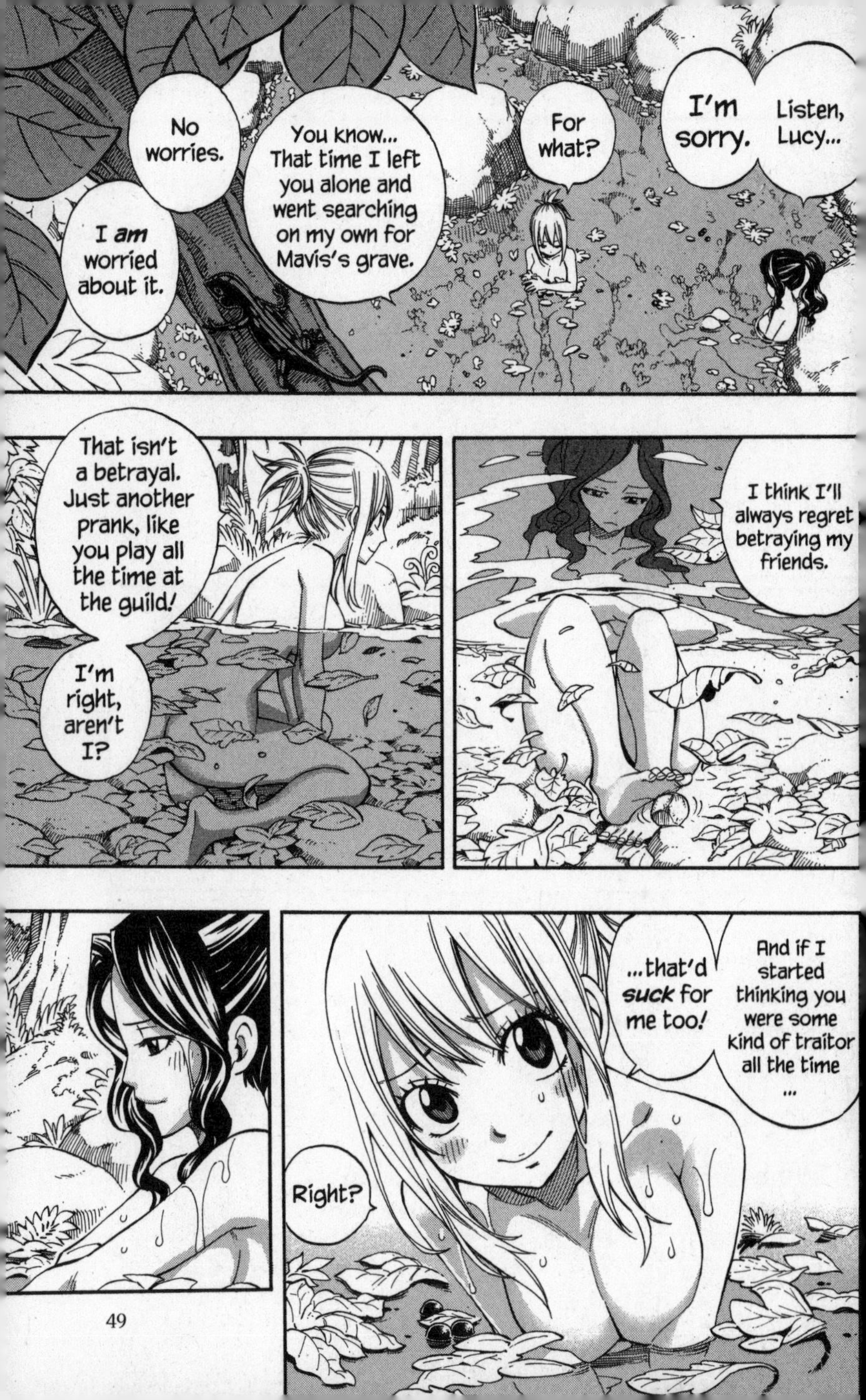
Listen, Lucy...
I'm sorry.
For what?
You know... That time I left you alone and went searching on my own for Mavis's grave.
No worries.
I *am* worried about it.
I think I'll always regret betraying my friends.
That isn't a betrayal. Just another prank, like you play all the time at the guild!
I'm right, aren't I?
And if I started thinking you were some kind of traitor all the time ...
...that'd *suck* for me too!
Right?

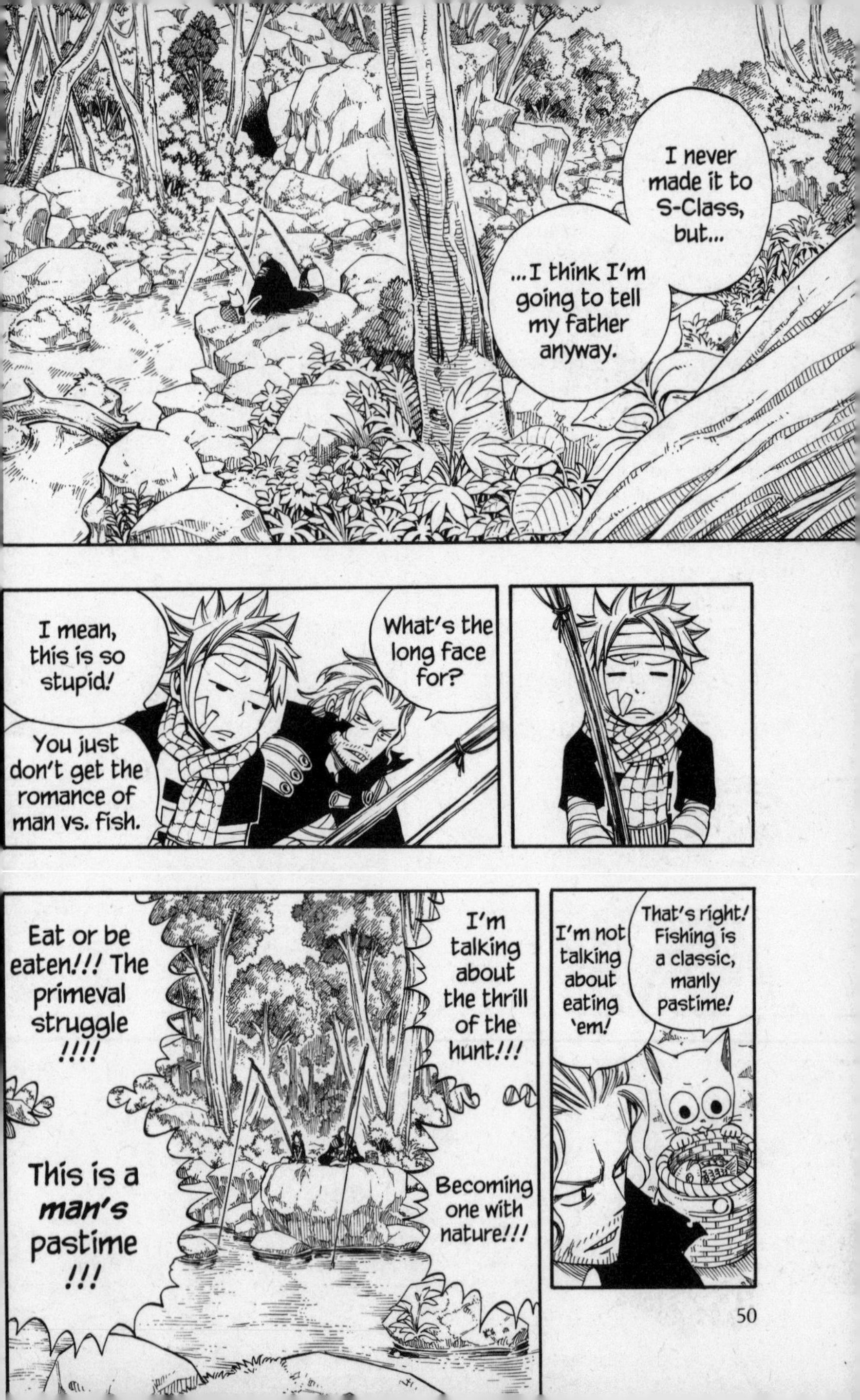
I never made it to S-Class, but...
...I think I'm going to tell my father anyway.
What's the long face for?
I mean, this is so stupid!
You just don't get the romance of man vs. fish.
That's right! Fishing is a classic, manly pastime!
I'm not talking about eating 'em!
I'm talking about the thrill of the hunt!!!
Eat or be eaten!!! The primeval struggle!!!!
Becoming one with nature!!!
This is a *man's* pastime!!!

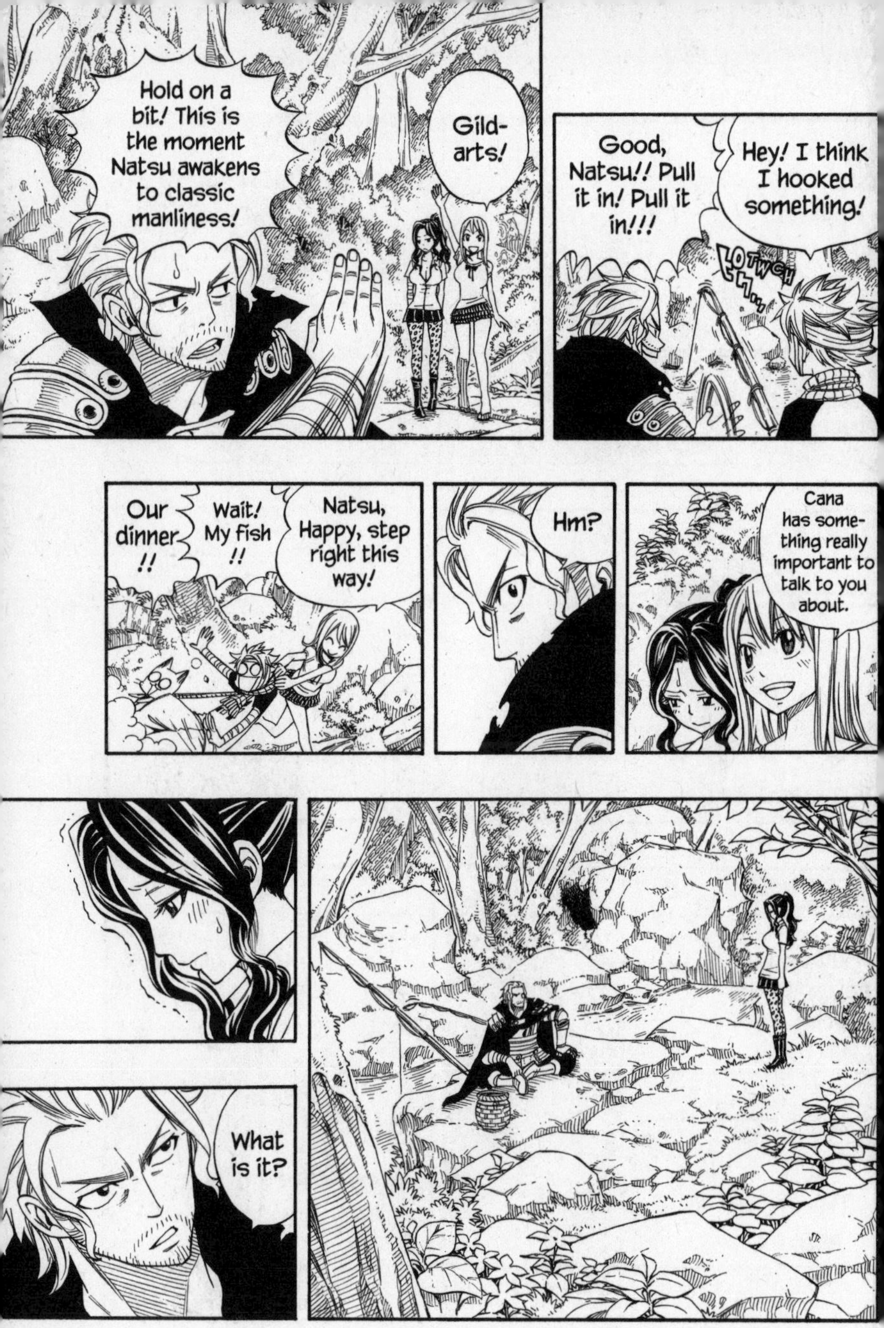
Hey! I think I hooked something!
TWITCH
Good, Natsu!! Pull it in! Pull it in!!!
Gild-arts!
Hold on a bit! This is the moment Natsu awakens to classic manliness!
Cana has some-thing really important to talk to you about.
Hm?
Natsu, Happy, step right this way!
Wait! My fish!!
Our dinner!!
What is it?

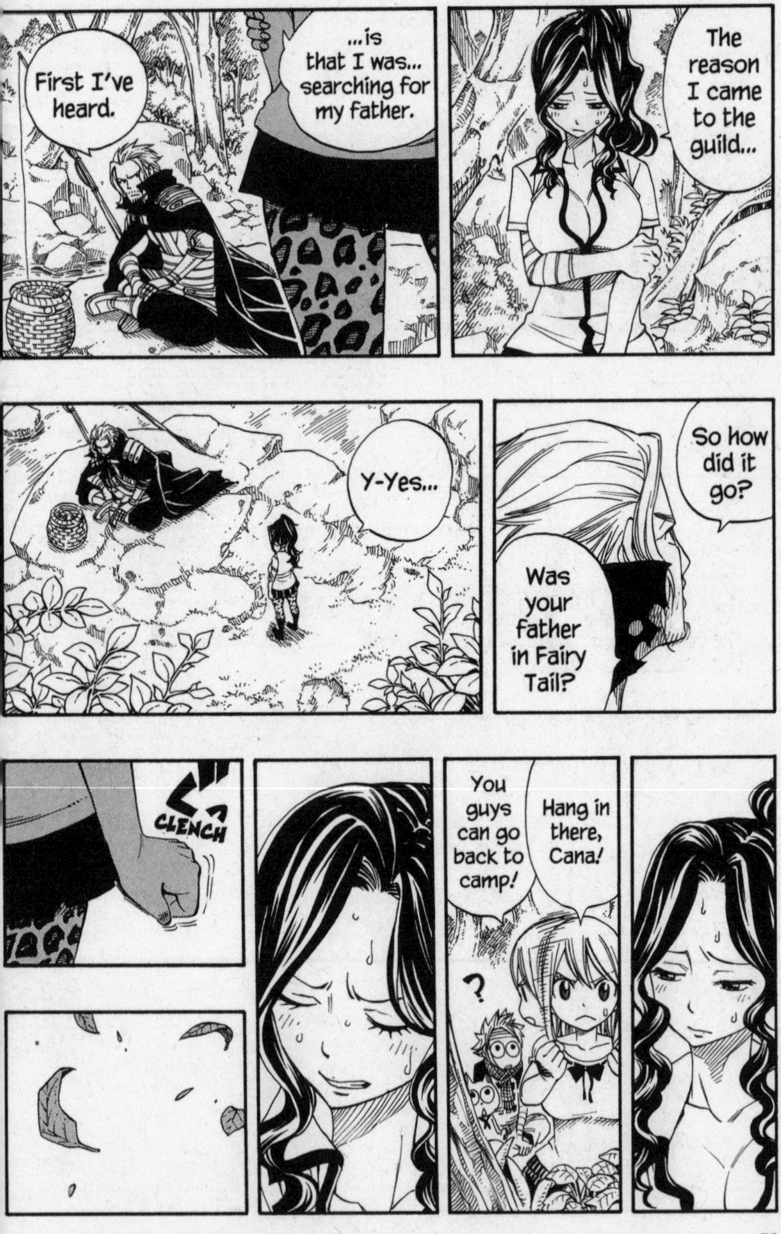
The reason I came to the guild...
...is that I was... searching for my father.
First I've heard.
So how did it go?
Was your father in Fairy Tail?
Y-Yes...
Hang in there, Cana!
You guys can go back to camp!
?
CLENCH

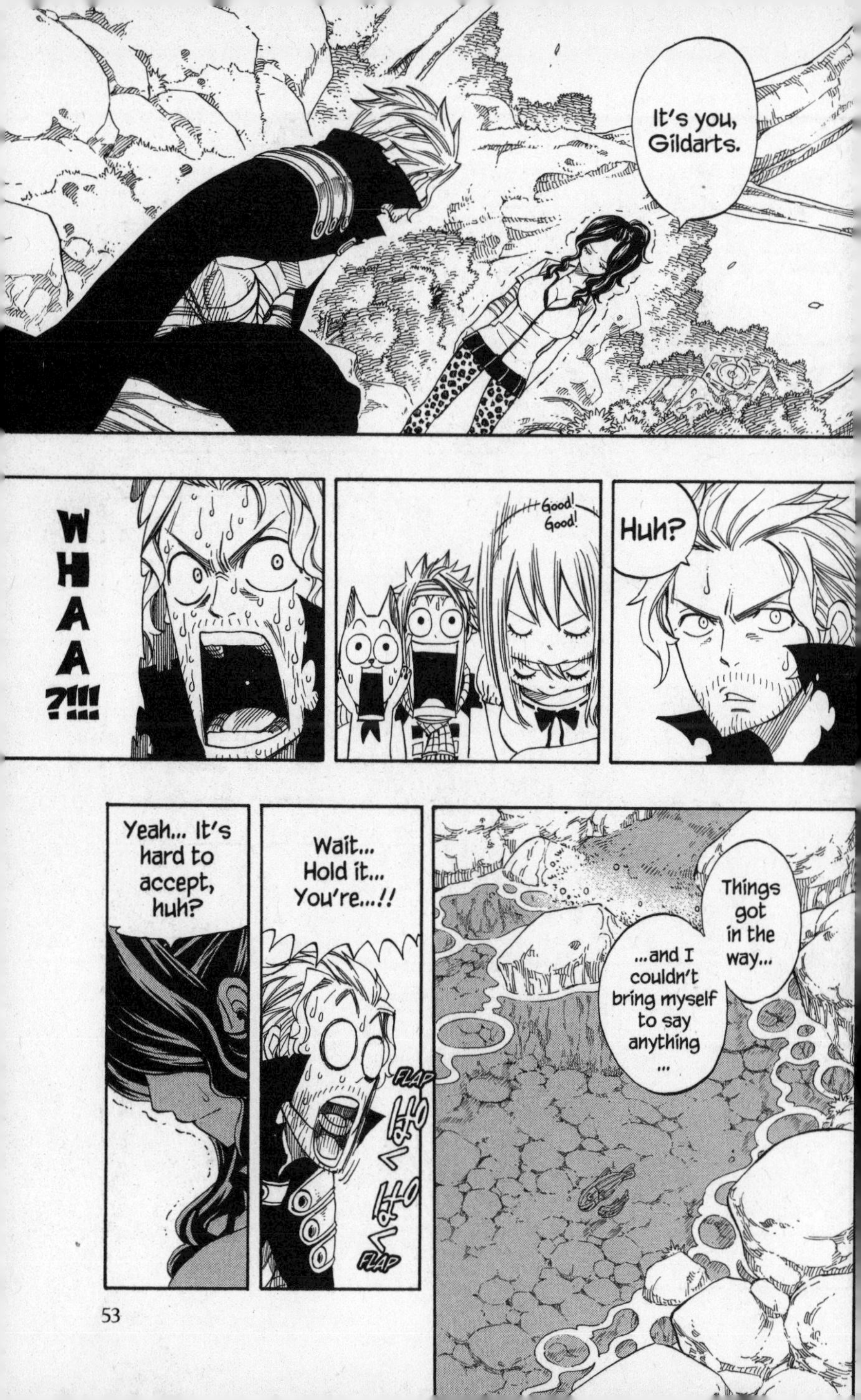
It's you, Gildarts.
Huh?
Good! Good!
WHAAA?!!!
Things got in the way...
...and I couldn't bring myself to say anything...
Wait... Hold it... You're...!!
FLAP
FLAP
Yeah... It's hard to accept, huh?

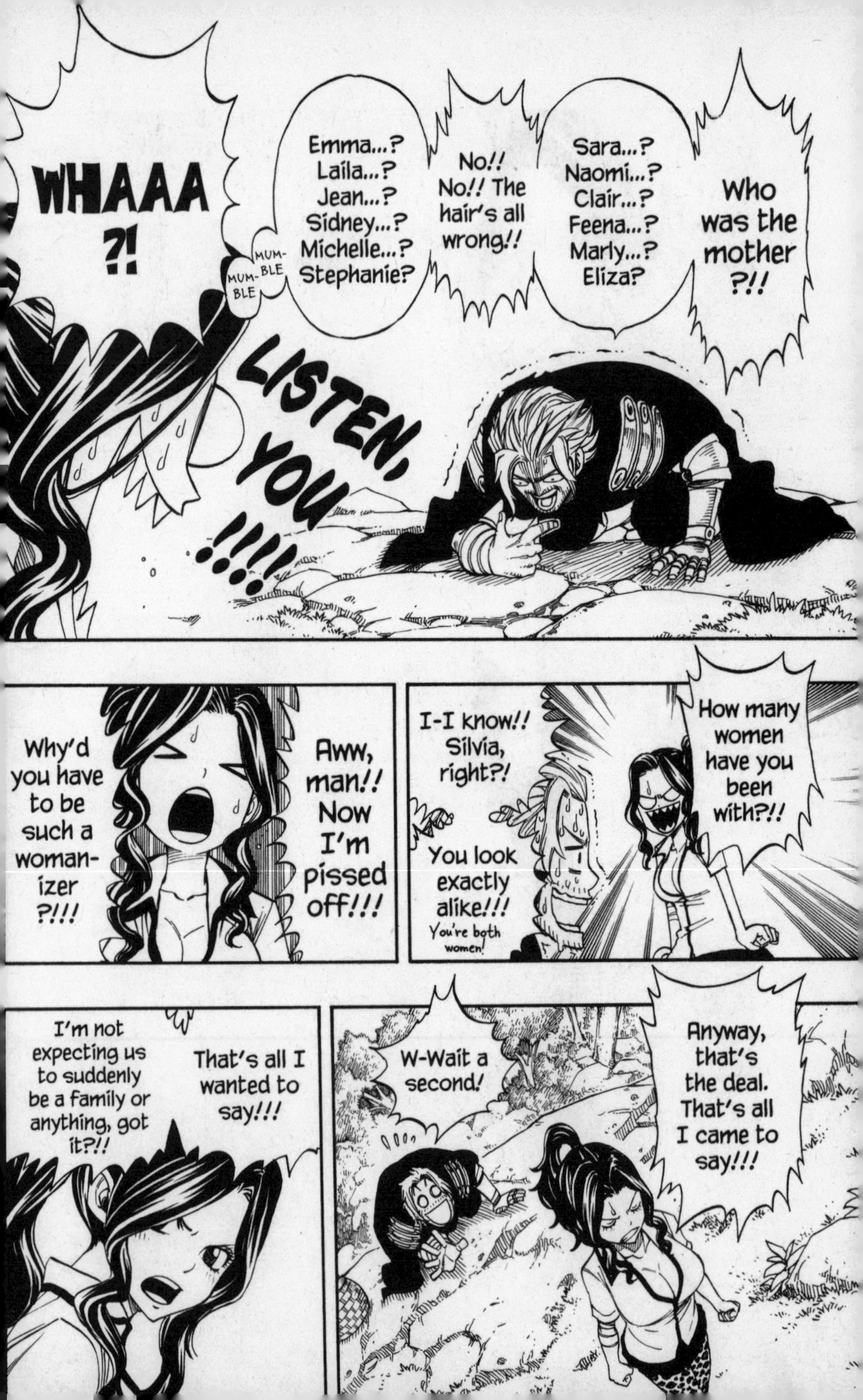

Who was the mother ?!!
Sara...? Naomi...? Clair...? Feena...? Marly...? Eliza?
No!! No!! The hair's all wrong!!
Emma...? Laila...? Jean...? Sidney...? Michelle...? Stephanie?
MUM-BLE MUM-BLE
WHAAA ?!
LISTEN, YOU !!!!
How many women have you been with?!!
I-I know!! Silvia, right?!
You look exactly alike!!!
You're both women!
Aww, man!! Now I'm pissed off!!!
Why'd you have to be such a woman-izer ?!!!
Anyway, that's the deal. That's all I came to say!!!
W-Wait a second!
That's all I wanted to say!!!
I'm not expecting us to suddenly be a family or anything, got it?!!

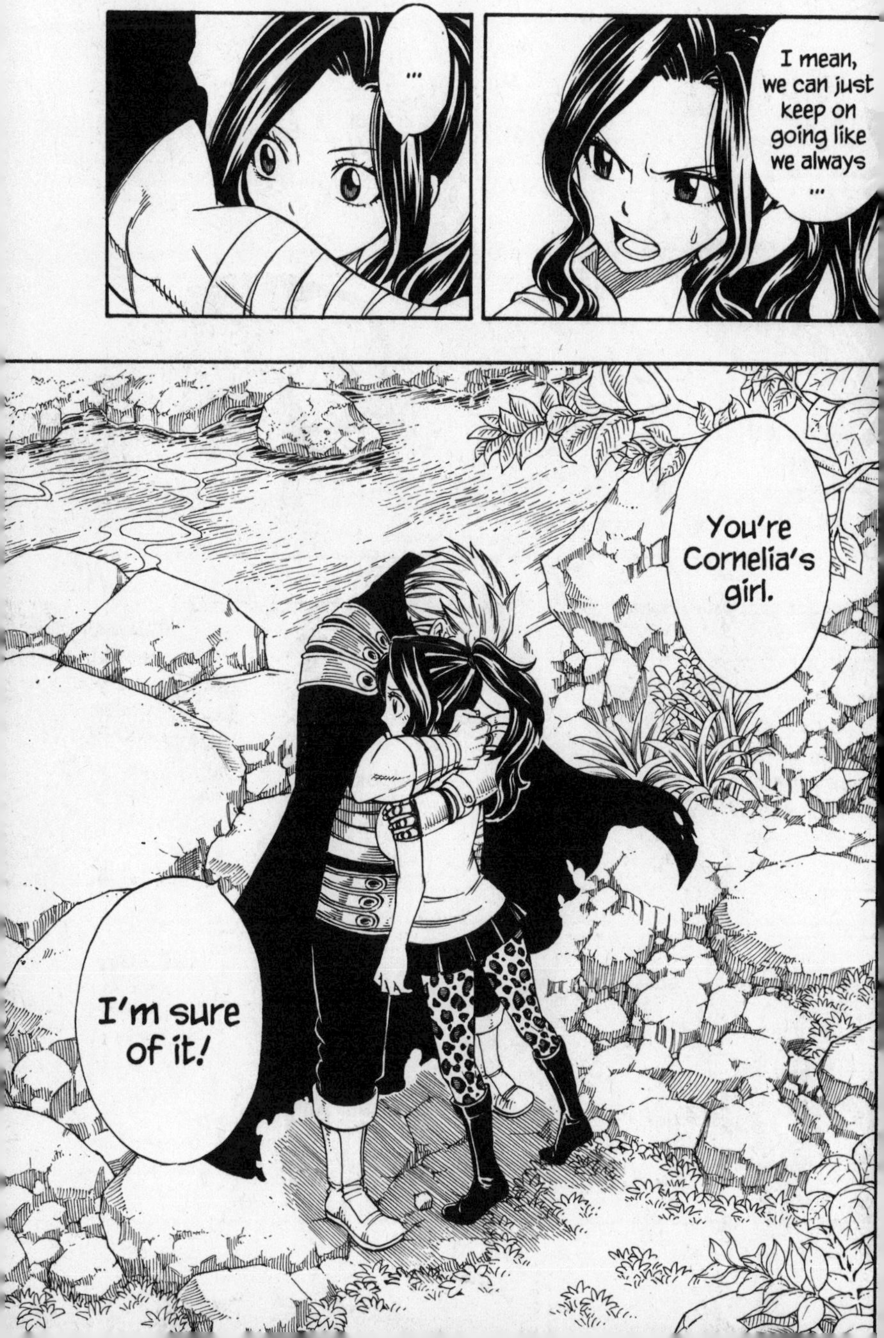
I mean, we can just keep on going like we always ...
...
You're Cornelia's girl.
I'm sure of it!

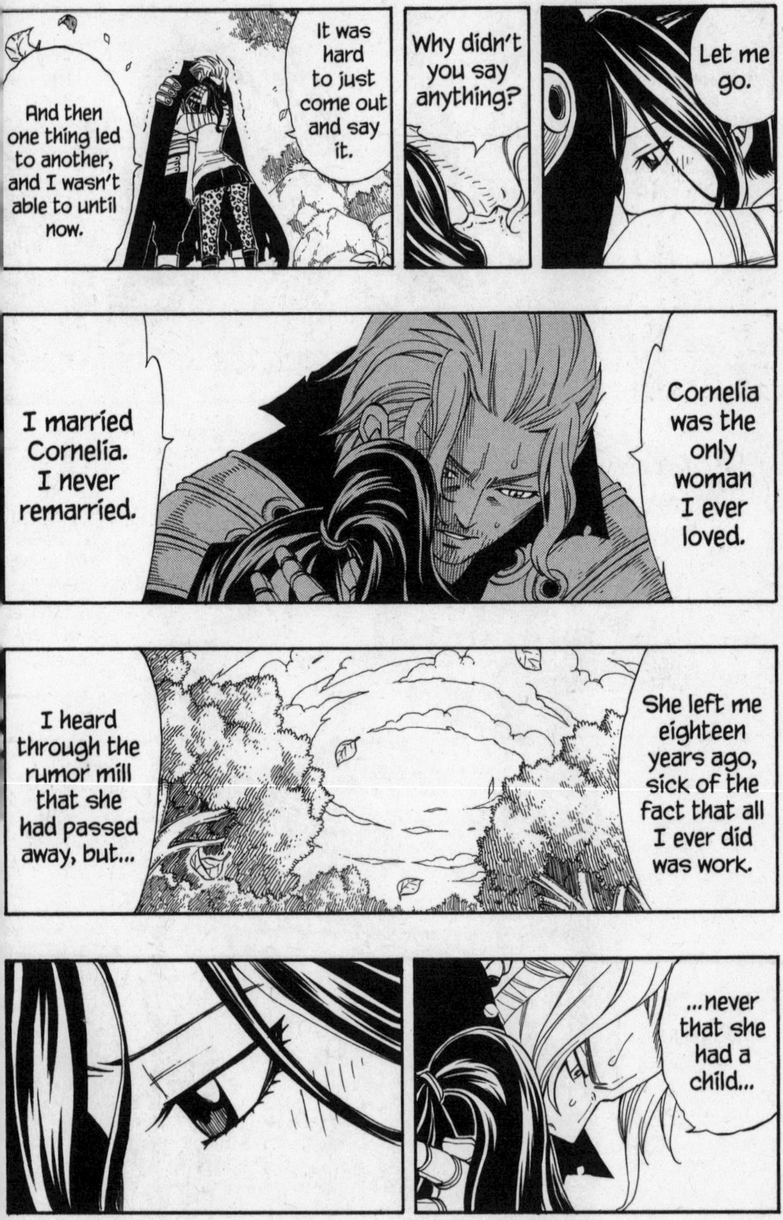
Let me go.
Why didn't you say anything?
It was hard to just come out and say it.
And then one thing led to another, and I wasn't able to until now.
Cornelia was the only woman I ever loved.
I married Cornelia. I never remarried.
She left me eighteen years ago, sick of the fact that all I ever did was work.
I heard through the rumor mill that she had passed away, but...
...never that she had a child...

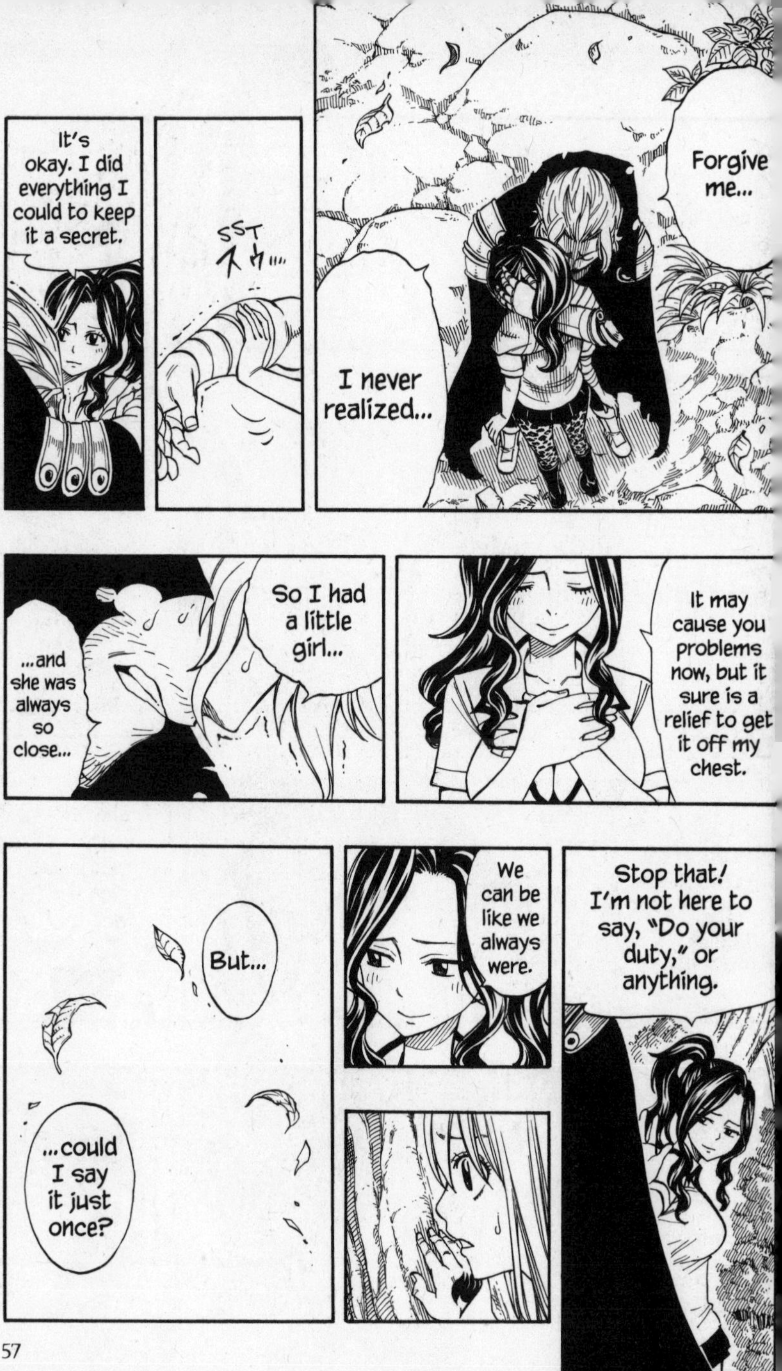
Forgive me...
I never realized...
SST
スゥ…
It's okay. I did everything I could to keep it a secret.
It may cause you problems now, but it sure is a relief to get it off my chest.
So I had a little girl...
...and she was always so close...
Stop that! I'm not here to say, "Do your duty," or anything.
We can be like we always were.
But...
...could I say it just once?

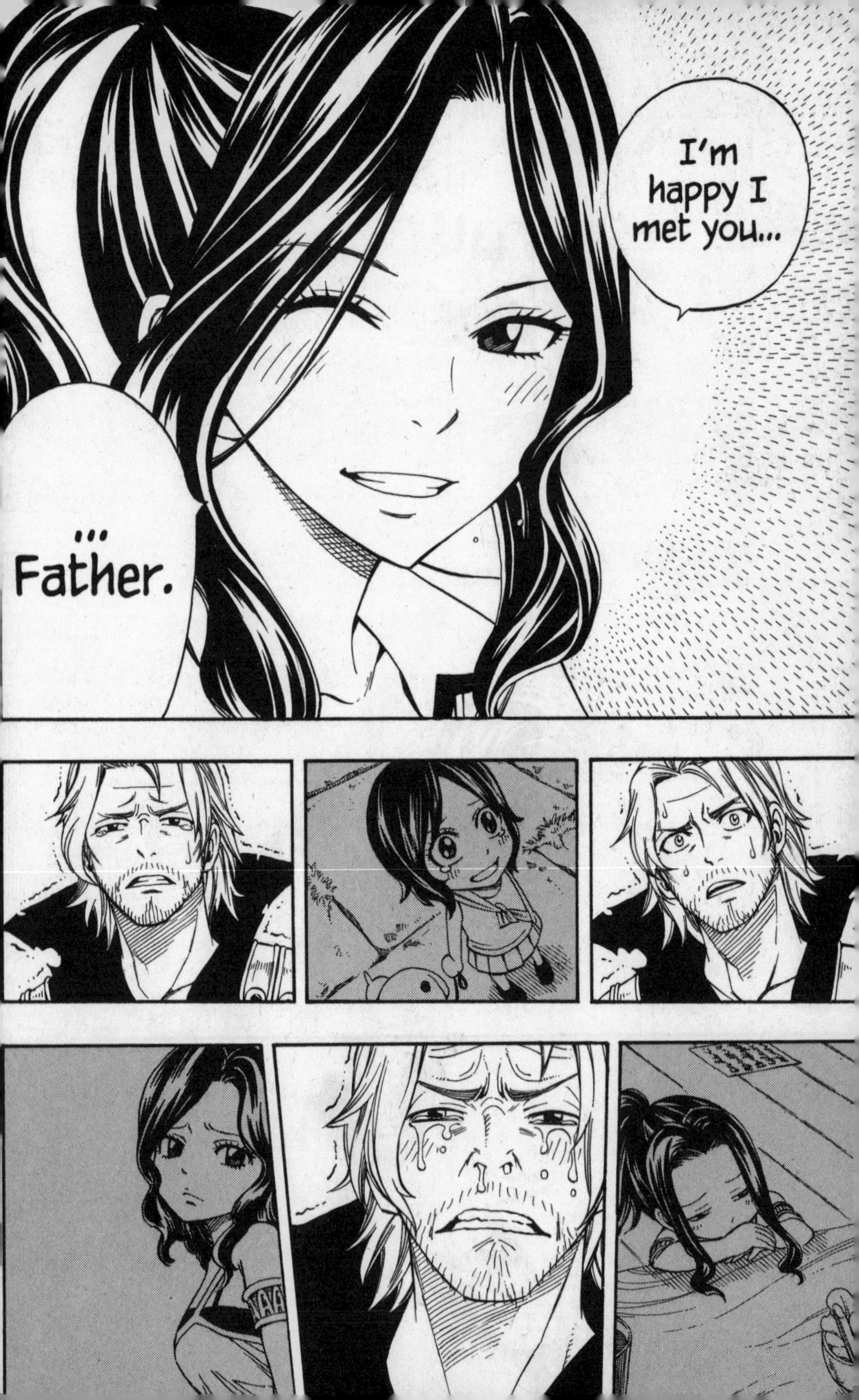
I'm happy I met you...
... Father.

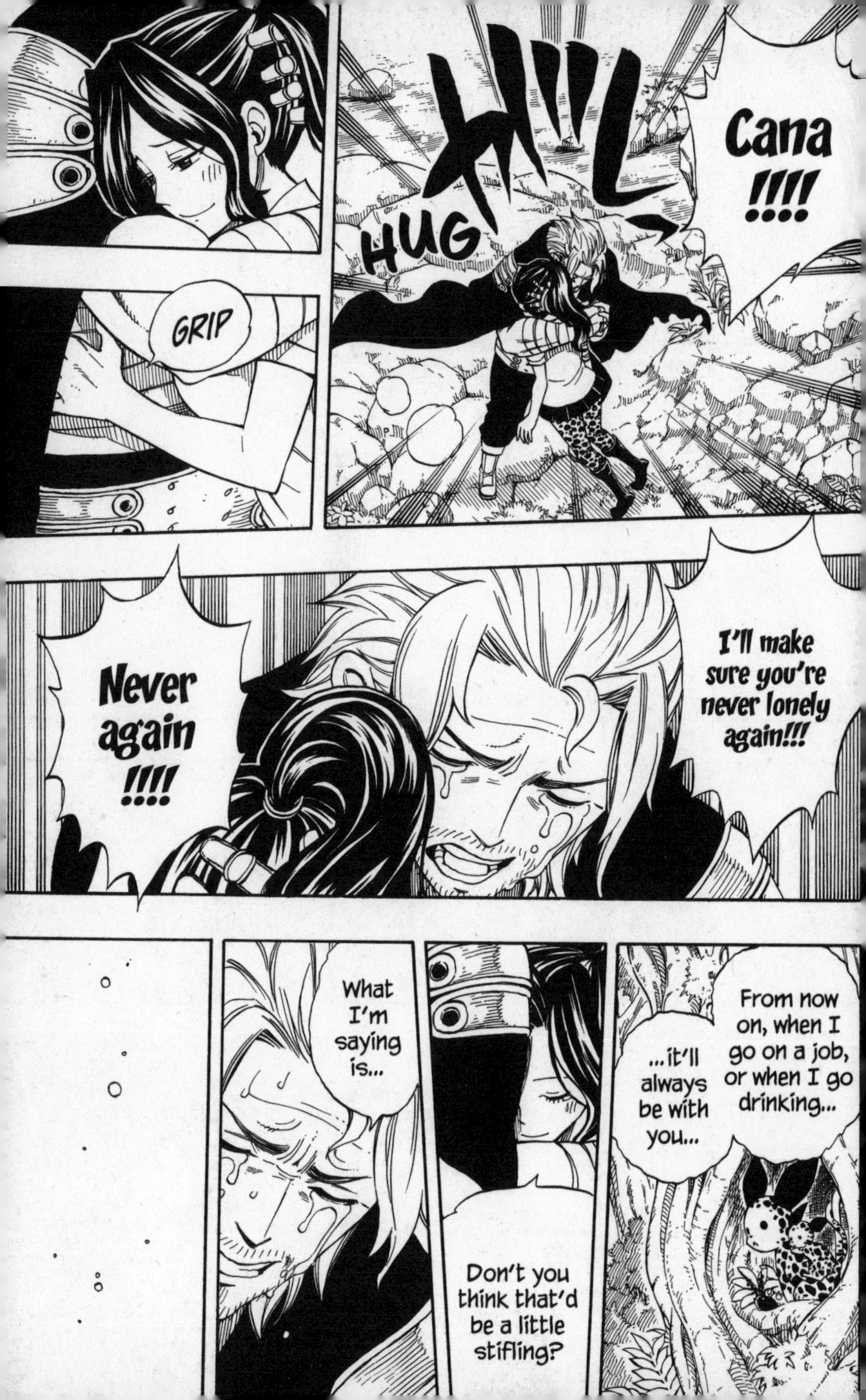
Cana!!!!
HUG
GRIP
I'll make sure you're never lonely again!!!
Never again!!!!
From now on, when I go on a job, or when I go drinking...
...it'll always be with you...
Don't you think that'd be a little stifling?
What I'm saying is...

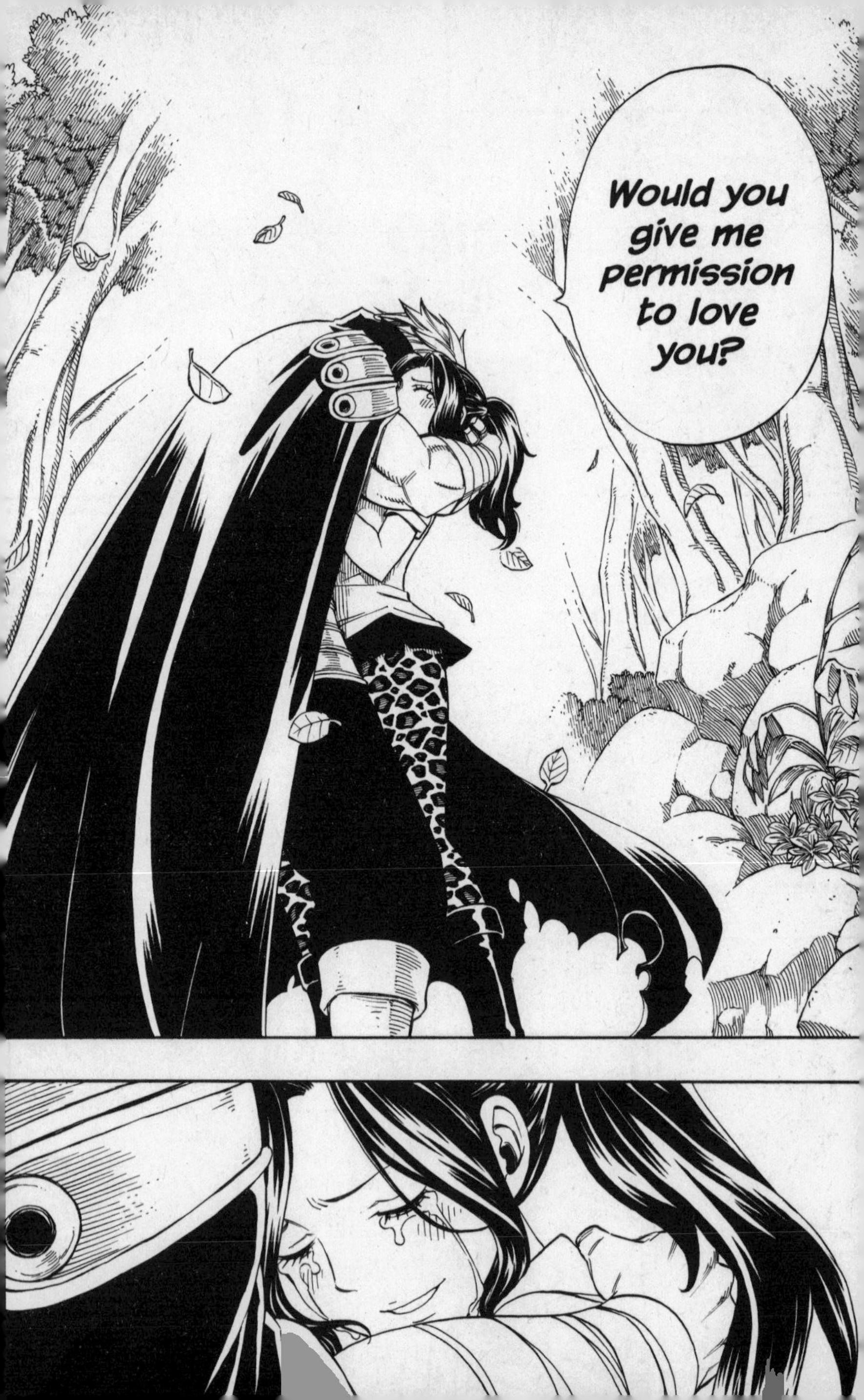
Would you give me permission to love you?

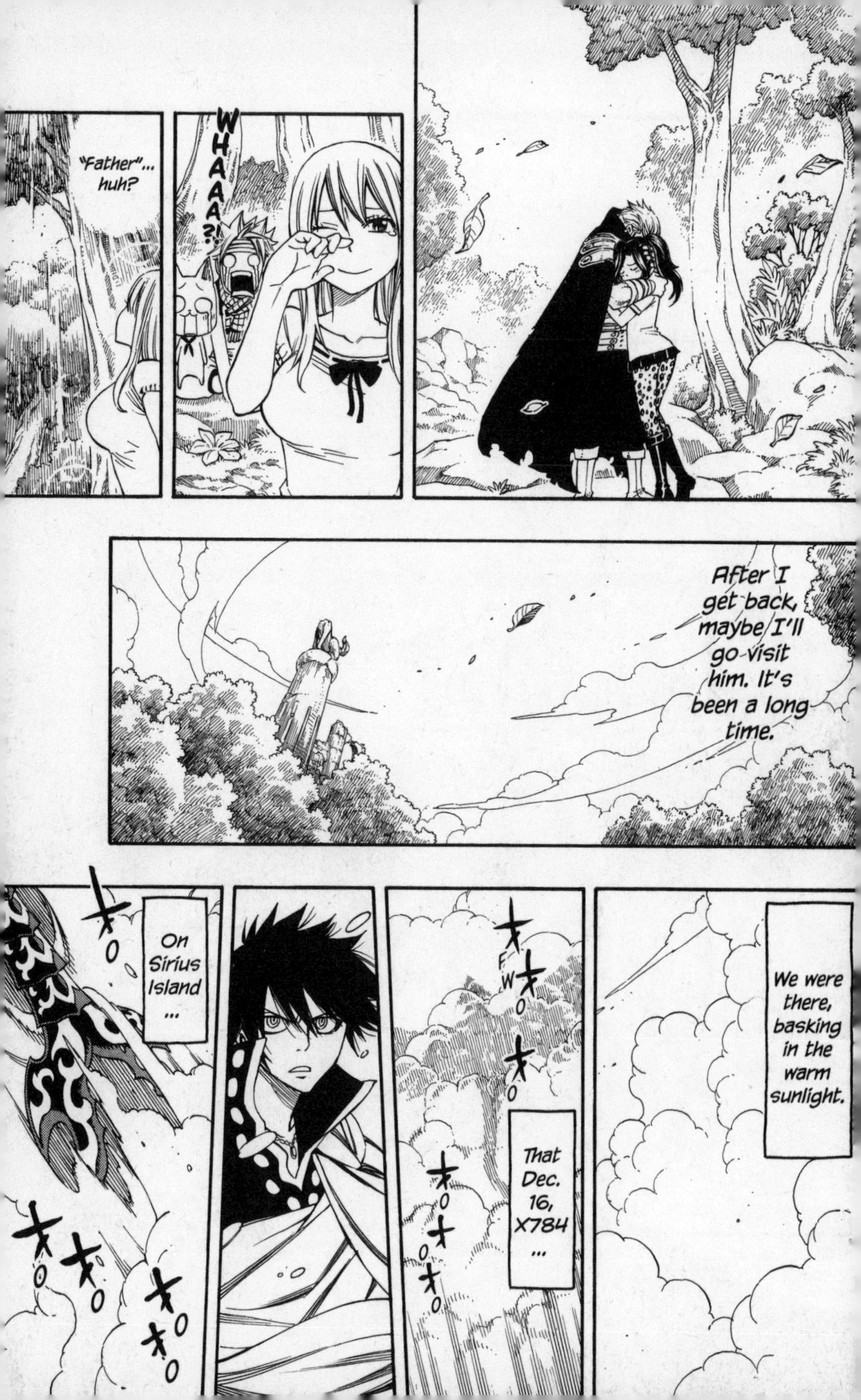

WHAAAA?!
"Father"... huh?
After I get back, maybe I'll go visit him. It's been a long time.
We were there, basking in the warm sunlight.
FWOO
That Dec. 16, X784 ...
On Sirius Island ...

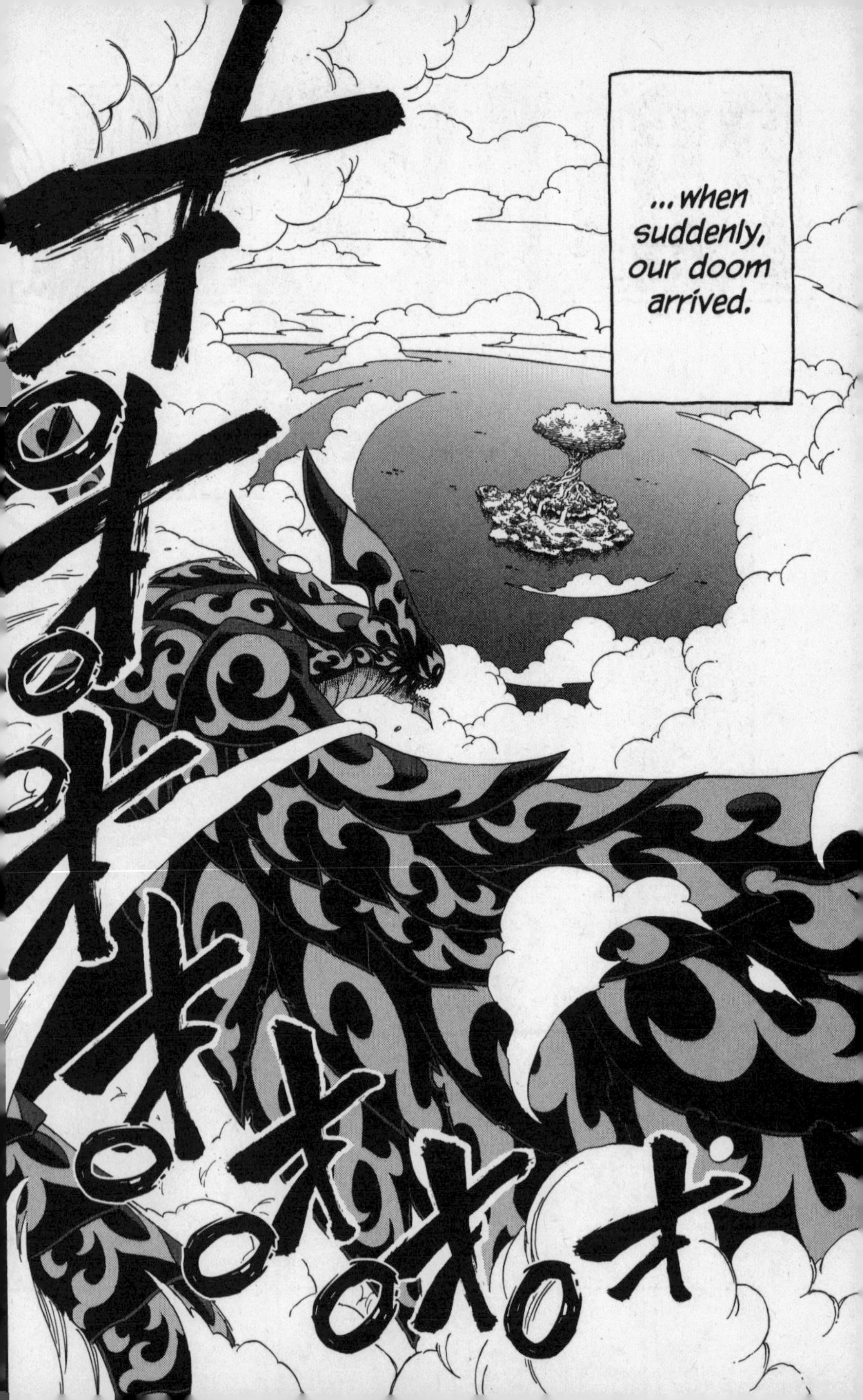
...when suddenly, our doom arrived.

FAIRY TAIL

フェアリーテイル

Chapter 252: To You Prideful Brats

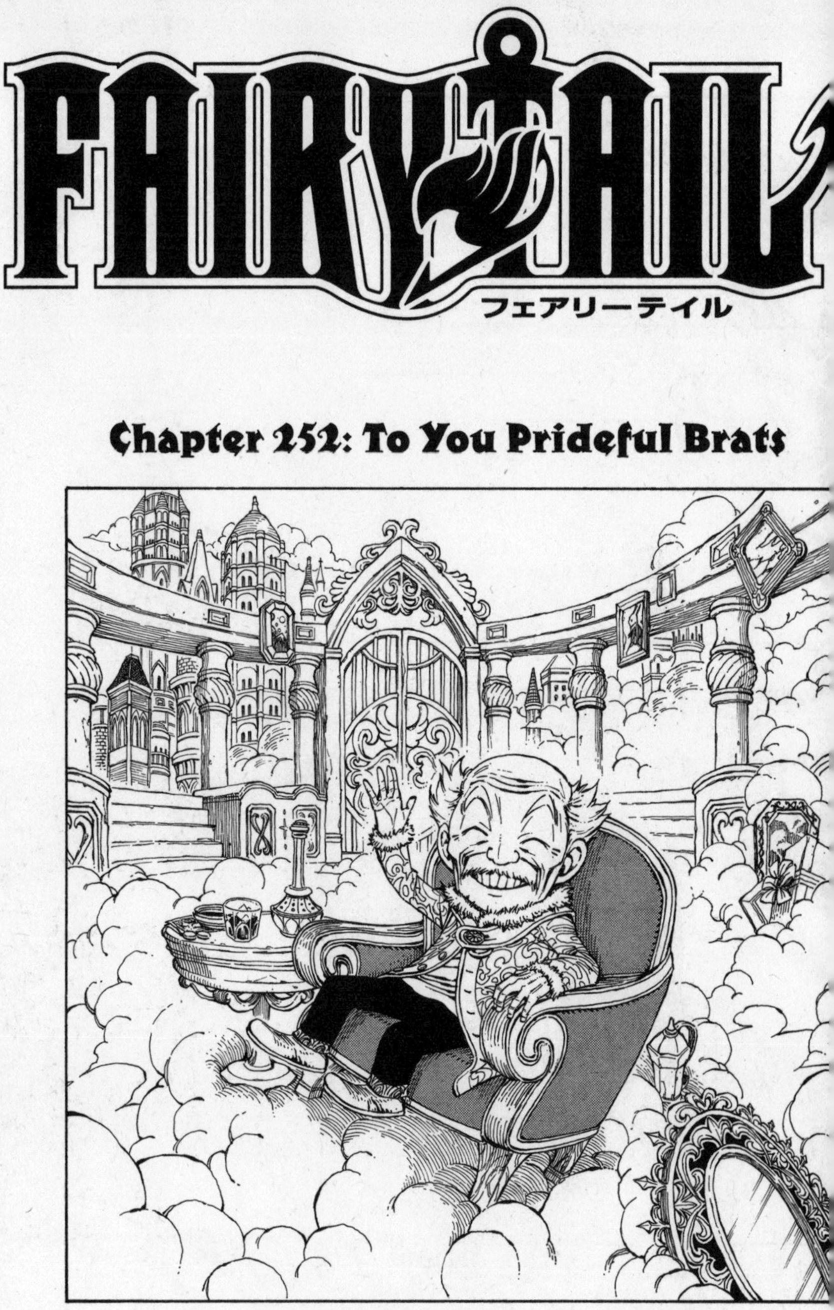

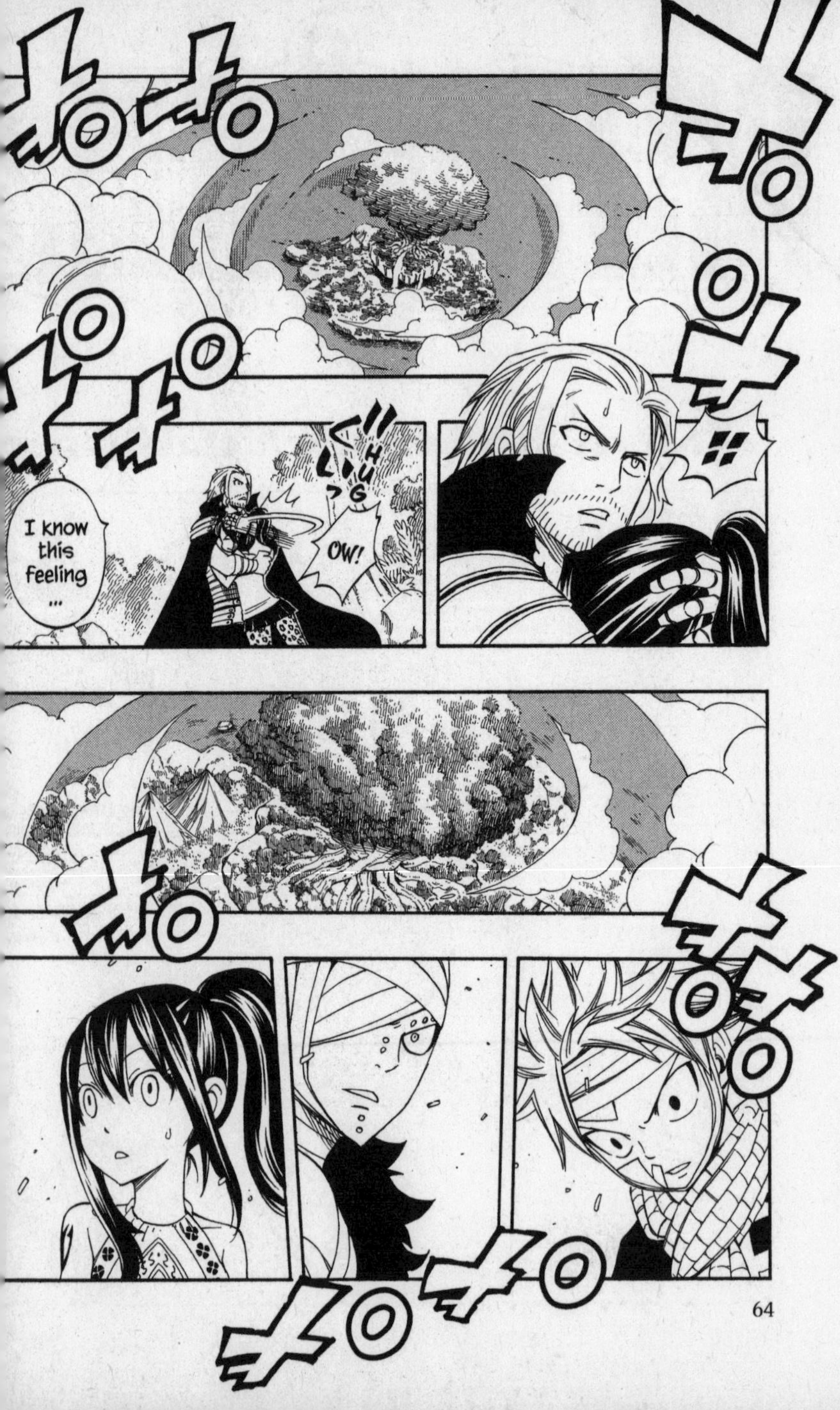
HUG
OW!
I know this feeling ...

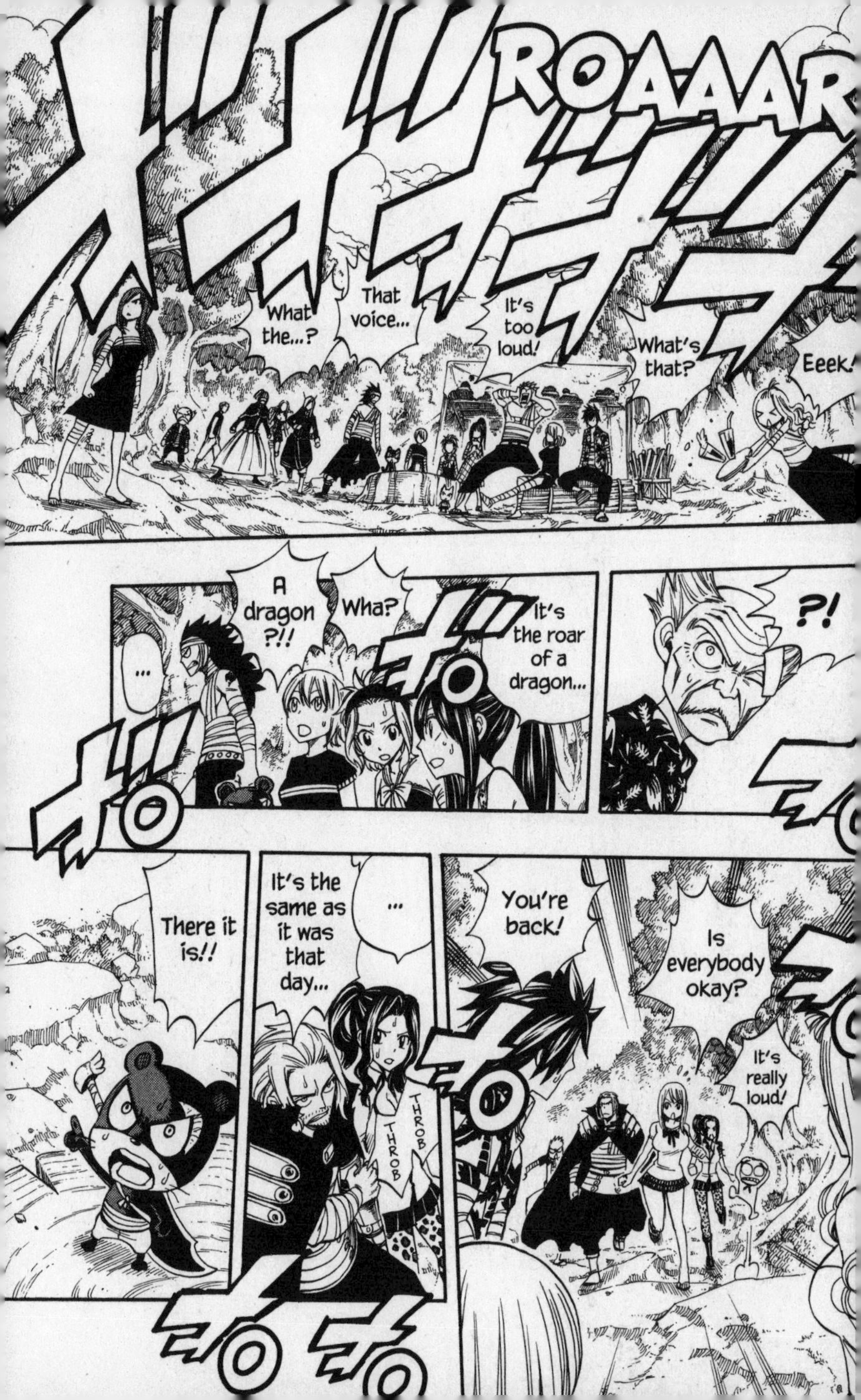
ROAAAR
Eeek!
What's that?
It's too loud!
That voice...
What the...?
?!
It's the roar of a dragon...
Wha?
A dragon?!!
...
Is everybody okay?
You're back!
It's really loud!
...
It's the same as it was that day...
THROB THROB
There it is!!

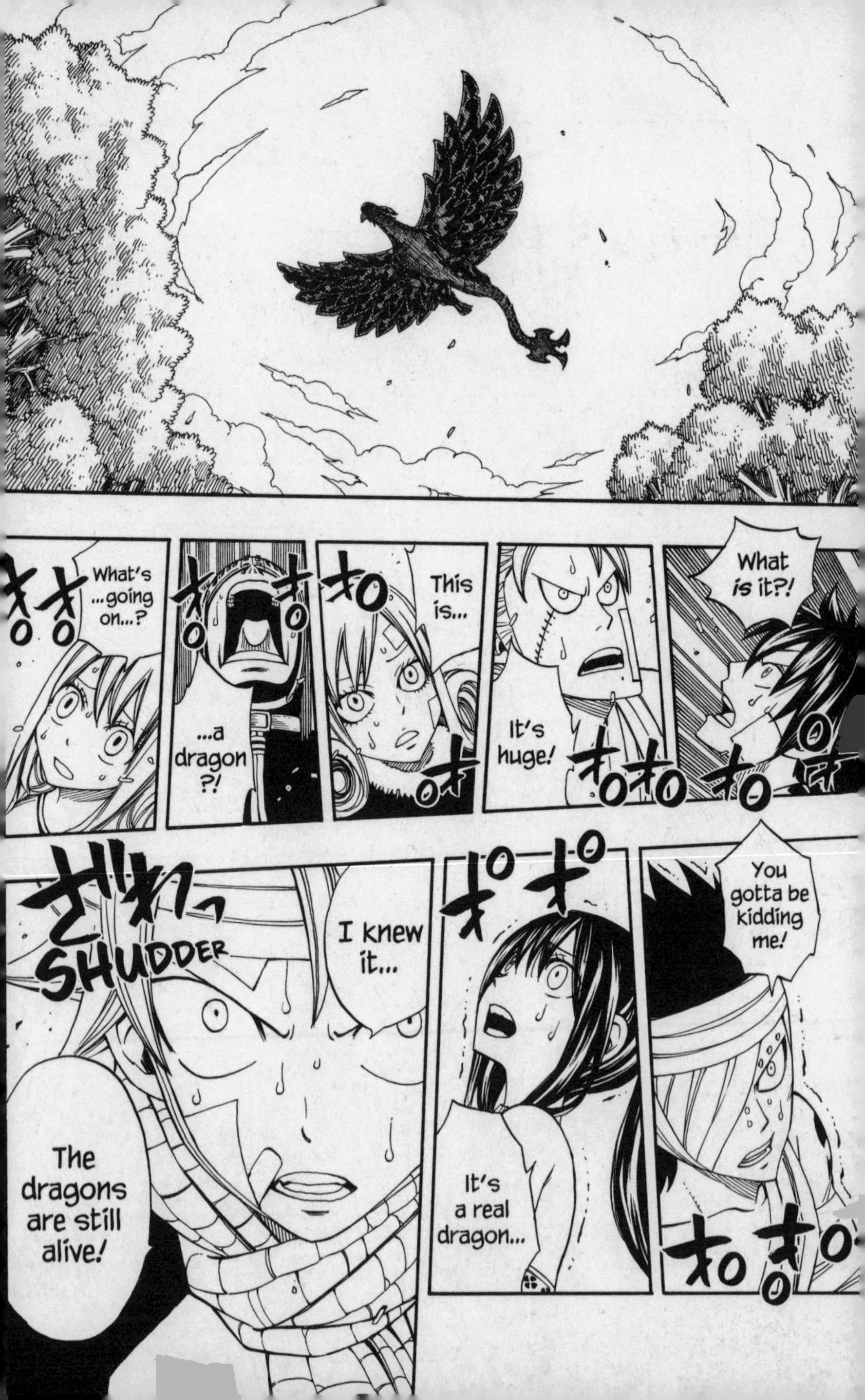
What is it?!
It's huge!
This is...
...a dragon?!
What's ...going on...?
You gotta be kidding me!
It's a real dragon...
I knew it...
SHUDDER
The dragons are still alive!

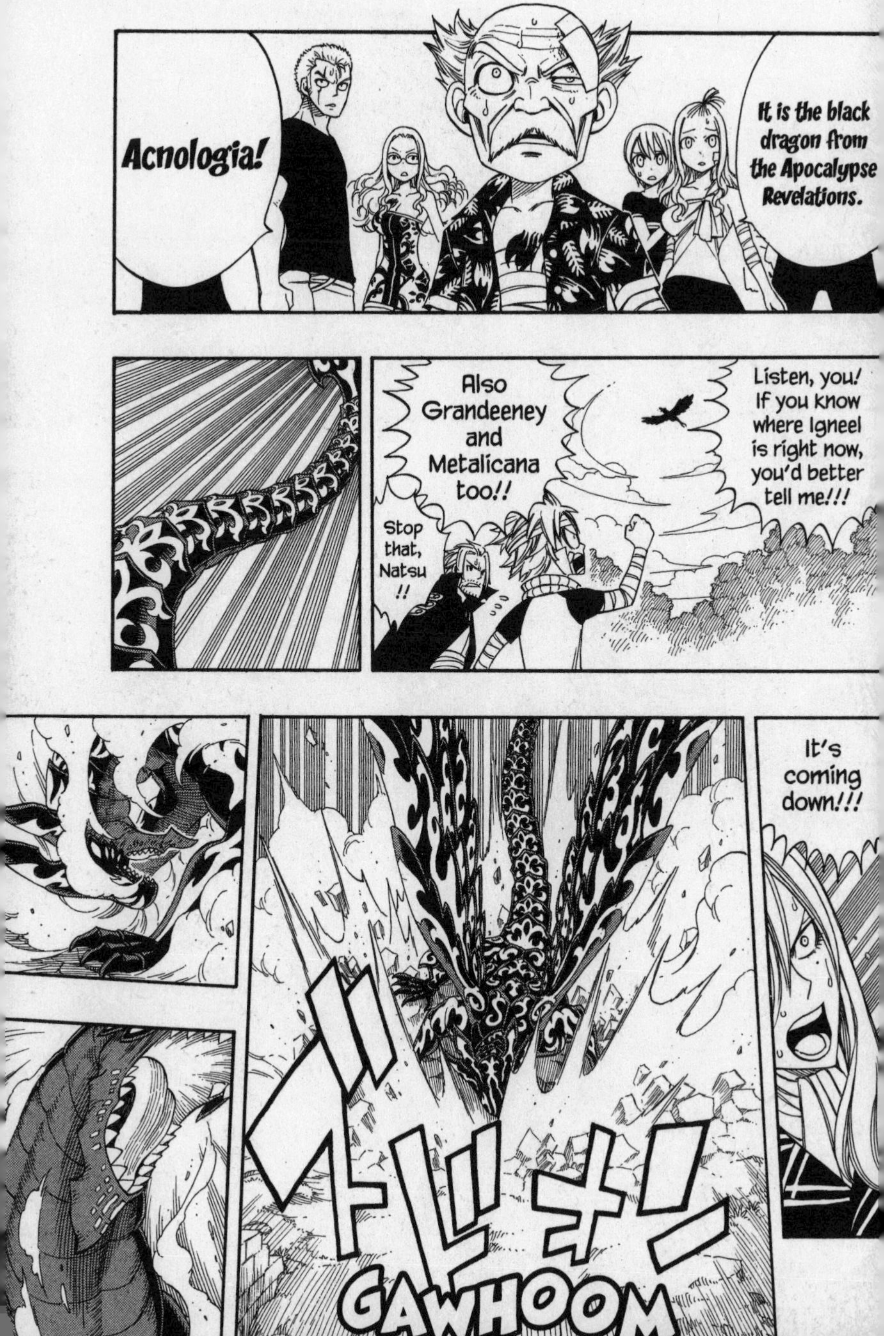
It is the black dragon from the Apocalypse Revelations.
Acnologia!
Listen, you! If you know where Igneel is right now, you'd better tell me!!!
Also Grandeeney and Metalicana too!!
Stop that, Natsu!!
It's coming down!!!
GAWHOOM

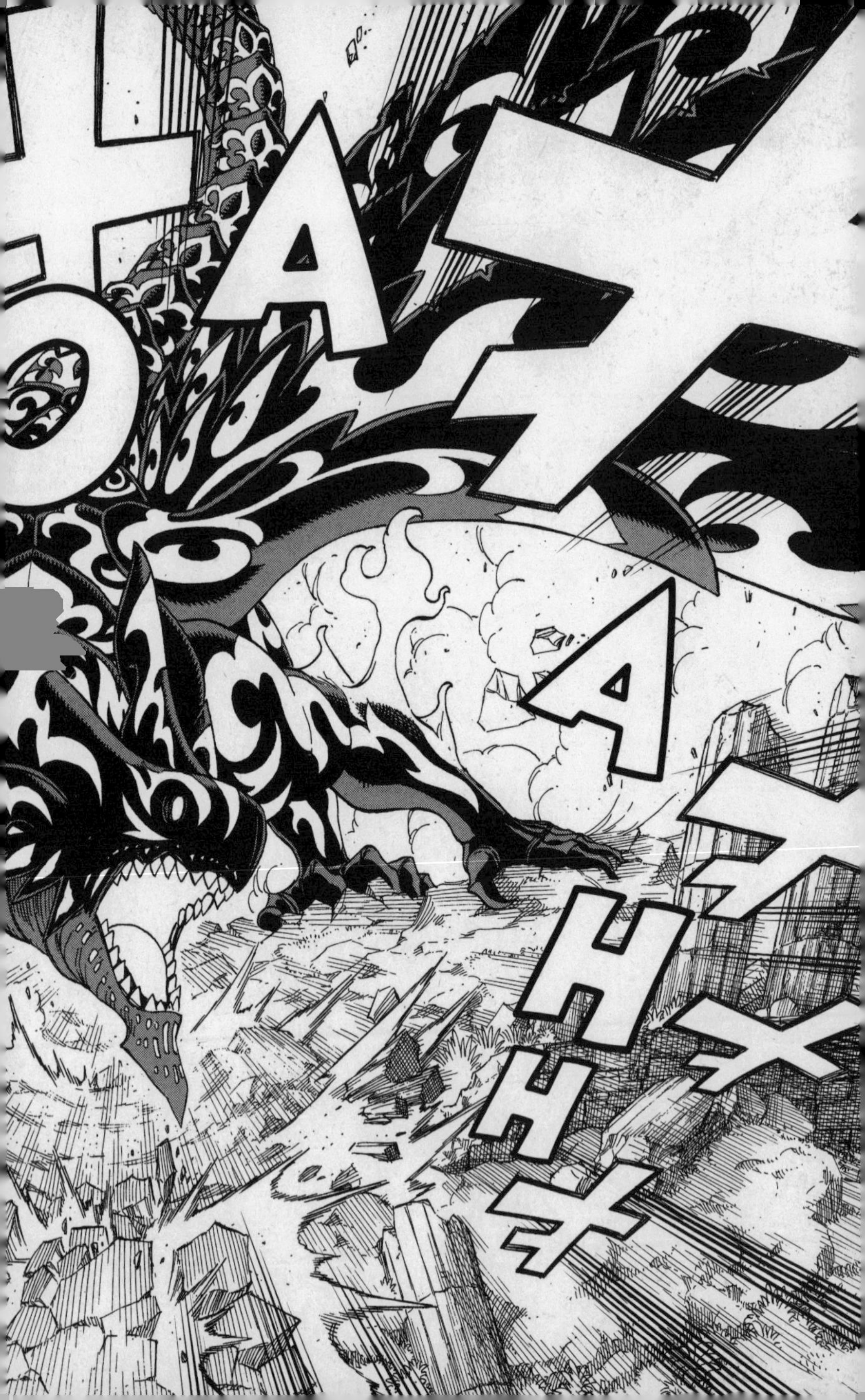

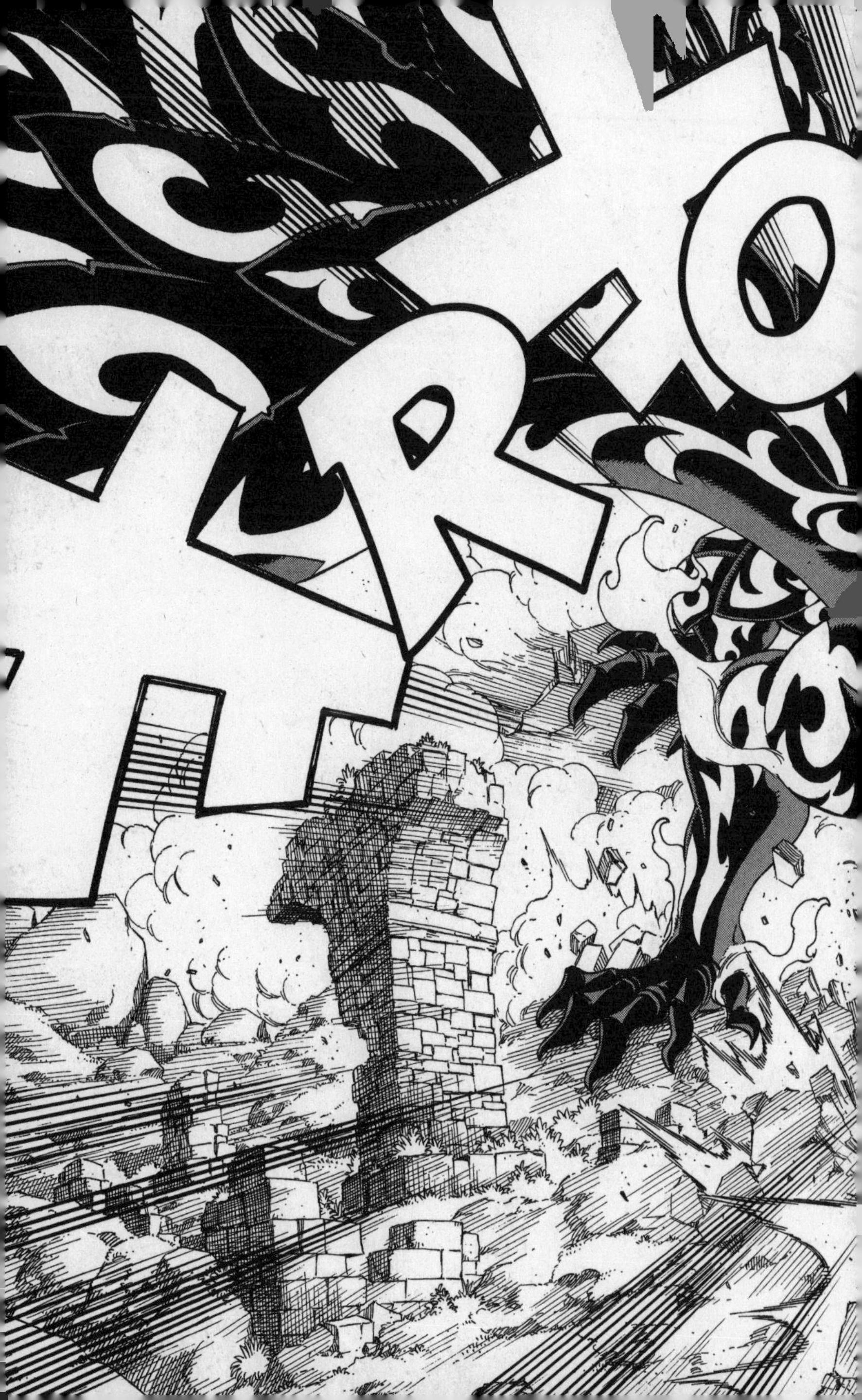

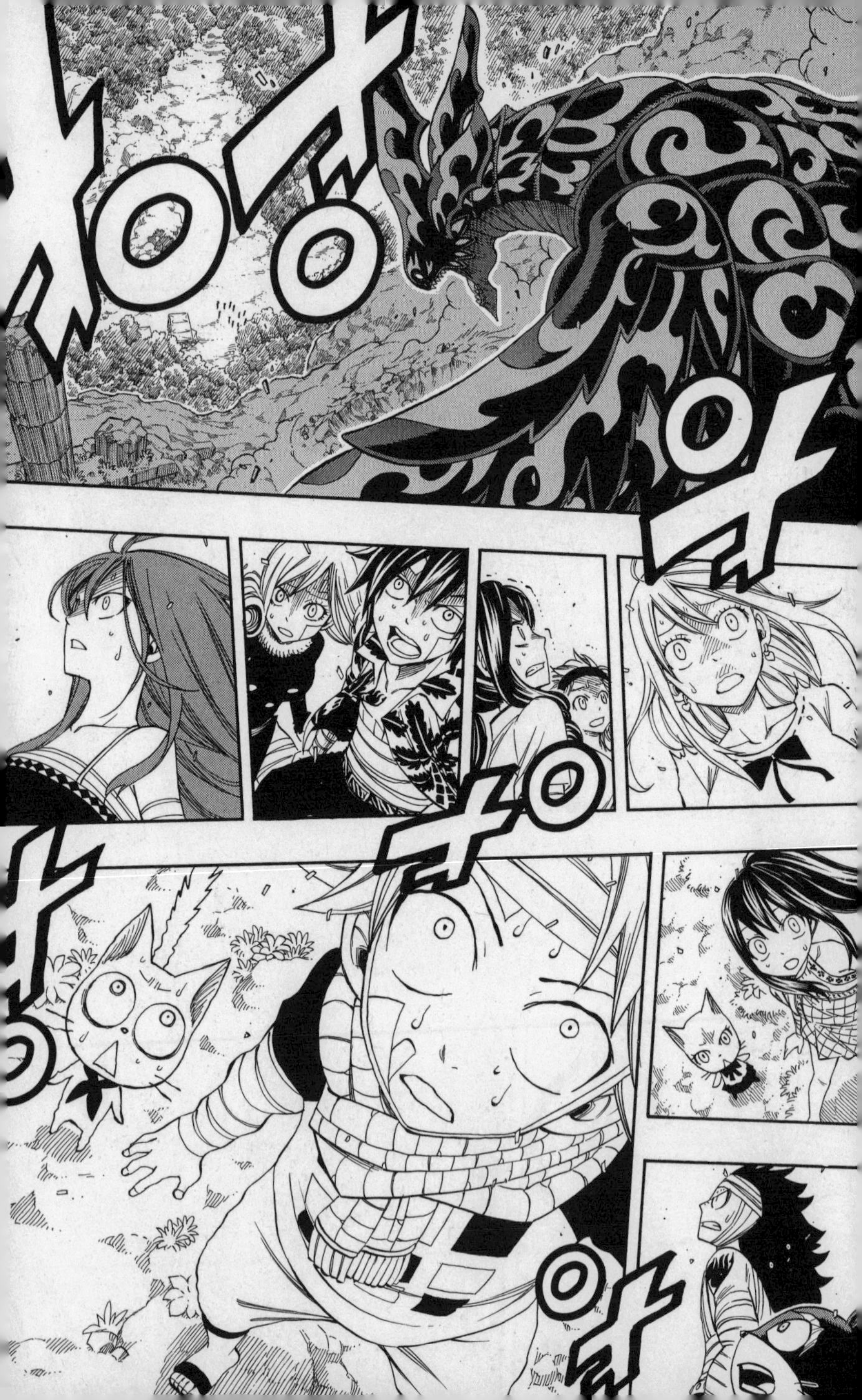

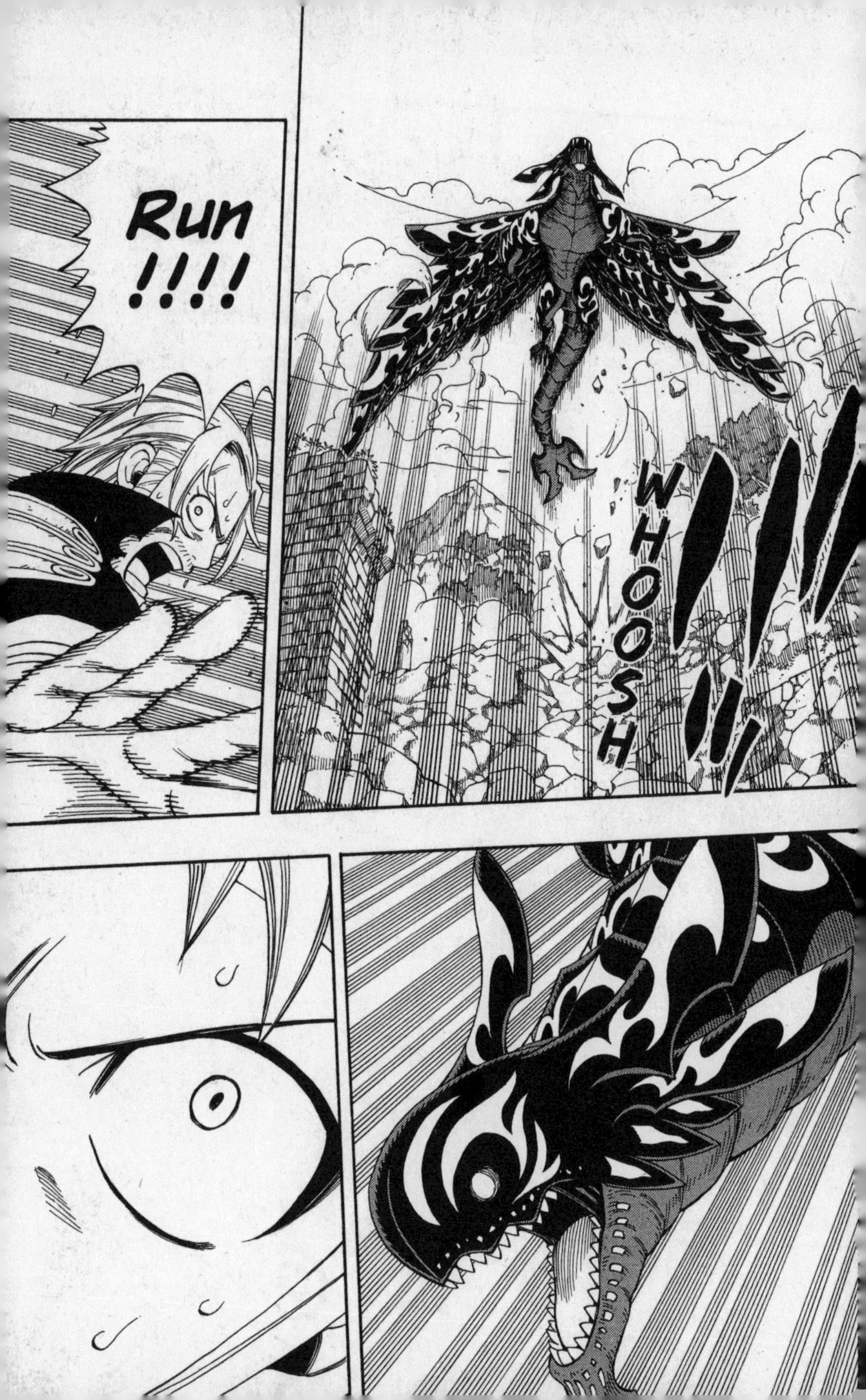
WHOOSH
Run !!!!

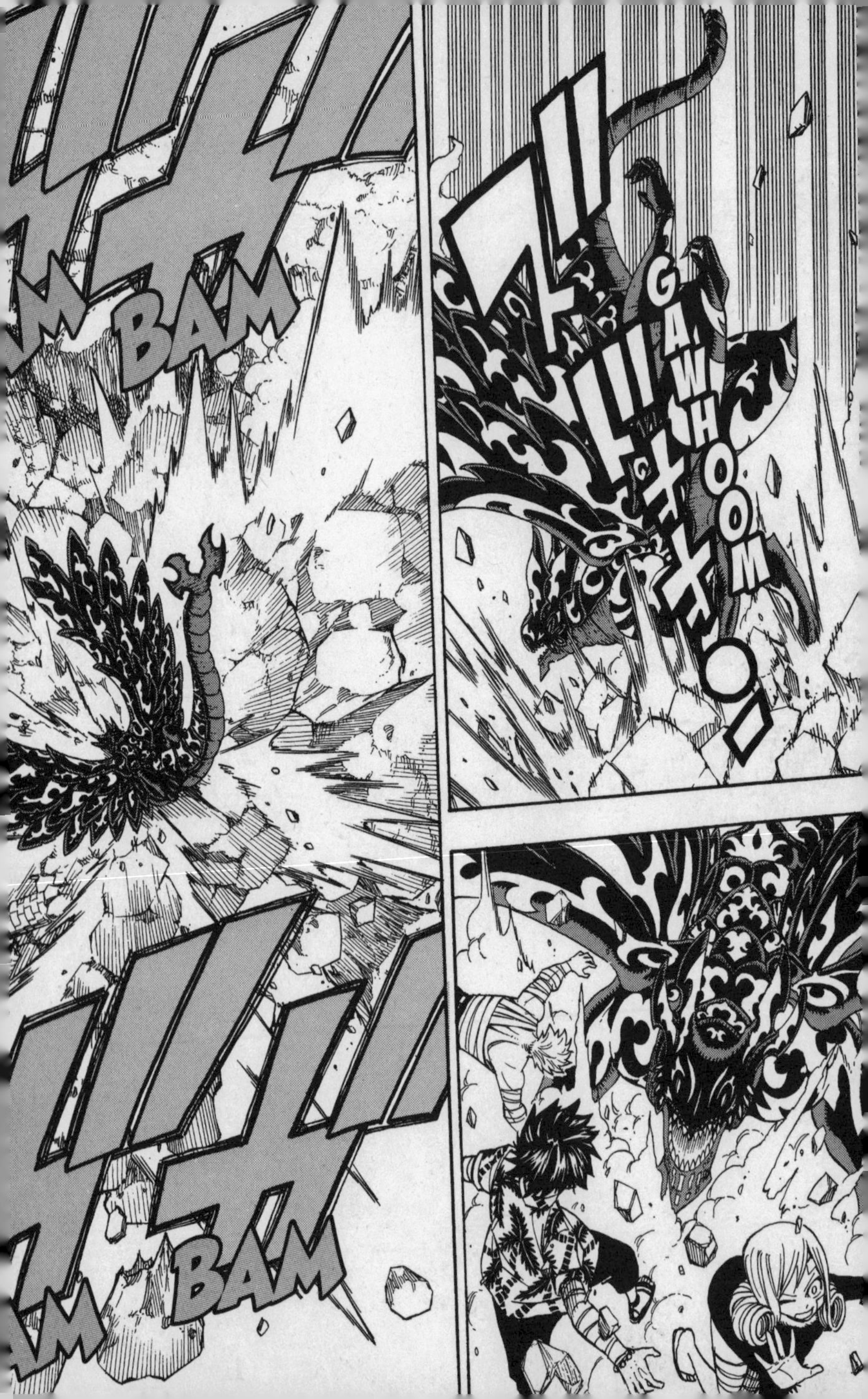
GAWHOOOM
BAM
BAM

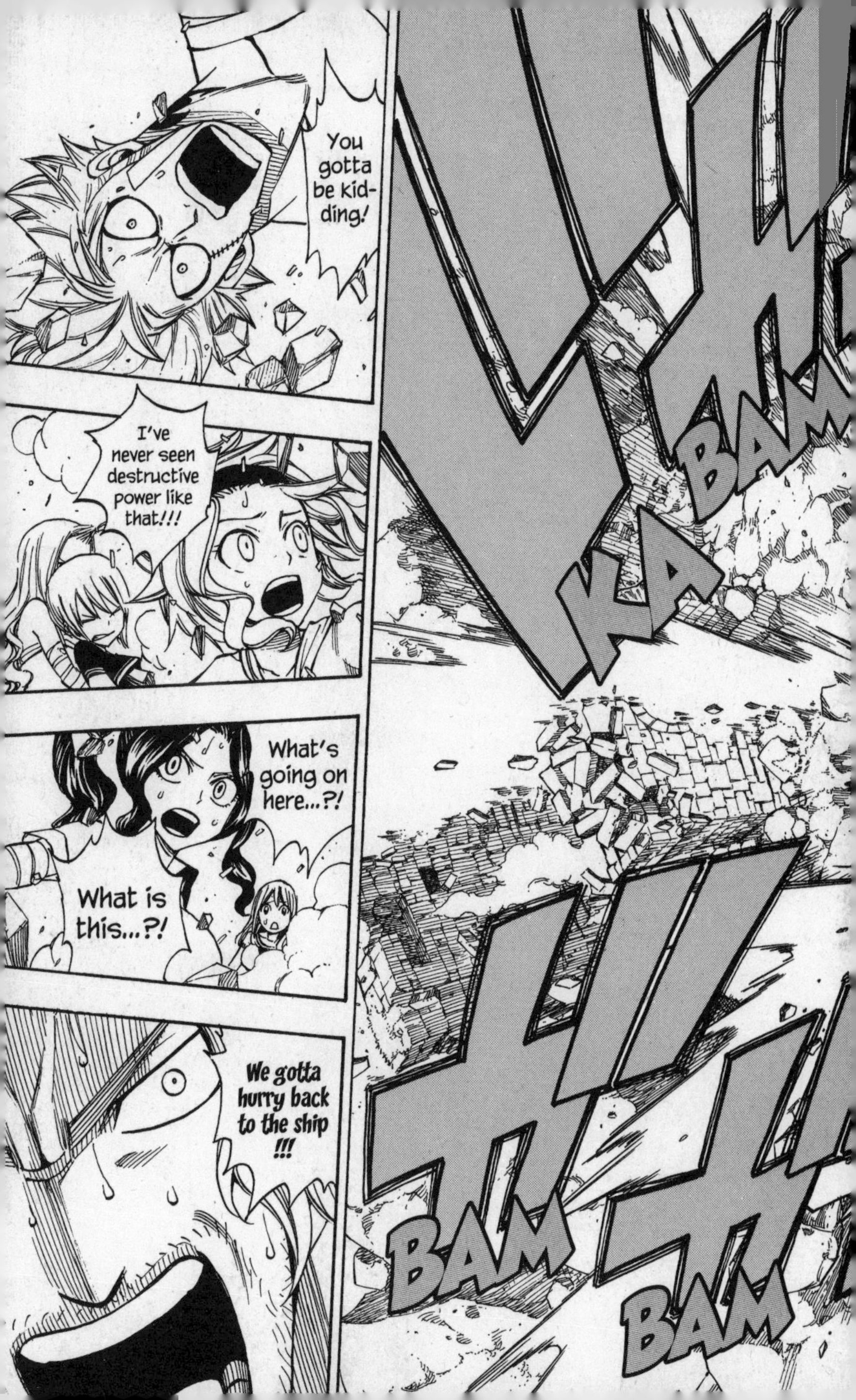
KABAM
BAM
BAM
You gotta be kid-ding!
I've never seen destructive power like that!!!
What's going on here...?!
What is this...?!
We gotta hurry back to the ship!!!

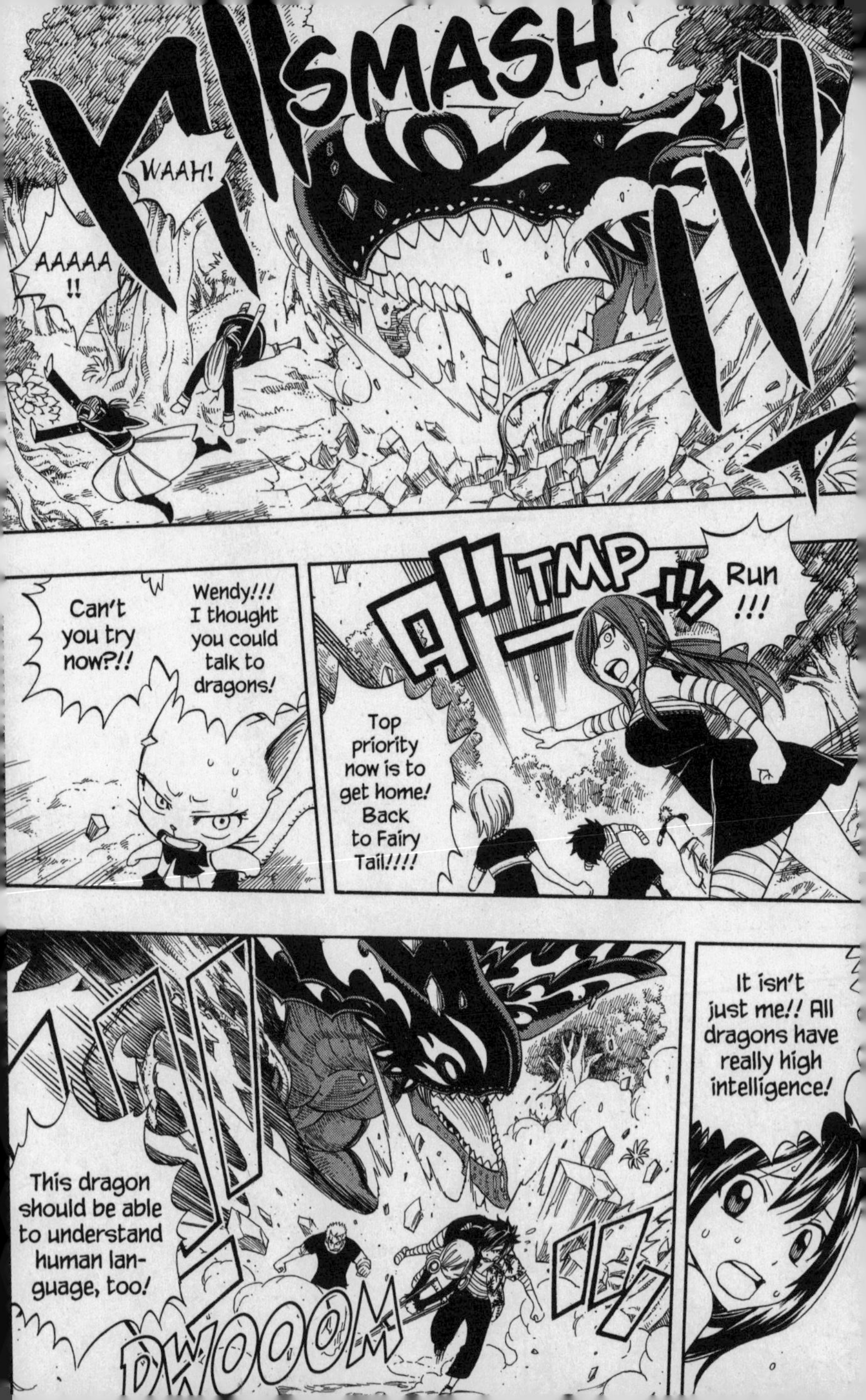
SMASH
WAAH!
AAAAA!!
Run!!!
TMP
Top priority now is to get home! Back to Fairy Tail!!!!
Wendy!!! I thought you could talk to dragons!
Can't you try now?!!
It isn't just me!! All dragons have really high intelligence!
This dragon should be able to understand human lan-guage, too!
DWOOOM

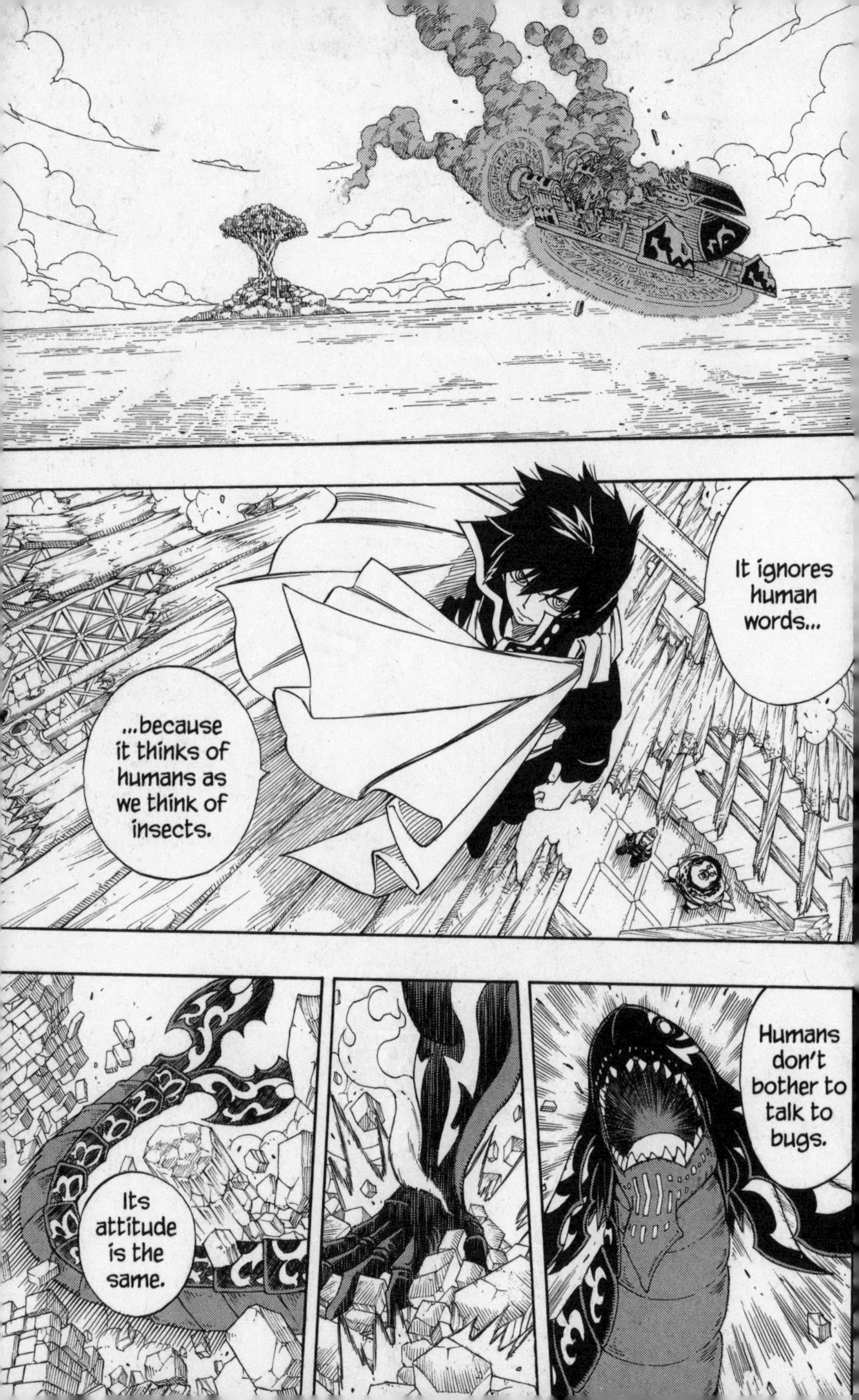
It ignores human words...
...because it thinks of humans as we think of insects.
Humans don't bother to talk to bugs.
Its attitude is the same.

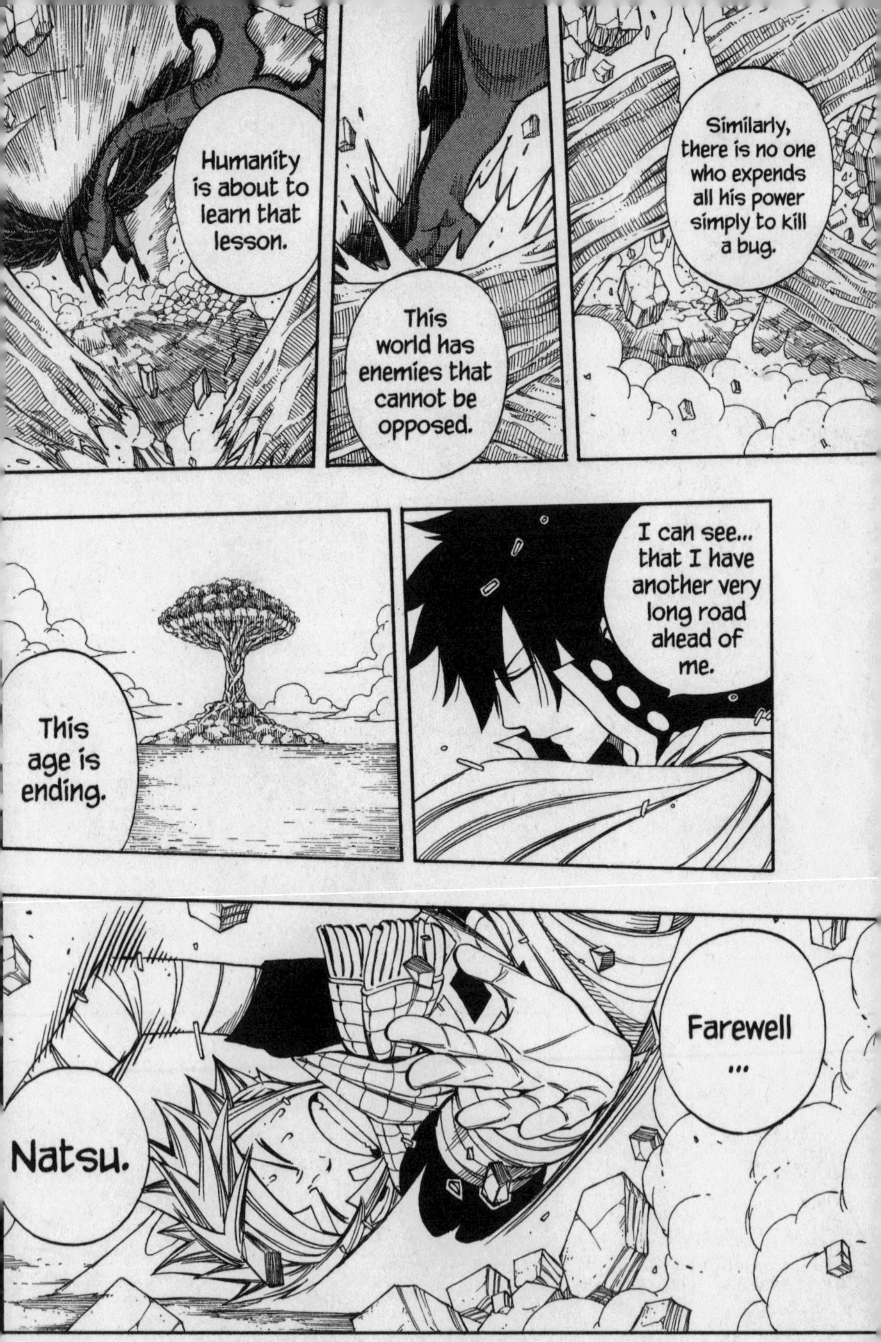
Similarly, there is no one who expends all his power simply to kill a bug.
This world has enemies that cannot be opposed.
Humanity is about to learn that lesson.
I can see... that I have another very long road ahead of me.
This age is ending.
Farewell ...
Natsu.

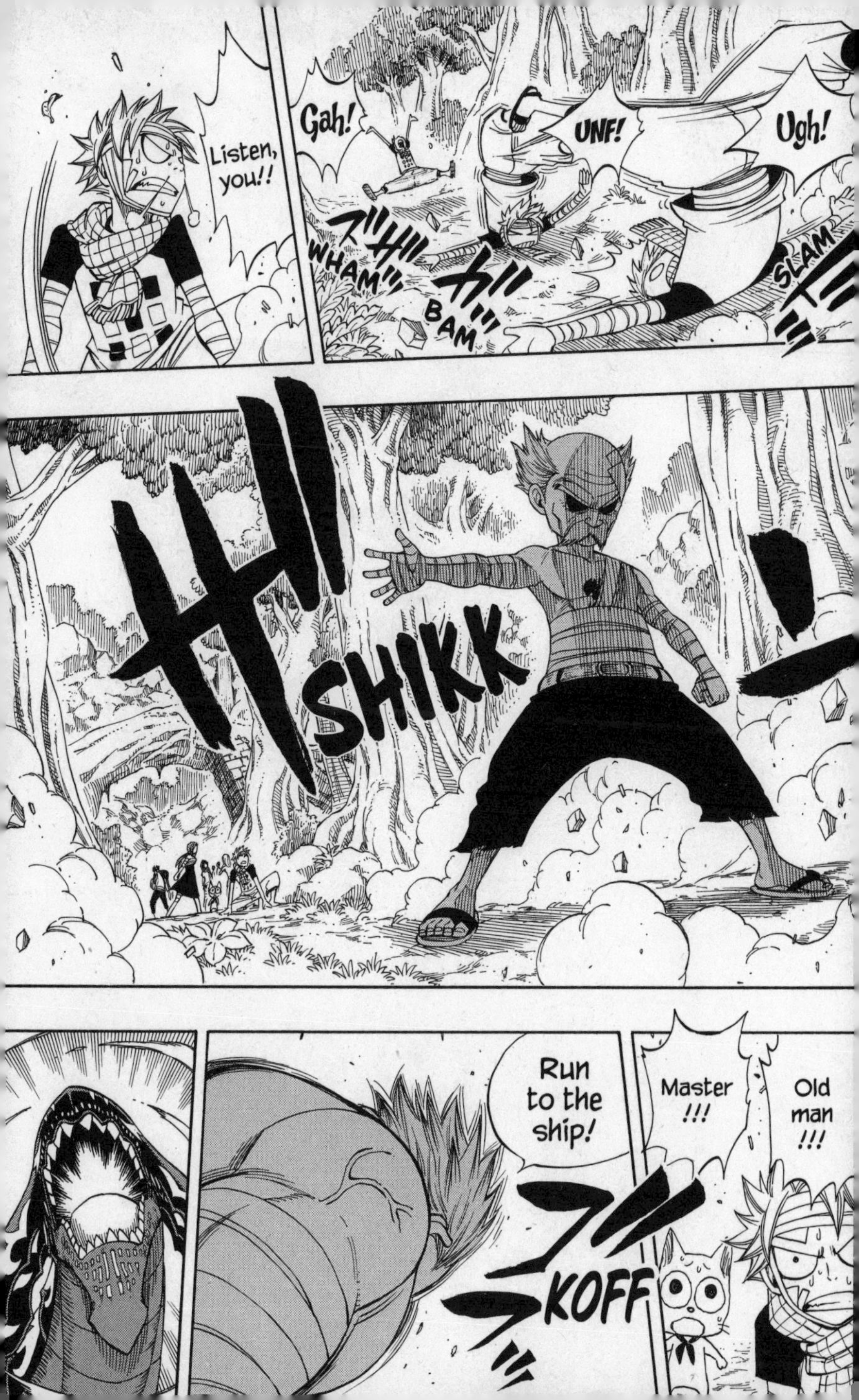

Ugh!
UNF!
Gah!
SLAM
WHAM
BAM
Listen, you!!
SHIKK
Old man!!!
Master!!!
Run to the ship!
KOFF

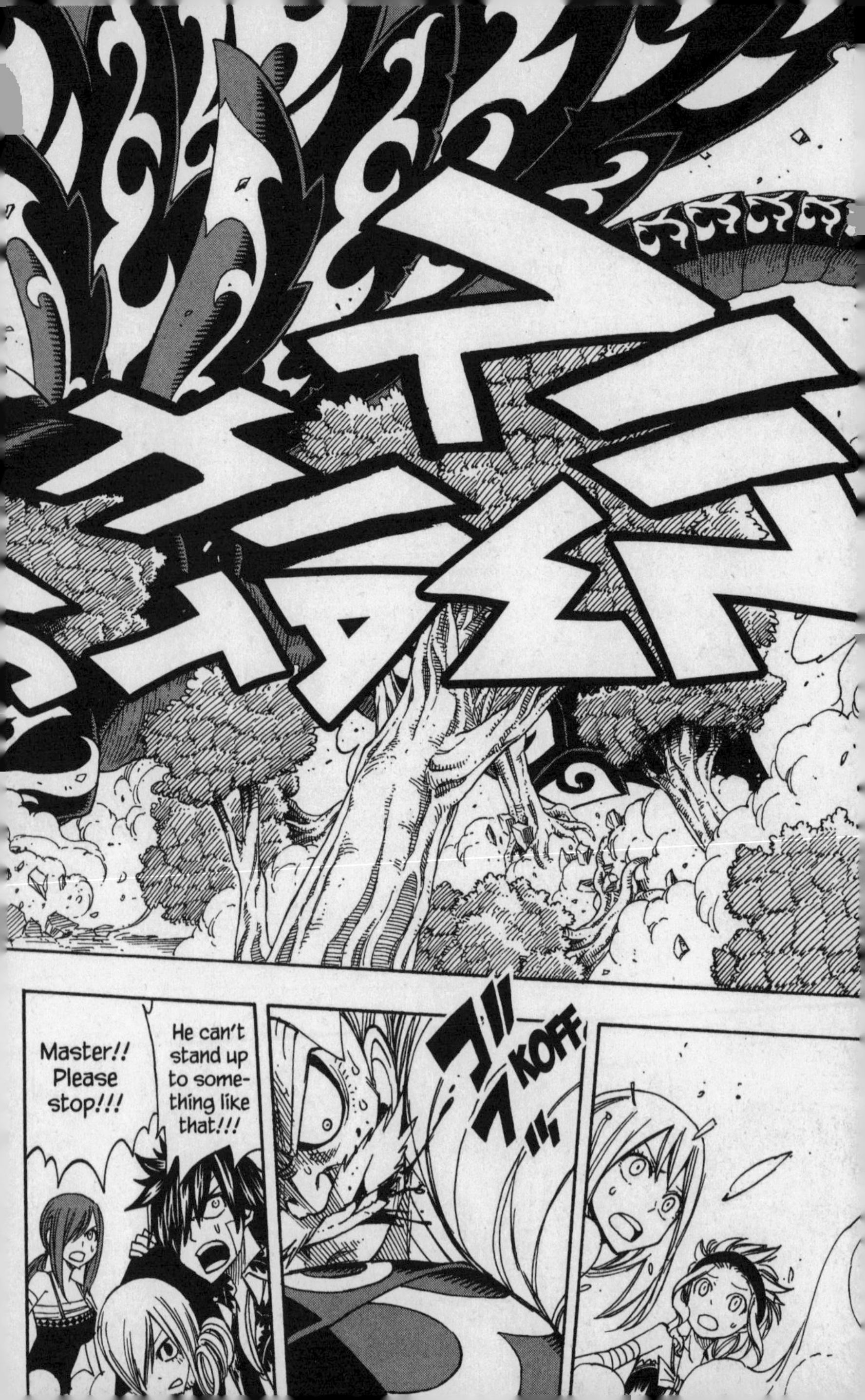
KOFF
He can't stand up to some-thing like that!!!
Master!! Please stop!!!

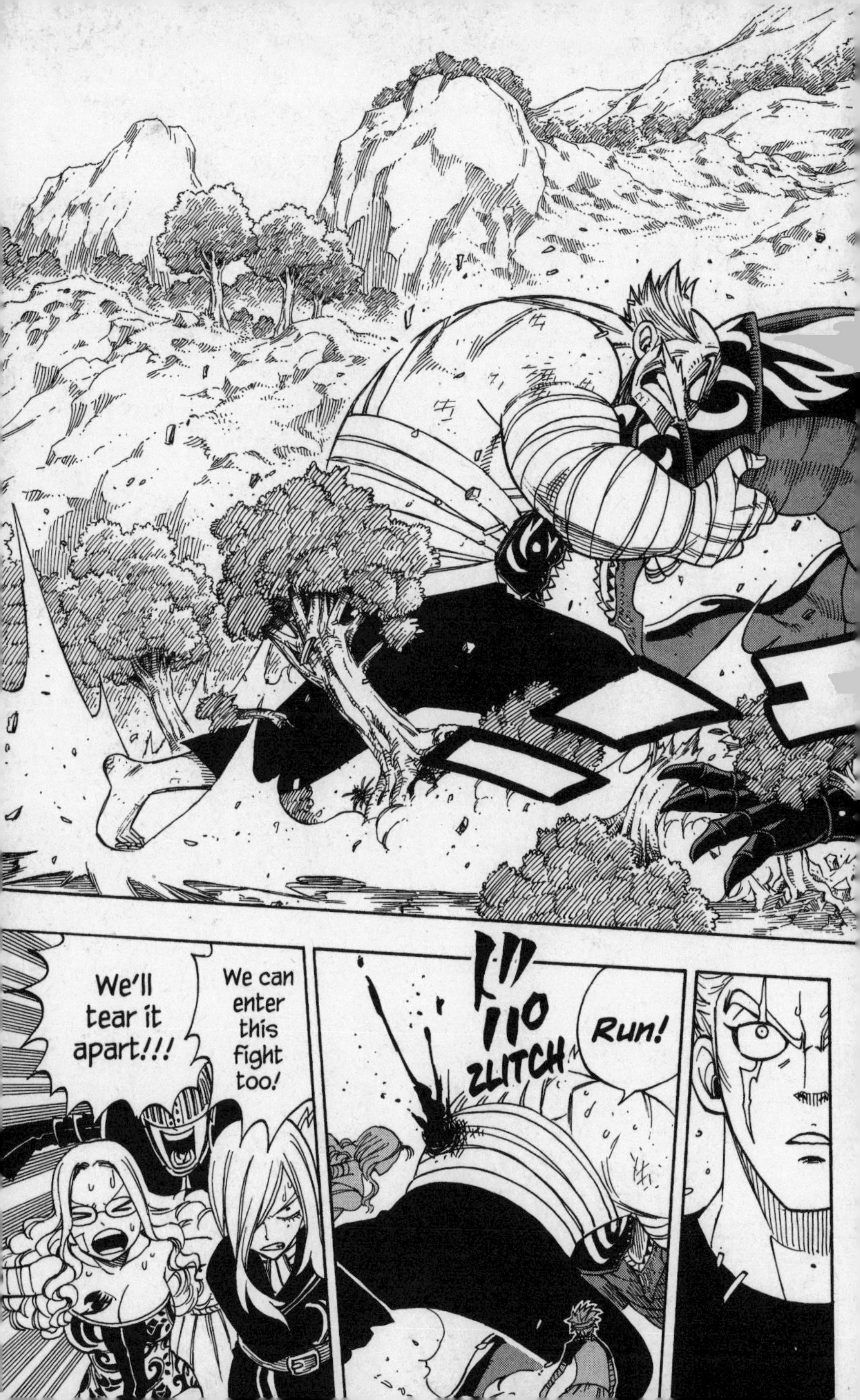
Run!
ZLITCH
We can enter this fight too!
We'll tear it apart!!!

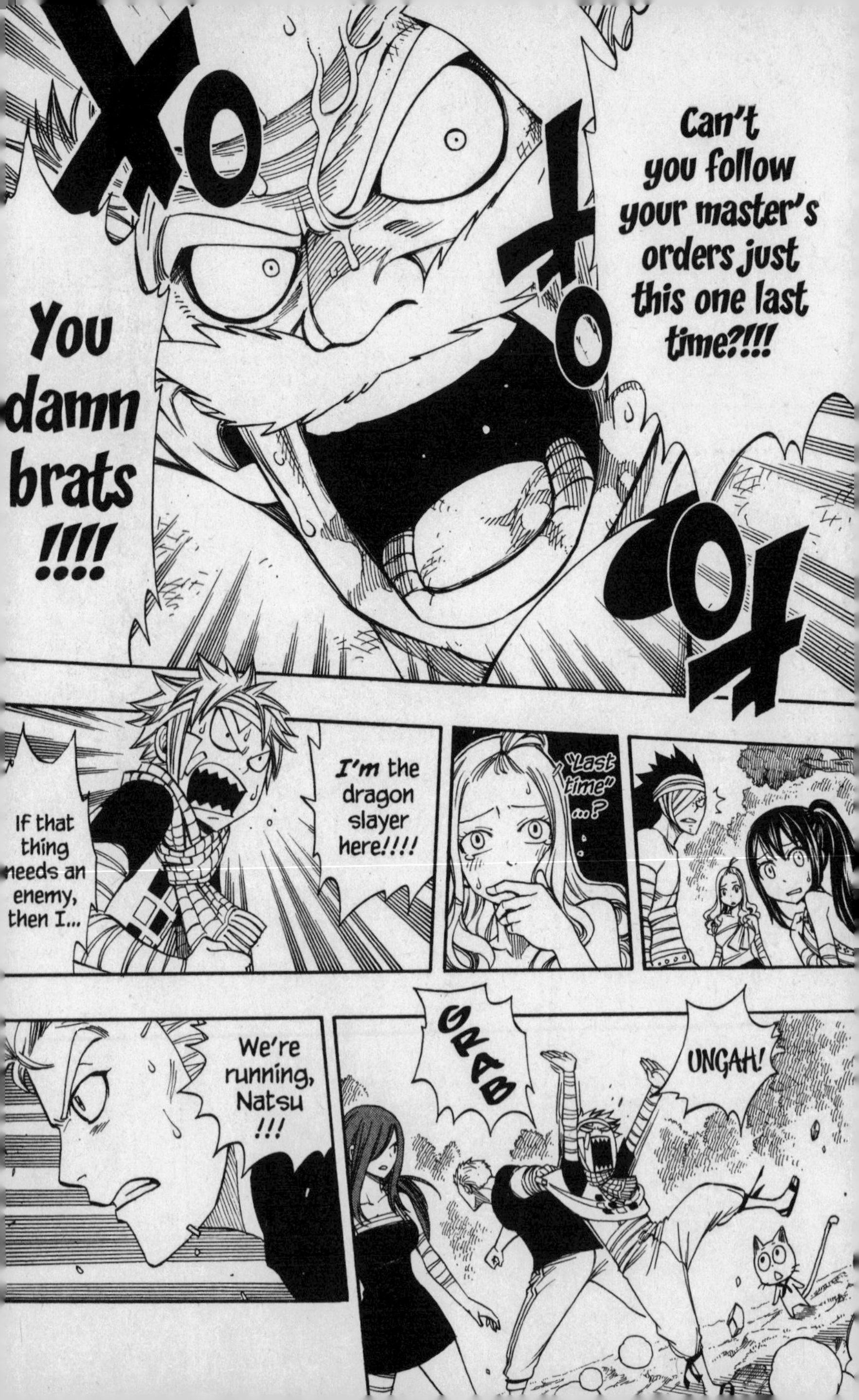
Can't you follow your master's orders just this one last time?!!!
You damn brats!!!!
"Last time"...?
I'm the dragon slayer here!!!!
If that thing needs an enemy, then I...
UNGAH!
GRAB
We're running, Natsu!!!

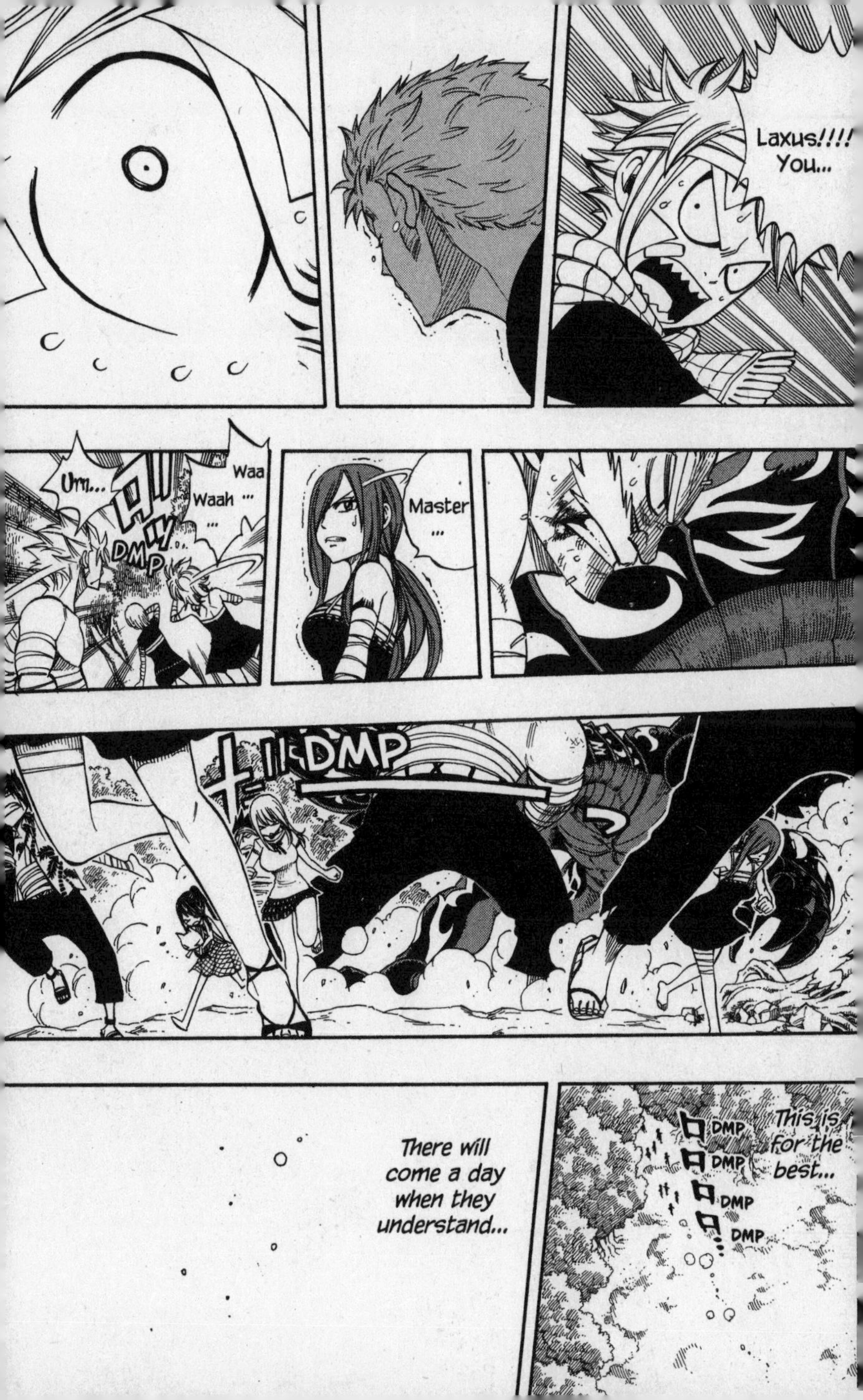
Laxus!!!! You...
Master ...
Waa Waah ... ...
Um...
DMP
DMP
This is for the best...
DMP
DMP
DMP
DMP
There will come a day when they understand...

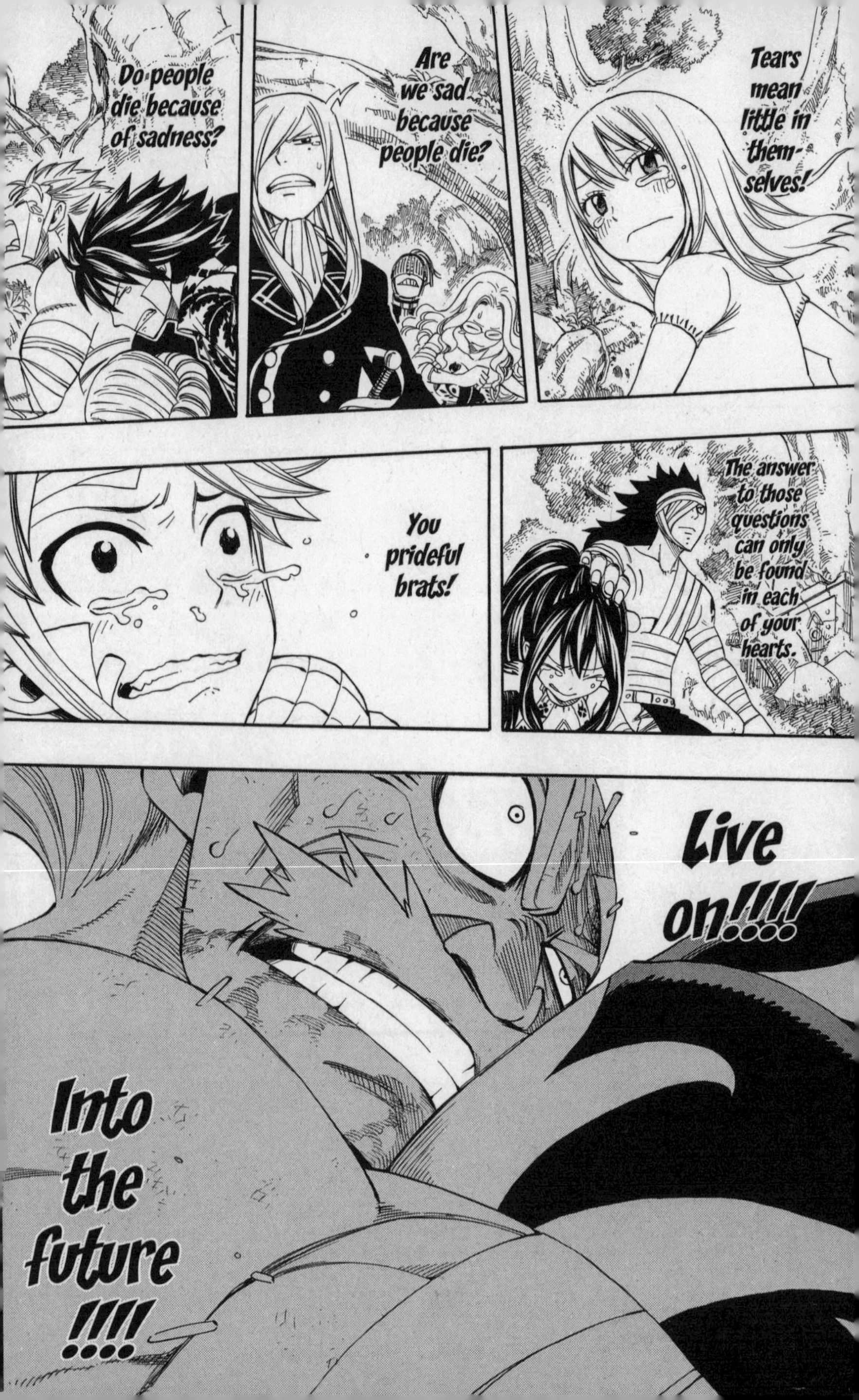
Tears mean little in them-selves!
Are we sad because people die?
Do people die because of sadness?
The answer to those questions can only be found in each of your hearts.
You prideful brats!
Live on!!!!
Into the future!!!!

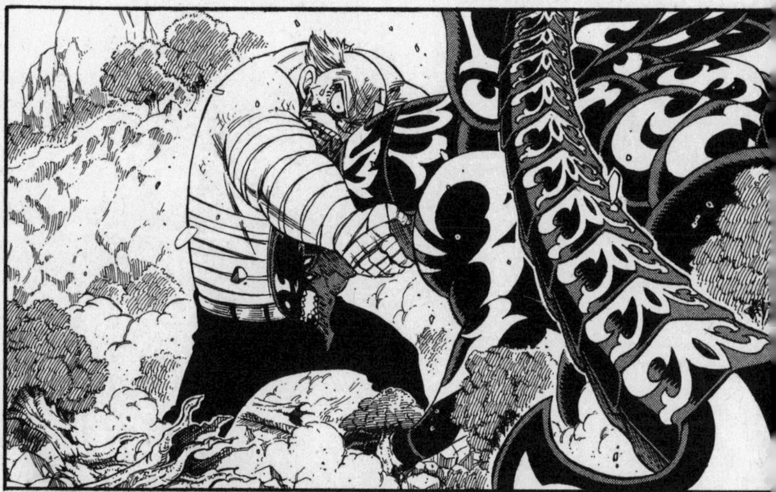

FAIRY TAIL

Chapter 253: Let's Join Hands

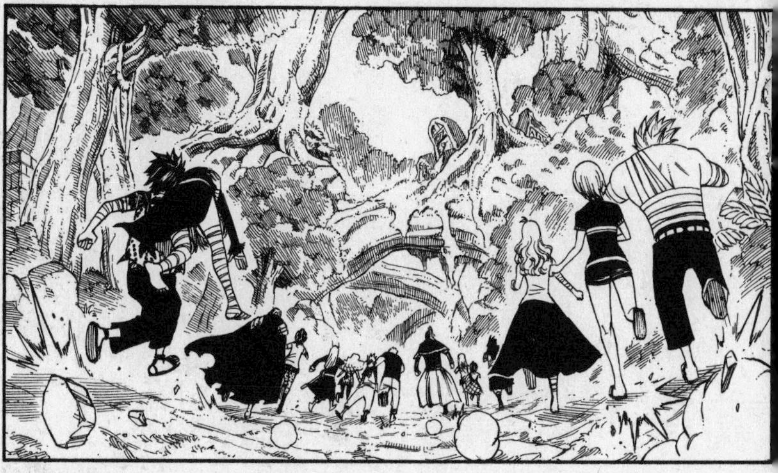

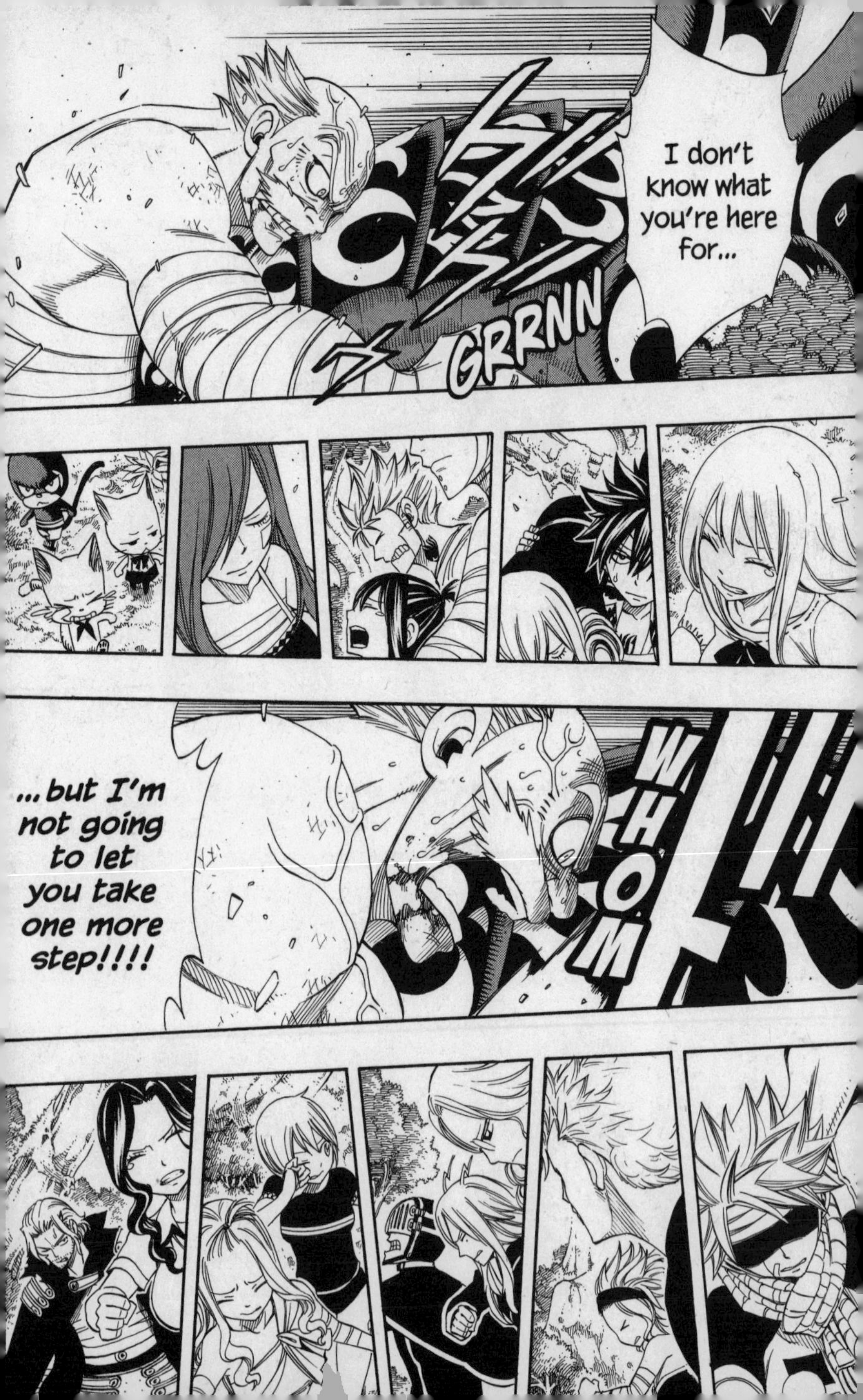
I don't know what you're here for...
GRRNN
WHOM
...but I'm not going to let you take one more step!!!!

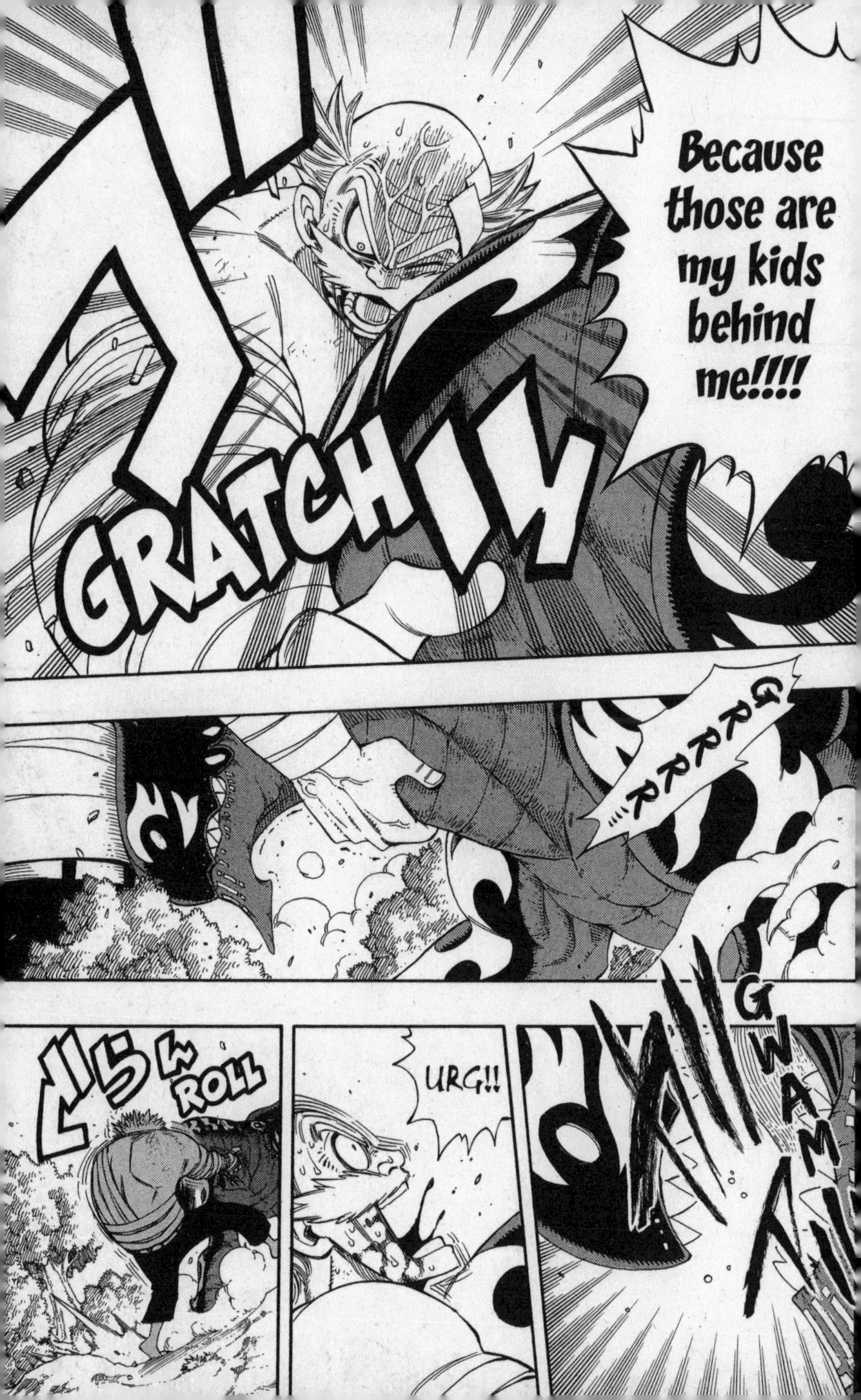
Because those are my kids behind me!!!!
GRATCH
GRRRR
GWAM
URG!!
ROLL

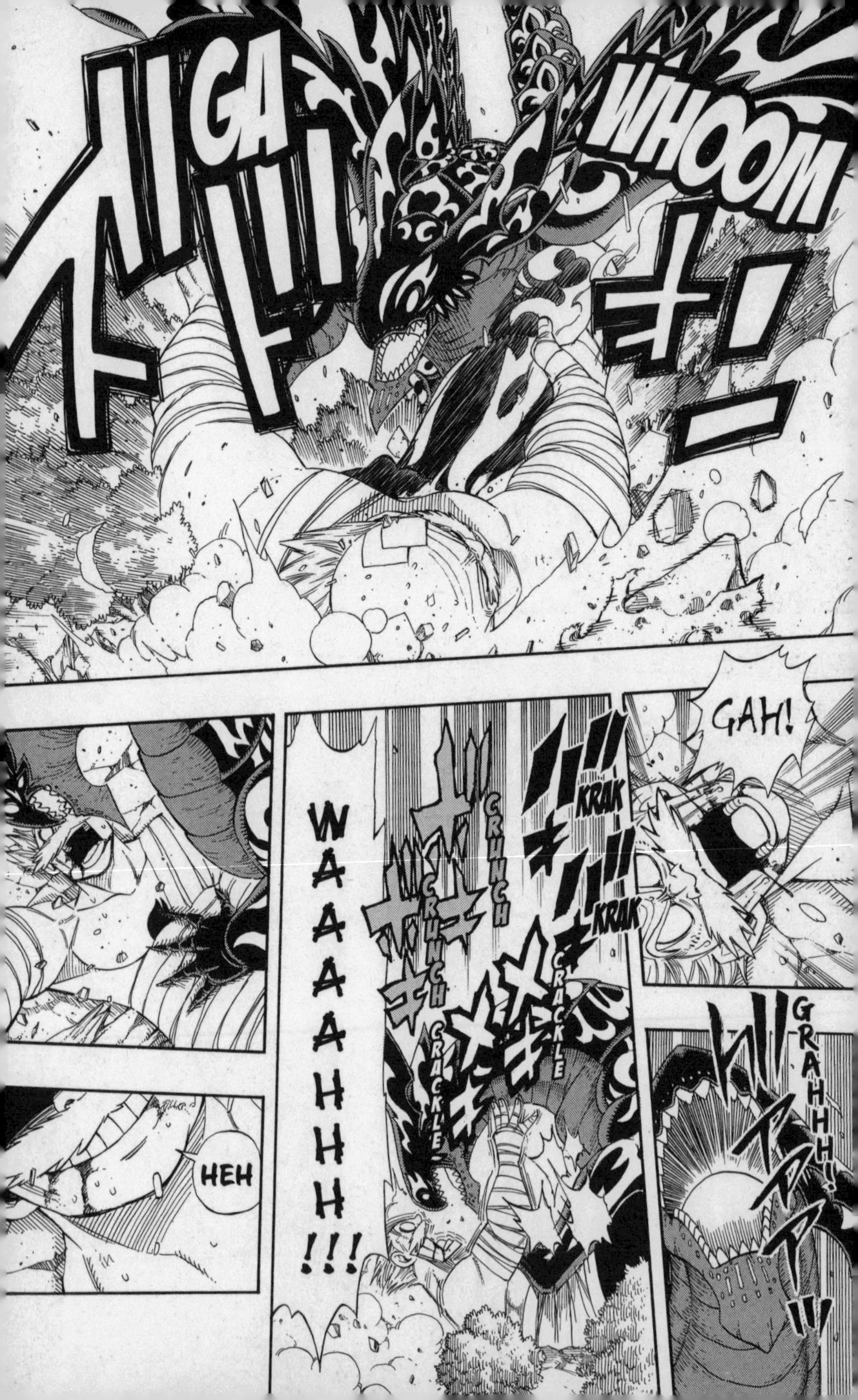
WHOOM
GA
GAH!
GRAHHH!!
KRAK
KRAK
CRUNCH
CRUNCH
CRACKLE
CRACKLE
WAAAAHHH!!!
HEH

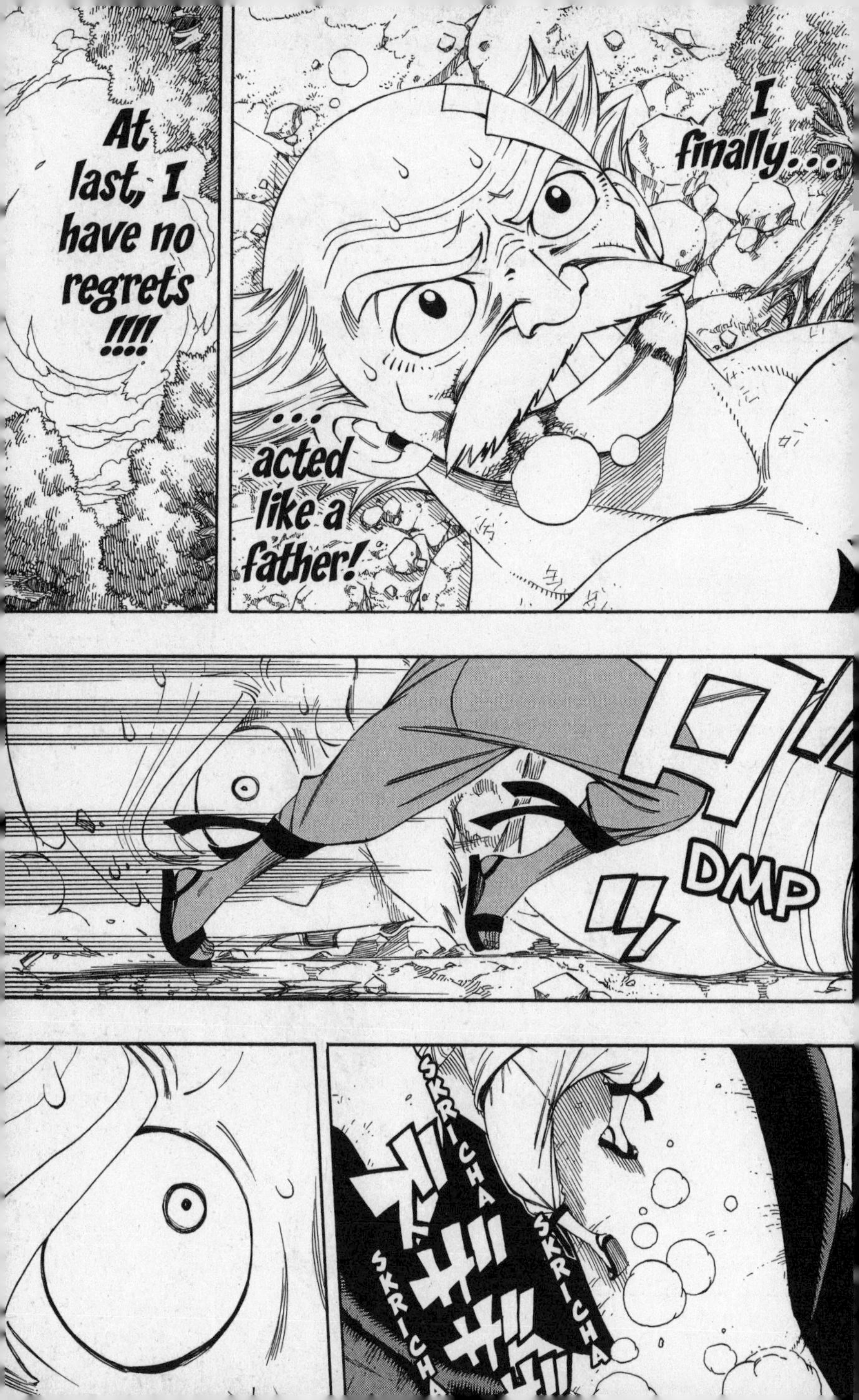
I finally...
...acted like a father!
At last, I have no regrets!!!!
DMP
SKRICHA
SKRICHA
SKRICHA

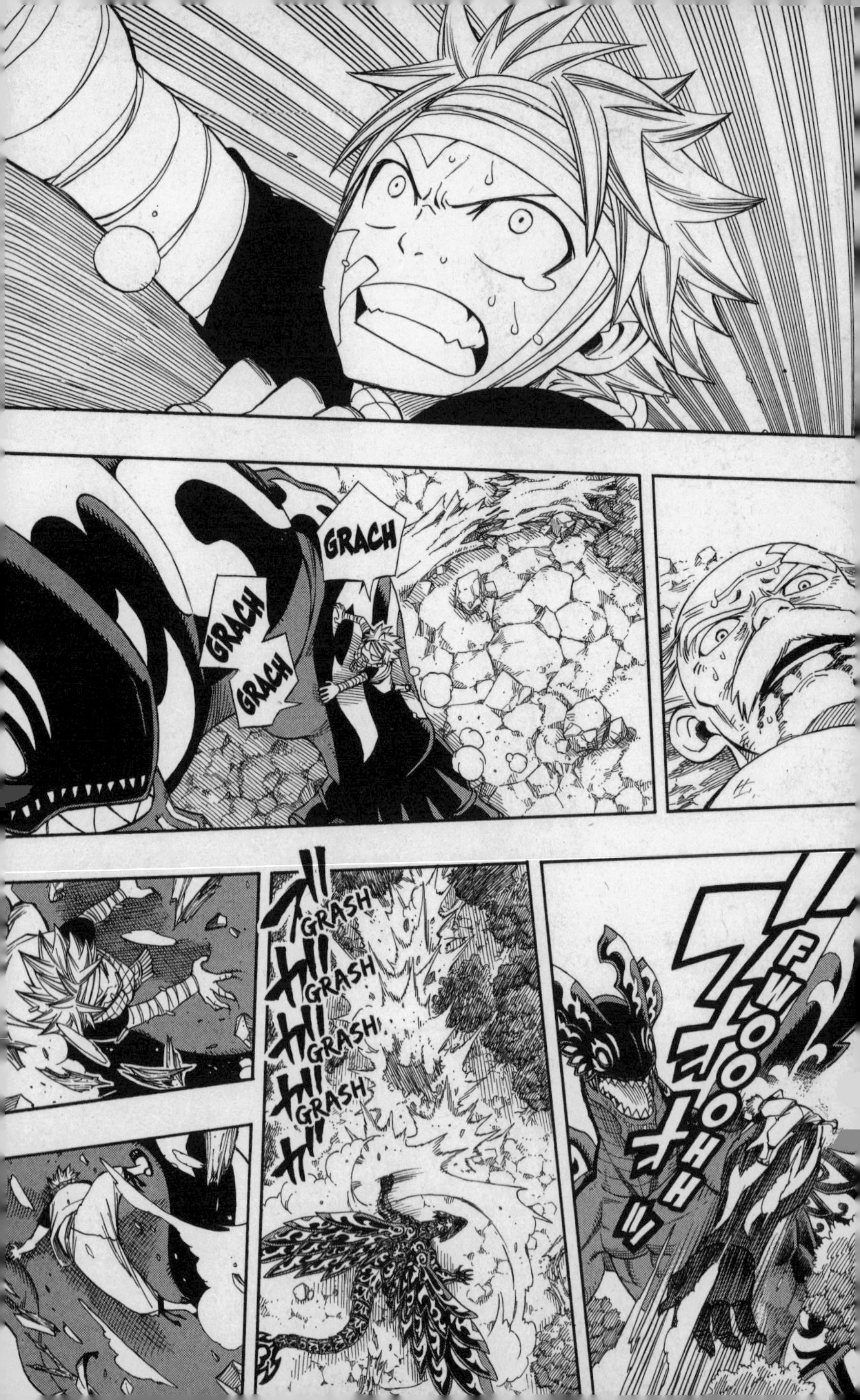
GRACH
GRACH
GRACH
FWOOOOHHH!!
GRASH
GRASH
GRASH
GRASH

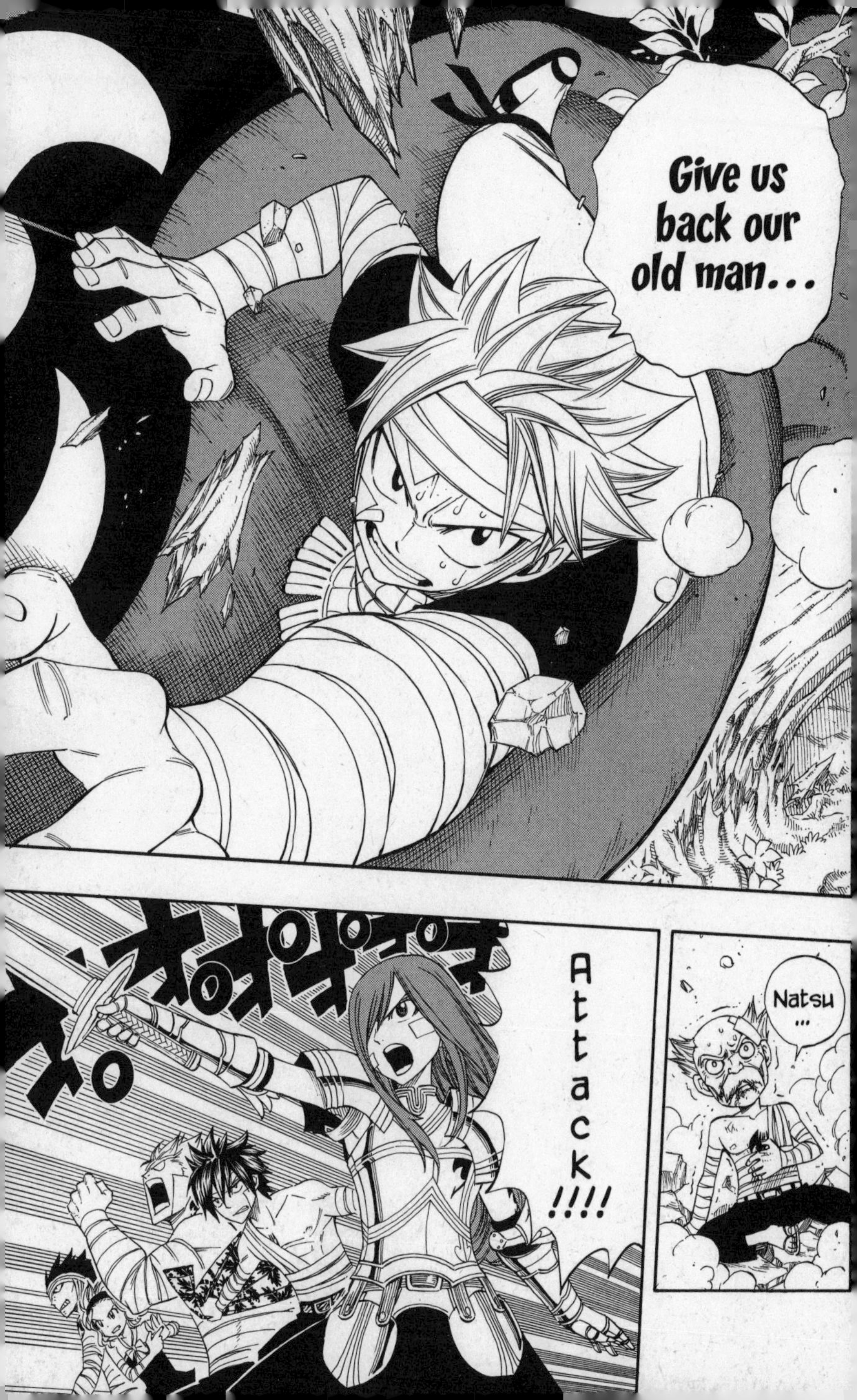
Give us back our old man...
Natsu...
Attack!!!!

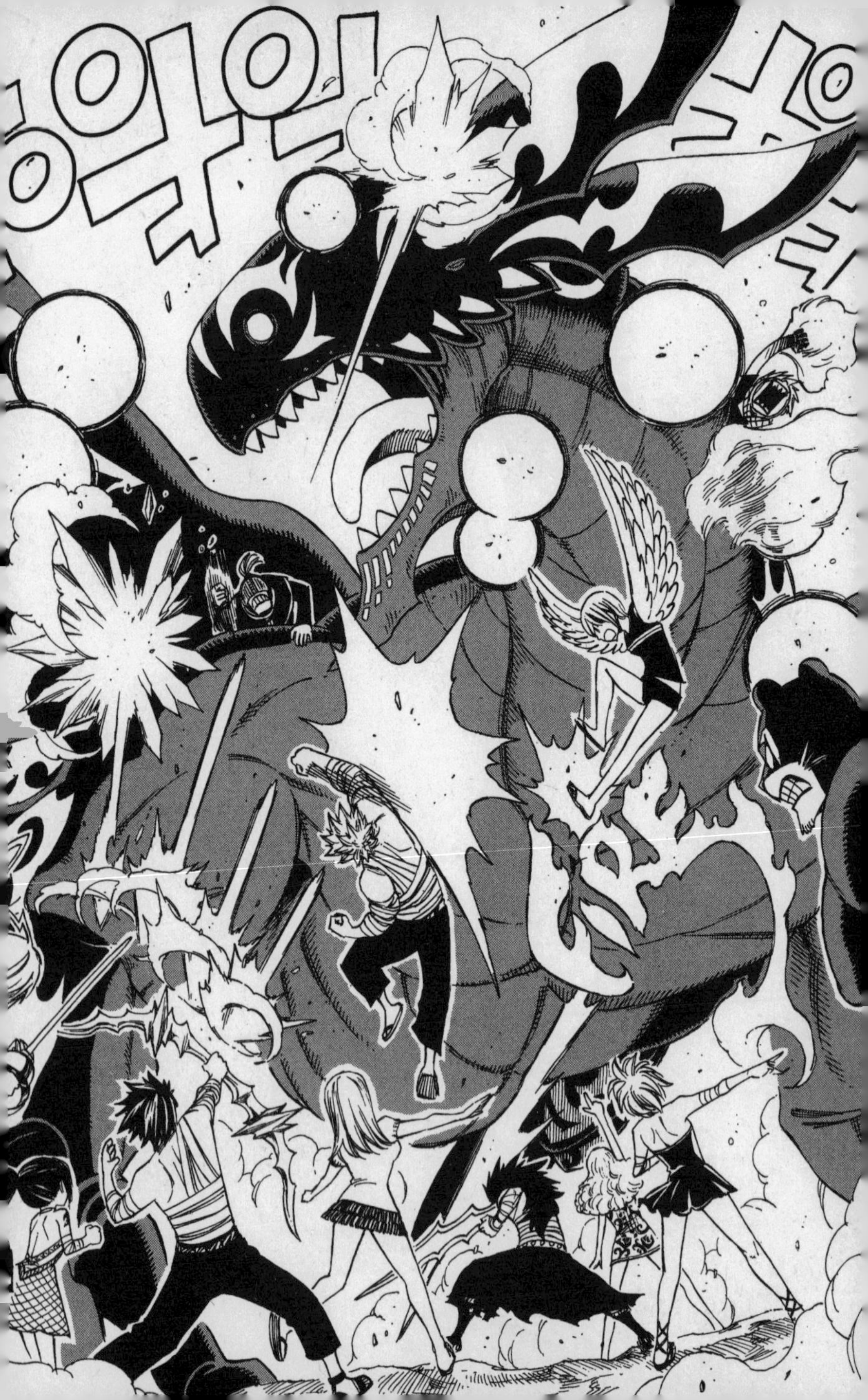

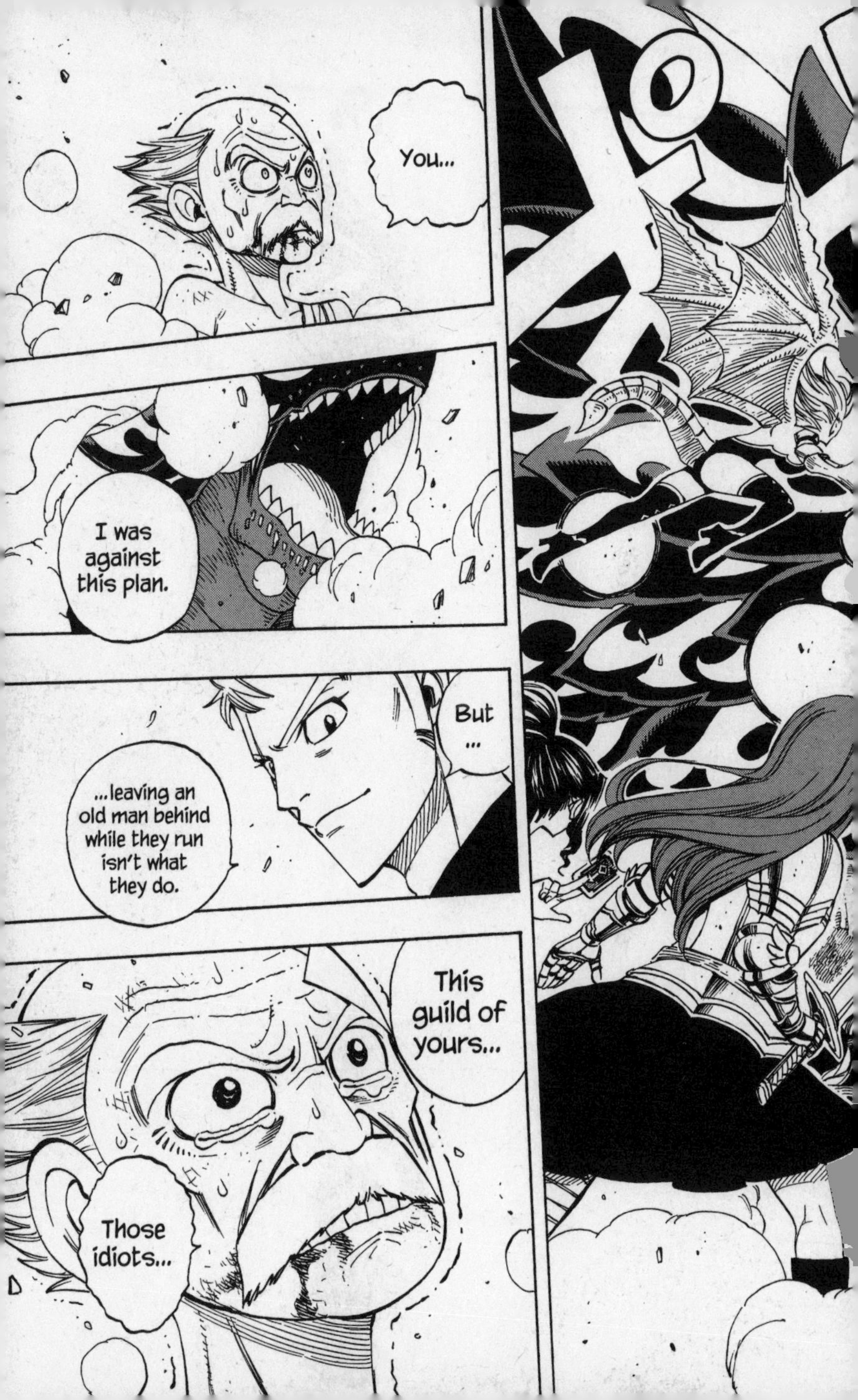
You...
I was against this plan.
But ...
...leaving an old man behind while they run isn't what they do.
This guild of yours...
Those idiots...

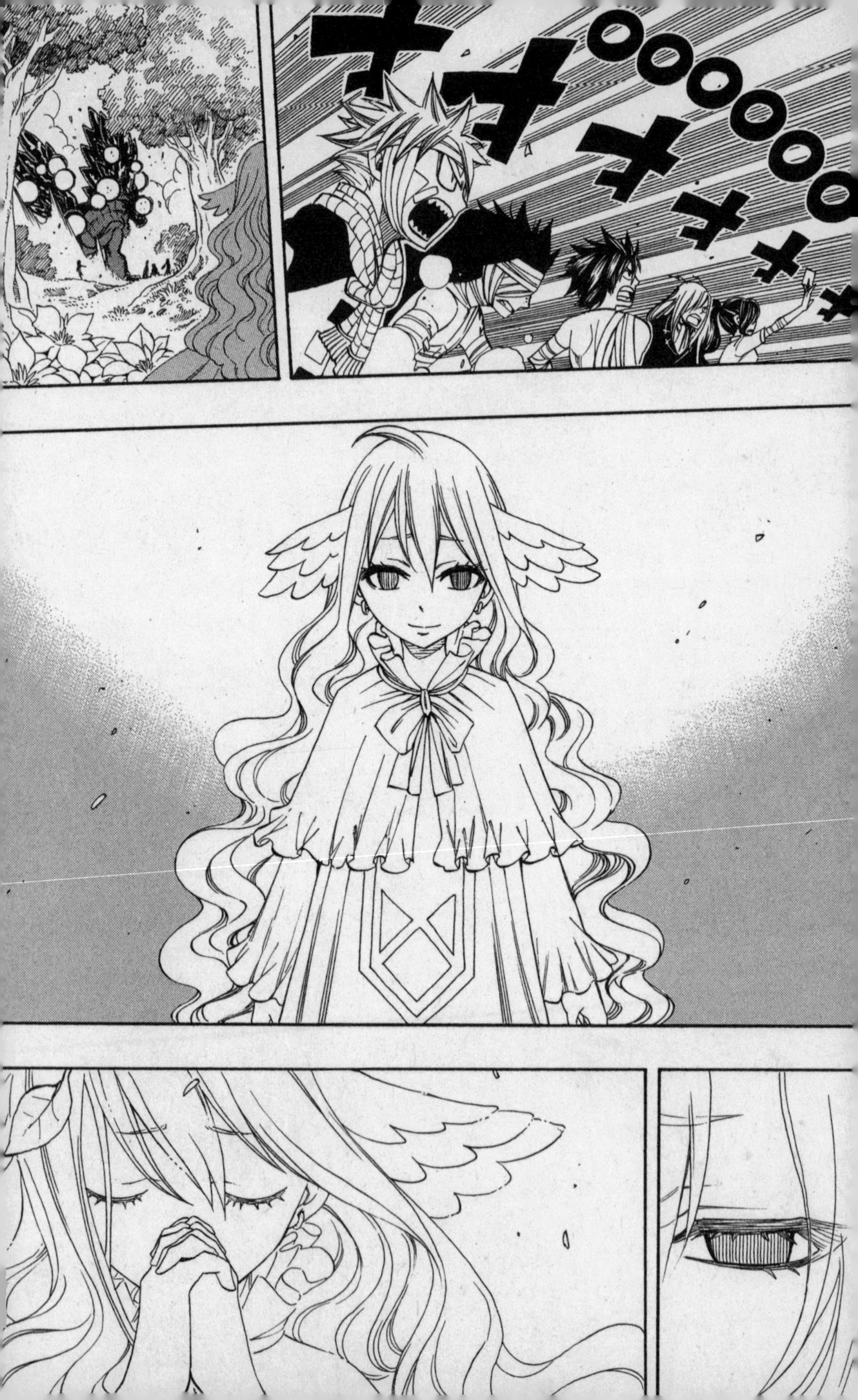
OOOOOOO

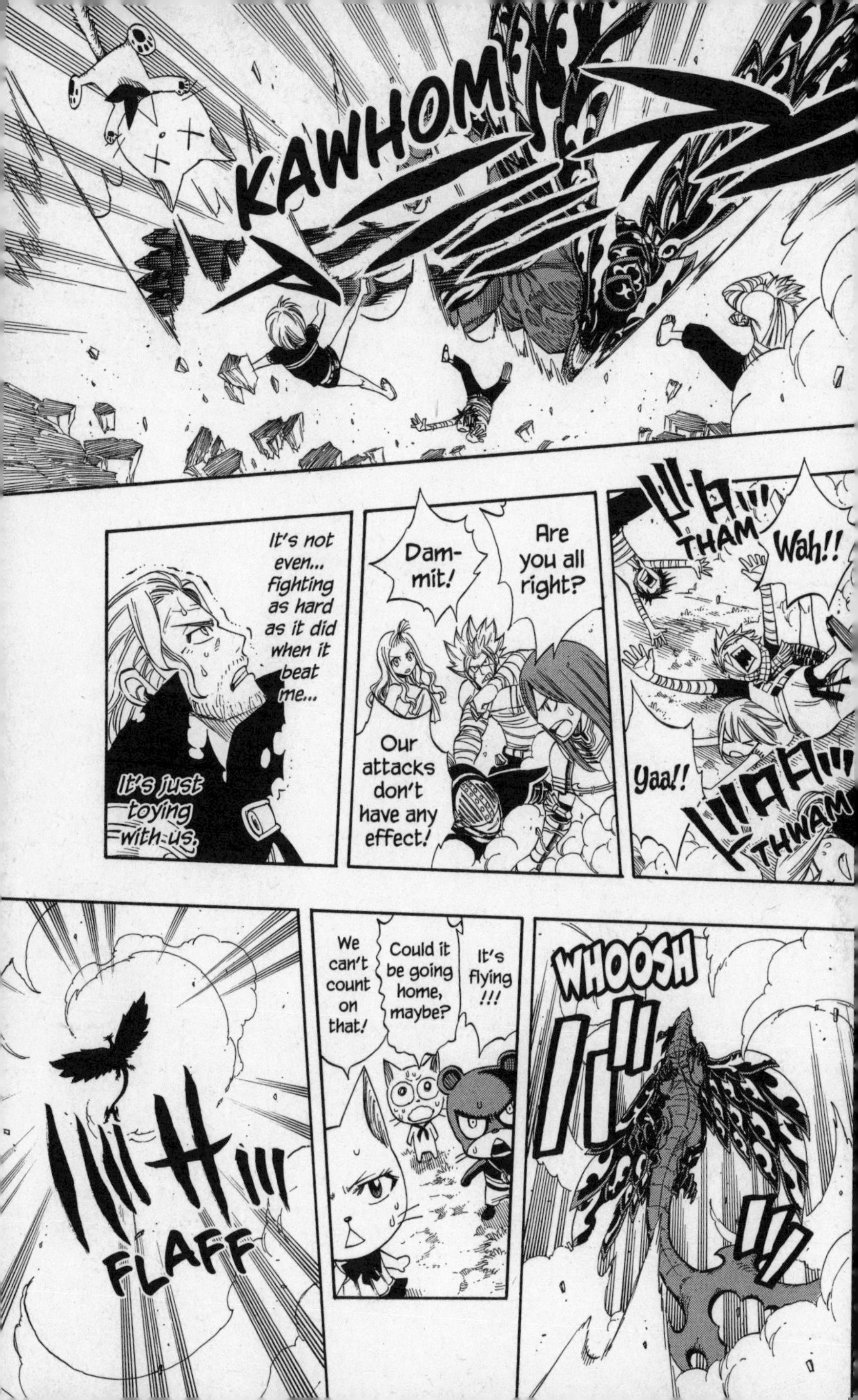
KAWHOM
THAM
Wah!!
Yaa!!
THWAM
Are you all right?
Dam-mit!
Our attacks don't have any effect!
It's not even... fighting as hard as it did when it beat me...
It's just toying with us.
WHOOSH
It's flying!!!
Could it be going home, maybe?
We can't count on that!
FLAFF

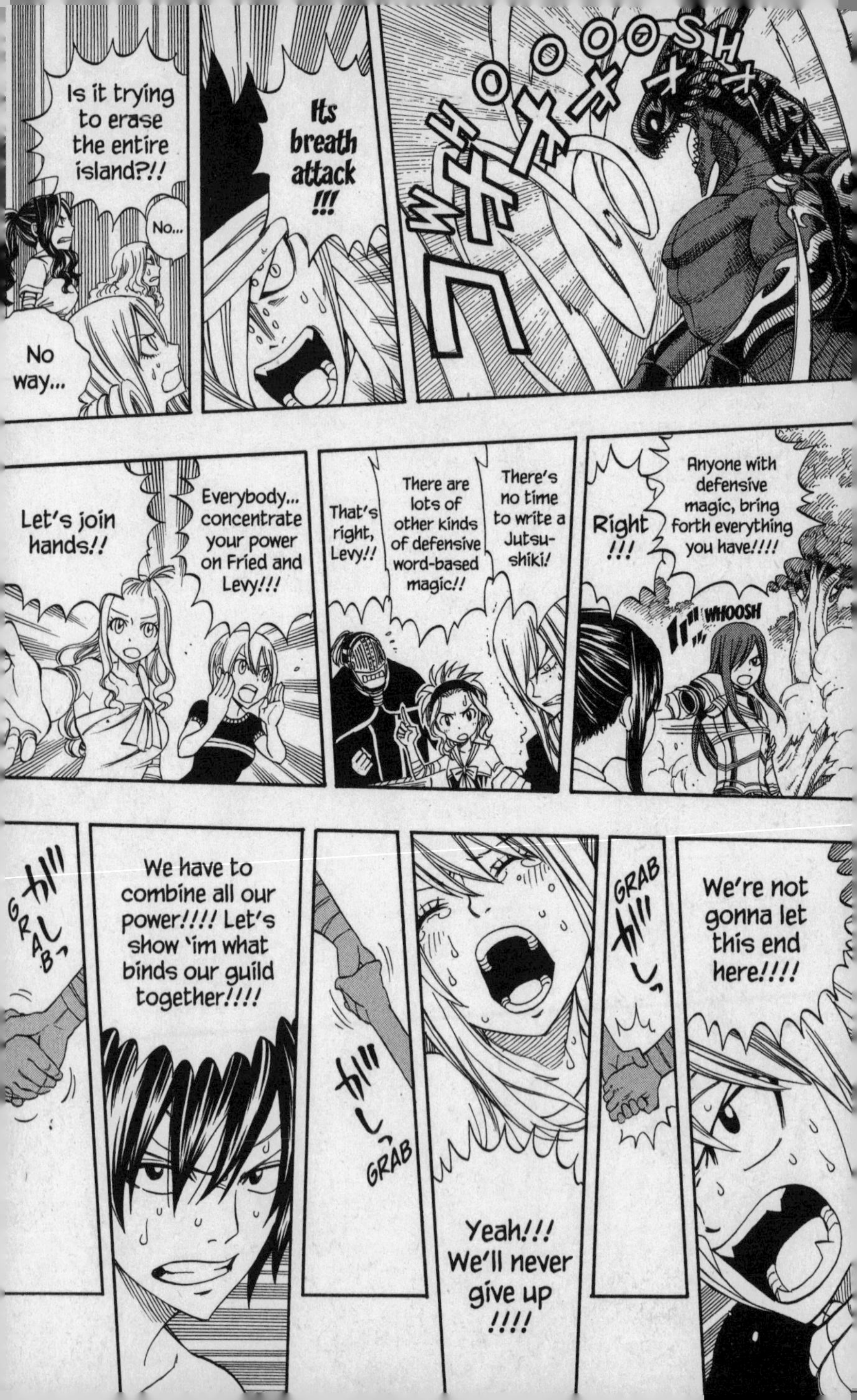
OOOOOSH
Its breath attack!!!
Is it trying to erase the entire island?!!
No...
No way...
Anyone with defensive magic, bring forth everything you have!!!!
Right!!!
WHOOSH
There's no time to write a Jutsu-shiki!
There are lots of other kinds of defensive word-based magic!!
That's right, Levy!!
Everybody... concentrate your power on Fried and Levy!!!
Let's join hands!!
We're not gonna let this end here!!!!
GRAB
Yeah!!! We'll never give up!!!!
GRAB
We have to combine all our power!!!! Let's show 'im what binds our guild together!!!!
GRAB

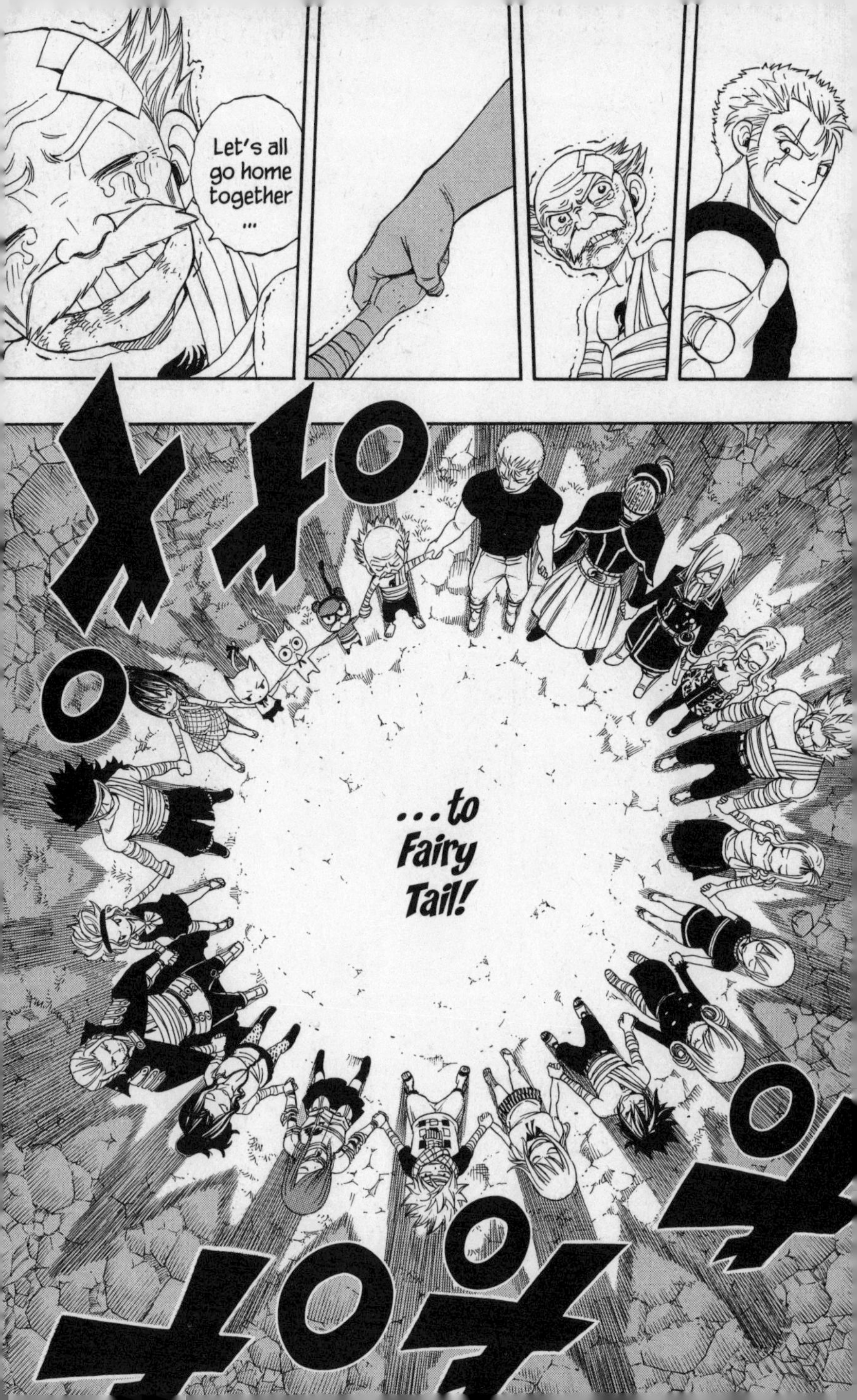
Let's all go home together ...
...to Fairy Tail!

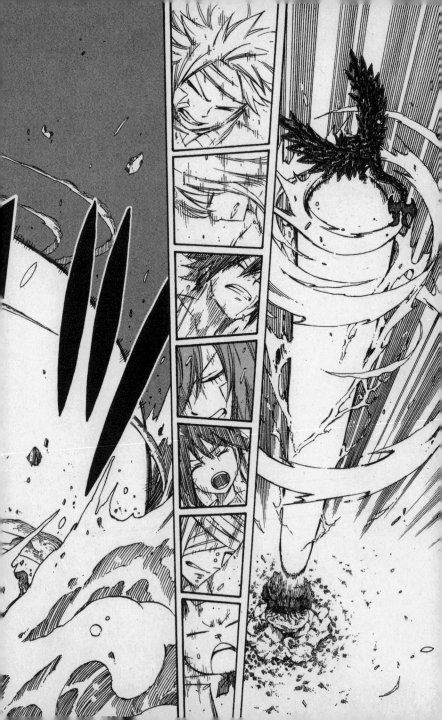

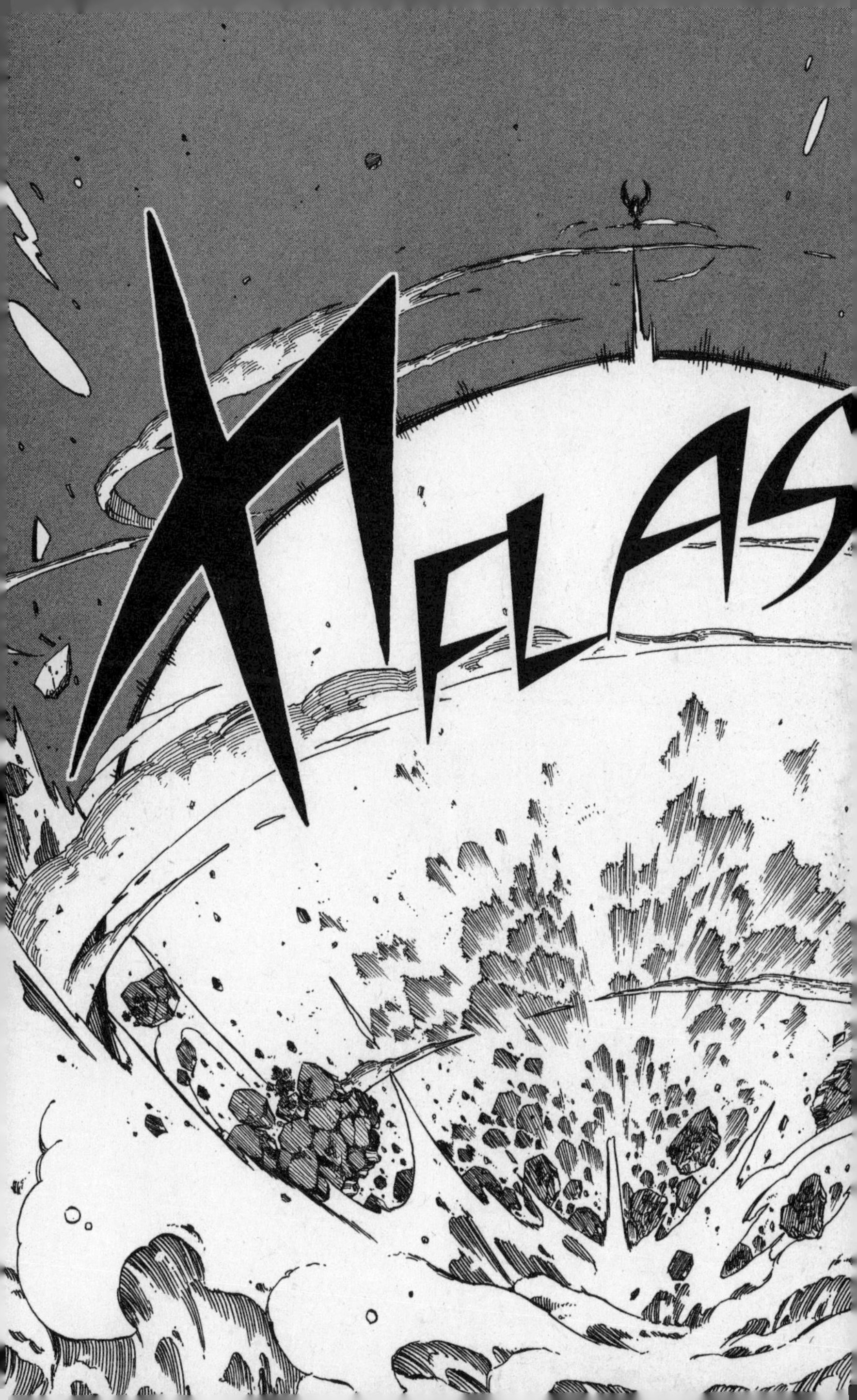
FLAS

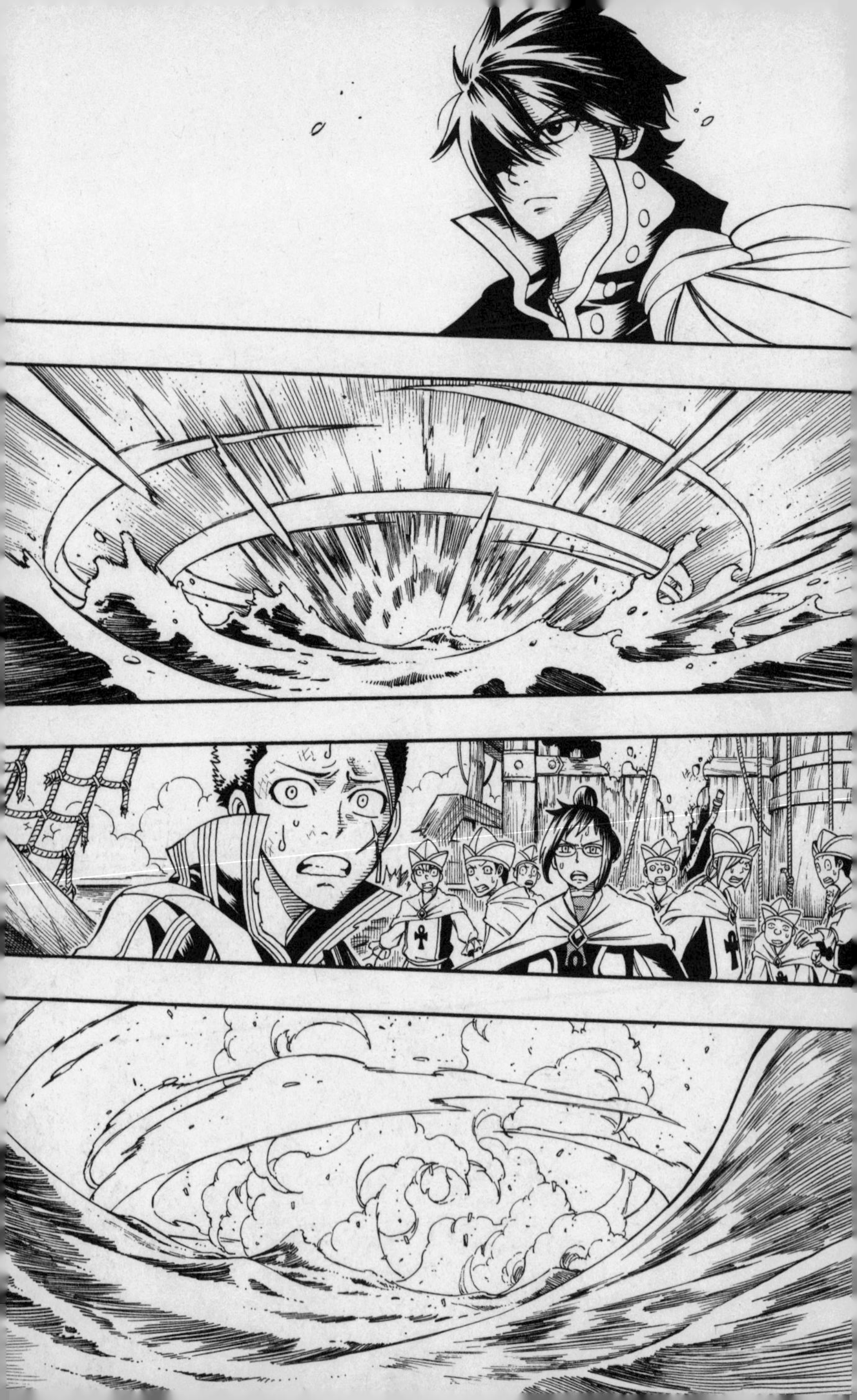

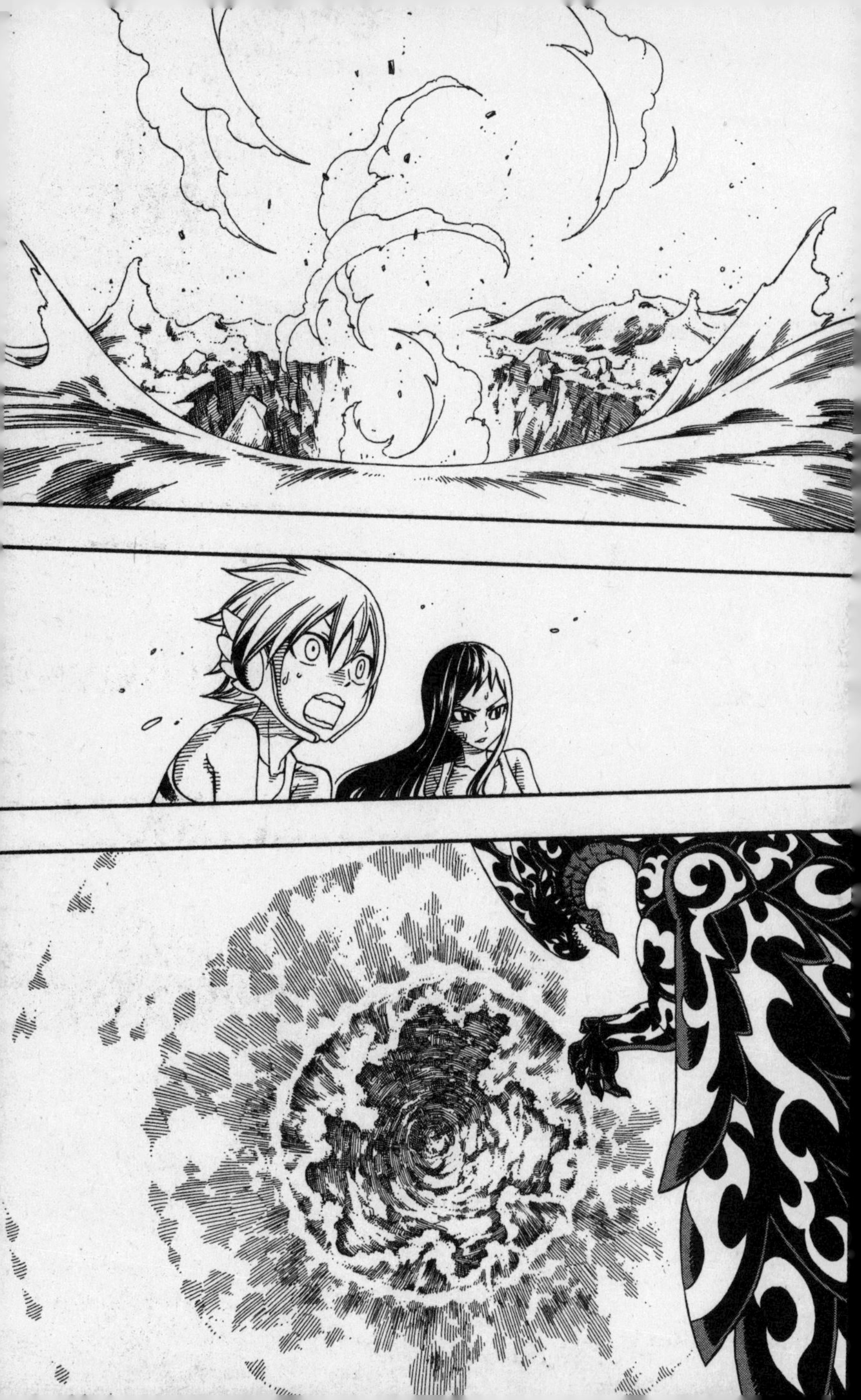

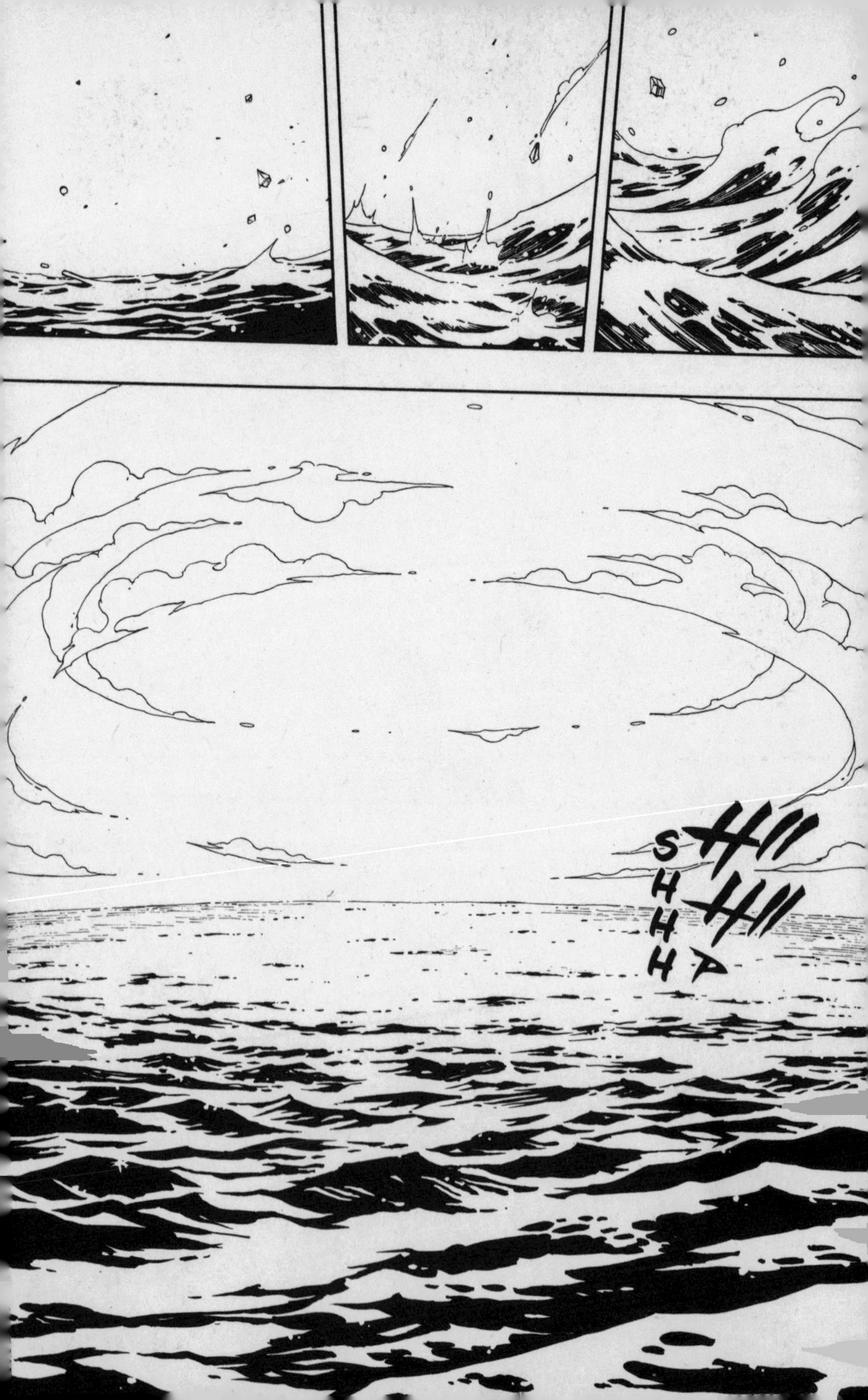
SHHH

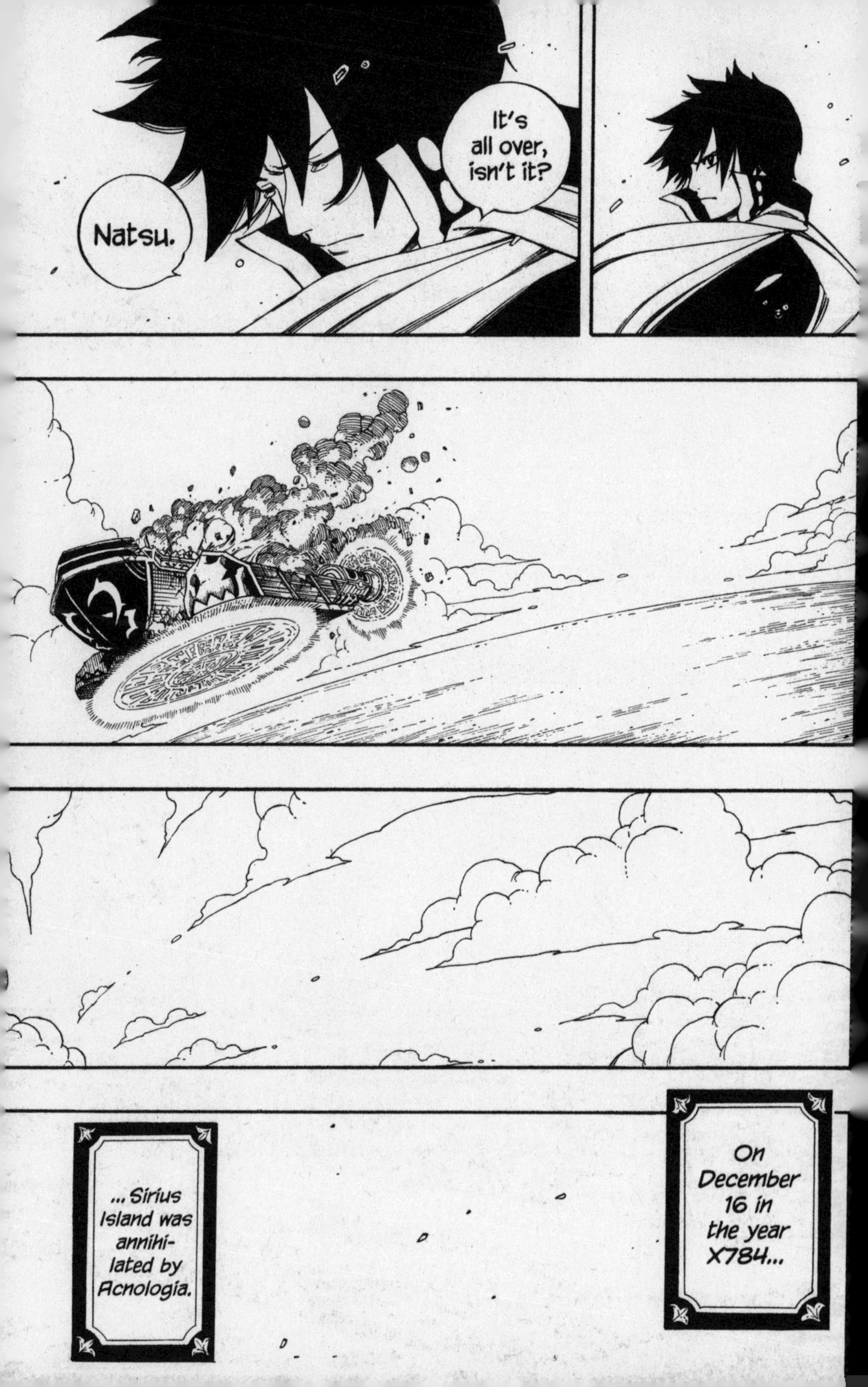
It's all over, isn't it?
Natsu.
On December 16 in the year X784...
...Sirius Island was annihilated by Acnologia.

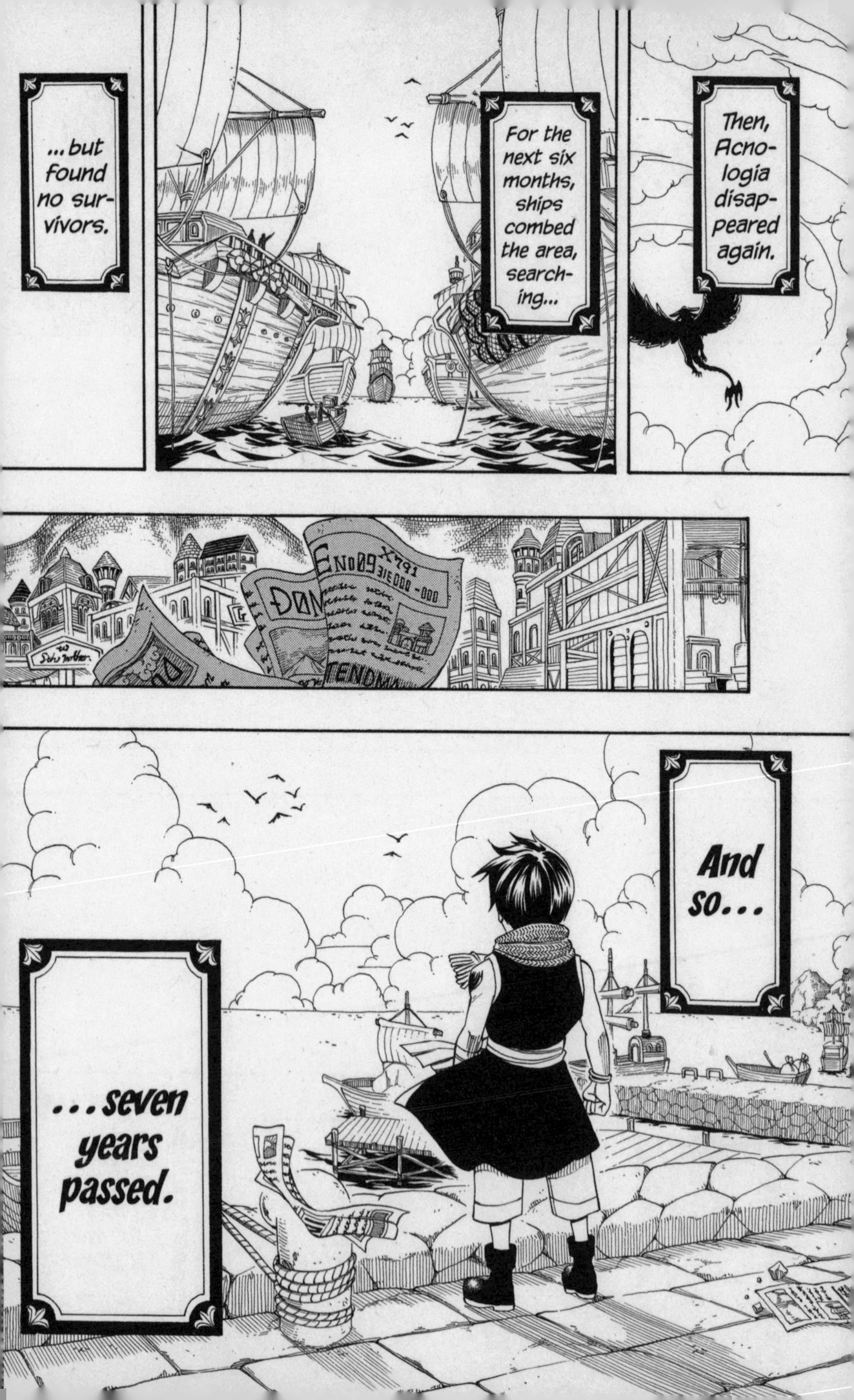

Then, Acnologia disappeared again.
For the next six months, ships combed the area, searching...
...but found no survivors.
And so...
...seven years passed.

FAIRY TAIL

Chapter 254:
Fairy Tail, X791

Hiro Mashima

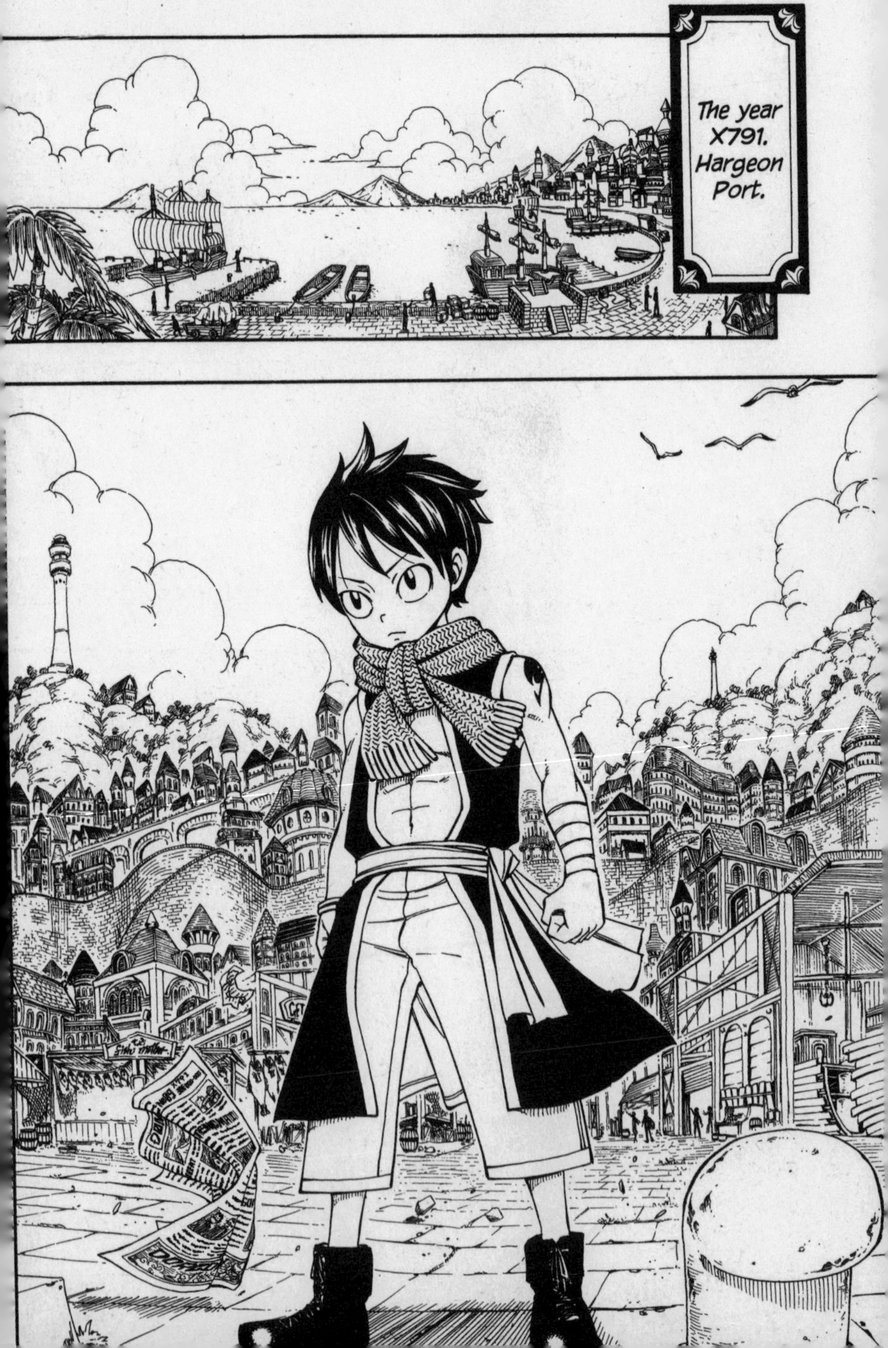
The year X791. Hargeon Port.

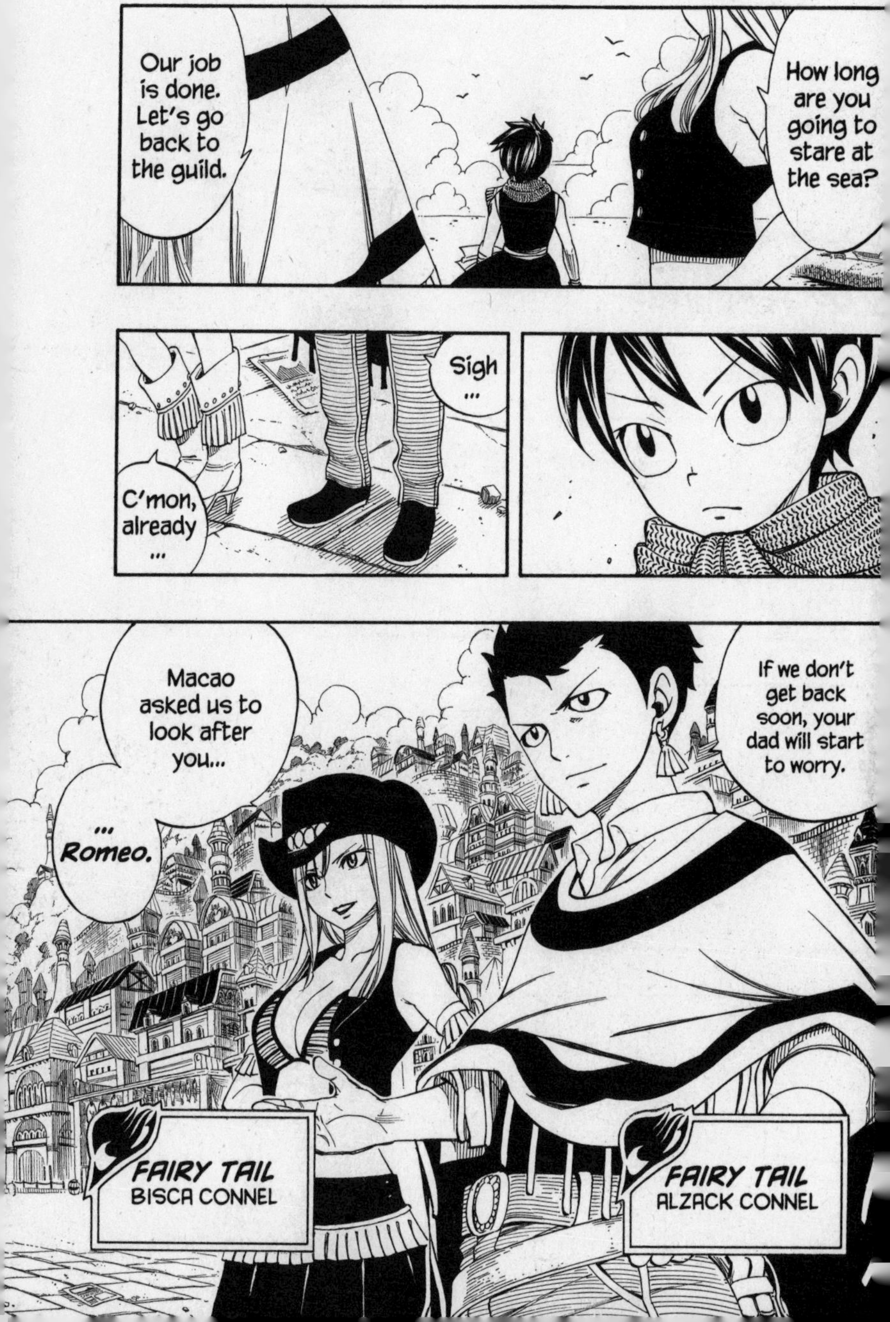
How long are you going to stare at the sea?
Our job is done. Let's go back to the guild.
Sigh ...
C'mon, already ...
If we don't get back soon, your dad will start to worry.
Macao asked us to look after you...
... Romeo.
FAIRY TAIL
ALZACK CONNEL
FAIRY TAIL
BISCA CONNEL

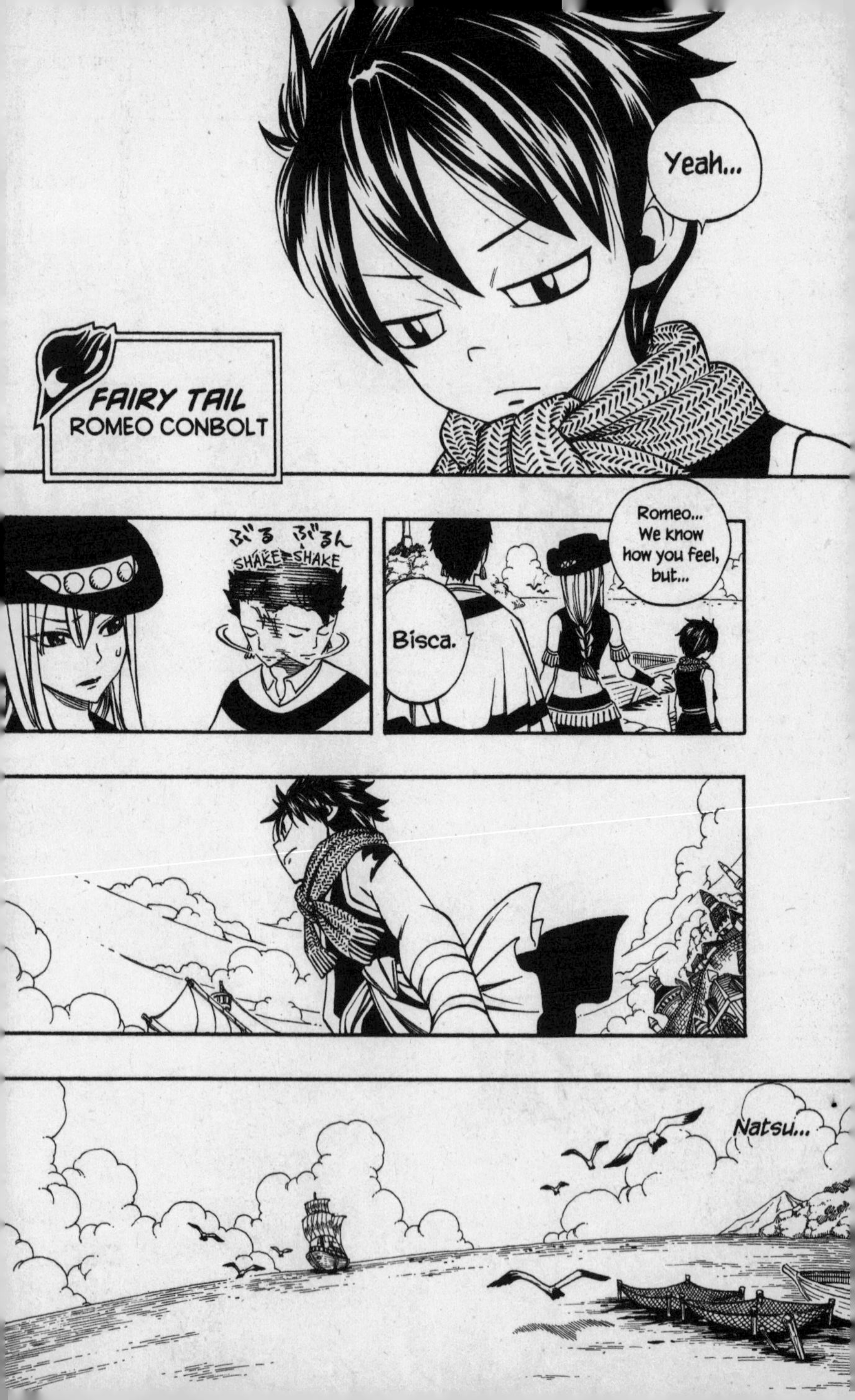
Yeah...
FAIRY TAIL
ROMEO CONBOLT
Romeo... We know how you feel, but...
Bisca.
ぶる ぶるん
SHAKE SHAKE
Natsu...

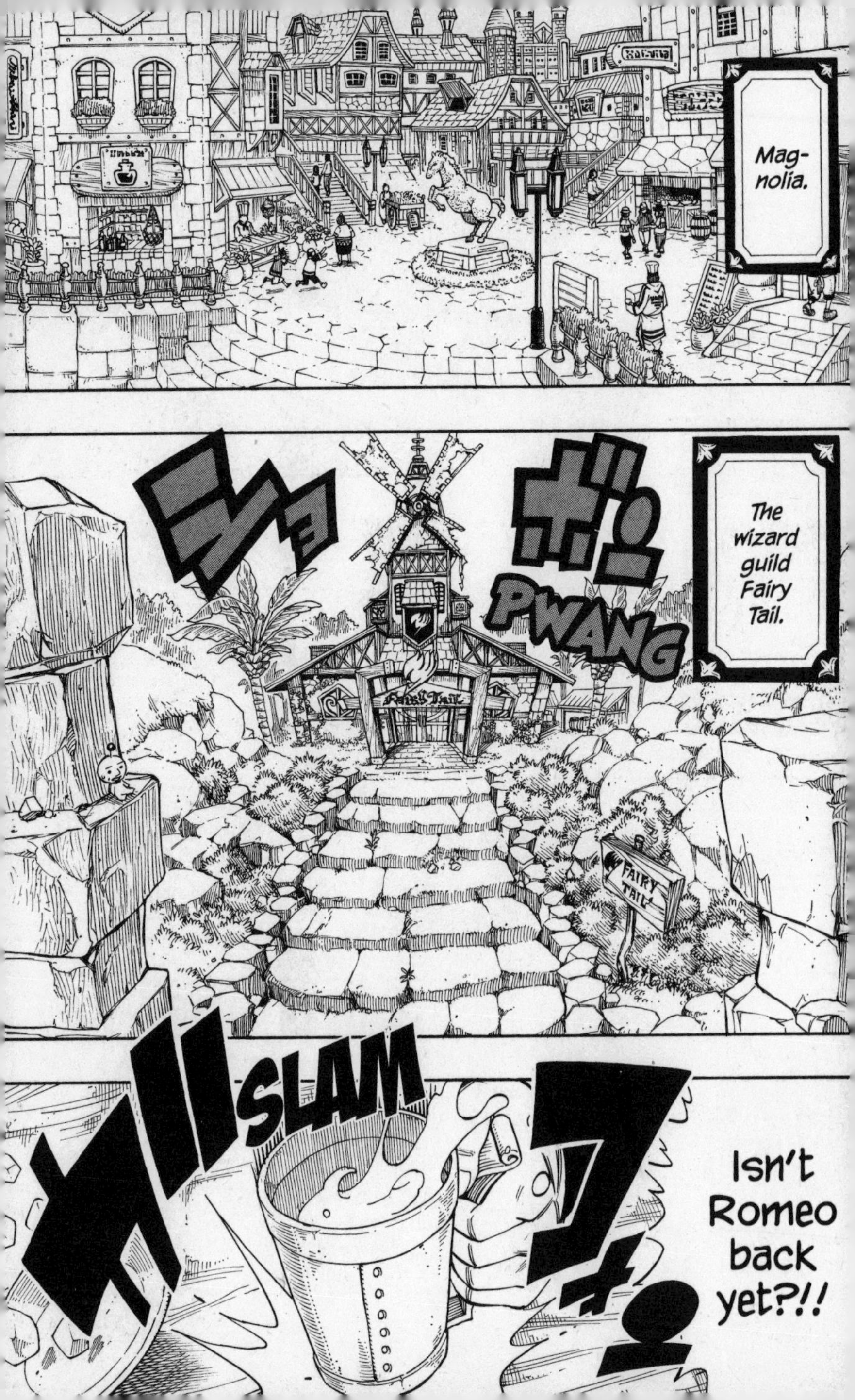
Mag-
nolia.
The wizard guild Fairy Tail.
PWANG
FAIRY TAIL
Isn't Romeo back yet?!!
SLAM

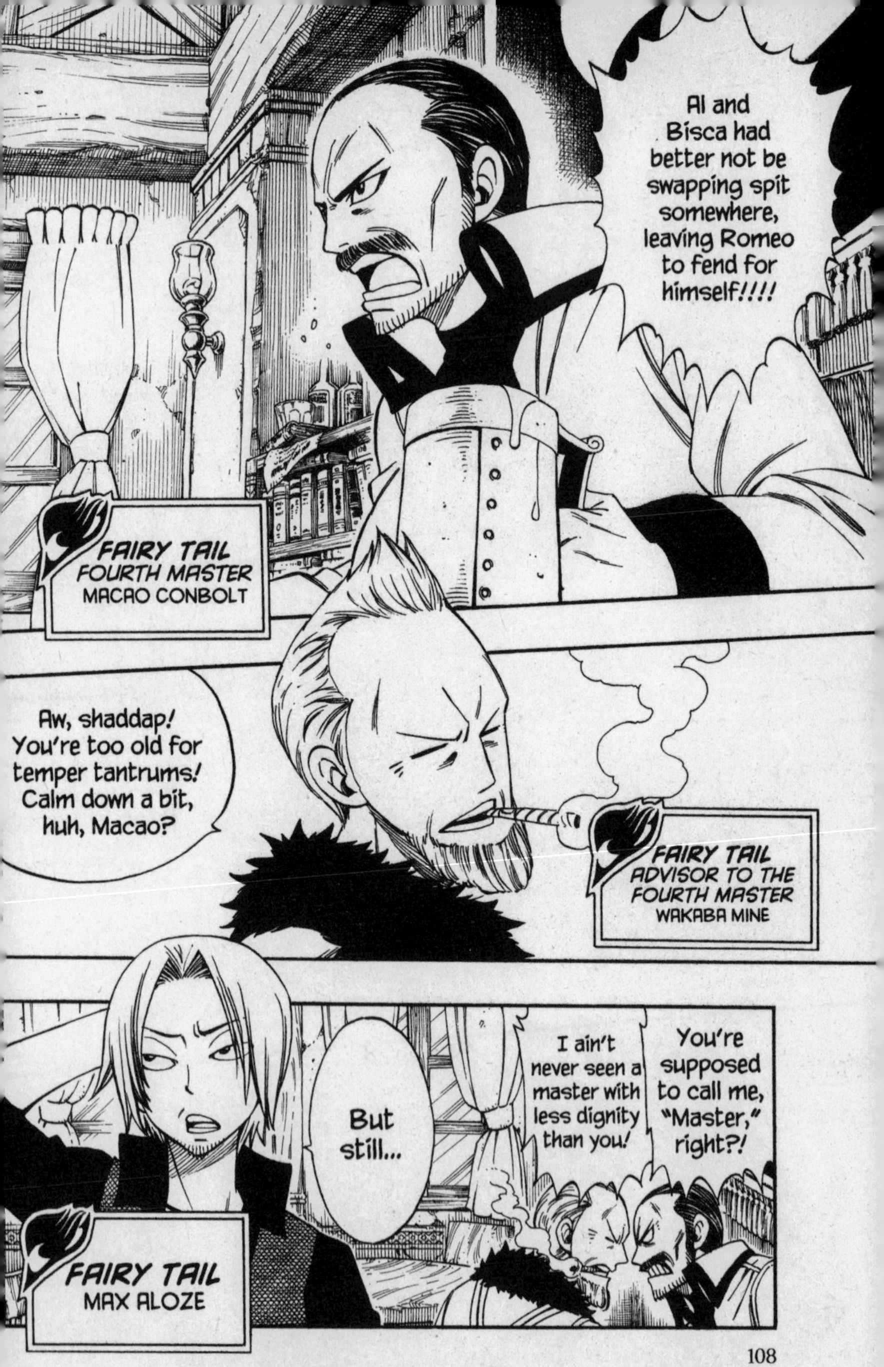
Al and Bisca had better not be swapping spit somewhere, leaving Romeo to fend for himself!!!!
FAIRY TAIL
FOURTH MASTER
MACAO CONBOLT
Aw, shaddap! You're too old for temper tantrums! Calm down a bit, huh, Macao?
FAIRY TAIL
ADVISOR TO THE FOURTH MASTER
WAKABA MINE
You're supposed to call me, "Master," right?!
I ain't never seen a master with less dignity than you!
But still...
FAIRY TAIL
MAX ALOZE

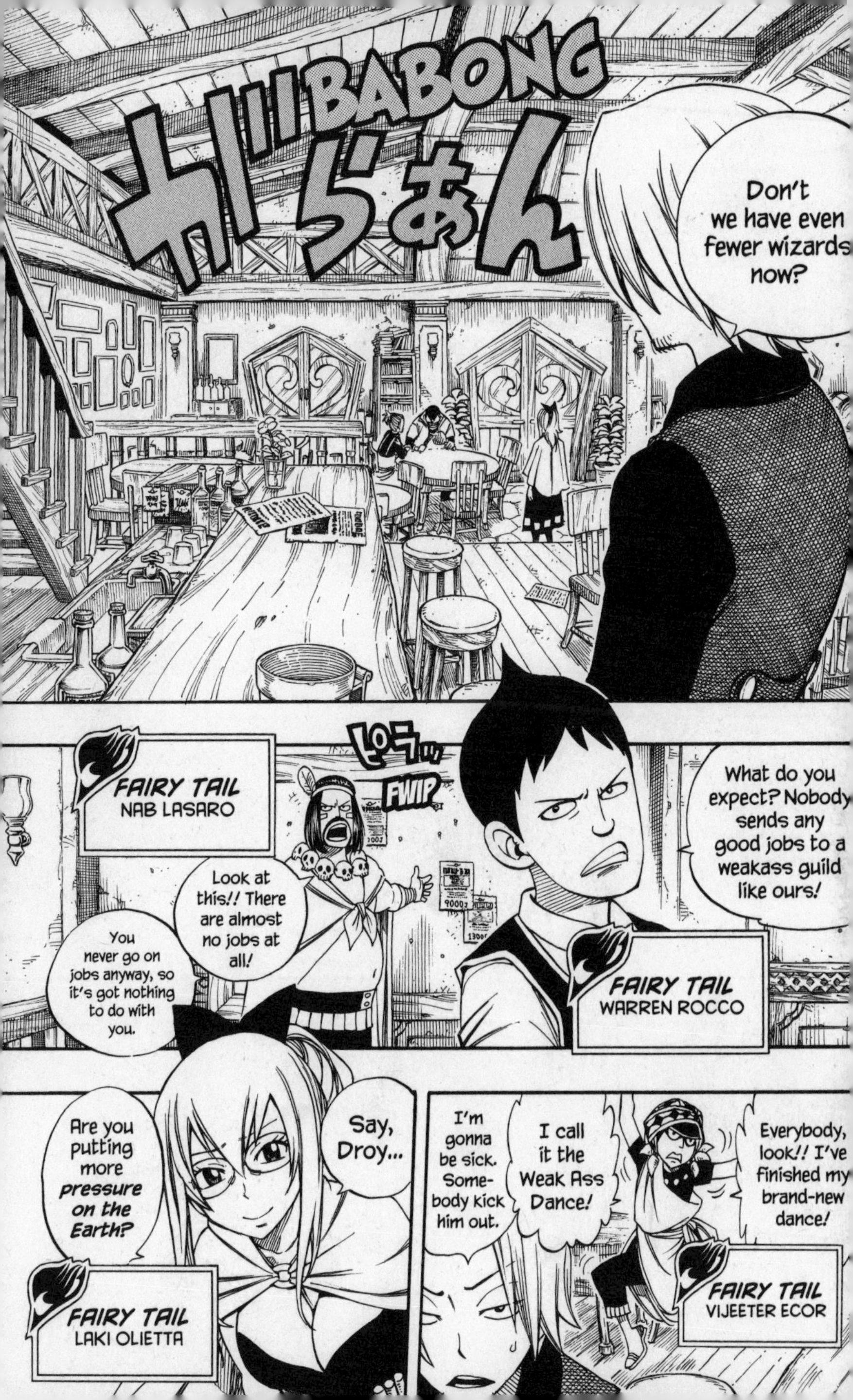
BABONG
Don't we have even fewer wizards now?
What do you expect? Nobody sends any good jobs to a weakass guild like ours!
FAIRY TAIL
WARREN ROCCO
FWIP
FAIRY TAIL
NAB LASARO
Look at this!! There are almost no jobs at all!
You never go on jobs anyway, so it's got nothing to do with you.
Everybody, look!! I've finished my brand-new dance!
FAIRY TAIL
VIJEETER ECOR
I call it the Weak Ass Dance!
I'm gonna be sick. Somebody kick him out.
Say, Droy...
Are you putting more pressure on the Earth?
FAIRY TAIL
LAKI OLIETTA

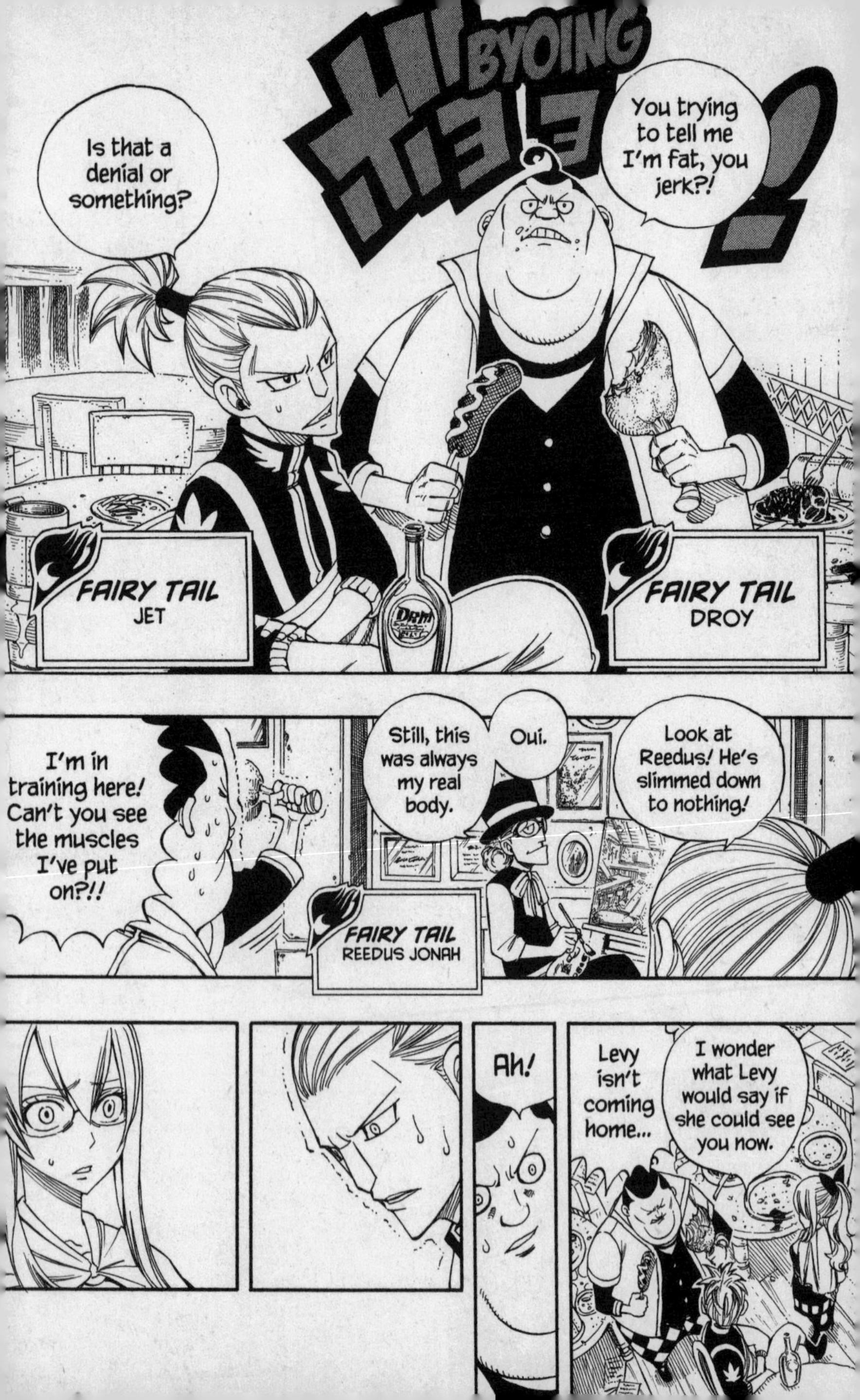
BYOING
You trying to tell me I'm fat, you jerk?!
Is that a denial or something?
FAIRY TAIL
DROY
FAIRY TAIL
JET
Look at Reedus! He's slimmed down to nothing!
Oui.
Still, this was always my real body.
FAIRY TAIL
REEDUS JONAH
I'm in training here! Can't you see the muscles I've put on?!!
I wonder what Levy would say if she could see you now.
Levy isn't coming home...
Ah!

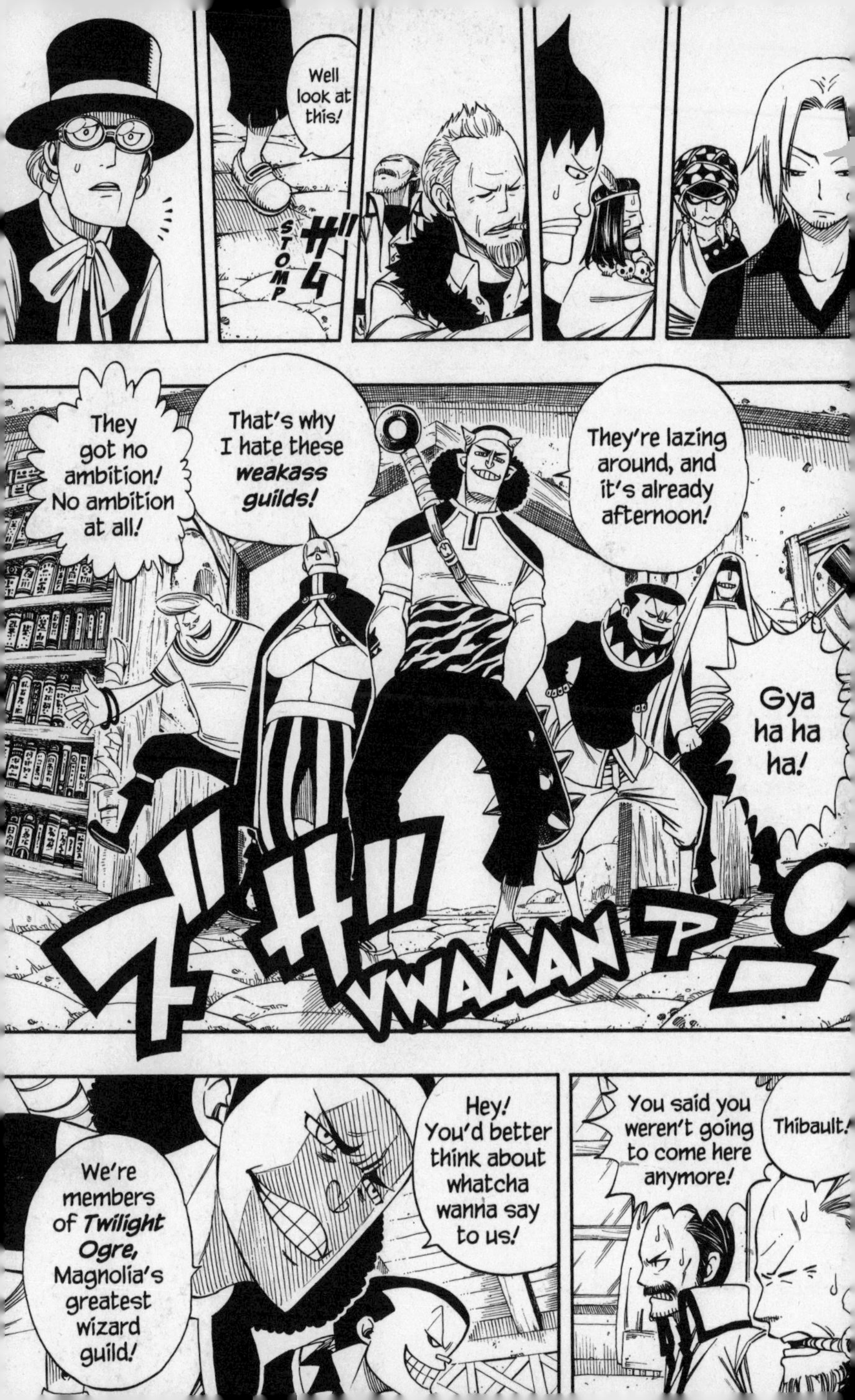
Well look at this!
STOMP
They're lazing around, and it's already afternoon!
Gya ha ha ha!
That's why I hate these *weakass guilds!*
They got no ambition! No ambition at all!
VWAAAN
Thibault!
You said you weren't going to come here anymore!
Hey! You'd better think about whatcha wanna say to us!
We're members of *Twilight Ogre,* Magnolia's greatest wizard guild!

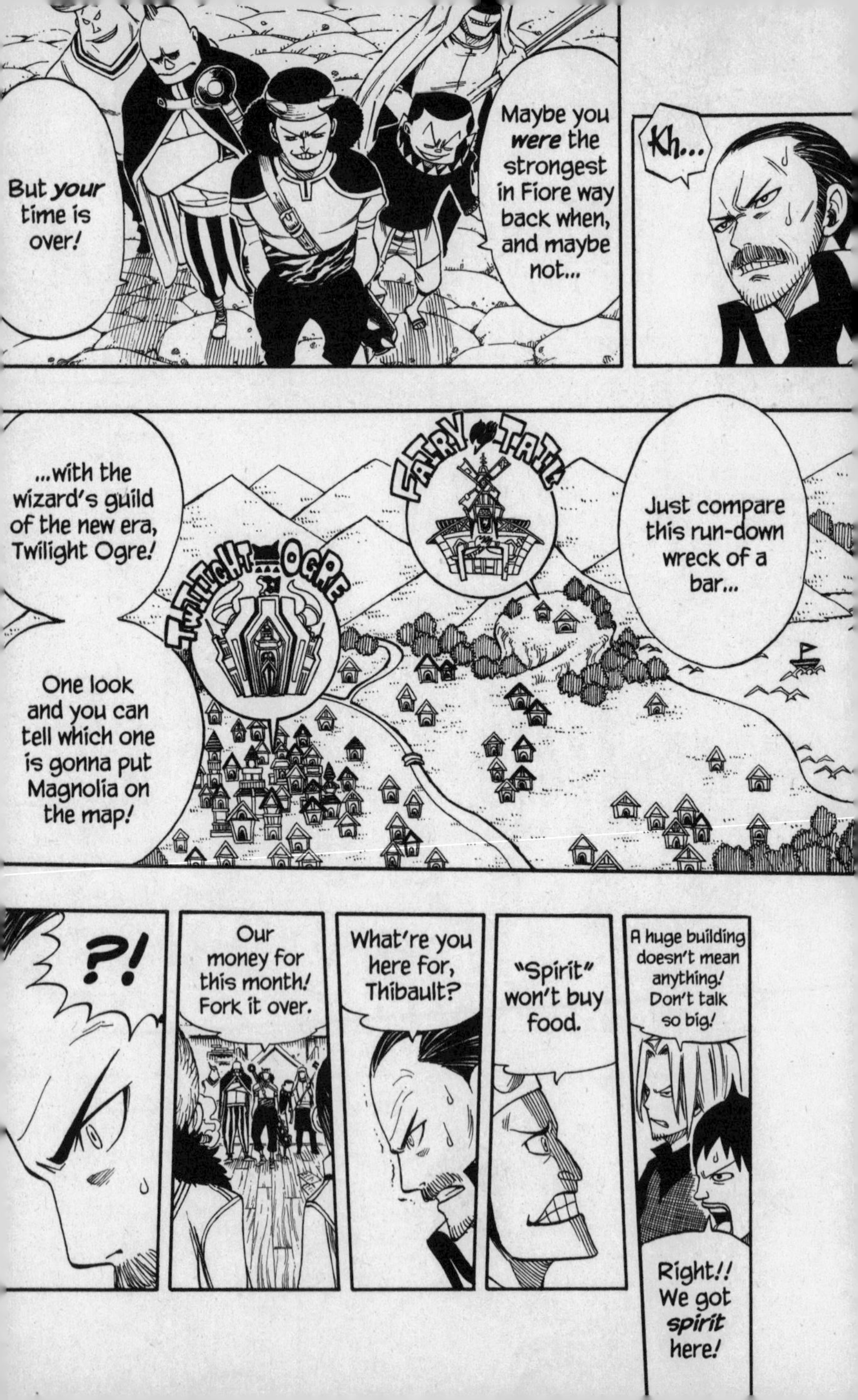
Kh...
Maybe you *were* the strongest in Fiore way back when, and maybe not...
But *your* time is over!
Just compare this run-down wreck of a bar...
FAIRY TAIL
TWILIGHT OGRE
...with the wizard's guild of the new era, Twilight Ogre!
One look and you can tell which one is gonna put Magnolia on the map!
A huge building doesn't mean anything! Don't talk so big!
Right!! We got *spirit* here!
"Spirit" won't buy food.
What're you here for, Thibault?
Our money for this month! Fork it over.
?!

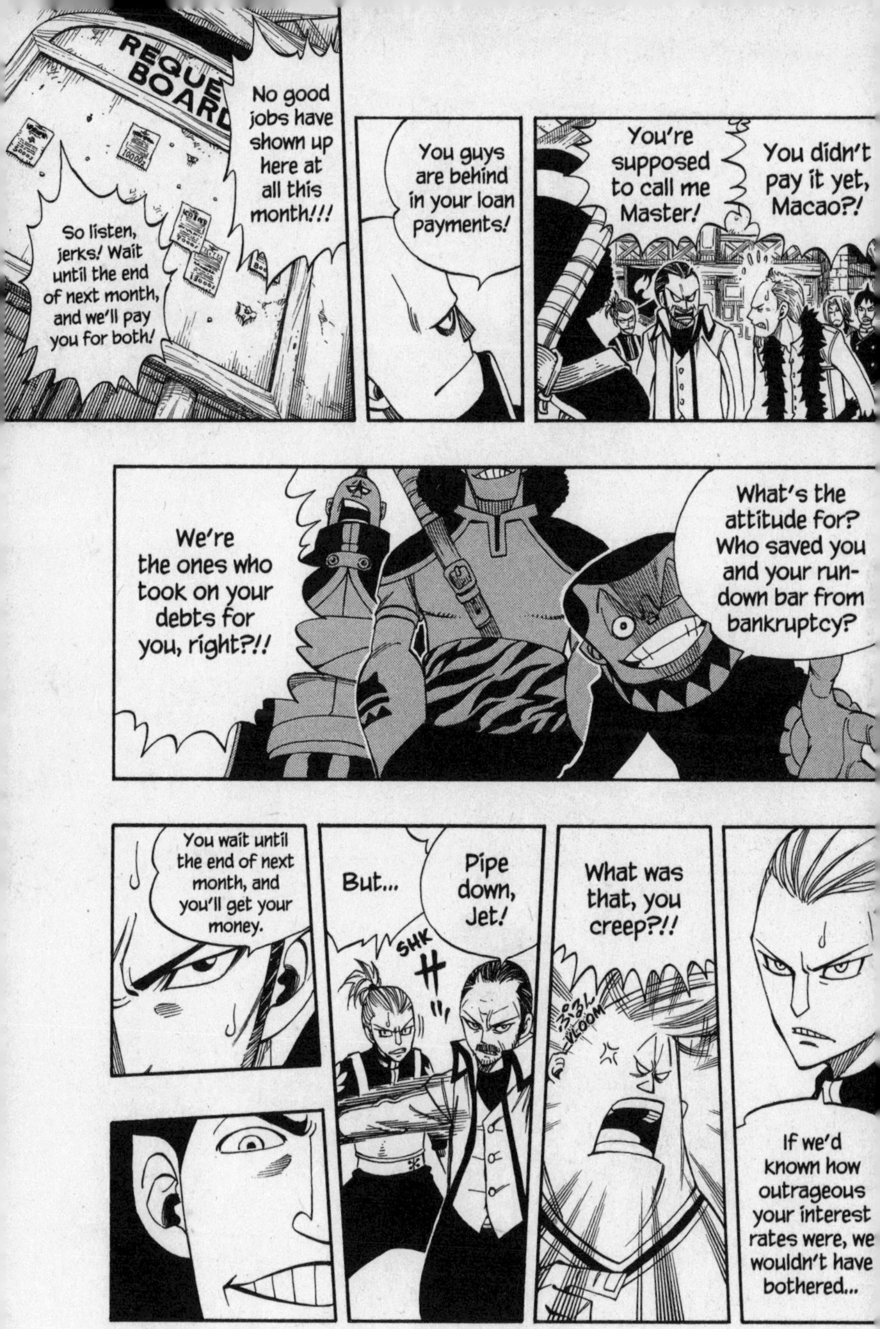
You didn't pay it yet, Macao?!
You're supposed to call me Master!
You guys are behind in your loan payments!
No good jobs have shown up here at all this month!!!
So listen, jerks! Wait until the end of next month, and we'll pay you for both!
What's the attitude for? Who saved you and your run-down bar from bankruptcy?
We're the ones who took on your debts for you, right?!!
If we'd known how outrageous your interest rates were, we wouldn't have bothered...
What was that, you creep?!!
VLOOM
Pipe down, Jet!
SHK
But...
You wait until the end of next month, and you'll get your money.

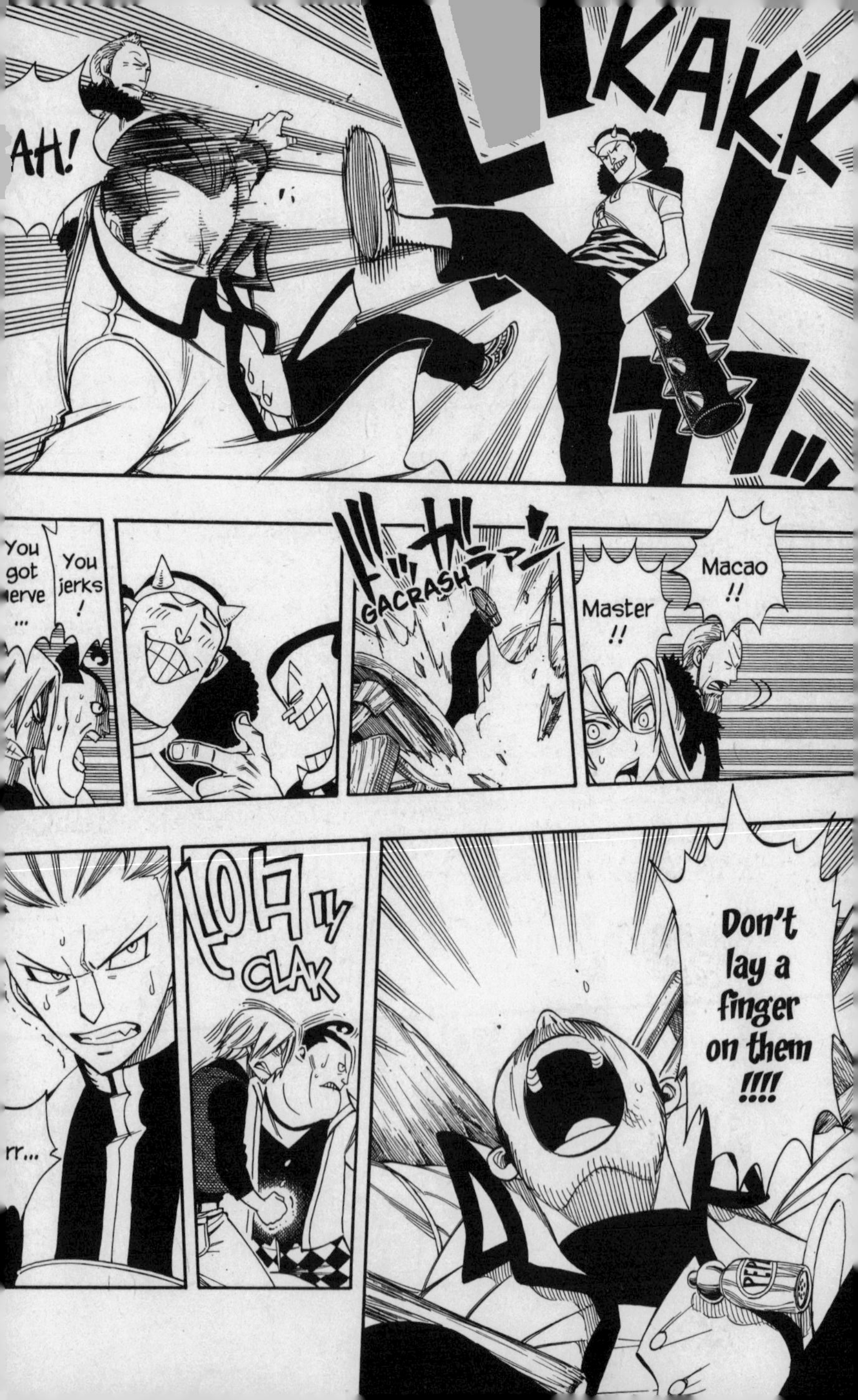
KAKK
AH!
GACRASH
Macao !!
Master !!
You jerks !
You got nerve ...
Don't lay a finger on them !!!!
CLAK
rr...

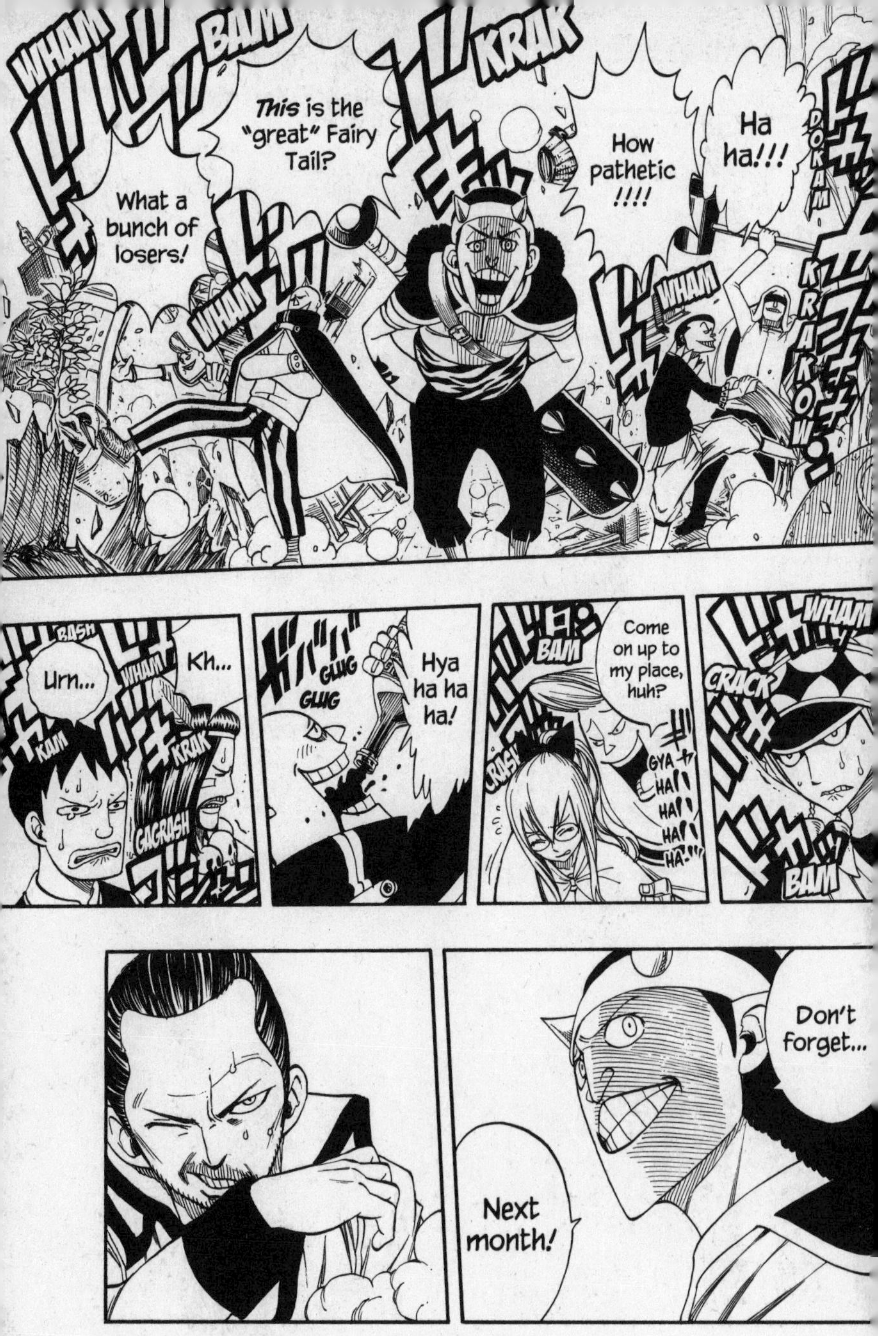

Ha ha!!!
DOKAM
KRAKOW!
How pathetic!!!!
WHAM
KRAK
This is the "great" Fairy Tail?
BAM
WHAM
What a bunch of losers!
WHAM
WHAM
CRACK
BAM
Come on up to my place, huh?
BAM
GYA HA! HA! HA! HA!!
CRASH
Hya ha ha ha!
GLUG
GLUG
Kh...
BASH
WHAM
Urn...
KRAK
KAM
GAGRASH
Don't forget...
Next month!

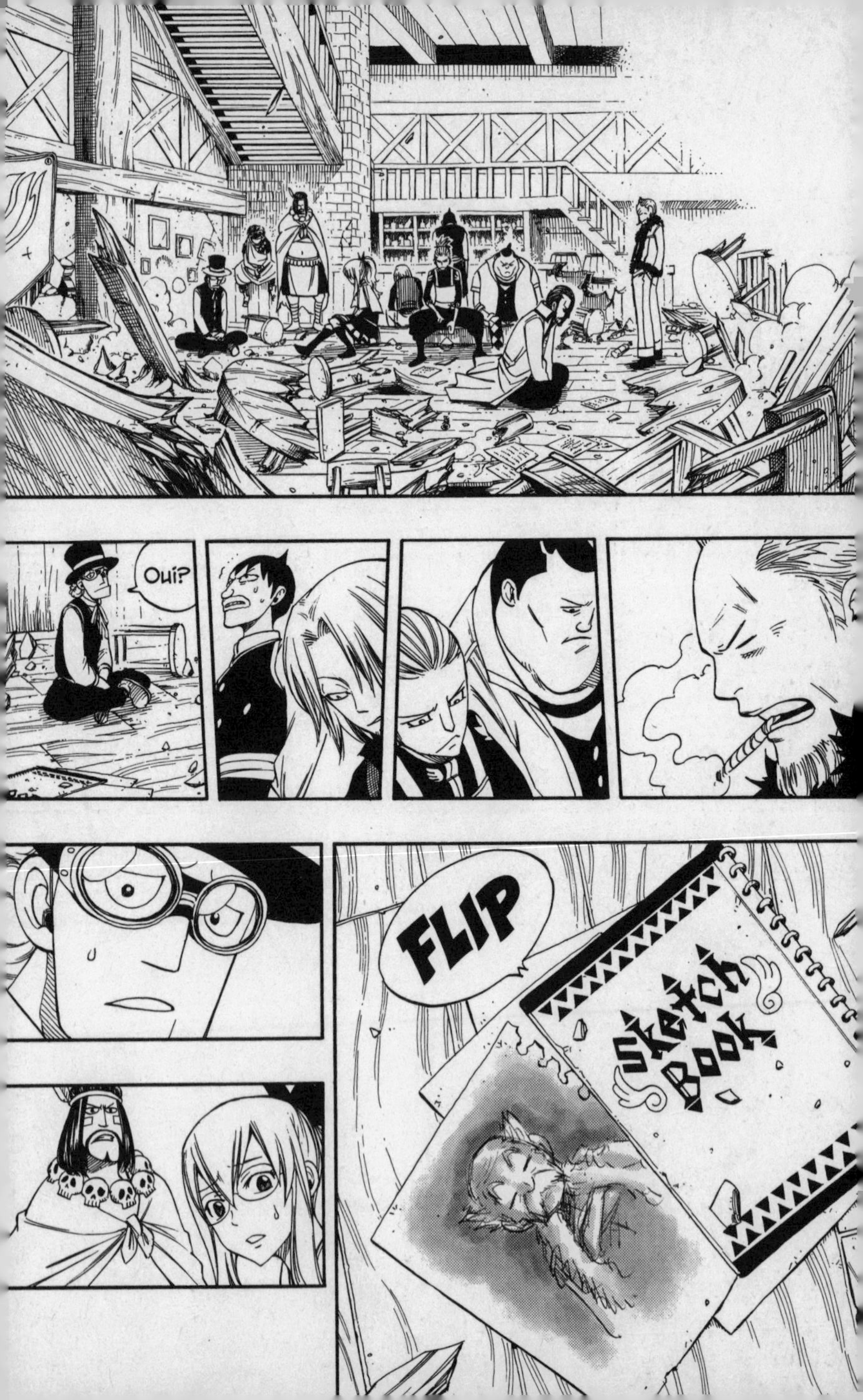
Oui?
FLIP
Sketch Book

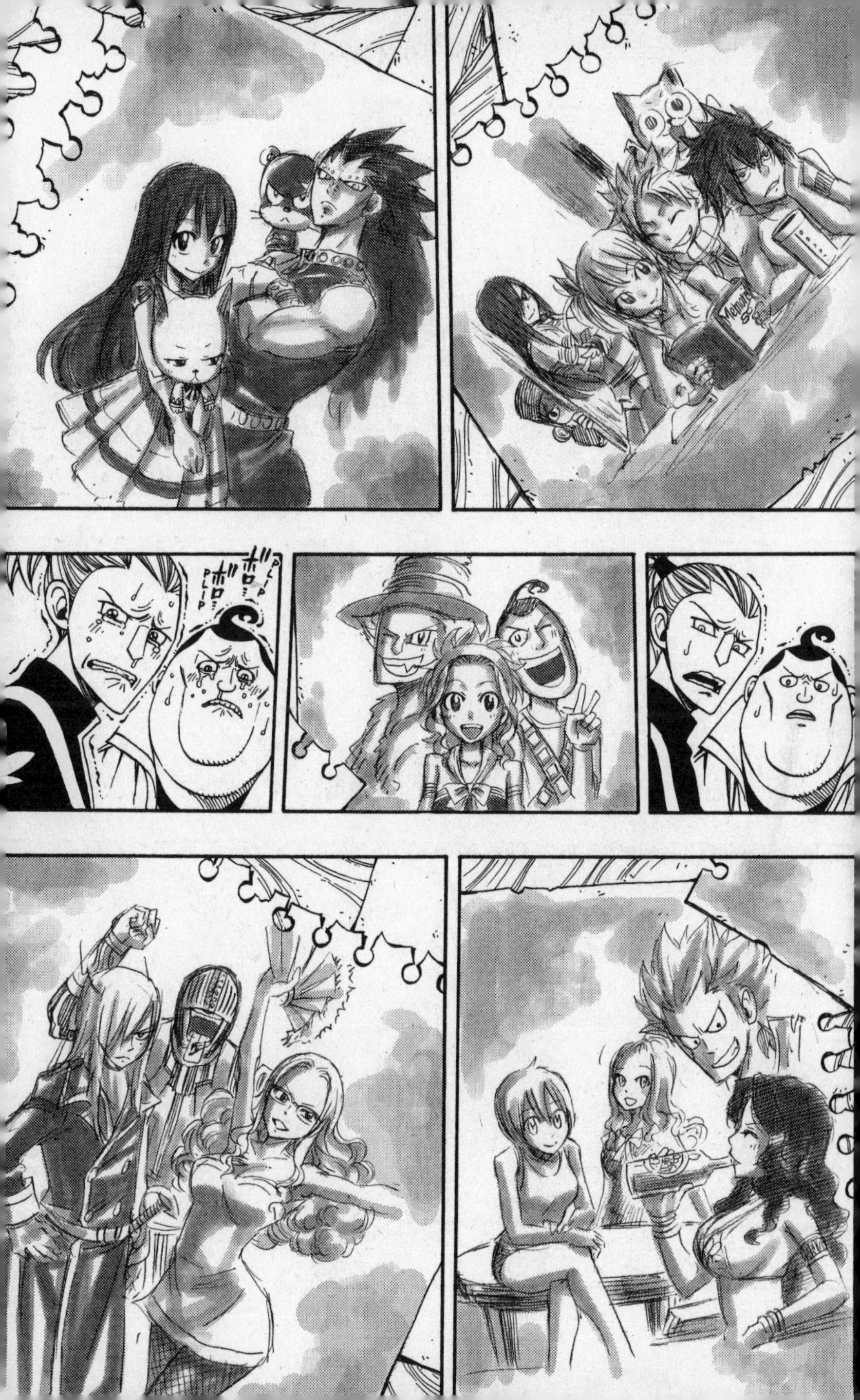
ボロ… PLIP
ボロ… PLIP

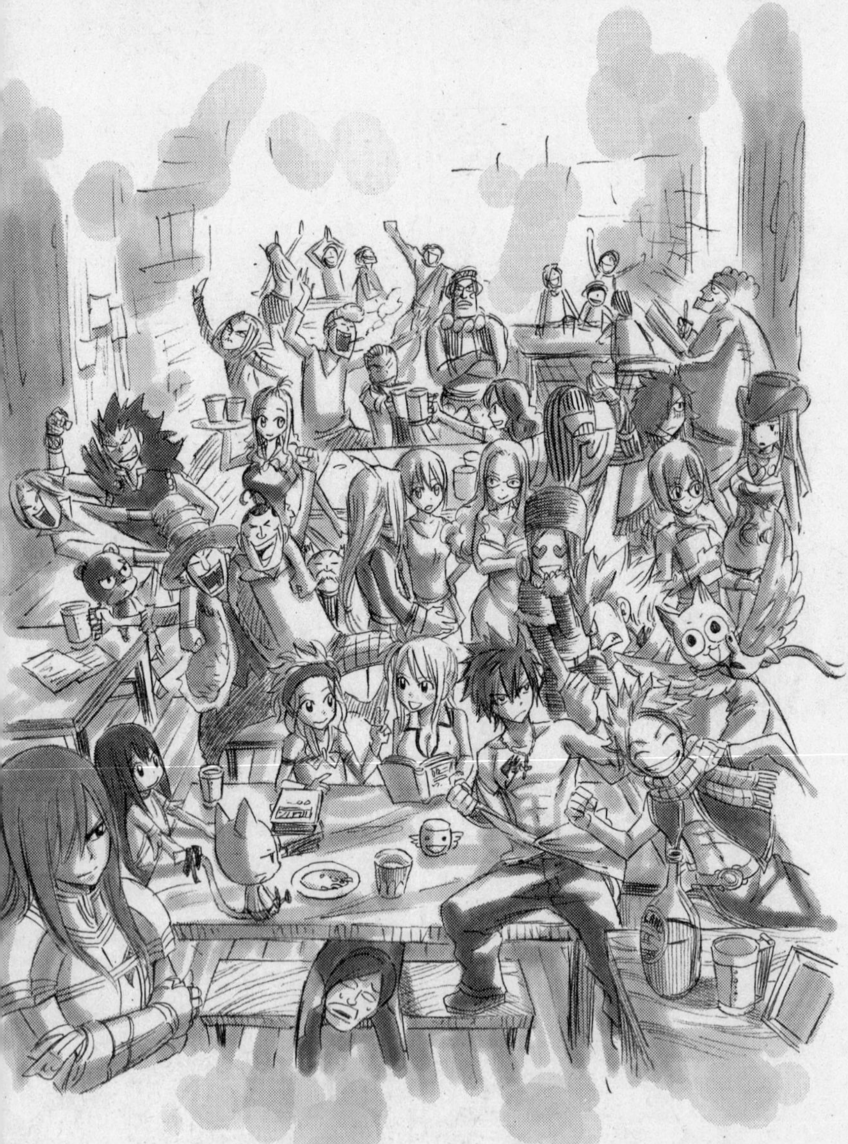

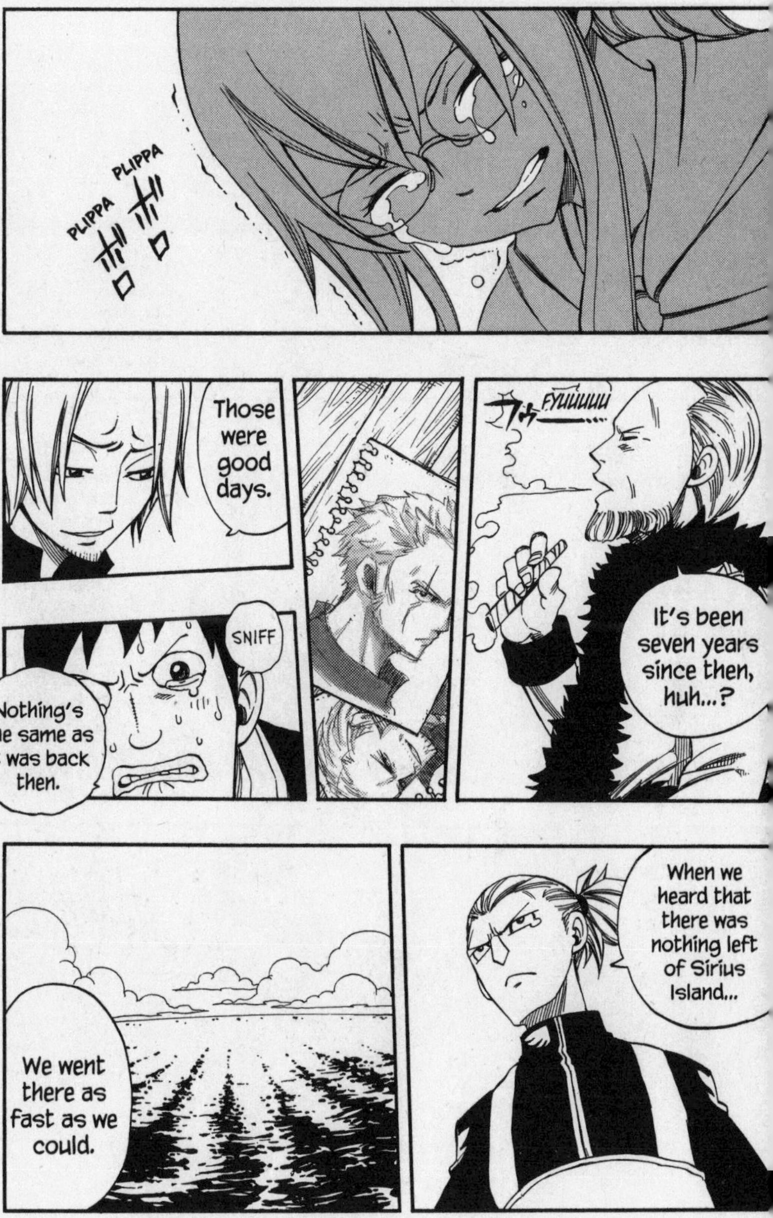
PLIPPA
PLIPPA
FYUUUUU
It's been seven years since then, huh...?
Those were good days.
SNIFF
Nothing's the same as it was back then.
When we heard that there was nothing left of Sirius Island...
We went there as fast as we could.

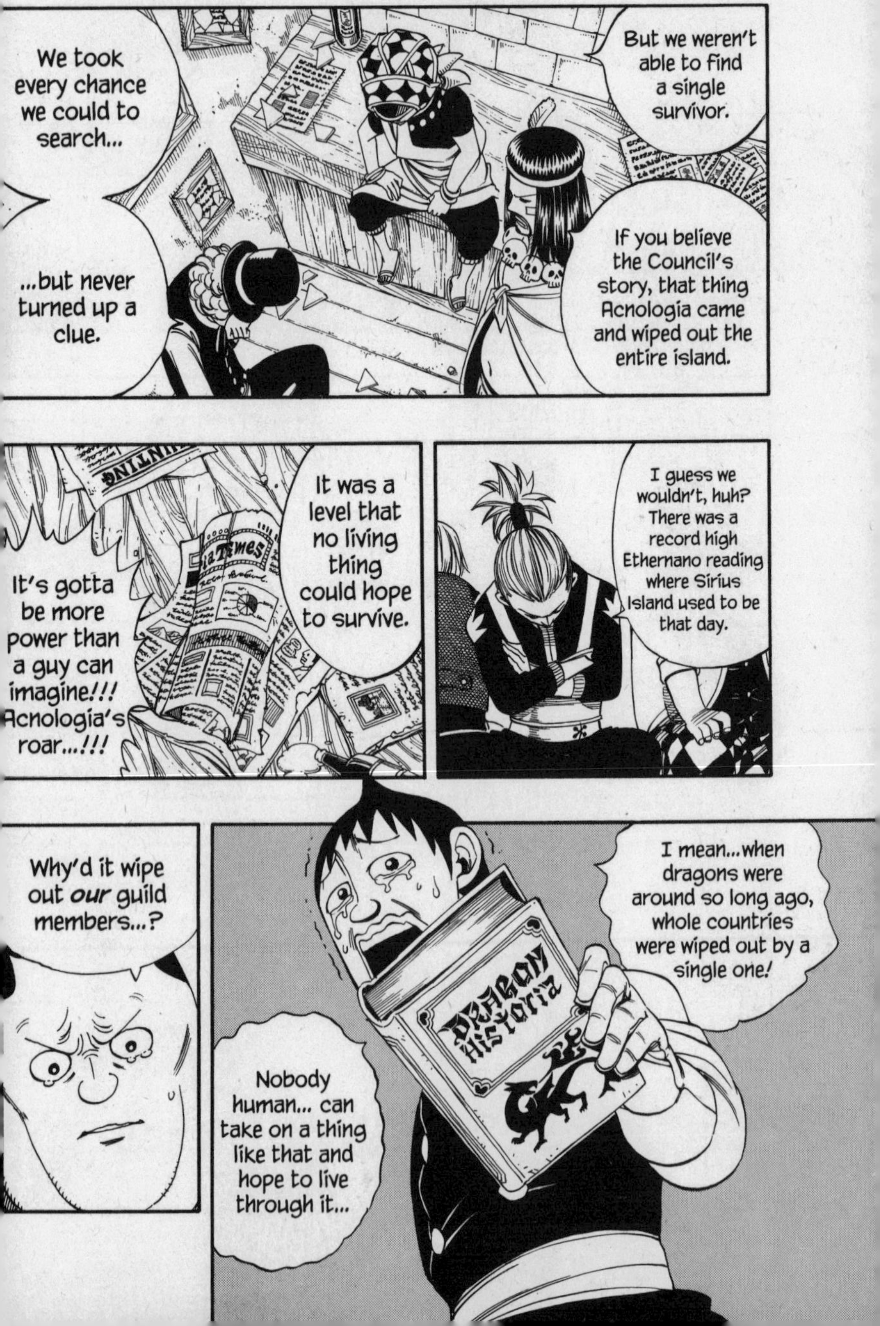

But we weren't able to find a single survivor.
We took every chance we could to search...
If you believe the Council's story, that thing Acnologia came and wiped out the entire island.
...but never turned up a clue.
I guess we wouldn't, huh? There was a record high Ethernano reading where Sirius Island used to be that day.
It was a level that no living thing could hope to survive.
It's gotta be more power than a guy can imagine!!! Acnologia's roar...!!!
I mean...when dragons were around so long ago, whole countries were wiped out by a single one!
DRAGON HISTORIA
Nobody human... can take on a thing like that and hope to live through it...
Why'd it wipe out *our* guild members...?

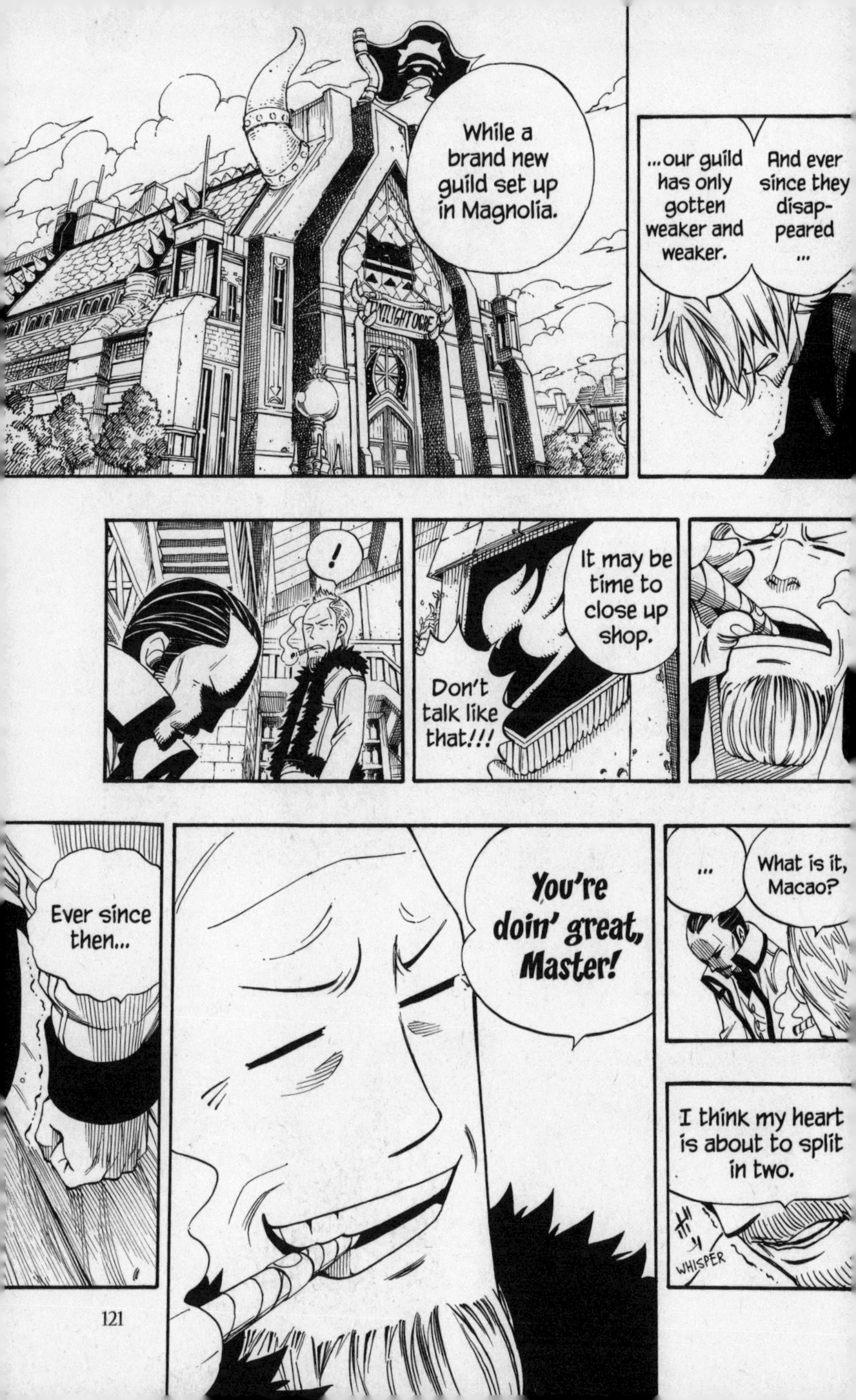
And ever since they disap- peared ...
...our guild has only gotten weaker and weaker.
While a brand new guild set up in Magnolia.
It may be time to close up shop.
Don't talk like that!!!
!
What is it, Macao?
...
I think my heart is about to split in two.
WHISPER
You're doin' great, Master!
Ever since then...

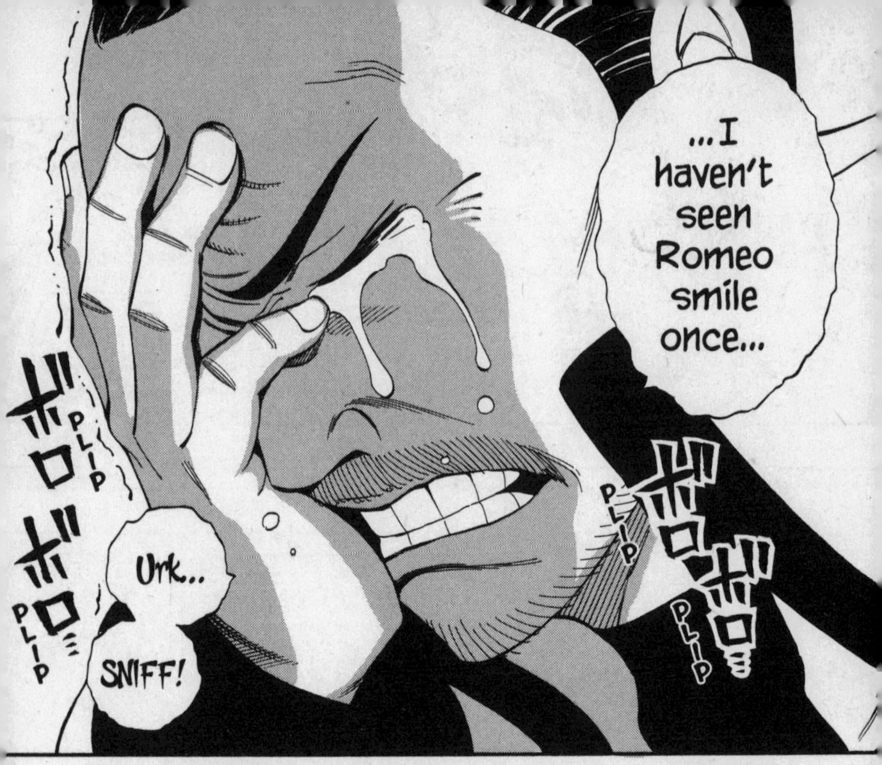
...I haven't seen Romeo smile once...
PLIP PLIP
PLIP PLIP
Urk...
SNIFF!

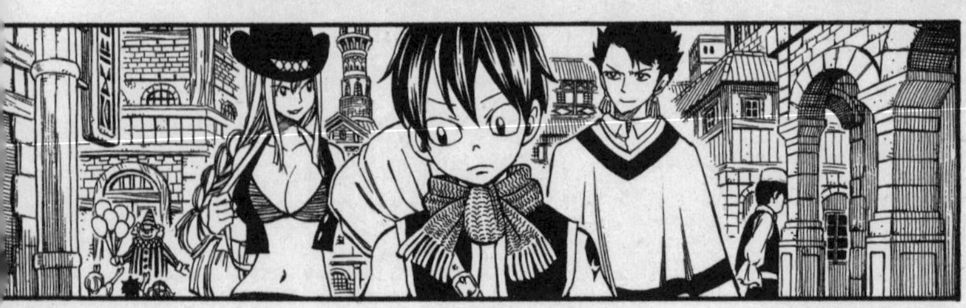

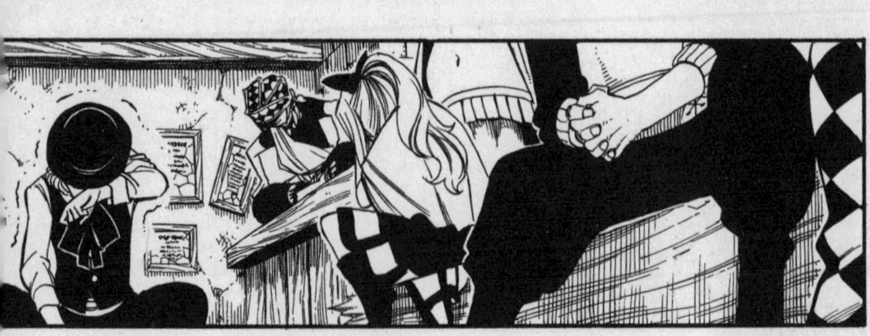

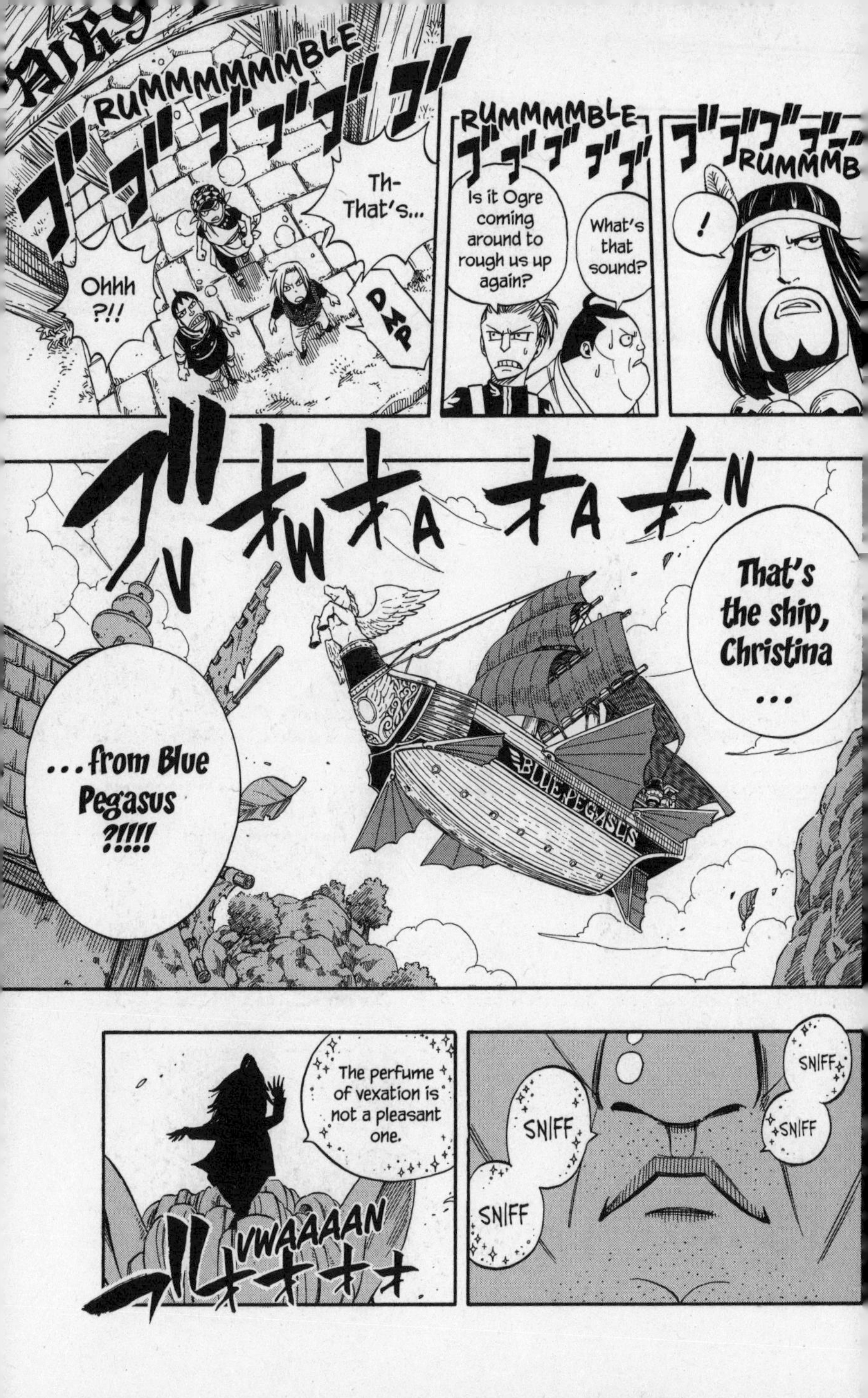
RUMMMMB
!
RUMMMMBLE
What's that sound?
Is it Ogre coming around to rough us up again?
RUMMMMMMMBLE
Th- That's...
DMP
Ohhh ?!!
VWAAAN
That's the ship, Christina...
...from Blue Pegasus ?!!!!
BLUE PEGASUS
SNIFF
SNIFF
SNIFF
SNIFF
The perfume of vexation is not a pleasant one.
VWAAAAN

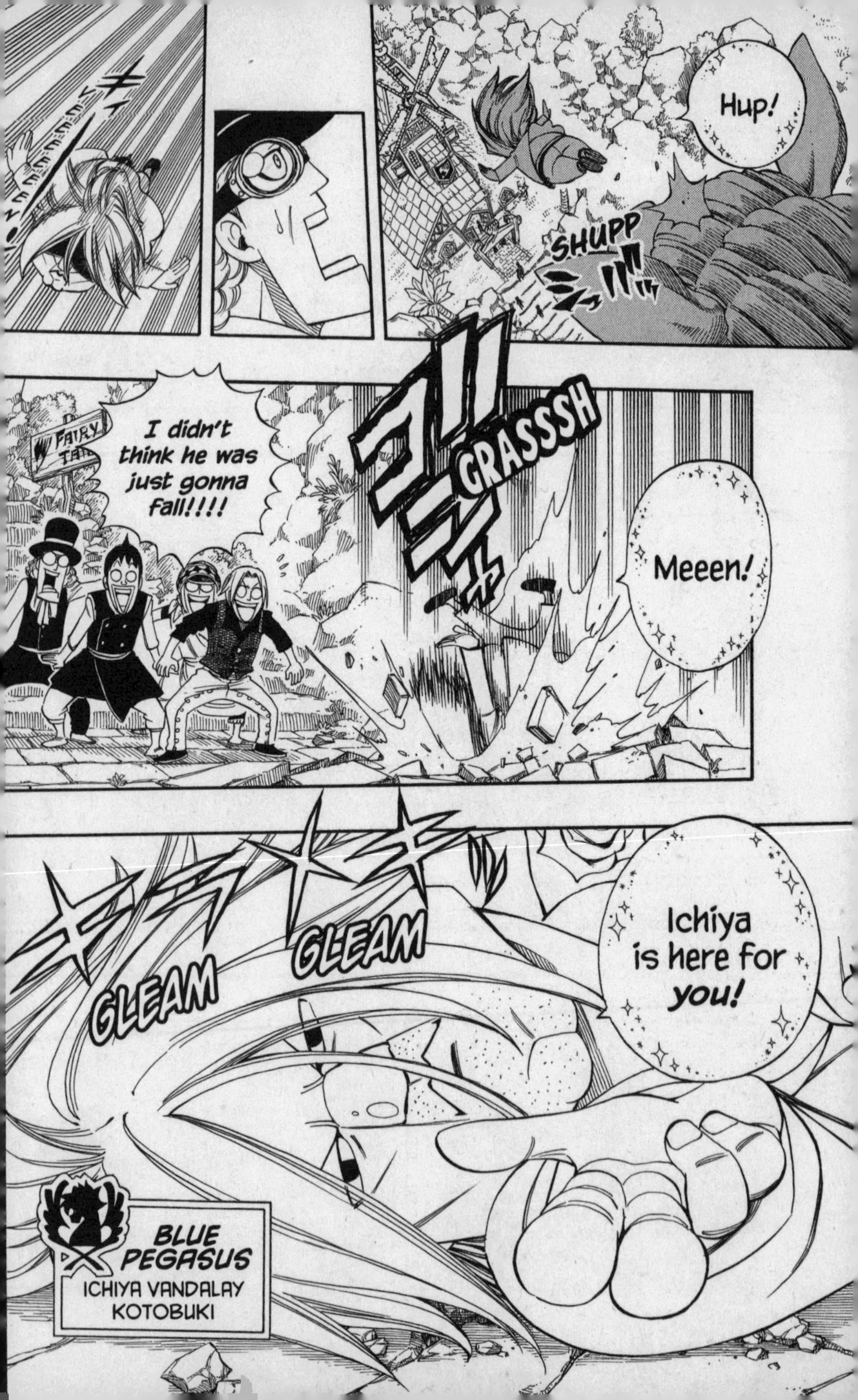
Hup!
SHUPP
GRASSSH
Meeen!
I didn't think he was just gonna fall!!!!
Ichiya is here for *you!*
GLEAM
GLEAM
BLUE PEGASUS
ICHIYA VANDALAY KOTOBUKI

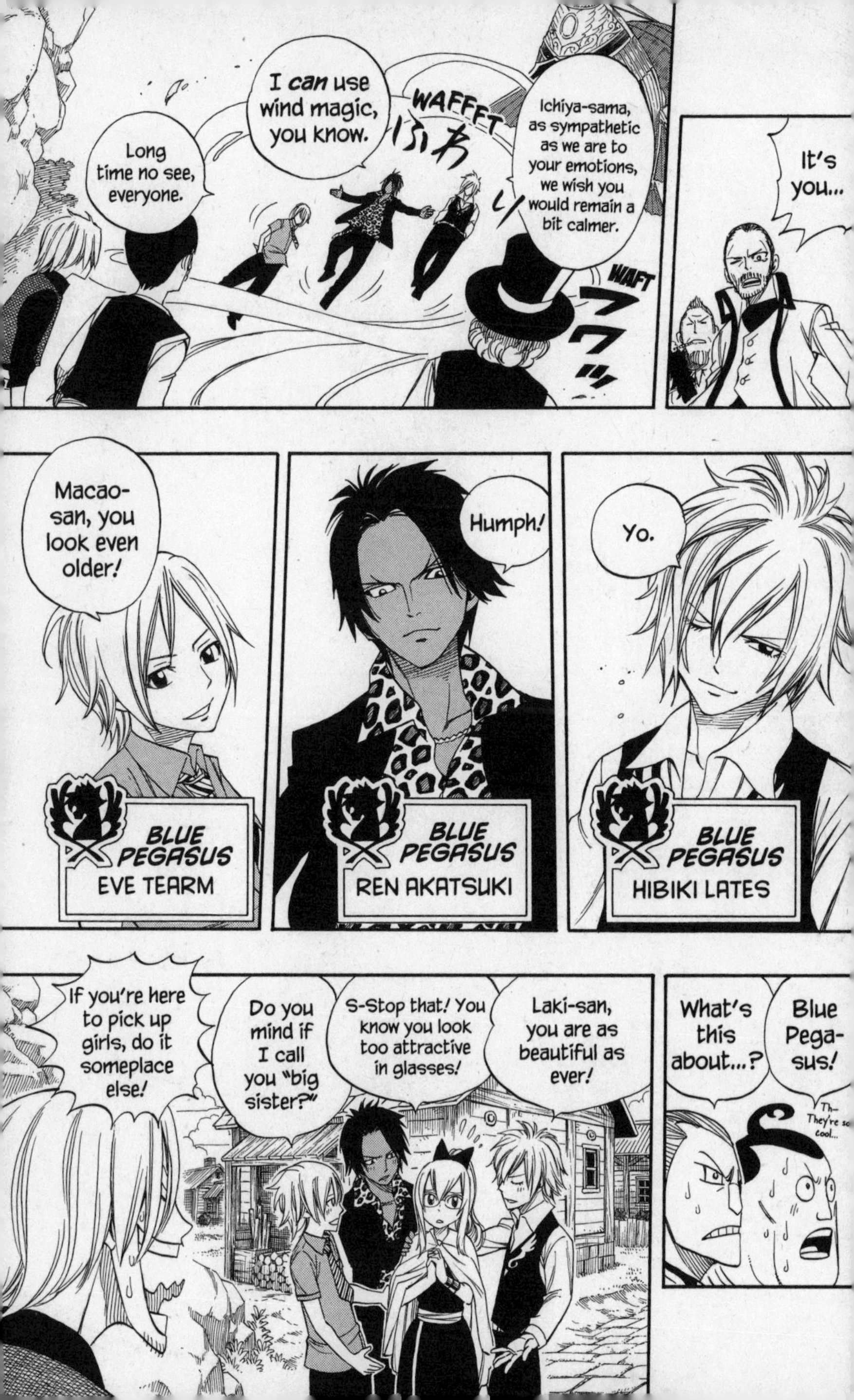
It's you...
Ichiya-sama, as sympathetic as we are to your emotions, we wish you would remain a bit calmer.
WAFFFT
I *can* use wind magic, you know.
Long time no see, everyone.
WAFT
Yo.
BLUE PEGASUS
HIBIKI LATES
Humph!
BLUE PEGASUS
REN AKATSUKI
Macao-san, you look even older!
BLUE PEGASUS
EVE TEARM
Blue Pega-sus!
What's this about...?
Th- They're so cool...
Laki-san, you are as beautiful as ever!
S-Stop that! You know you look too attractive in glasses!
Do you mind if I call you "big sister?"
If you're here to pick up girls, do it someplace else!

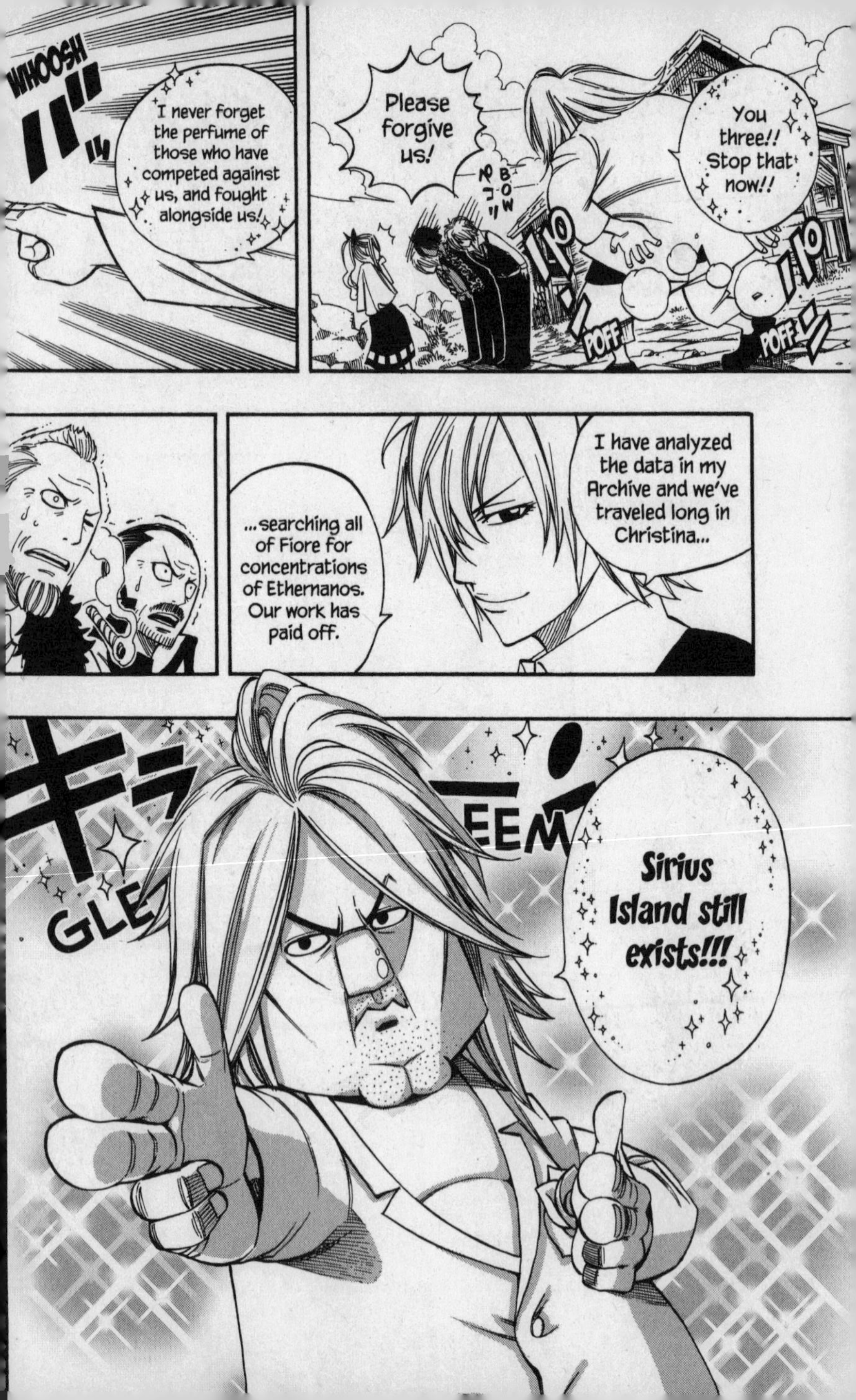
You three!! Stop that now!!
Please forgive us!
BOW
POFF
POFF
WHOOSH
I never forget the perfume of those who have competed against us, and fought alongside us!
I have analyzed the data in my Archive and we've traveled long in Christina...
...searching all of Fiore for concentrations of Ethernanos. Our work has paid off.
Sirius Island still exists!!!
EEM
GLE

FAIRY TAIL

フェアリーテイル

Chapter 255: Fairy Sphere

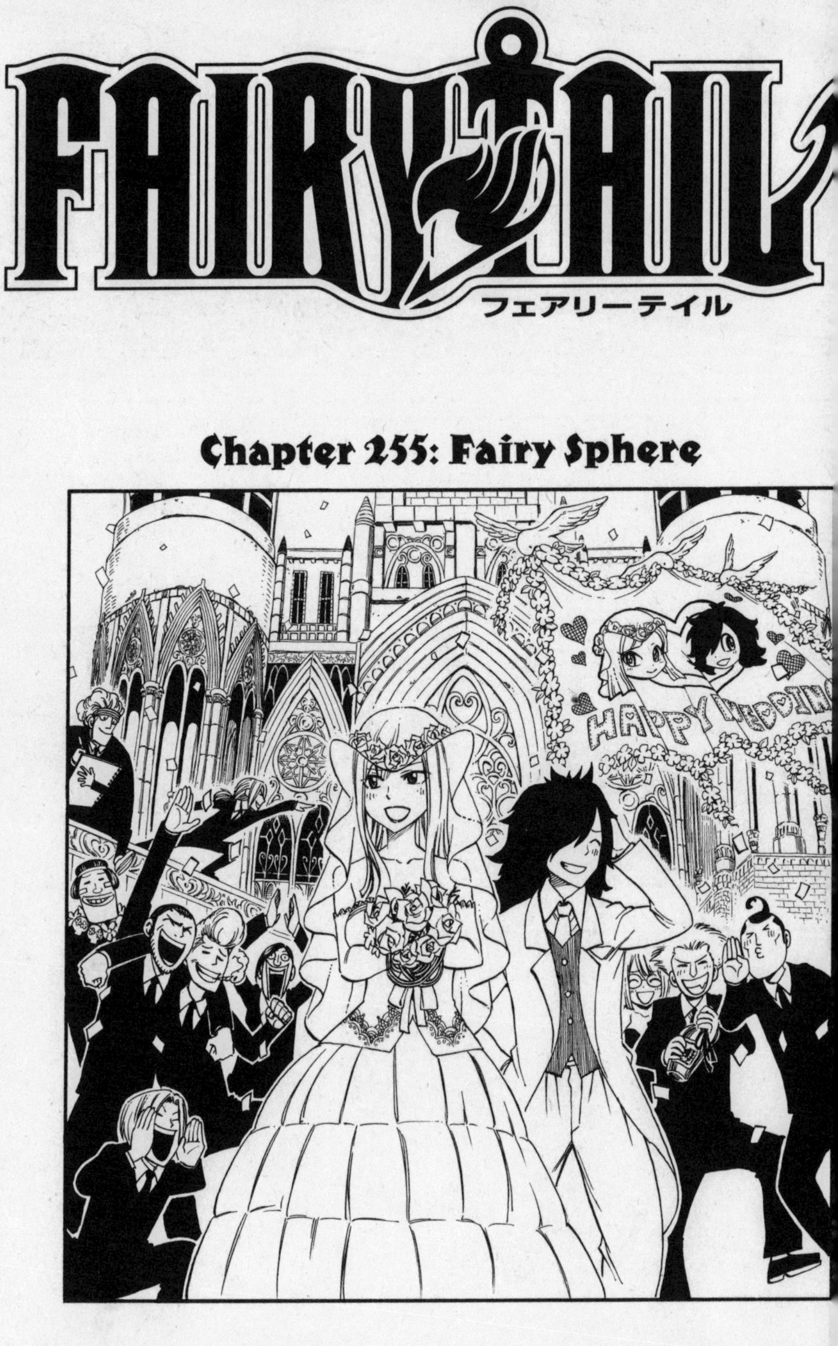
HAPPY WEDDIN

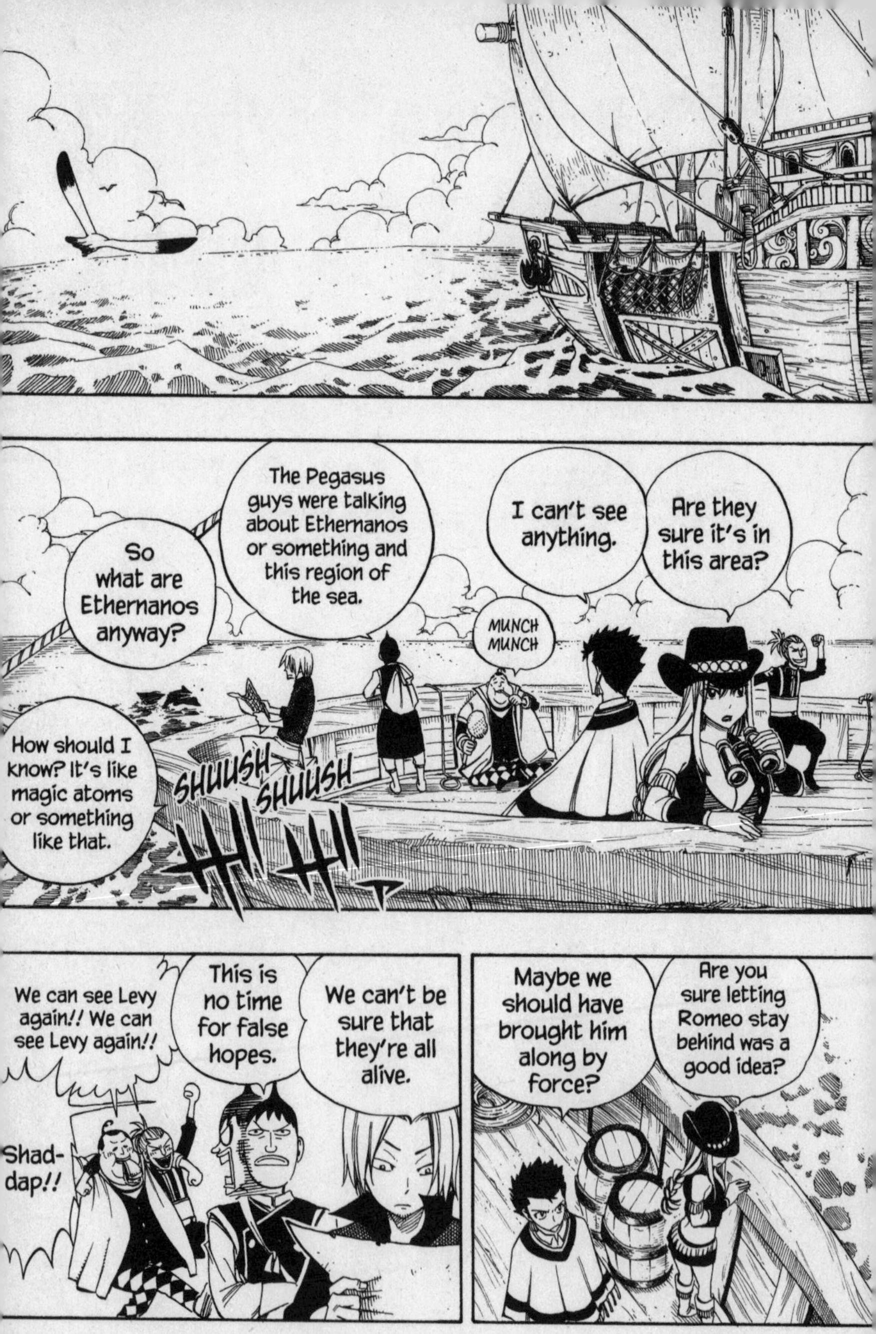
Are they sure it's in this area?
I can't see anything.
MUNCH MUNCH
The Pegasus guys were talking about Ethernanos or something and this region of the sea.
So what are Ethernanos anyway?
How should I know? It's like magic atoms or something like that.
SHUUSH SHUUSH
Are you sure letting Romeo stay behind was a good idea?
Maybe we should have brought him along by force?
We can't be sure that they're all alive.
This is no time for false hopes.
We can see Levy again!! We can see Levy again!!
Shad-dap!!

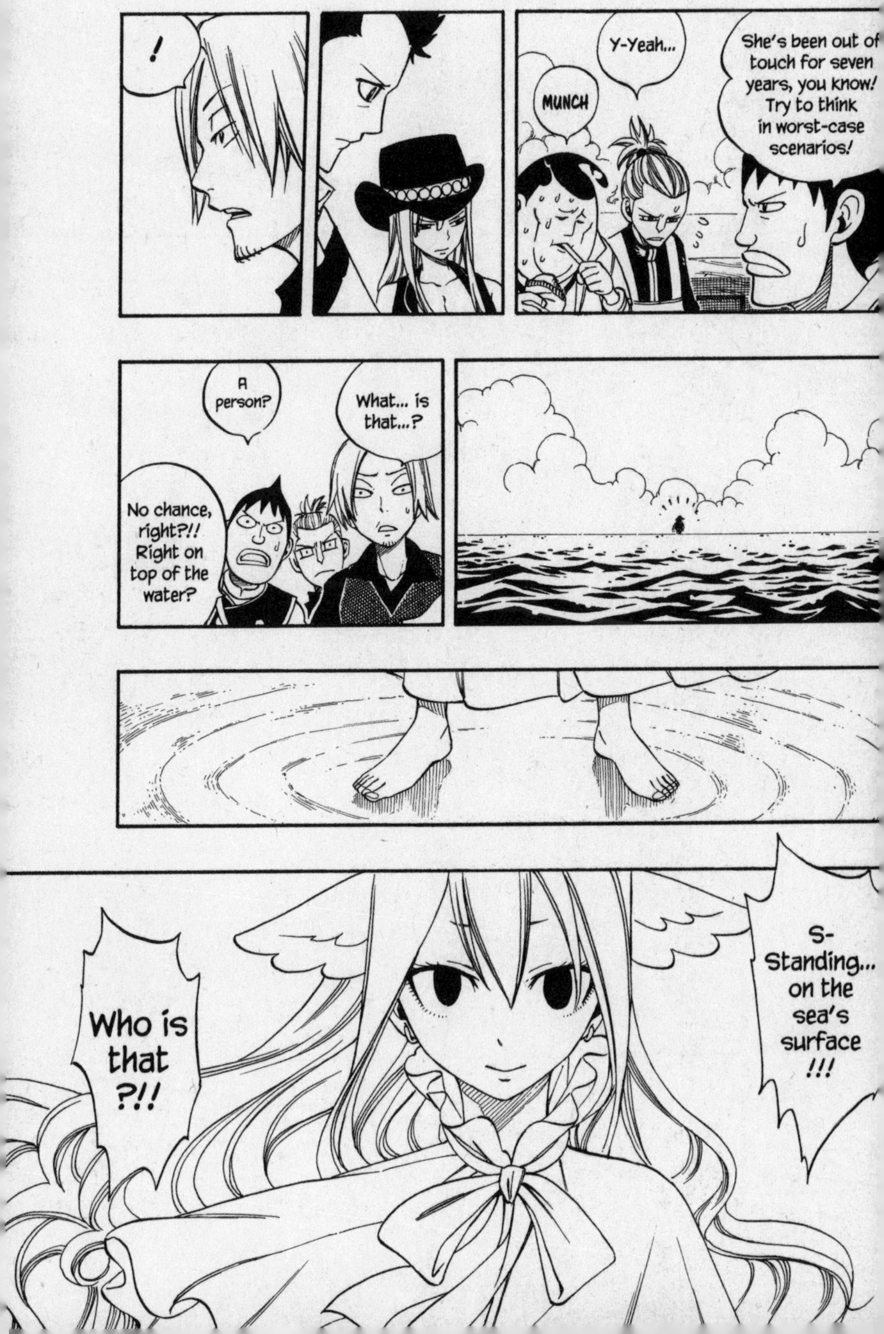
She's been out of touch for seven years, you know! Try to think in worst-case scenarios!
Y-Yeah...
MUNCH
!
What... is that...?
A person?
No chance, right?!! Right on top of the water?
S-Standing... on the sea's surface!!!
Who is that?!!

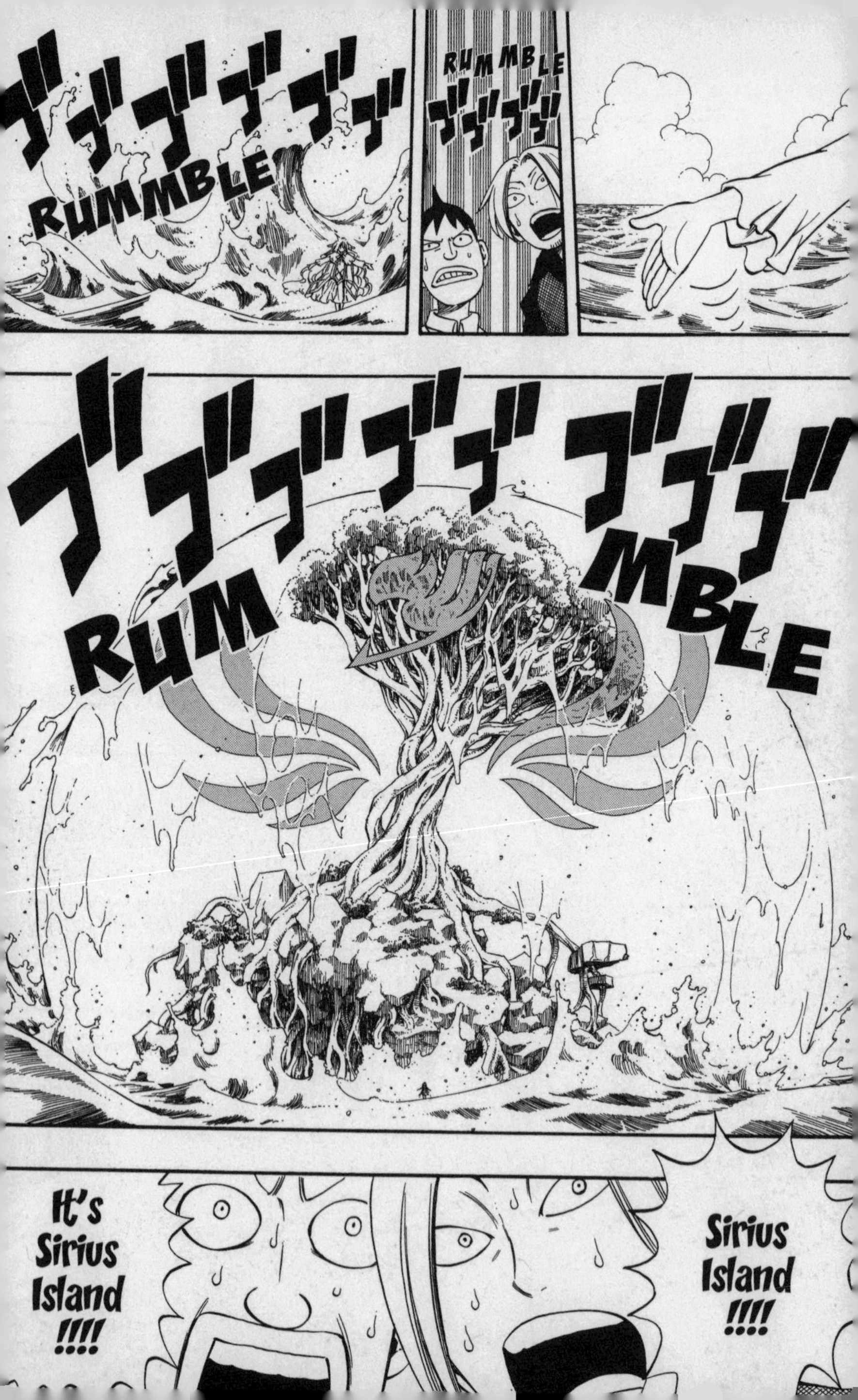
RUMMBLE
RUMMBLE
RUMMBLE
Sirius Island!!!!
It's Sirius Island!!!!

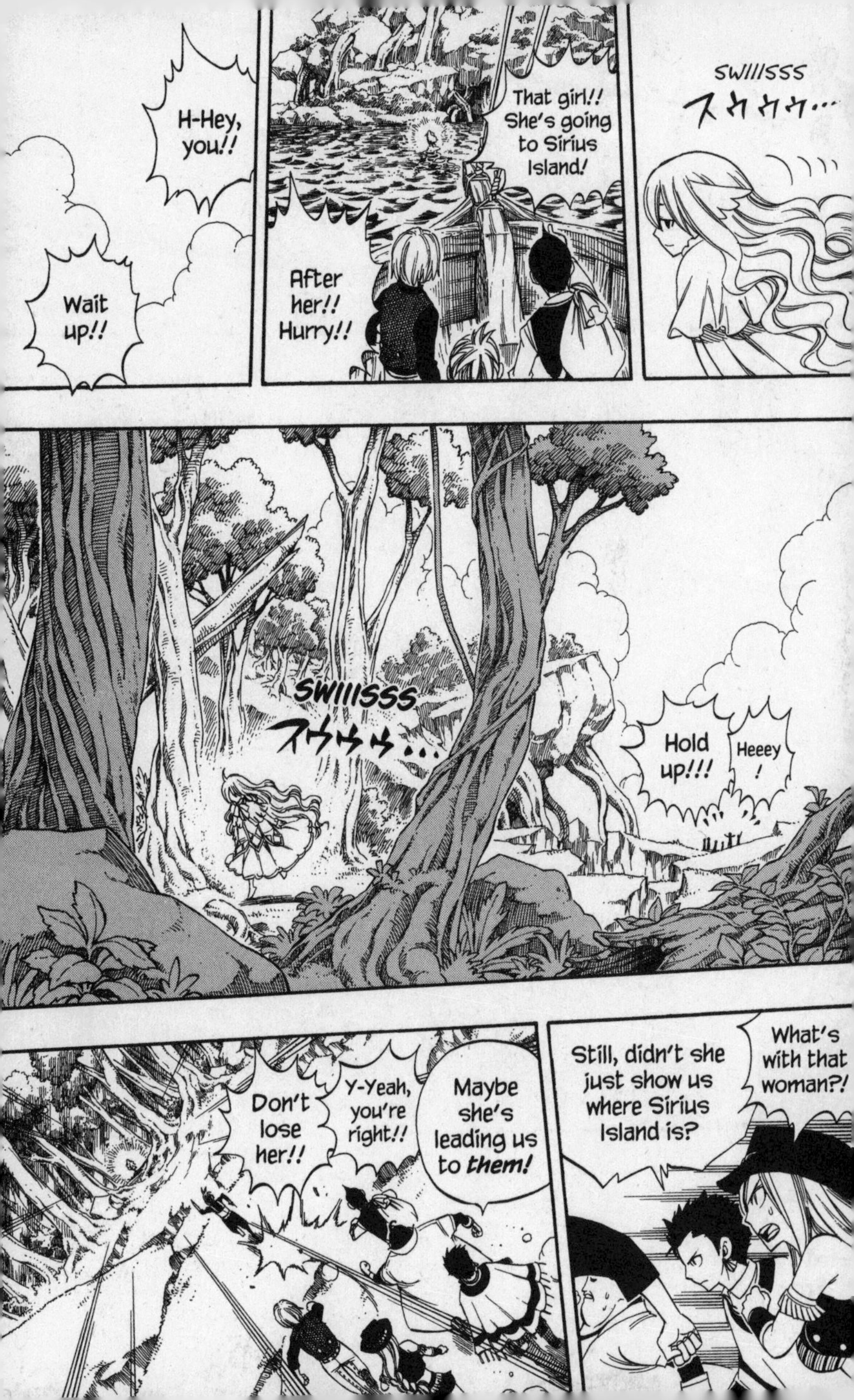
SWIIISSS
スゥゥゥ…
That girl!! She's going to Sirius Island!
After her!! Hurry!!
H-Hey, you!!
Wait up!!
Heeey!
Hold up!!!
SWIIISSS
スゥゥゥ…
What's with that woman?!
Still, didn't she just show us where Sirius Island is?
Maybe she's leading us to *them*!
Y-Yeah, you're right!!
Don't lose her!!

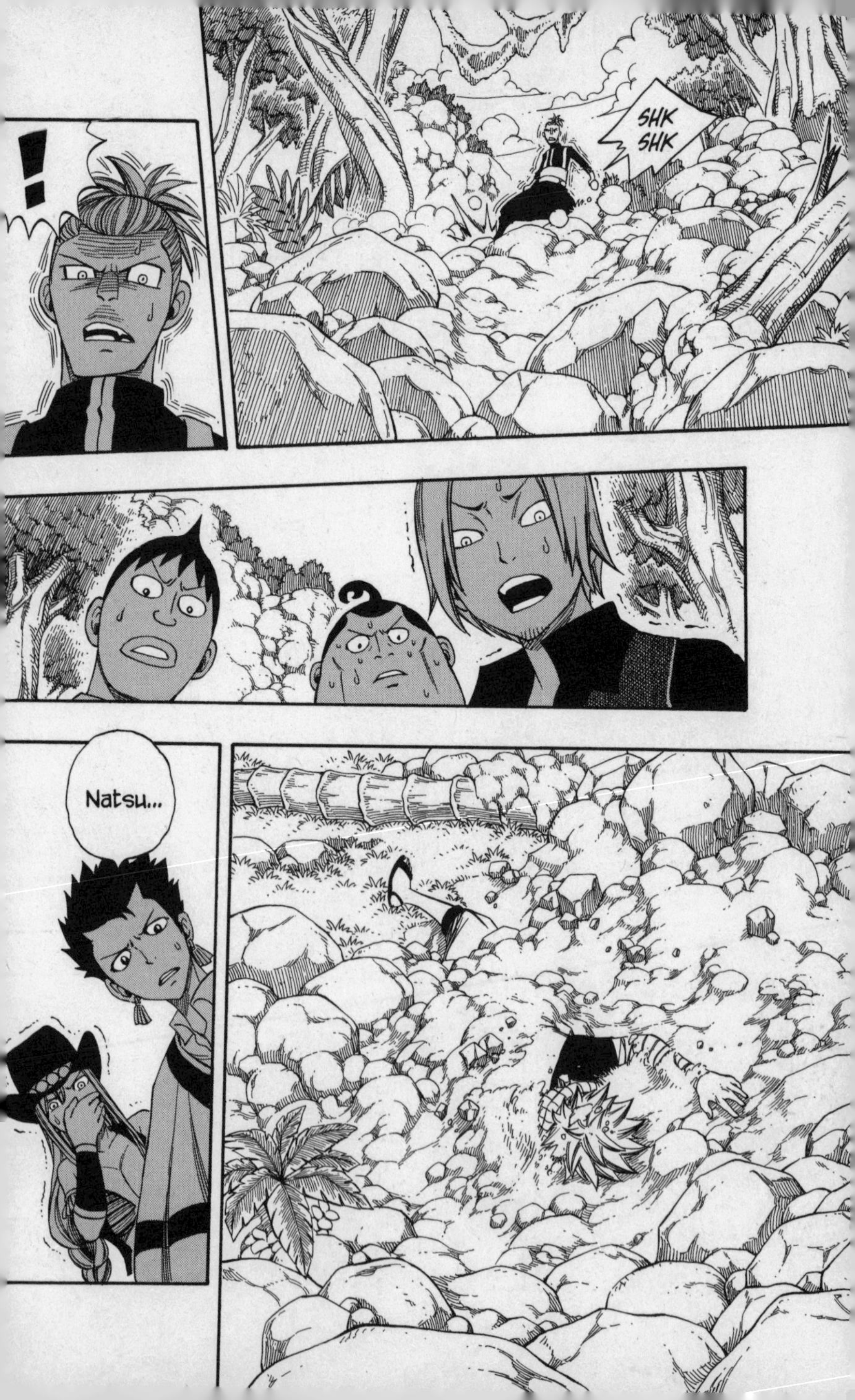
SHK SHK
!
Natsu...

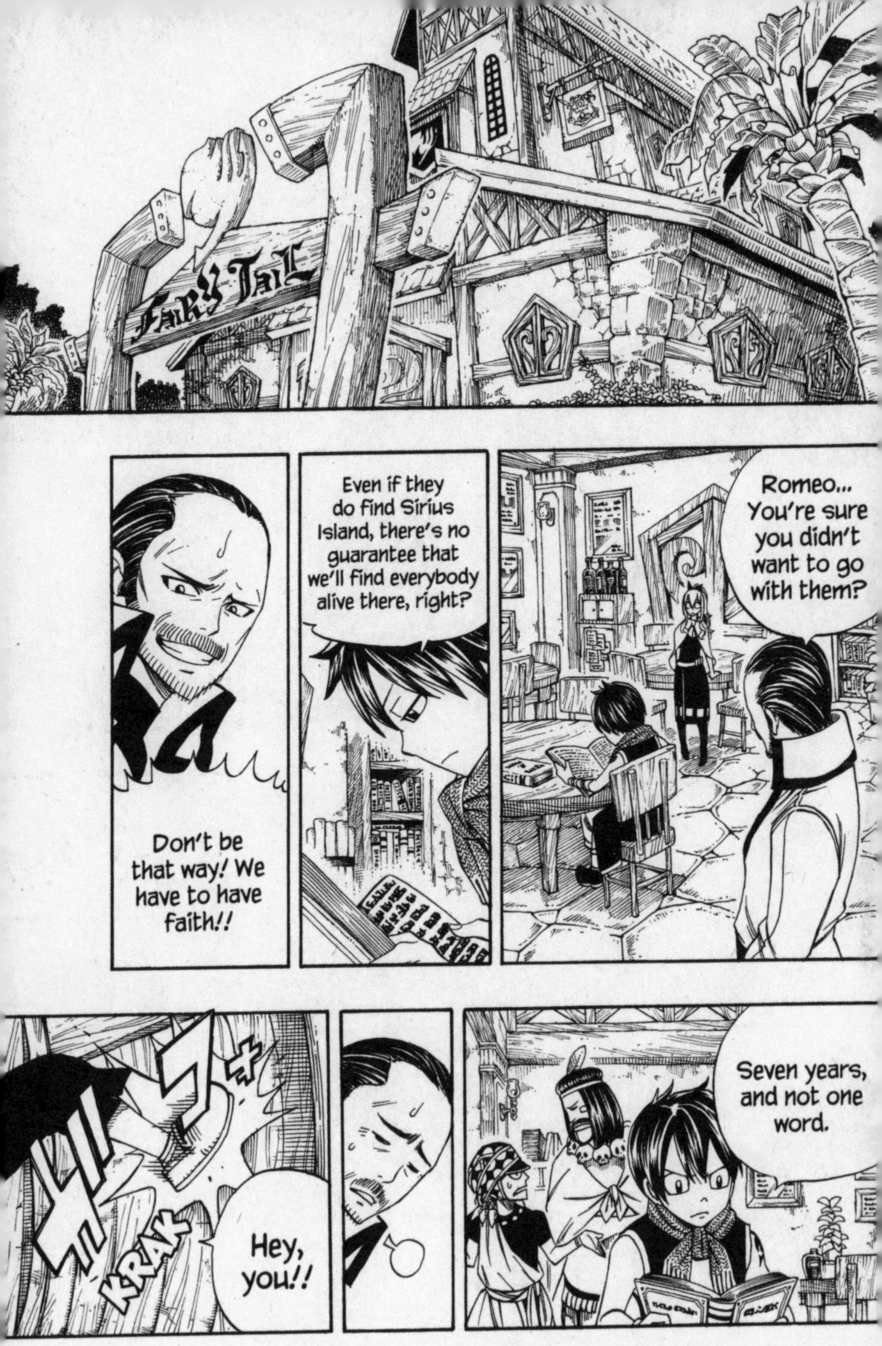
FAIRY TAIL
Romeo... You're sure you didn't want to go with them?
Even if they do find Sirius Island, there's no guarantee that we'll find everybody alive there, right?
Don't be that way! We have to have faith!!
Seven years, and not one word.
Hey, you!!
KRAK

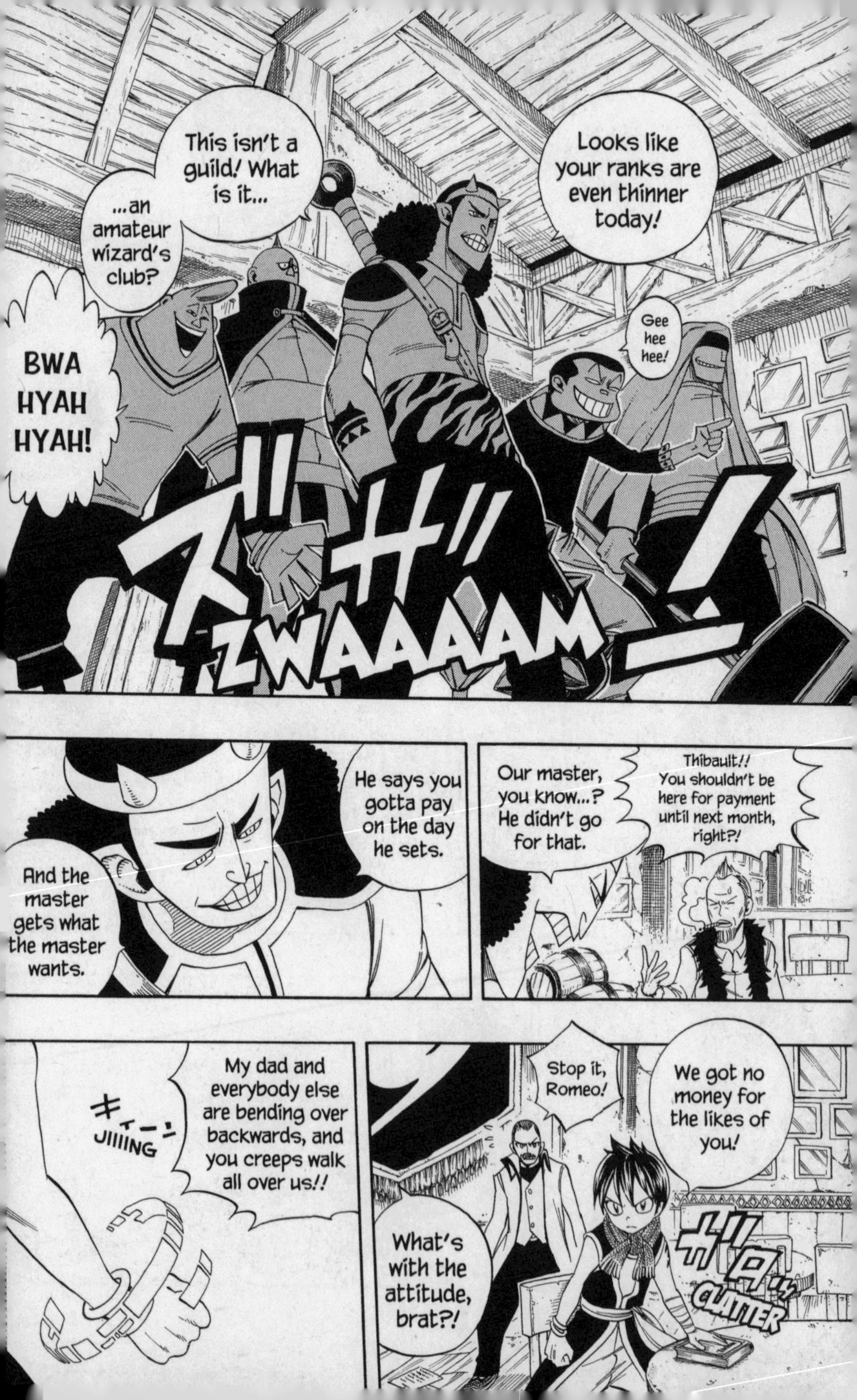

Looks like your ranks are even thinner today!
Gee hee hee!
This isn't a guild! What is it...
...an amateur wizard's club?
BWA HYAH HYAH!
ZWAAAAM
Thibault!! You shouldn't be here for payment until next month, right?!
Our master, you know...? He didn't go for that.
He says you gotta pay on the day he sets.
And the master gets what the master wants.
We got no money for the likes of you!
Stop it, Romeo!
What's with the attitude, brat?!
CLATTER
My dad and everybody else are bending over backwards, and you creeps walk all over us!!
JIIIING

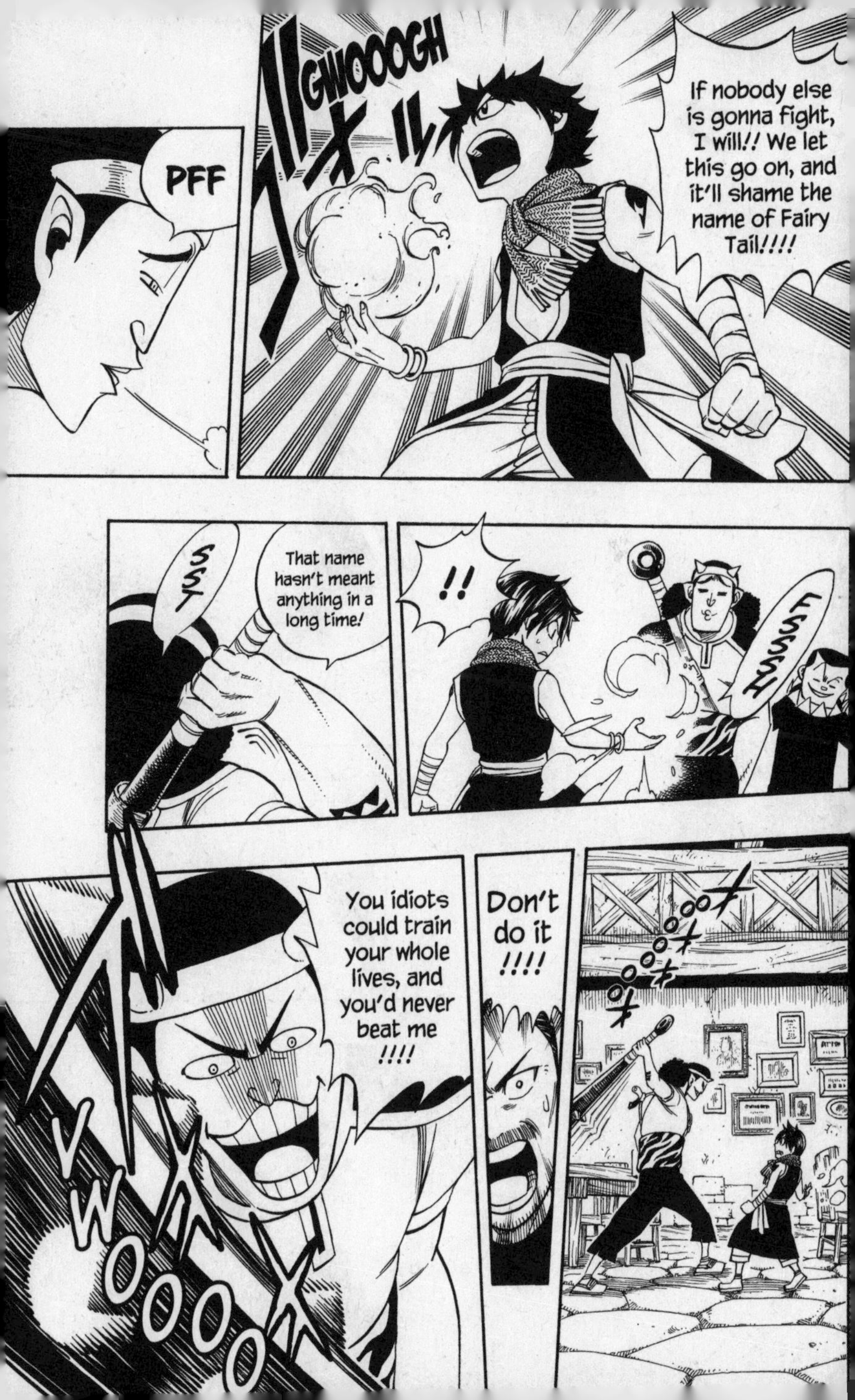
GWOOOGH
If nobody else is gonna fight, I will!! We let this go on, and it'll shame the name of Fairy Tail!!!!
PFF
!!
HSSSSH
That name hasn't meant anything in a long time!
SST
Don't do it!!!!
You idiots could train your whole lives, and you'd never beat me!!!!
VWOOOO

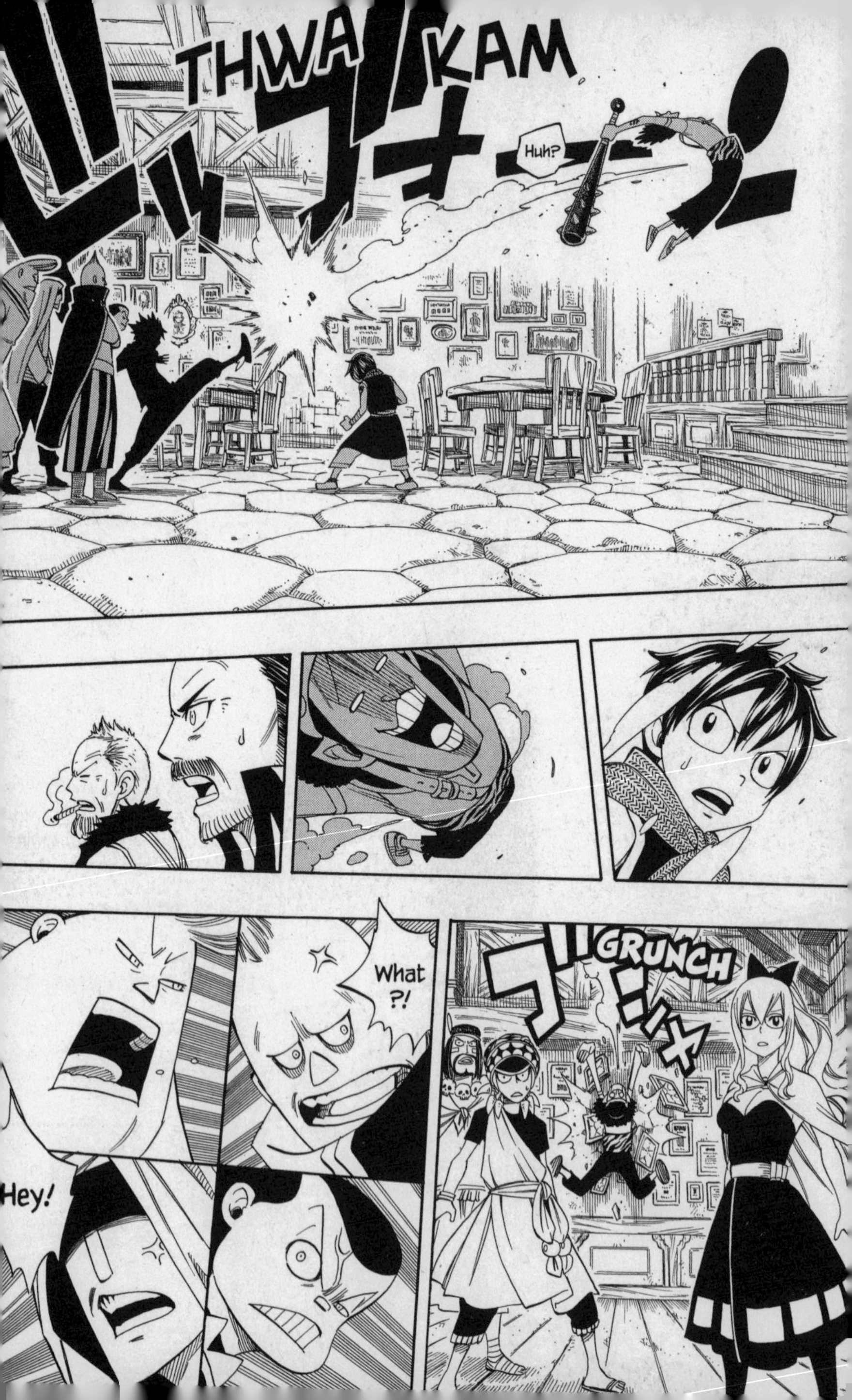
THWA KAM
Huh?
GRUNCH
What ?!
Hey!

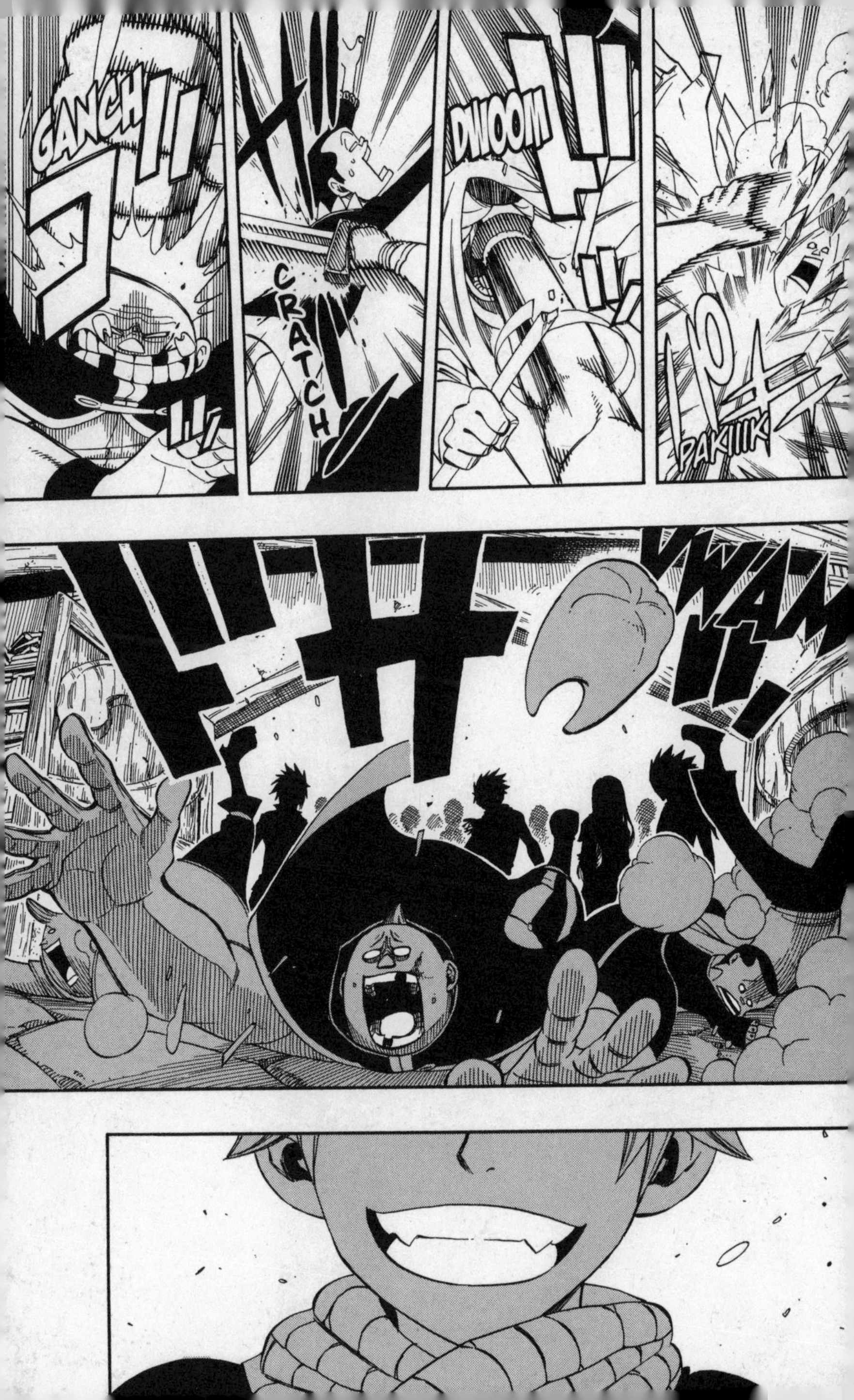
PAKIIIK
DWOOM
CRATCH
GANCH
WAM

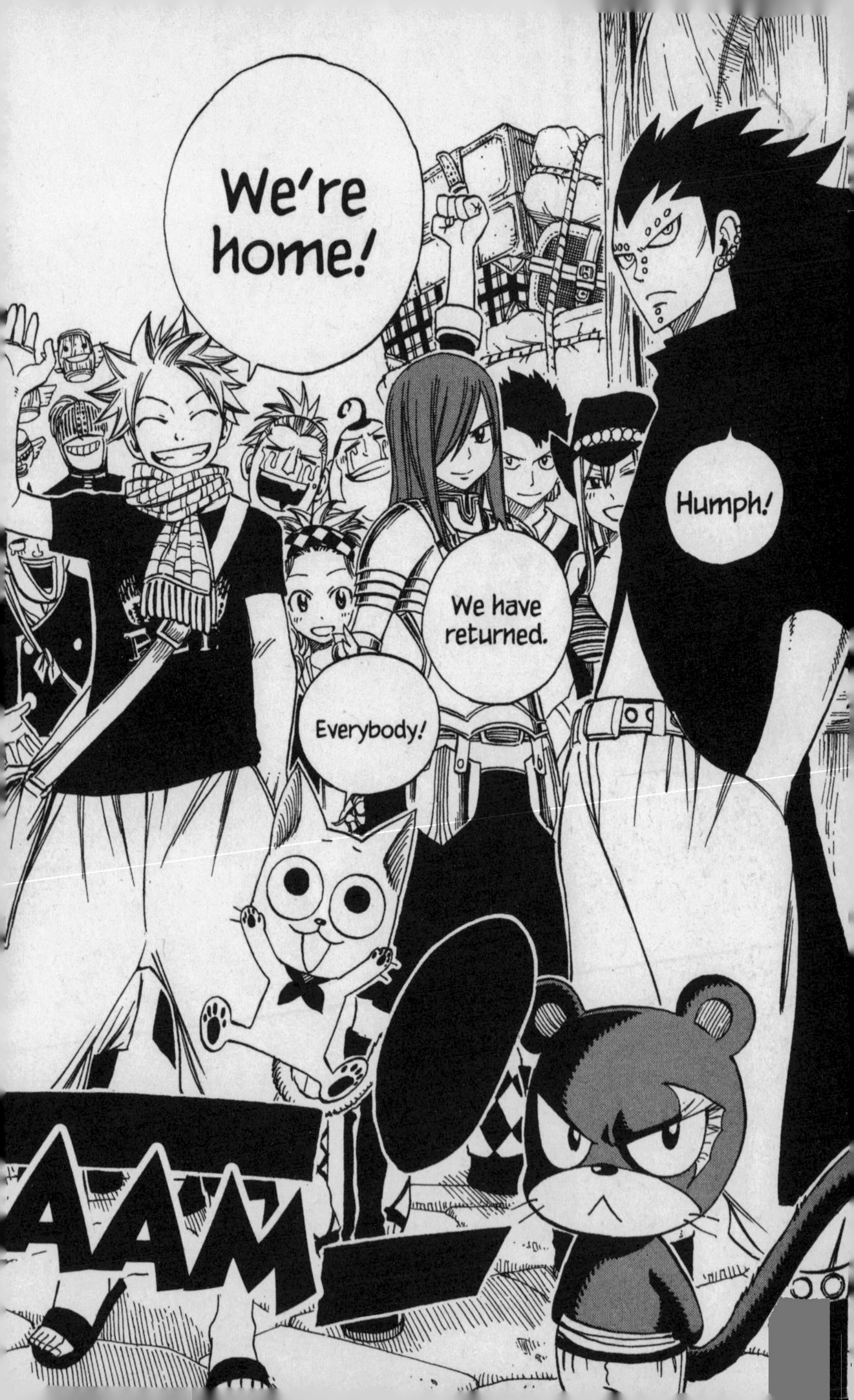
We're home!
Humph!
We have returned.
Everybody!
AAM

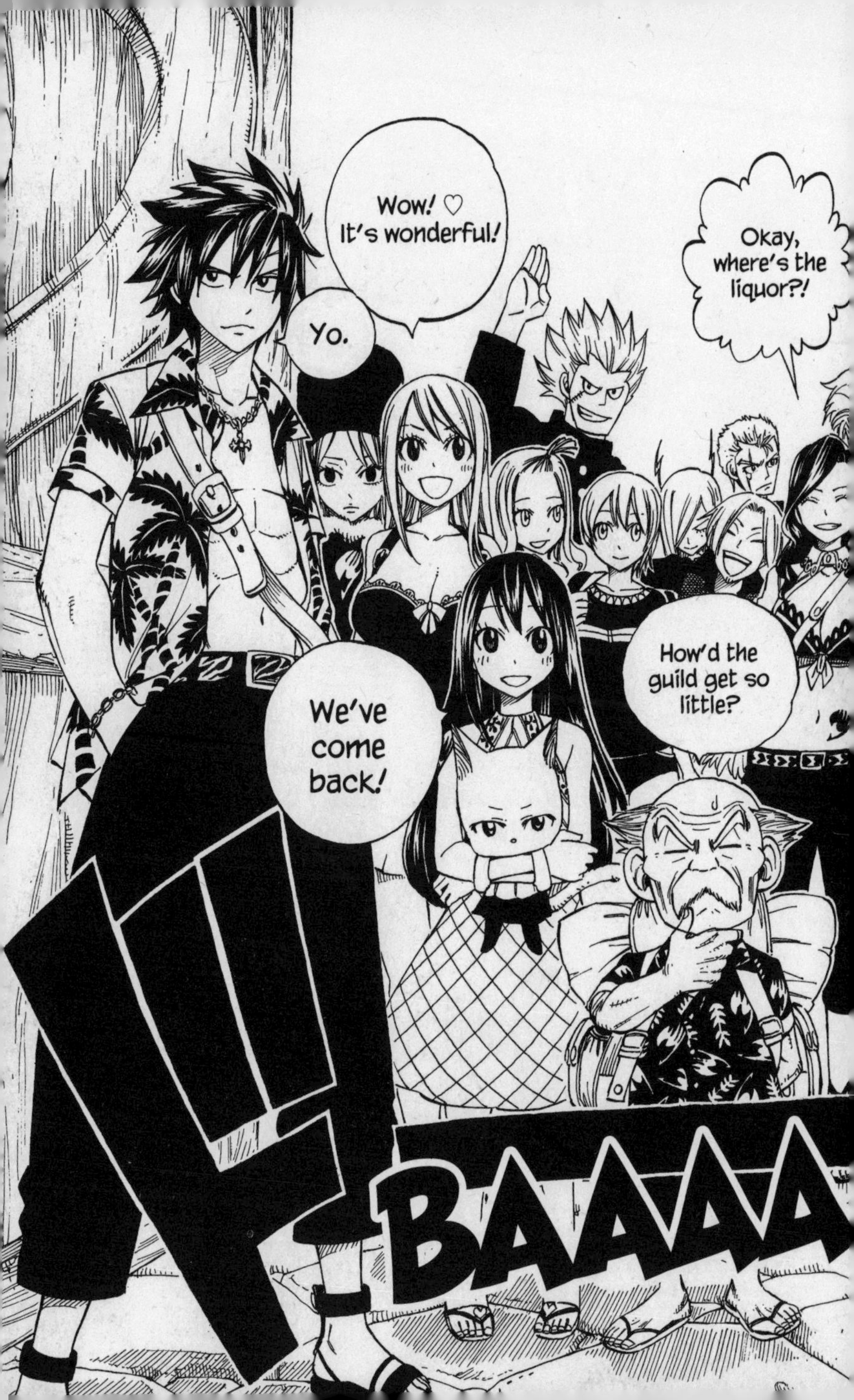
Okay, where's the liquor?!
Wow! ♡ It's wonderful!
Yo.
How'd the guild get so little?
We've come back!
BAAA

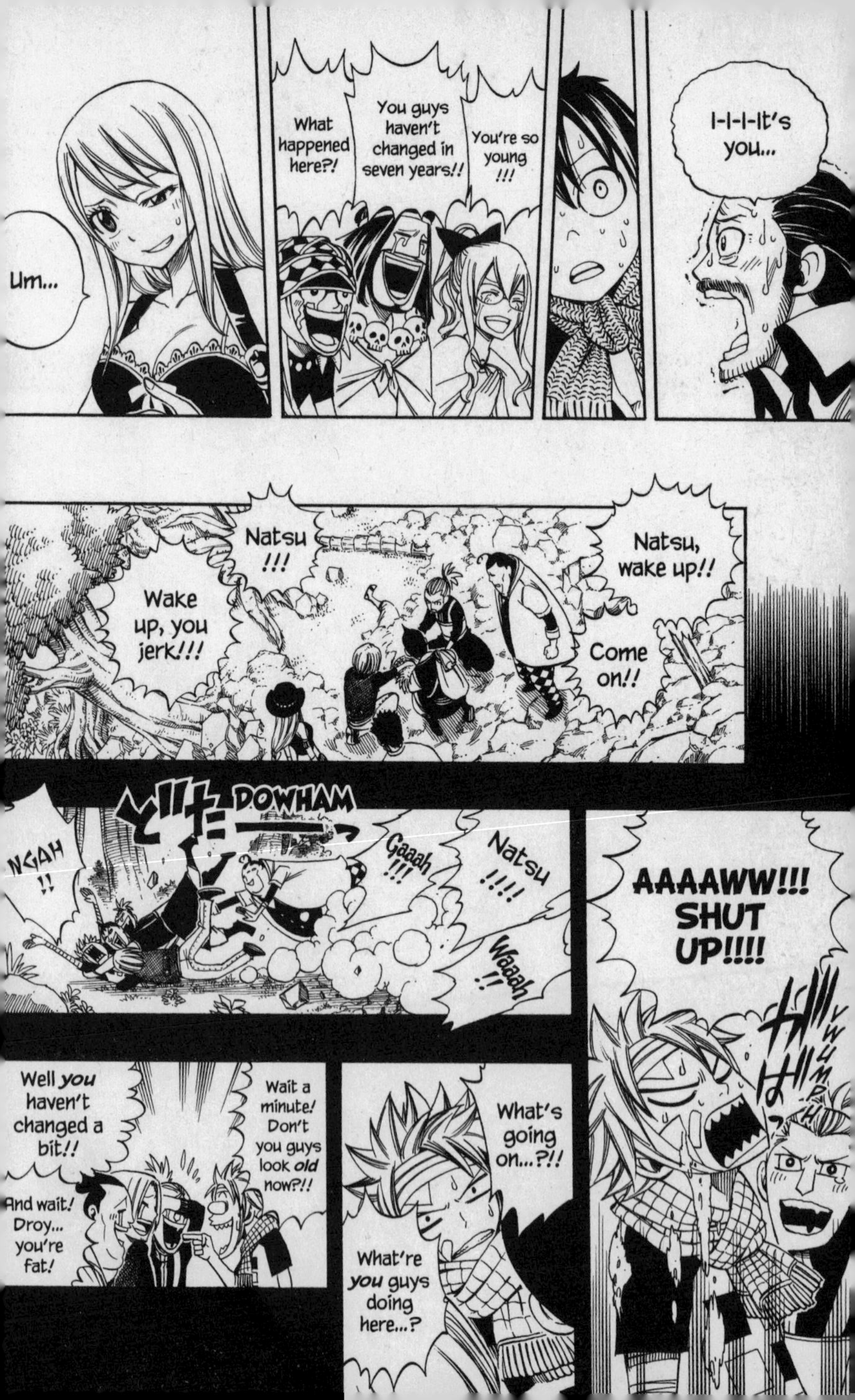
I-I-I-It's you...
You're so young!!!
You guys haven't changed in seven years!!
What happened here?!
Um...
Natsu, wake up!!
Come on!!
Natsu!!!
Wake up, you jerk!!!
AAAAWW!!! SHUT UP!!!!
VWUMPH
Natsu!!!!
Waaah!!
Gaaah!!!
DOWHAM
NGAH!!
What's going on...?!!
What're *you* guys doing here...?
Wait a minute! Don't you guys look *old* now?!!
Well *you* haven't changed a bit!!
And wait! Droy... you're fat!

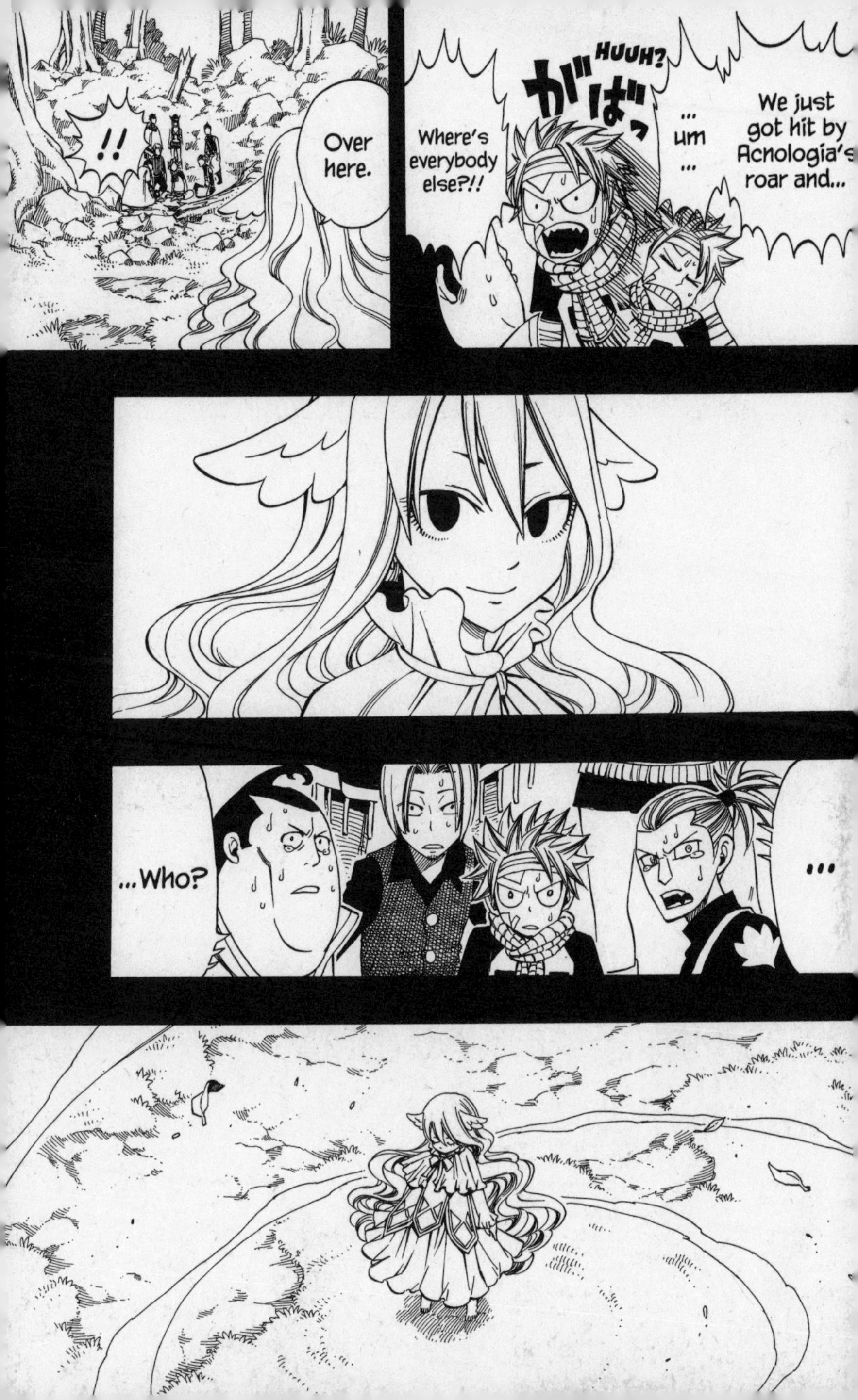
We just got hit by Acnologia's roar and...
... um ...
HUUH?
がばっ
Where's everybody else?!!
Over here.
!!
...
...Who?

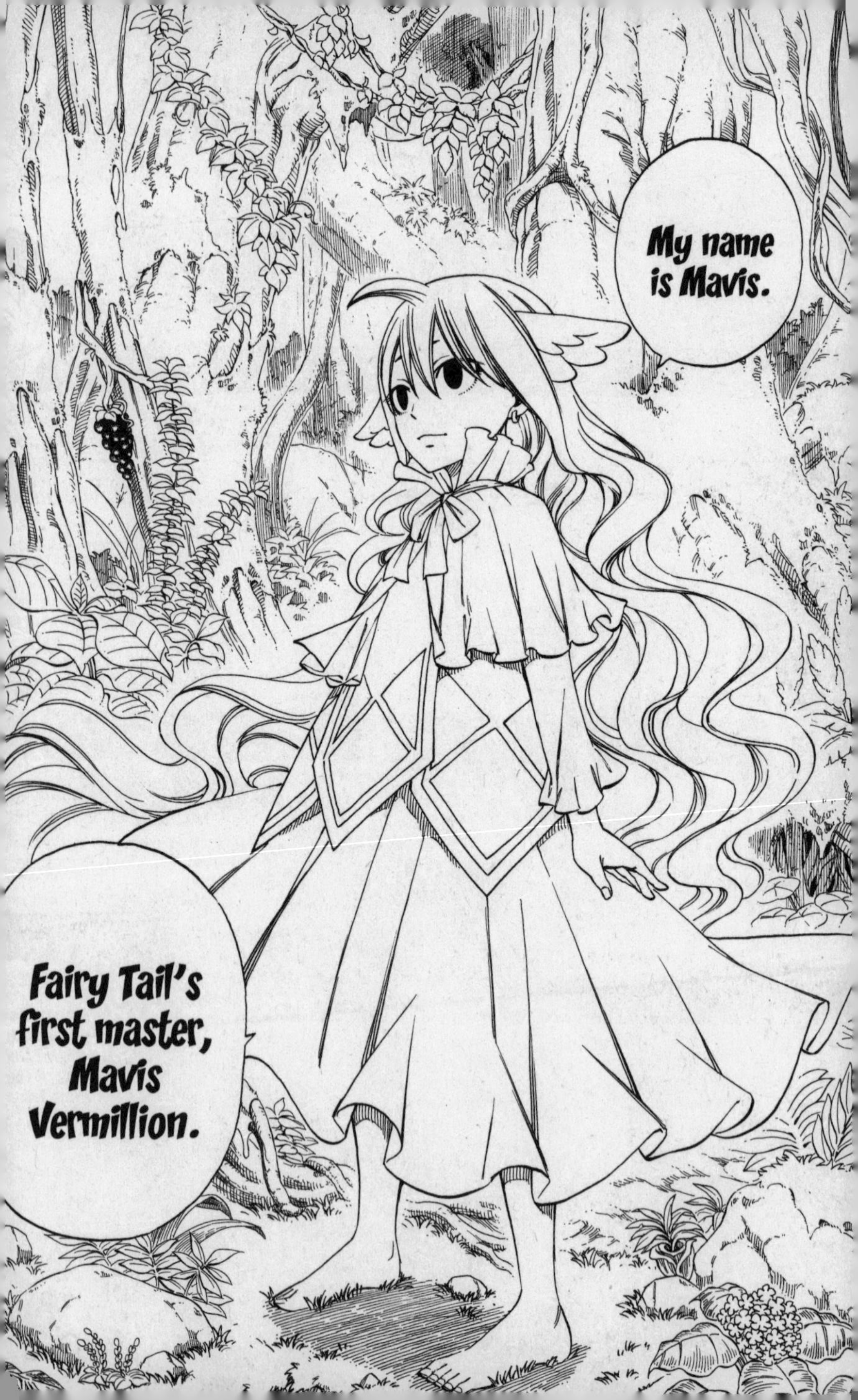
My name is Mavis.
Fairy Tail's first master, Mavis Vermillion.

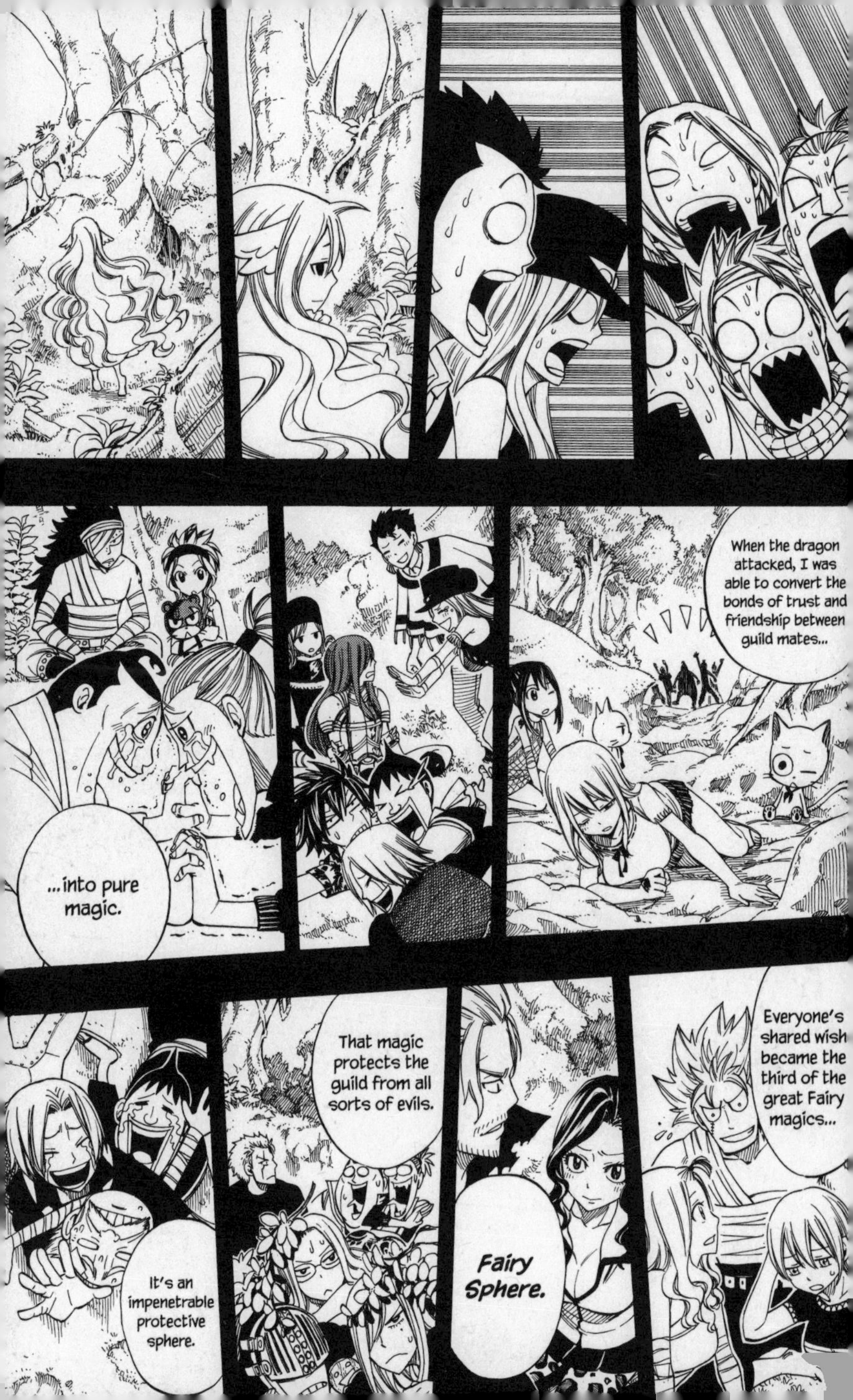
When the dragon attacked, I was able to convert the bonds of trust and friendship between guild mates...
...into pure magic.
Everyone's shared wish became the third of the great Fairy magics...
Fairy Sphere.
That magic protects the guild from all sorts of evils.
It's an impenetrable protective sphere.

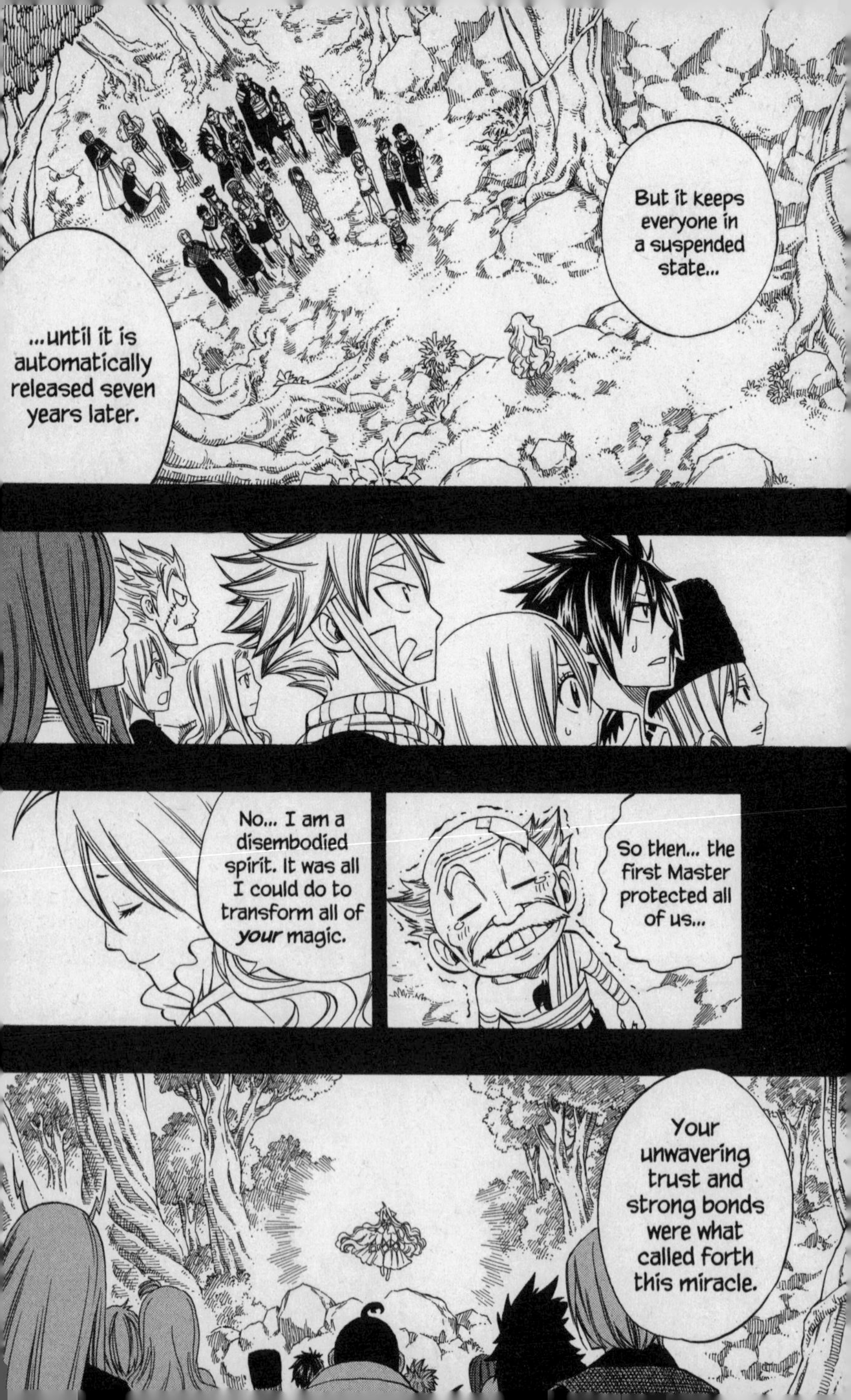
But it keeps everyone in a suspended state...
...until it is automatically released seven years later.
So then... the first Master protected all of us...
No... I am a disembodied spirit. It was all I could do to transform all of *your* magic.
Your unwavering trust and strong bonds were what called forth this miracle.

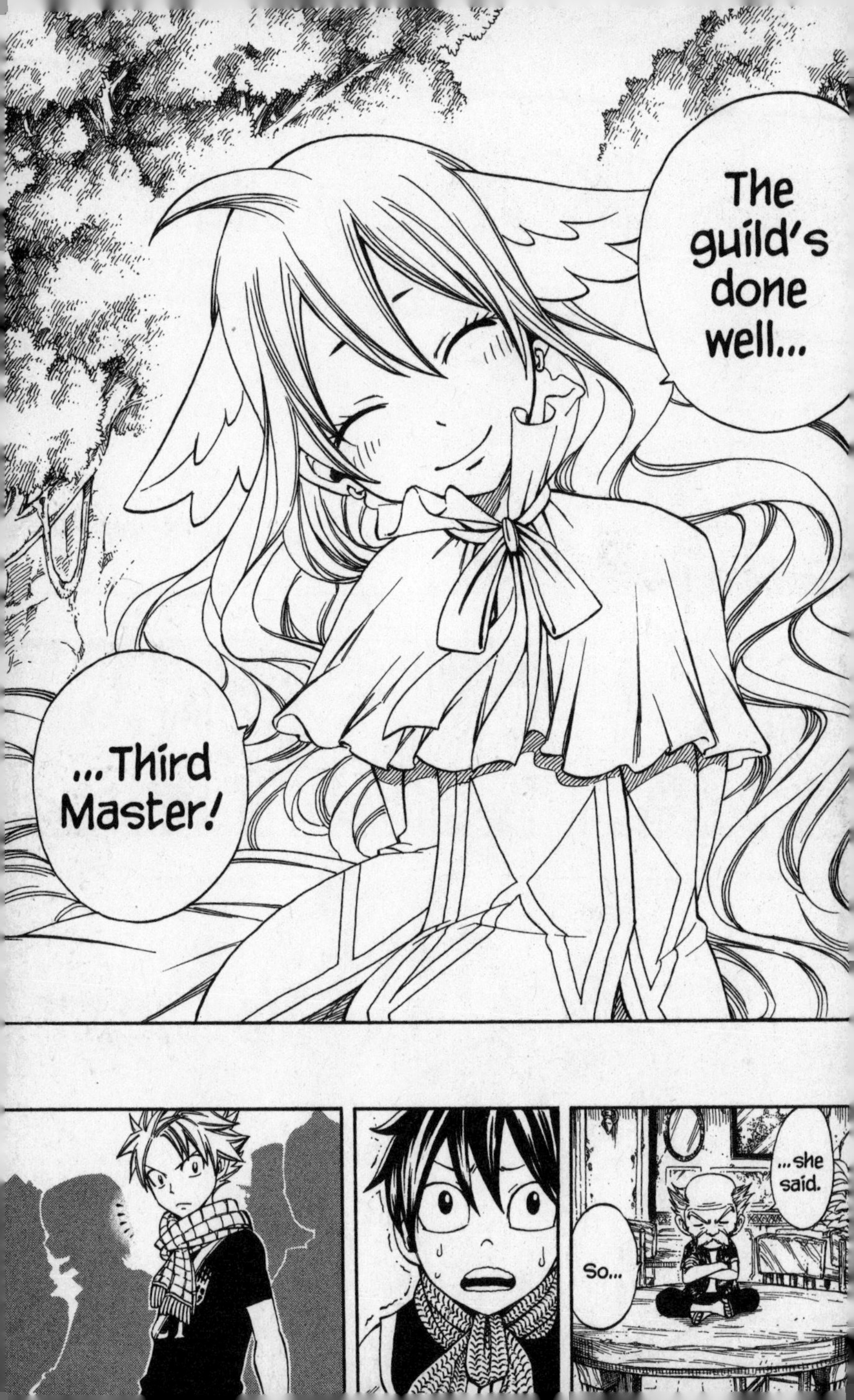
The guild's done well...
...Third Master!
...she said.
So...

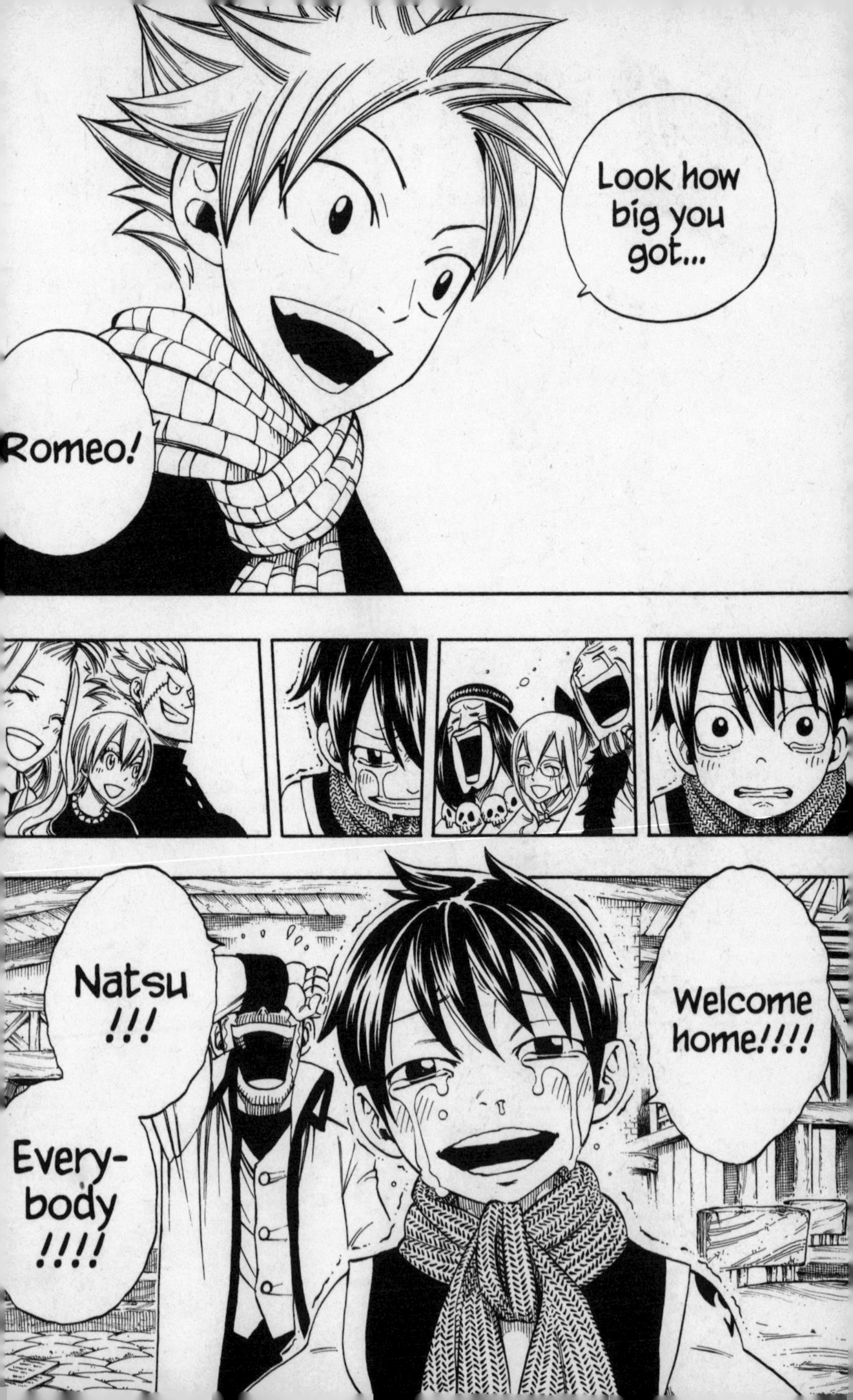
Look how big you got...
Romeo!
Welcome home!!!!
Natsu!!!
Every-body!!!!

FAIRY TAIL

FAIRY TAIL

Name: **Macao Conbolt** Age: **43**

Magic: **Purple Flare**

Likes: **Romeo**   Dislikes: **Loans**

WIZARD GUILD BUST

Chapter 256: Seven Empty Years

Remarks

The fourth master of Fairy Tail. For the first year after the disappearance of Sirius Island, he was only "acting master," but the Council reluctantly made him the fourth master of the guild. Ever since, he's been gravely worried about how his son has never smiled since Sirius Island was lost, but when the island returned, his son's smile did as well.

He would tell people that he was going off to a meeting, but instead go to Blue Pegasus because of all the beauties there. Since then, Master Bob has taken a liking to him.

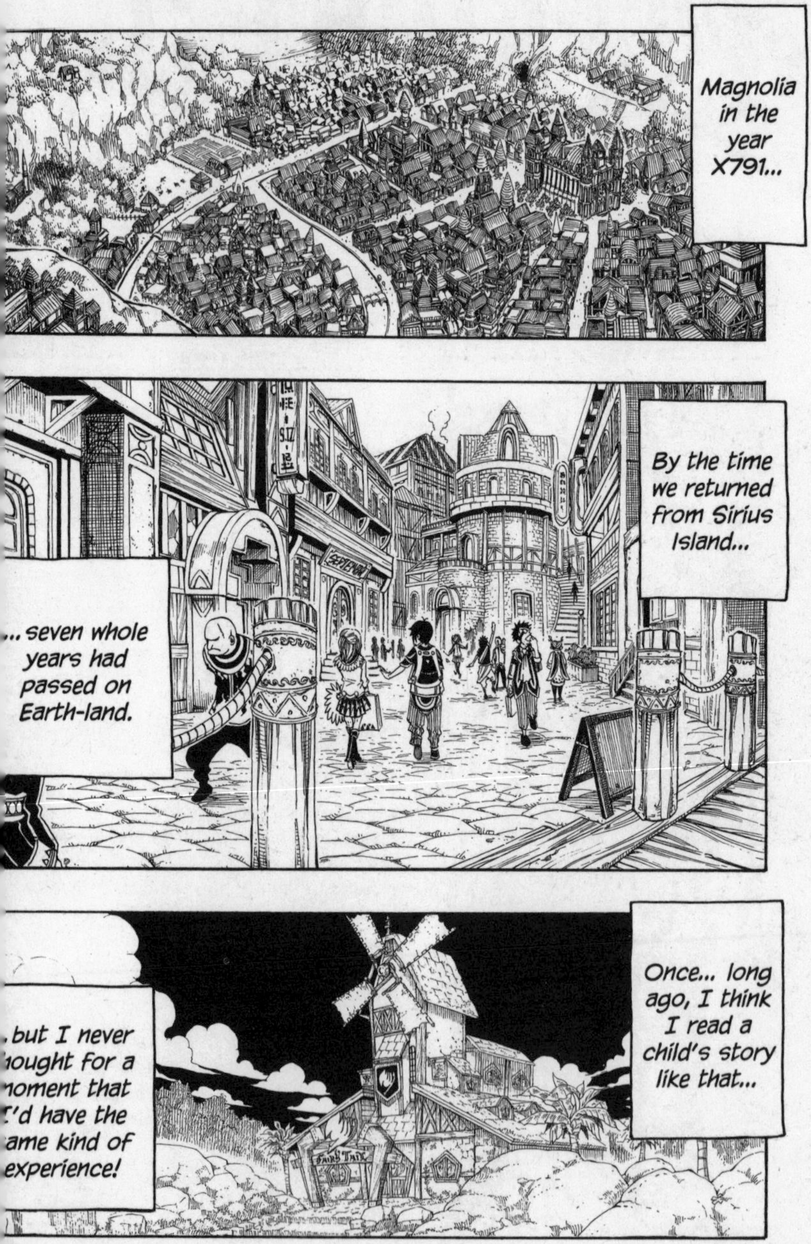
Magnolia in the year X791...
By the time we returned from Sirius Island...
...seven whole years had passed on Earth-land.
Once... long ago, I think I read a child's story like that...
.but I never hought for a noment that 'd have the ame kind of experience!
FAIRY TAIL

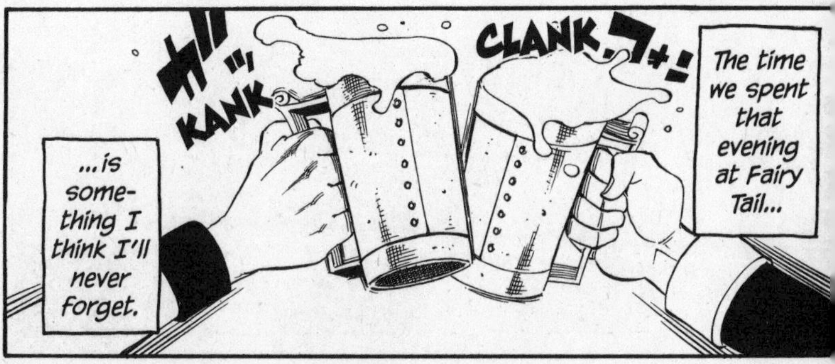
The time we spent that evening at Fairy Tail...
CLANK
KANK
...is something I think I'll never forget.

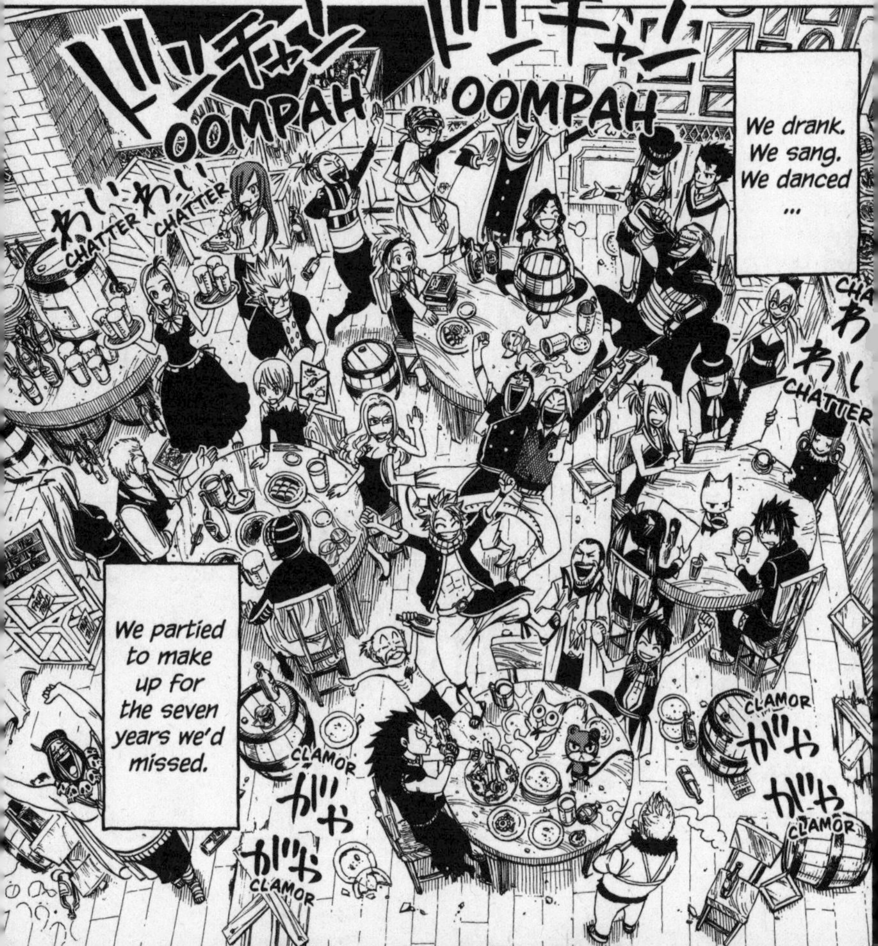
We drank. We sang. We danced ...
OOMPAH
OOMPAH
CHATTER
CHATTER
CHATTER
CLAMOR
CLAMOR
We partied to make up for the seven years we'd missed.
CLAMOR
CLAMOR

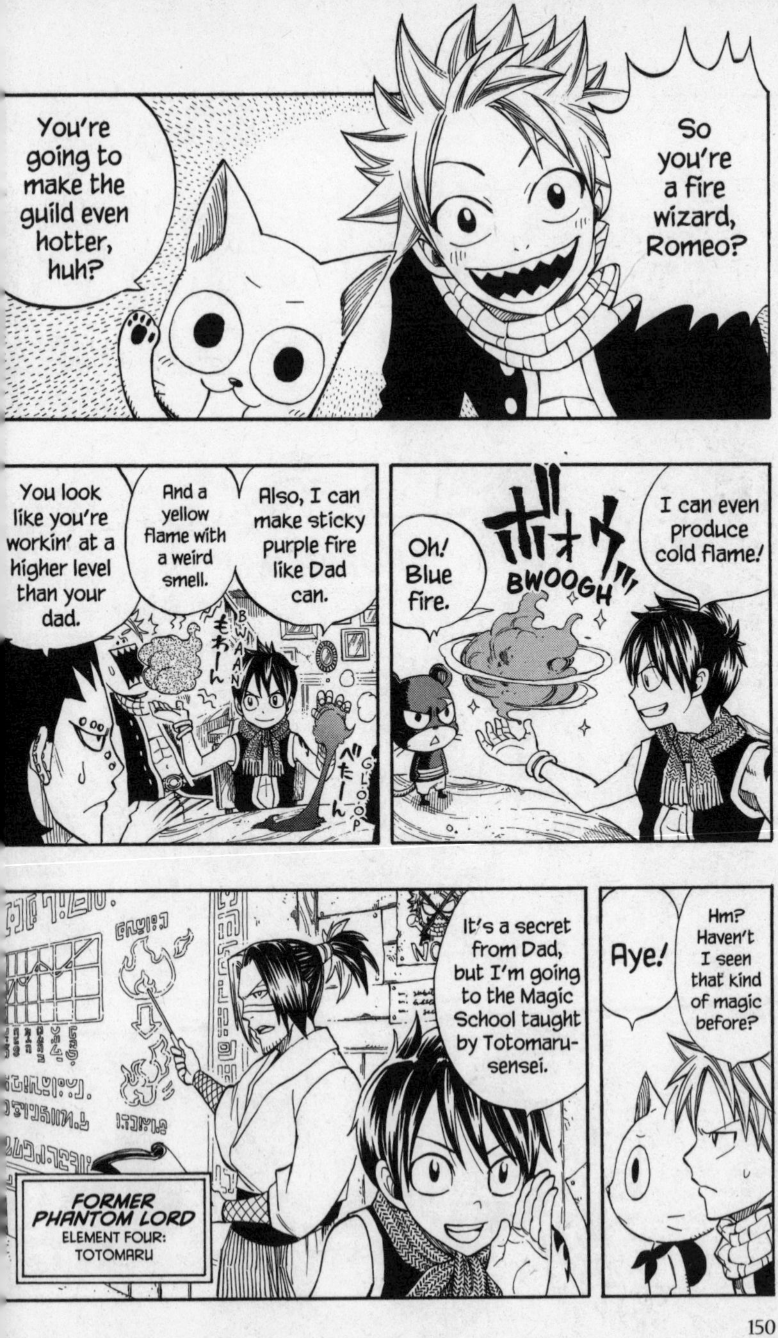
So you're a fire wizard, Romeo?
You're going to make the guild even hotter, huh?
I can even produce cold flame!
ボォウ
BWOOGH
Oh! Blue fire.
Also, I can make sticky purple fire like Dad can.
And a yellow flame with a weird smell.
もわーん
BWAAN
べたーん
GLOOP
You look like you're workin' at a higher level than your dad.
Hm? Haven't I seen that kind of magic before?
Aye!
It's a secret from Dad, but I'm going to the Magic School taught by Totomaru-sensei.
FORMER PHANTOM LORD
ELEMENT FOUR: TOTOMARU

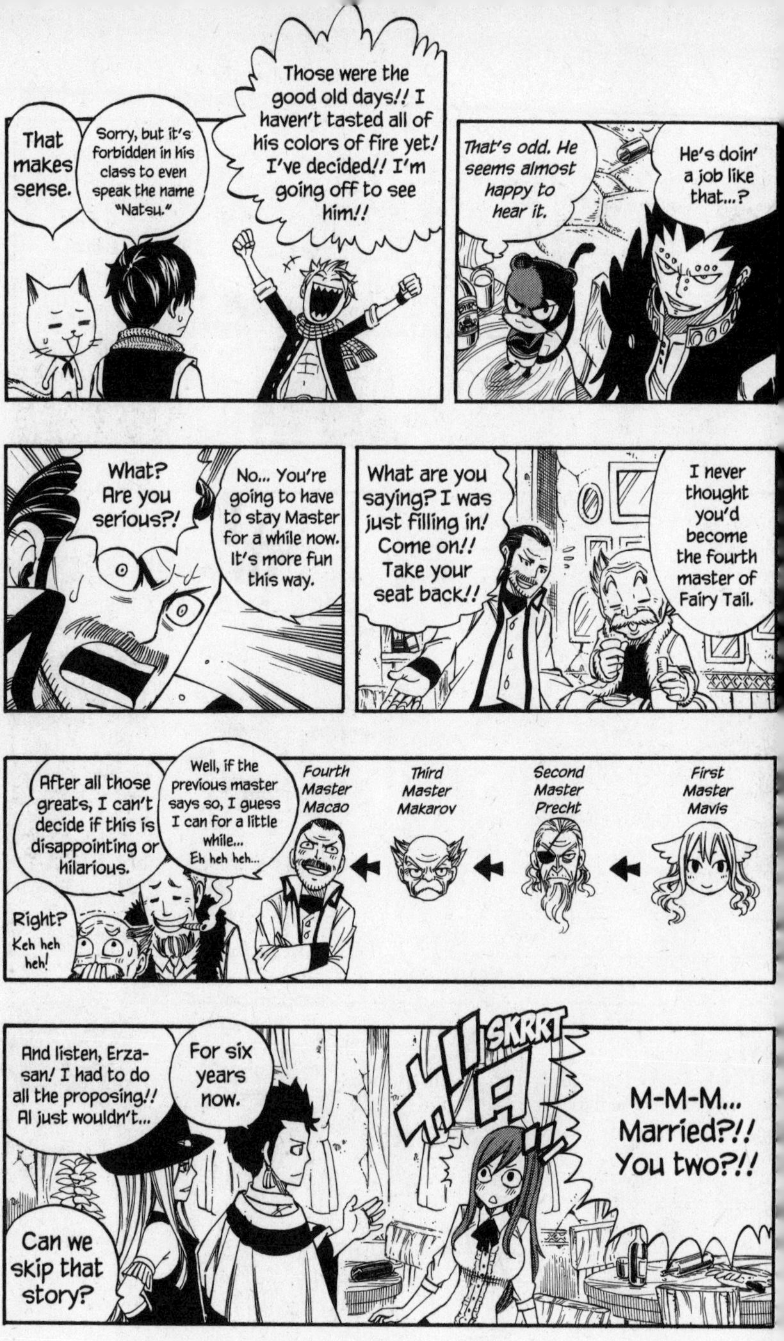
He's doin' a job like that...?
That's odd. He seems almost happy to hear it.
Those were the good old days!! I haven't tasted all of his colors of fire yet! I've decided!! I'm going off to see him!!
Sorry, but it's forbidden in his class to even speak the name "Natsu."
That makes sense.
I never thought you'd become the fourth master of Fairy Tail.
What are you saying? I was just filling in! Come on!! Take your seat back!!
No... You're going to have to stay Master for a while now. It's more fun this way.
What? Are you serious?!
First Master Mavis
Second Master Precht
Third Master Makarov
Fourth Master Macao
Well, if the previous master says so, I guess I can for a little while... Eh heh heh...
After all those greats, I can't decide if this is disappointing or hilarious.
Right? Keh heh heh!
M-M-M... Married?!! You two?!!
SKRRT
For six years now.
And listen, Erza-san! I had to do all the proposing!! Al just wouldn't...
Can we skip that story?

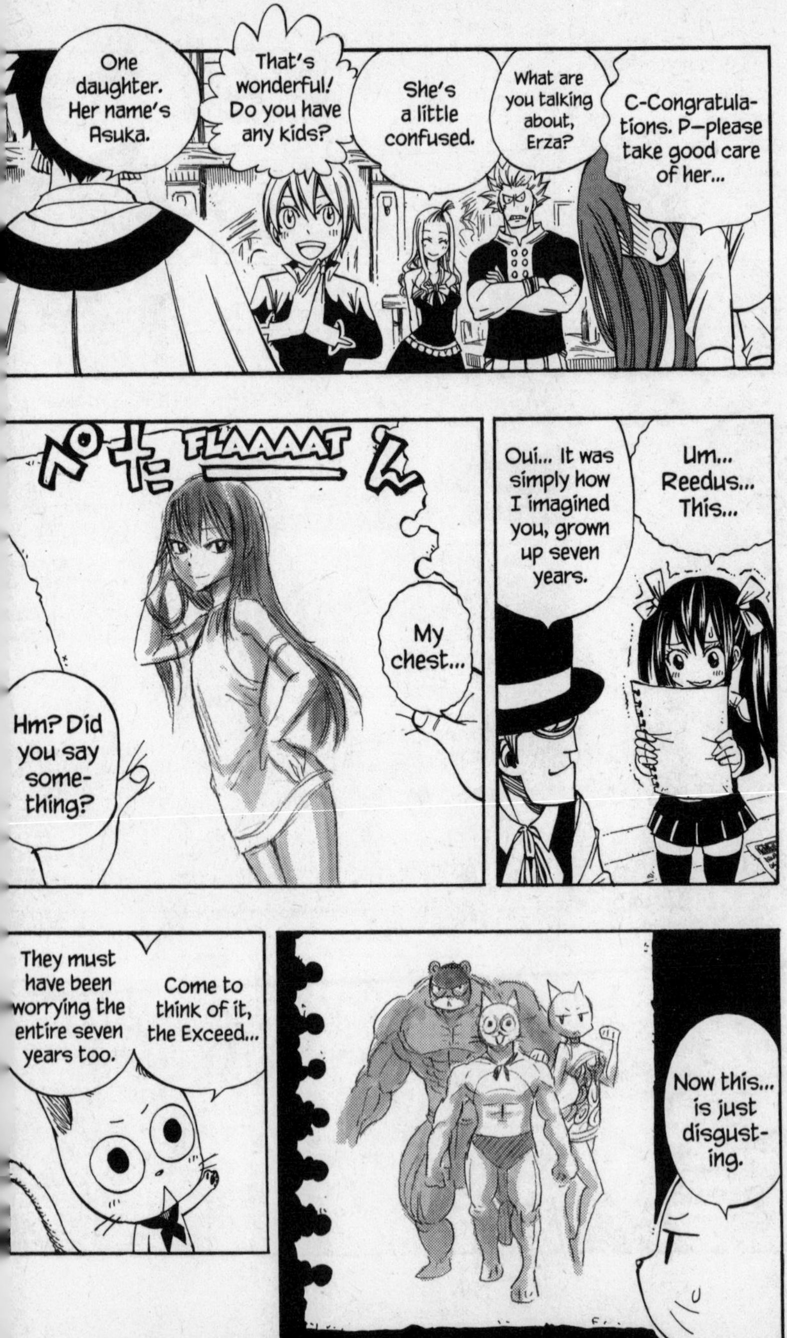
C-Congratula-tions. P—please take good care of her...
What are you talking about, Erza?
She's a little confused.
That's wonderful! Do you have any kids?
One daughter. Her name's Asuka.
Um... Reedus... This...
Oui... It was simply how I imagined you, grown up seven years.
FLAAAAT
My chest...
Hm? Did you say some-thing?
Now this... is just disgust-ing.
Come to think of it, the Exceed...
They must have been worrying the entire seven years too.

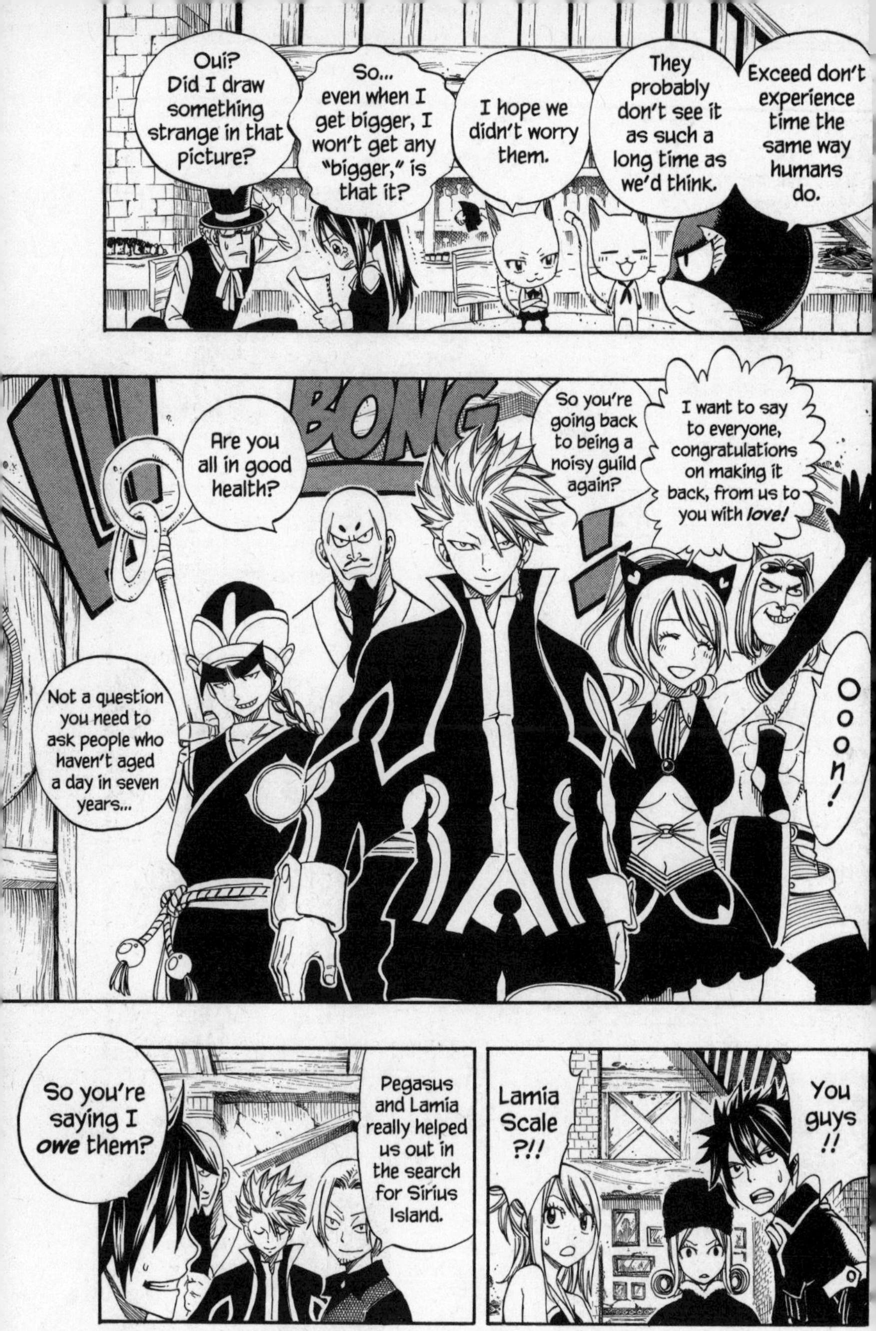
Exceed don't experience time the same way humans do.
They probably don't see it as such a long time as we'd think.
I hope we didn't worry them.
So... even when I get bigger, I won't get any "bigger," is that it?
Oui? Did I draw something strange in that picture?
BONG
I want to say to everyone, congratulations on making it back, from us to you with *love!*
So you're going back to being a noisy guild again?
Are you all in good health?
Ooon!
Not a question you need to ask people who haven't aged a day in seven years...
You guys!!
Lamia Scale?!!
Pegasus and Lamia really helped us out in the search for Sirius Island.
So you're saying I *owe* them?

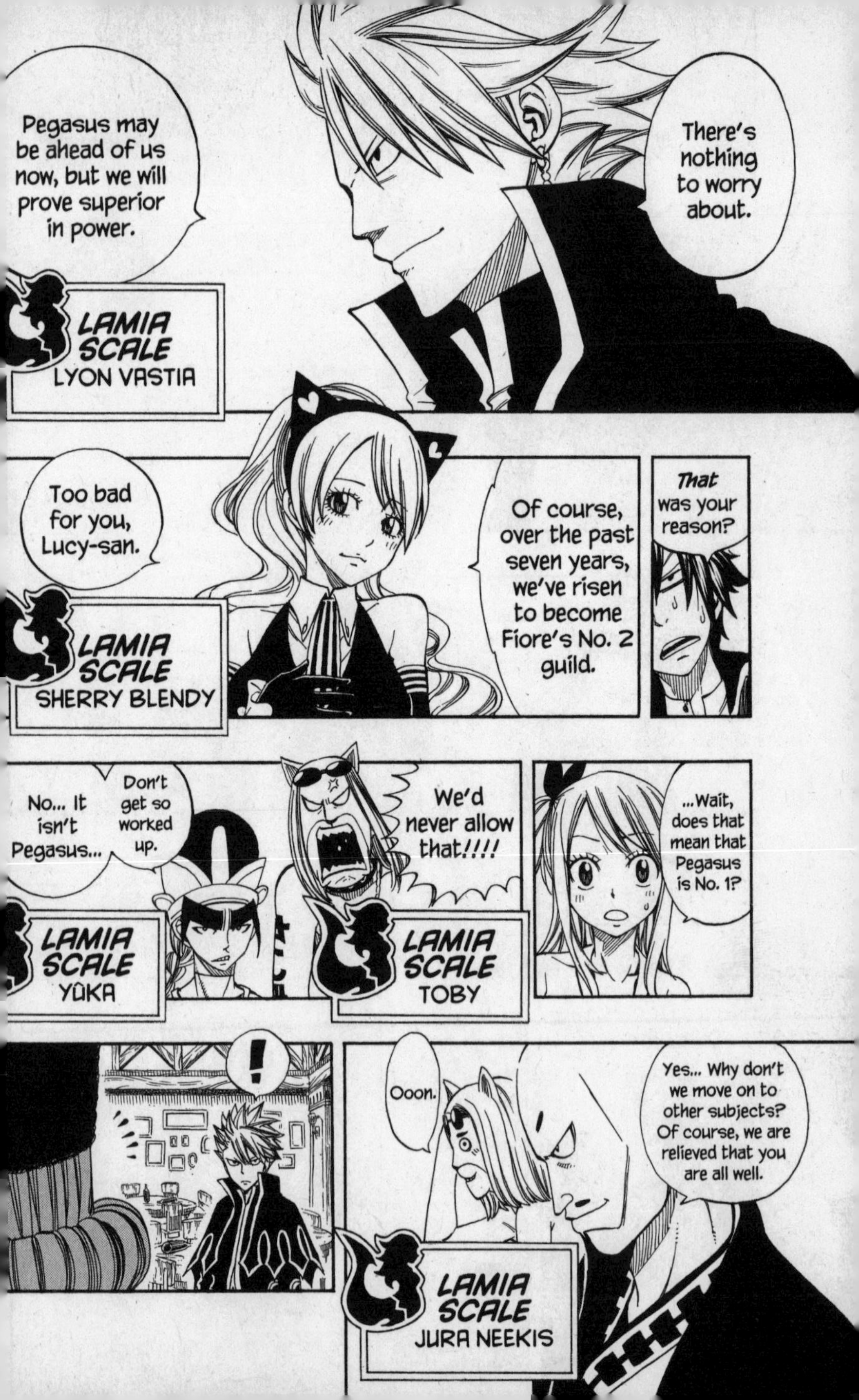
There's nothing to worry about.
Pegasus may be ahead of us now, but we will prove superior in power.
LAMIA SCALE
LYON VASTIA
That was your reason?
Of course, over the past seven years, we've risen to become Fiore's No. 2 guild.
Too bad for you, Lucy-san.
LAMIA SCALE
SHERRY BLENDY
...Wait, does that mean that Pegasus is No. 1?
We'd never allow that!!!!
Don't get so worked up.
No... It isn't Pegasus...
LAMIA SCALE
TOBY
LAMIA SCALE
YÛKA
Yes... Why don't we move on to other subjects? Of course, we are relieved that you are all well.
Ooon.
LAMIA SCALE
JURA NEEKIS
!

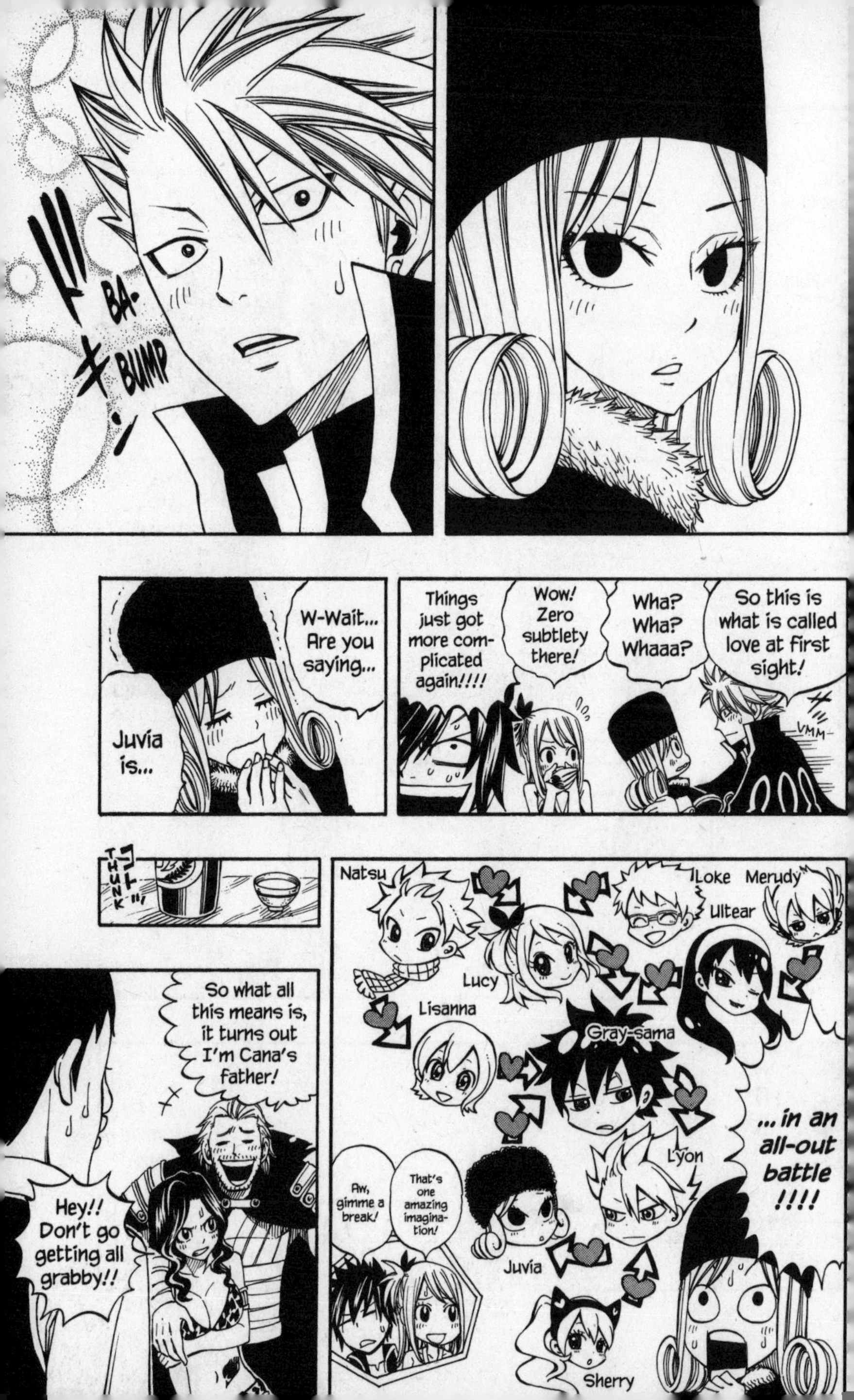
BA-BUMP
So this is what is called love at first sight!
VMM
Wha? Wha? Whaaa?
Wow! Zero subtlety there!
Things just got more complicated again!!!!
W-Wait... Are you saying...
Juvia is...
Merudy
Loke
Ultear
Natsu
Lucy
Lisanna
Gray-sama
Lyon
...in an all-out battle!!!!
Juvia
Sherry
That's one amazing imagination!
Aw, gimme a break!
THUNK
So what all this means is, it turns out I'm Cana's father!
Hey!! Don't go getting all grabby!!

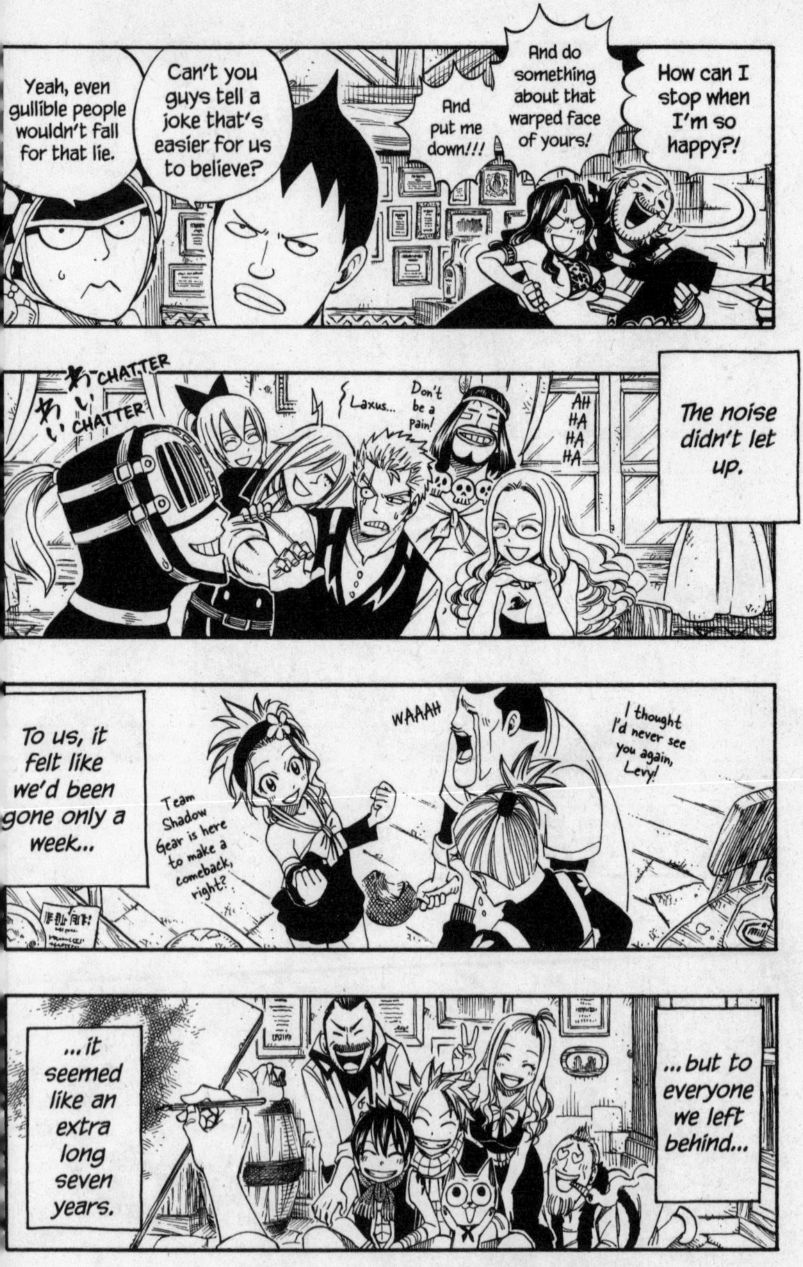
How can I stop when I'm so happy?!
And do something about that warped face of yours!
And put me down!!!
Can't you guys tell a joke that's easier for us to believe?
Yeah, even gullible people wouldn't fall for that lie.
The noise didn't let up.
AH HA HA HA
Don't be a pain!
Laxus...
CHATTER
CHATTER
I thought I'd never see you again, Levy!
WAAAH
Team Shadow Gear is here to make a comeback, right?
To us, it felt like we'd been gone only a week...
...but to everyone we left behind...
...it seemed like an extra long seven years.

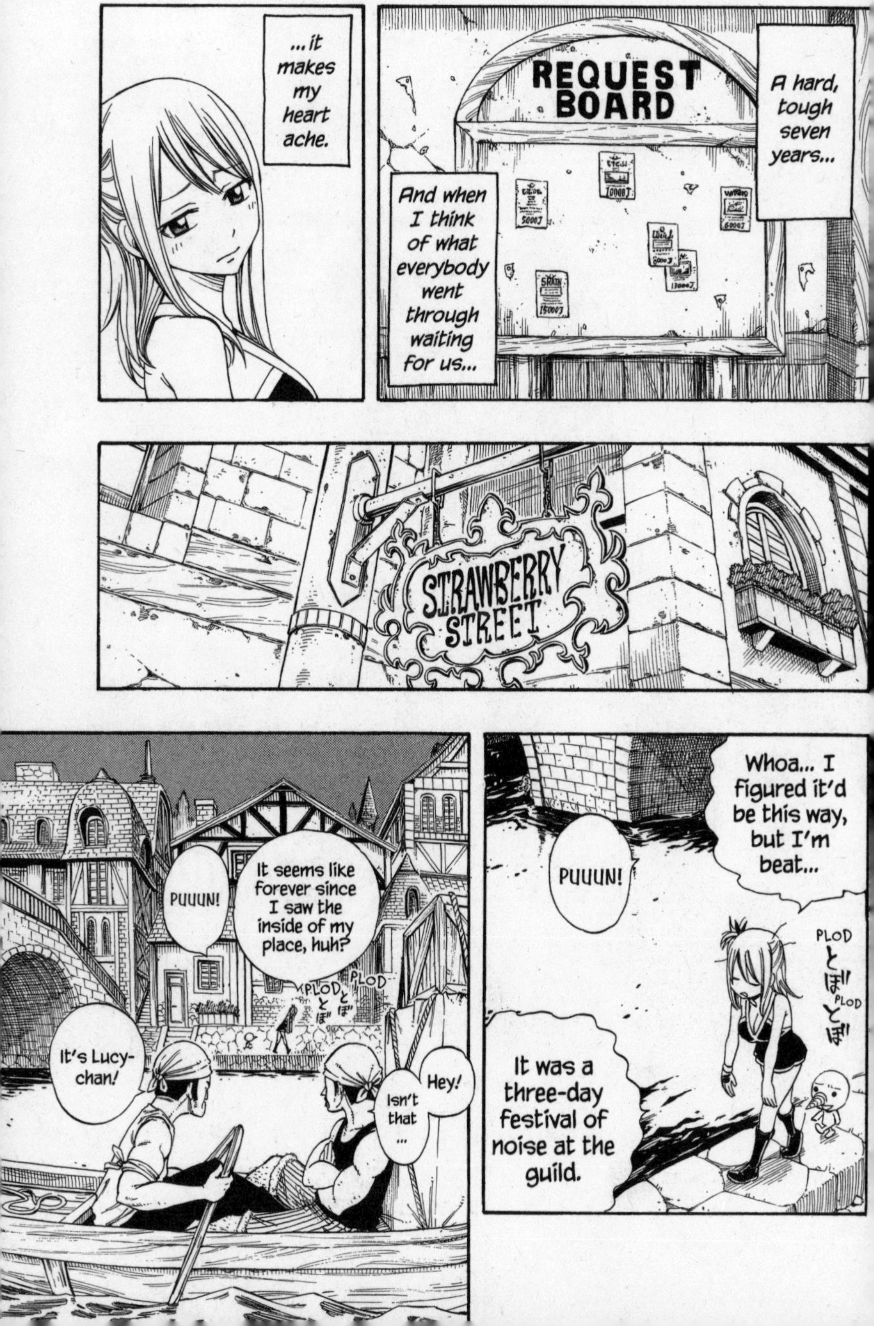
A hard, tough seven years...
REQUEST BOARD
And when I think of what everybody went through waiting for us...
...it makes my heart ache.
STRAWBERRY STREET
Whoa... I figured it'd be this way, but I'm beat...
PLOD とぼ PLOD とぼ
PUUUN!
It was a three-day festival of noise at the guild.
Hey!
Isn't that ...
It's Lucy-chan!
It seems like forever since I saw the inside of my place, huh?
PUUUN!
PLOD とぼ PLOD

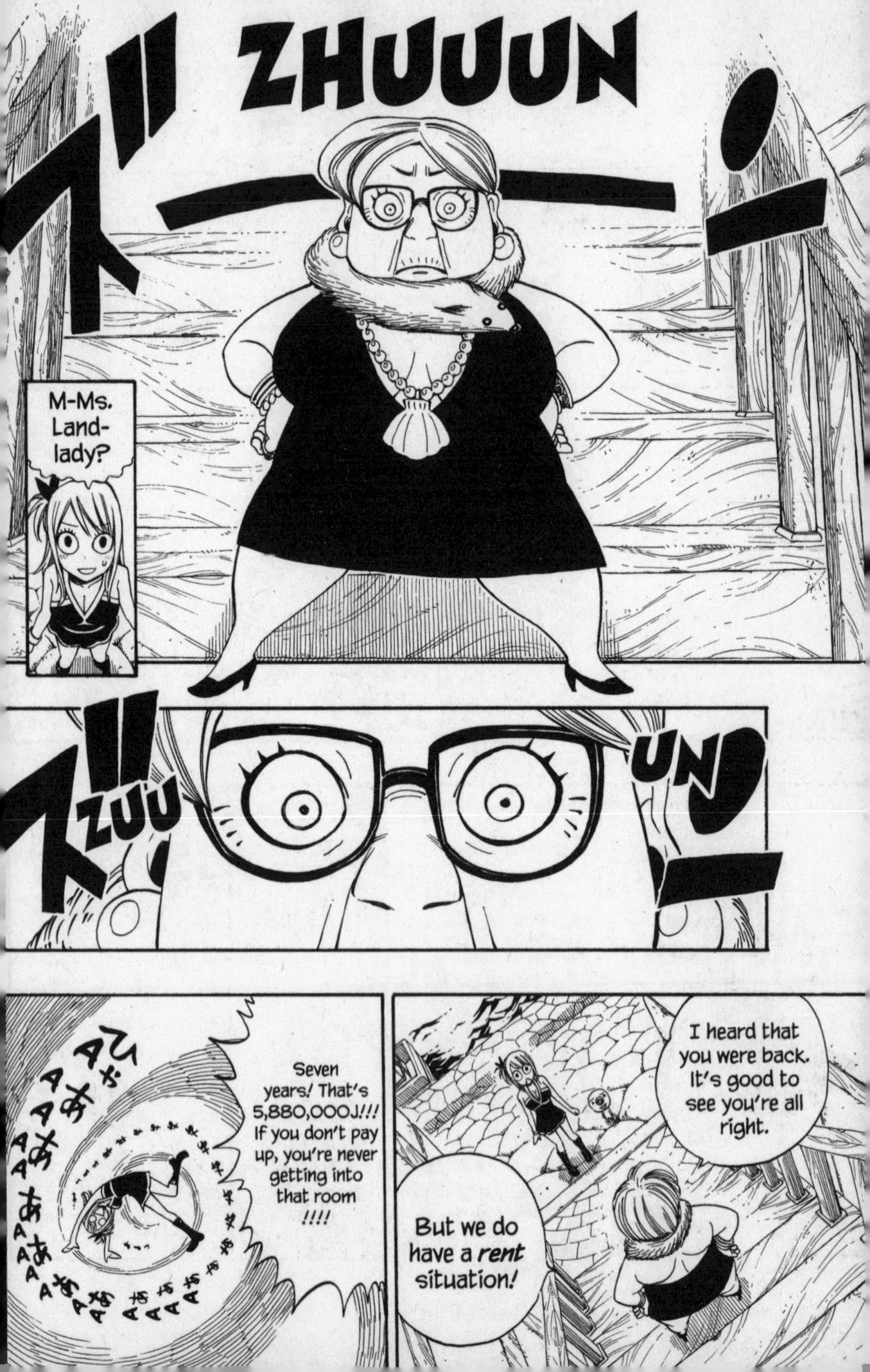
ZHUUUN
M-Ms. Land-lady?
ZUU UN
I heard that you were back. It's good to see you're all right.
But we do have a *rent* situation!
Seven years! That's 5,880,000J!!! If you don't pay up, you're never getting into that room !!!!

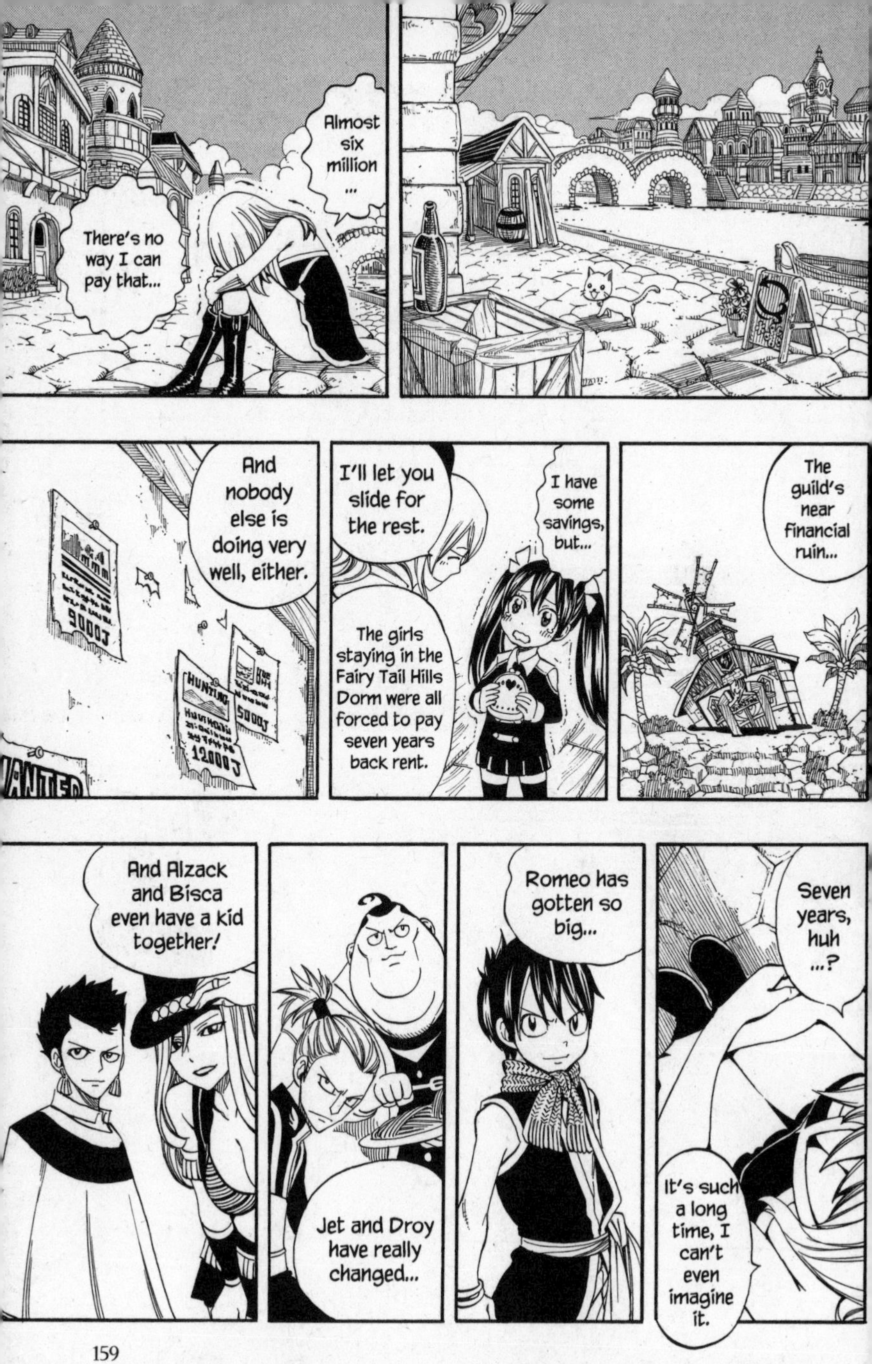
Almost six million ...
There's no way I can pay that...
The guild's near financial ruin...
I have some savings, but...
I'll let you slide for the rest.
The girls staying in the Fairy Tail Hills Dorm were all forced to pay seven years back rent.
And nobody else is doing very well, either.
9000J
HUNTING
5000J
12000J
Seven years, huh ...?
It's such a long time, I can't even imagine it.
Romeo has gotten so big...
Jet and Droy have really changed...
And Alzack and Bisca even have a kid together!

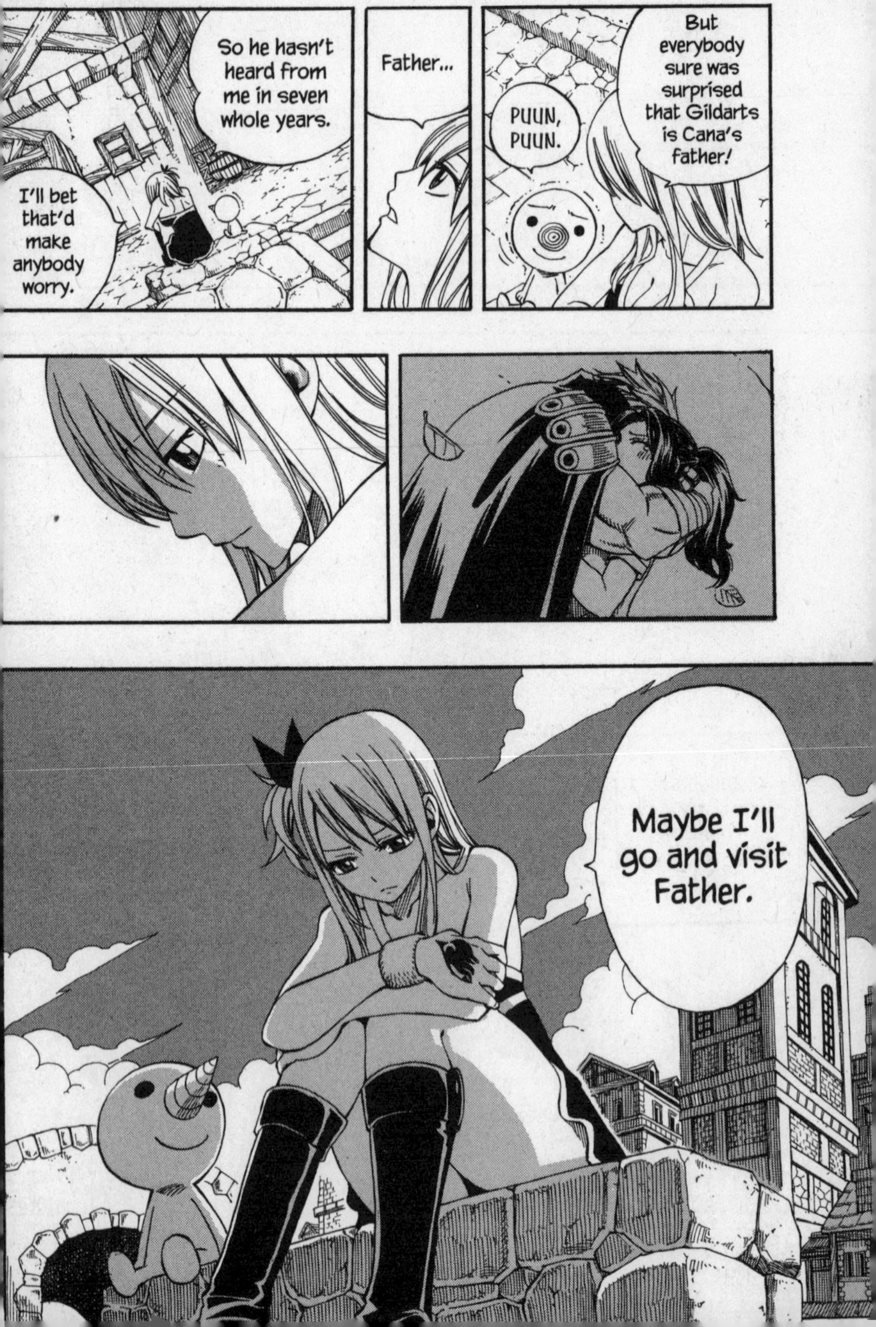
But everybody sure was surprised that Gildarts is Cana's father!
PUUN, PUUN.
Father...
So he hasn't heard from me in seven whole years.
I'll bet that'd make anybody worry.
Maybe I'll go and visit Father.

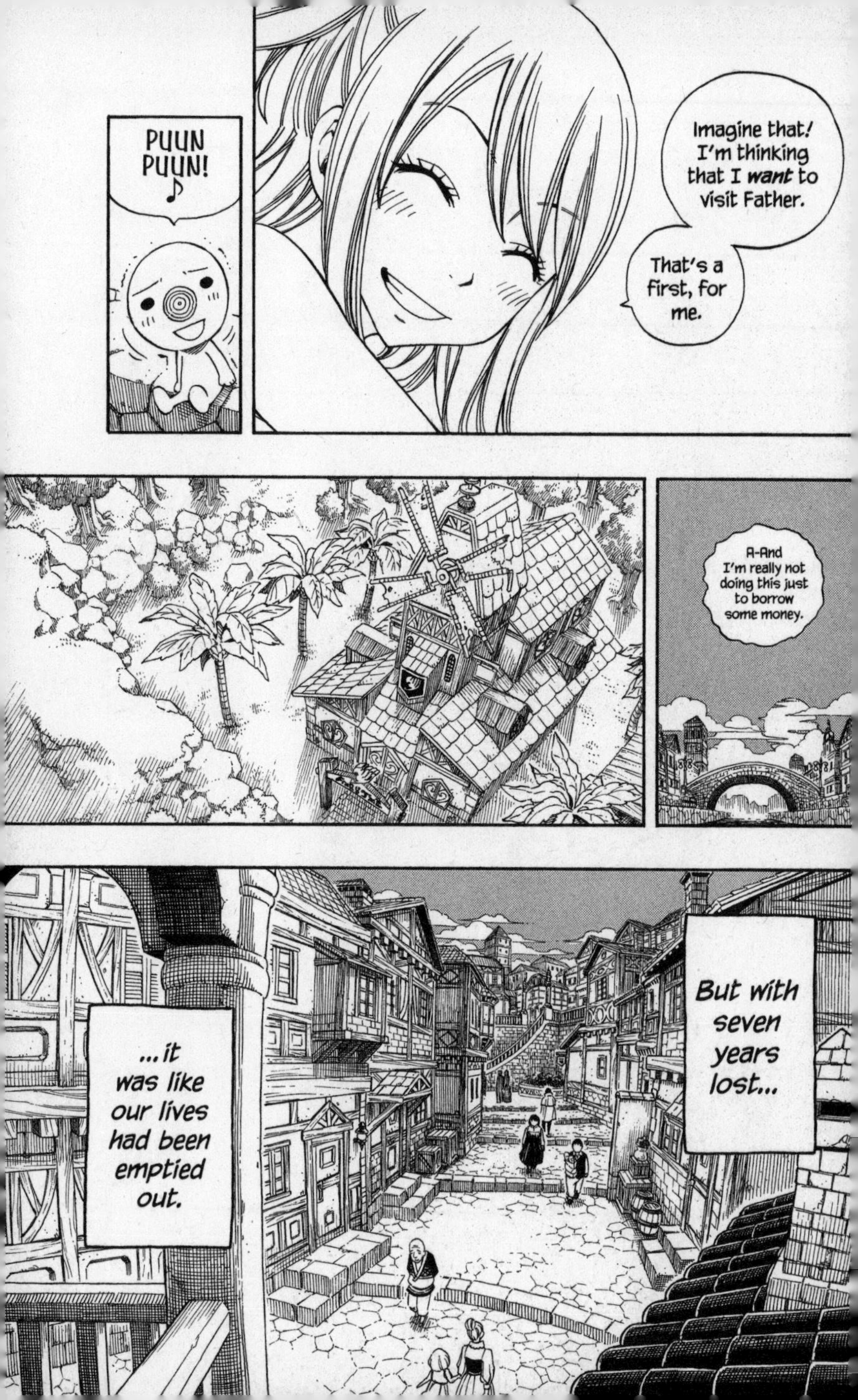
Imagine that! I'm thinking that I *want* to visit Father.
That's a first, for me.
PUUN PUUN! ♪
A-And I'm really not doing this just to borrow some money.
But with seven years lost...
...it was like our lives had been emptied out.

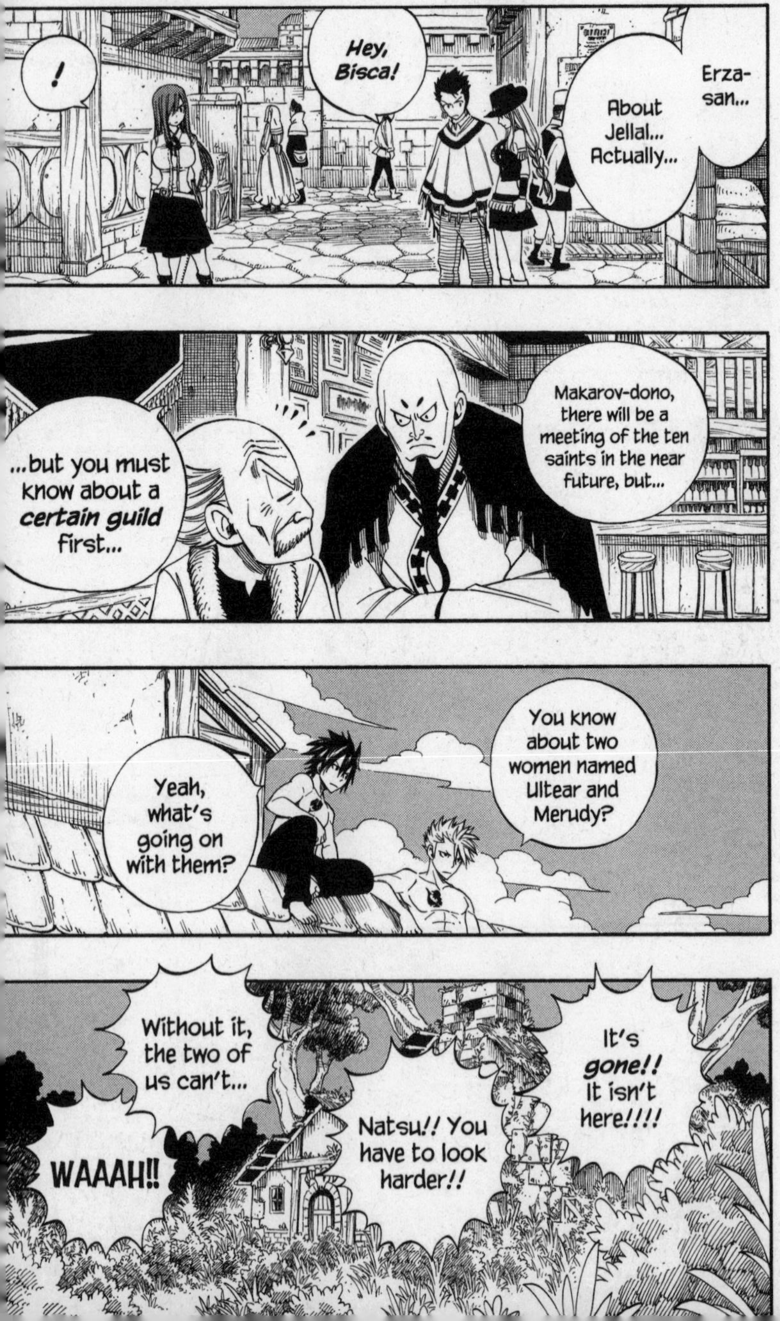
Erza-san...
About Jellal... Actually...
Hey, Bisca!
!
Makarov-dono, there will be a meeting of the ten saints in the near future, but...
...but you must know about a certain guild first...
You know about two women named Ultear and Merudy?
Yeah, what's going on with them?
It's gone!! It isn't here!!!!
Without it, the two of us can't...
Natsu!! You have to look harder!!
WAAAH!!

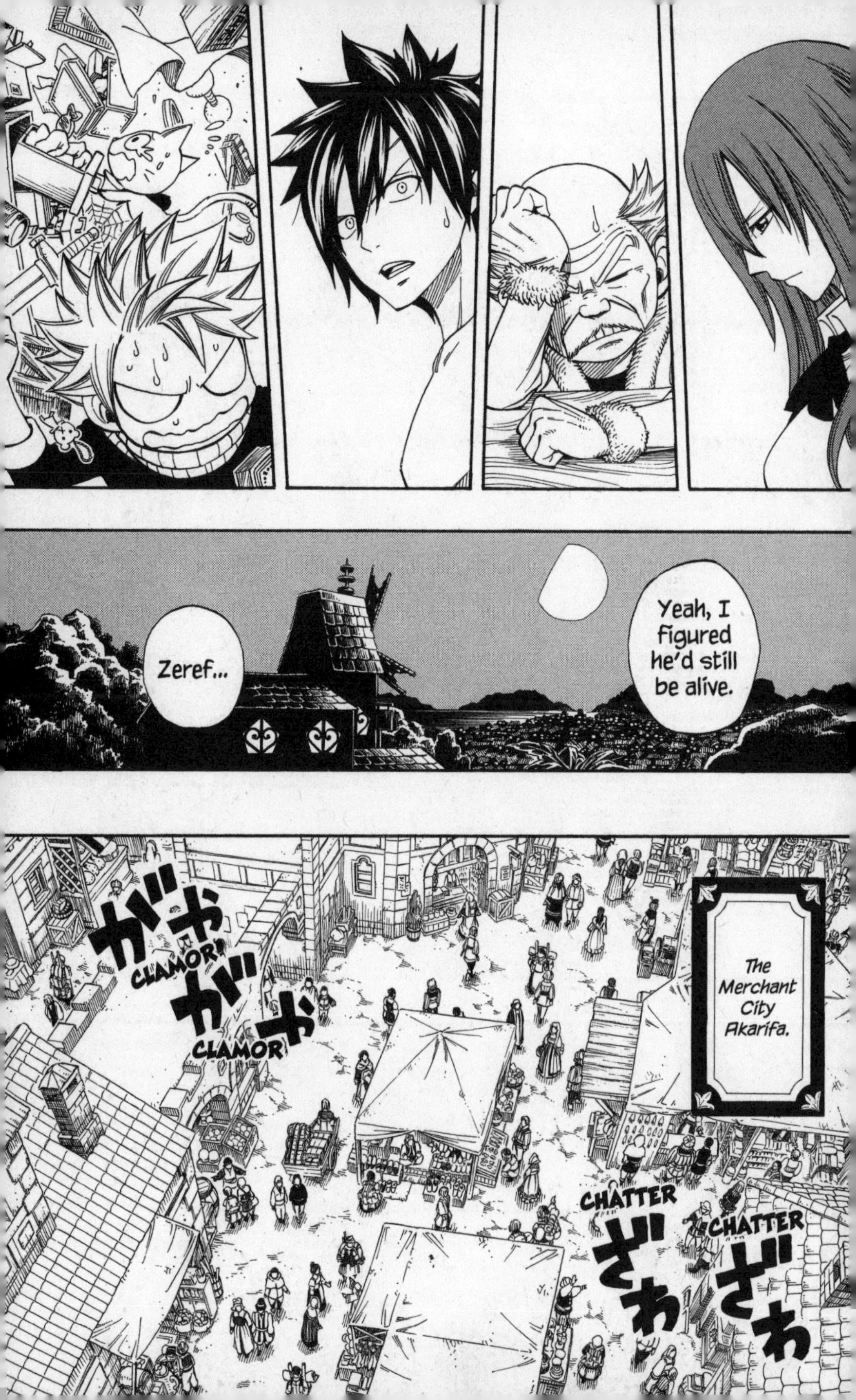
Yeah, I figured he'd still be alive.
Zeref...
The Merchant City Akarifa.
CHATTER
CHATTER
CLAMOR
CLAMOR

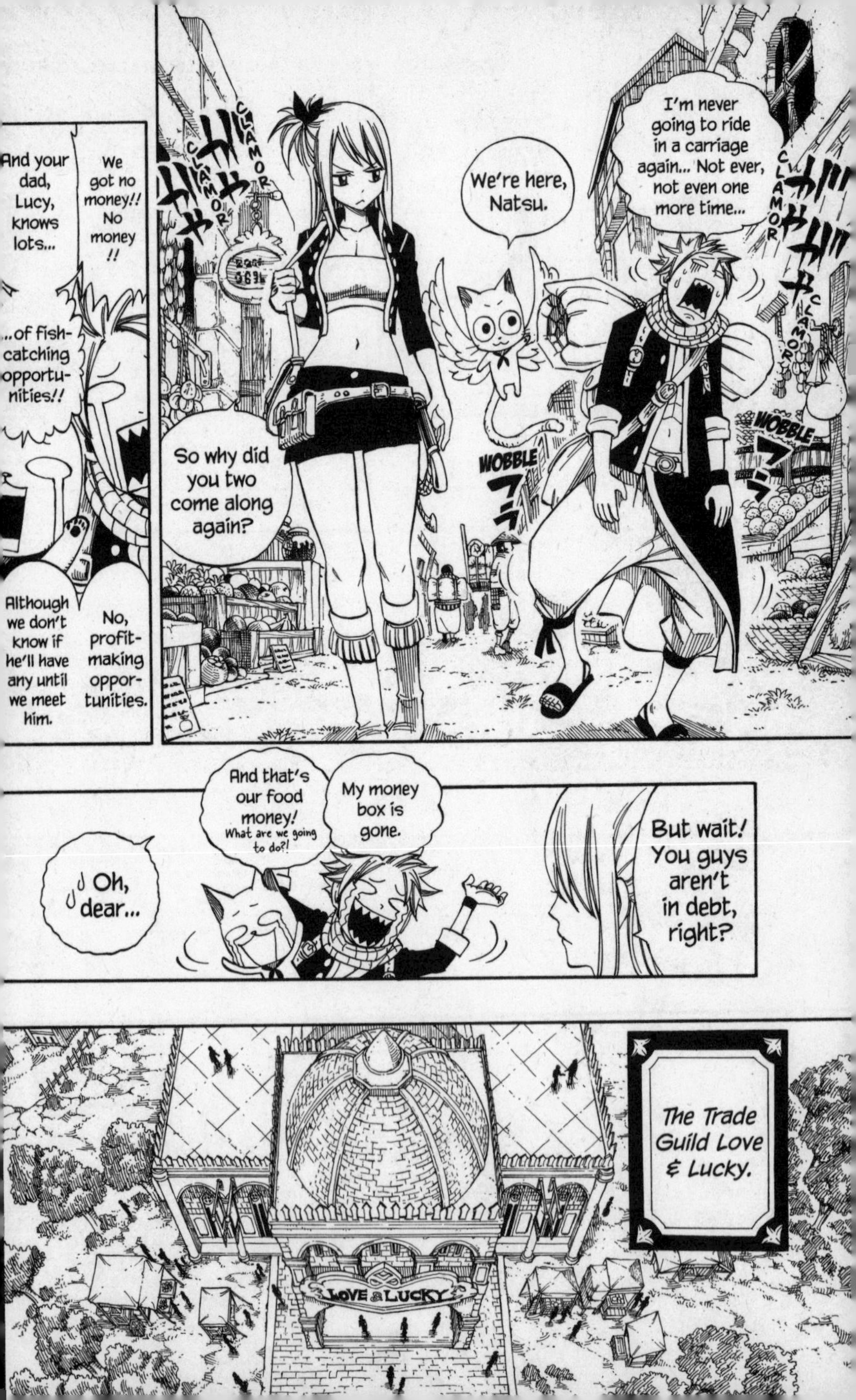
I'm never going to ride in a carriage again... Not ever, not even one more time...
CLAMOR
We're here, Natsu.
CLAMOR
CLAMOR
WOBBLE
WOBBLE
So why did you two come along again?
We got no money!! No money!!
And your dad, Lucy, knows lots...
...of fish-catching opportunities!!
No, profit-making opportunities.
Although we don't know if he'll have any until we meet him.
But wait! You guys aren't in debt, right?
My money box is gone.
And that's our food money! What are we going to do?!
Oh, dear...
The Trade Guild Love & Lucky.
LOVE & LUCKY

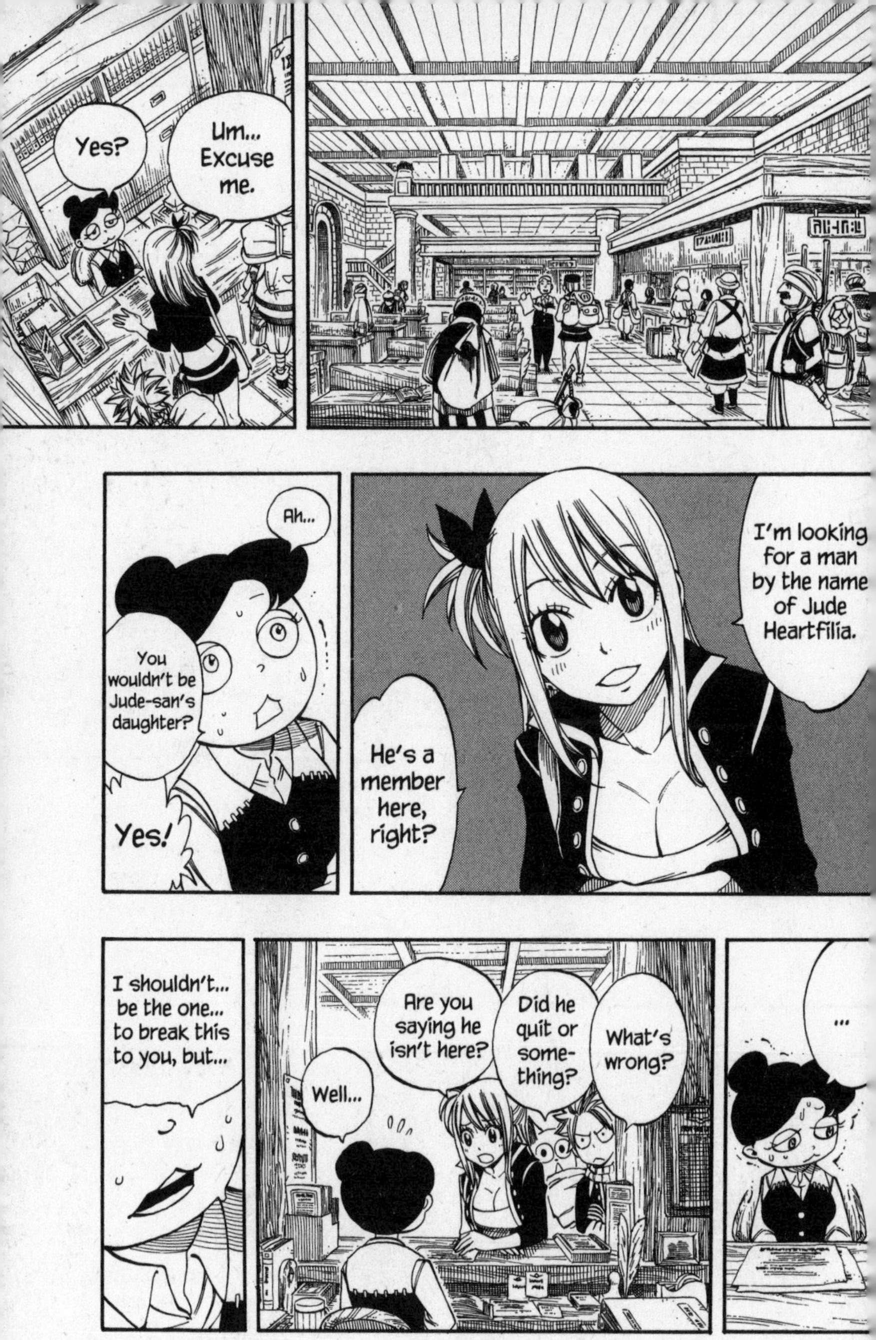
Um... Excuse me.
Yes?
I'm looking for a man by the name of Jude Heartfilia.
He's a member here, right?
Ah...
You wouldn't be Jude-san's daughter?
Yes!
...
What's wrong?
Did he quit or some-thing?
Are you saying he isn't here?
Well...
I shouldn't... be the one... to break this to you, but...

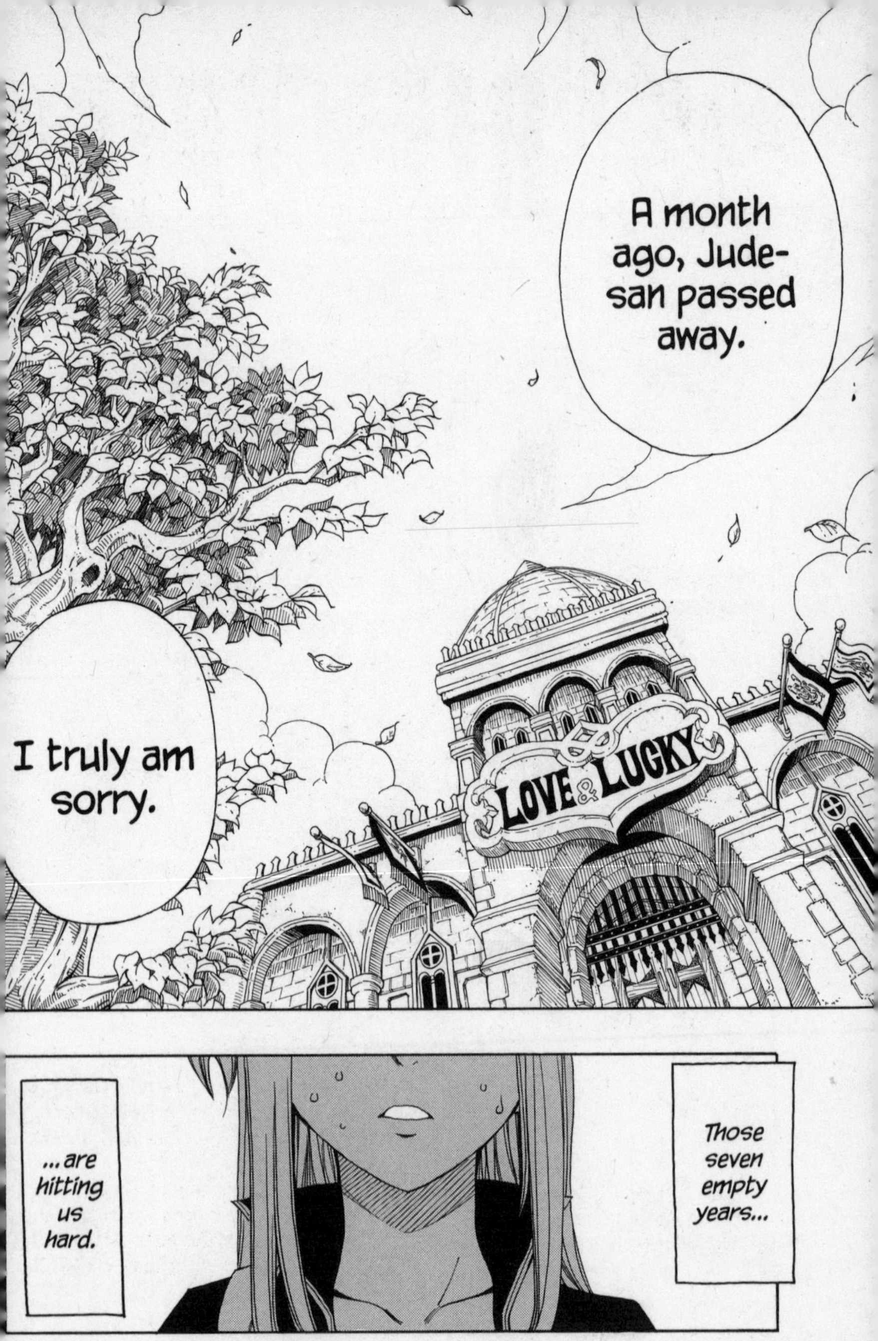

A month ago, Jude-san passed away.
LOVE & LUCKY
I truly am sorry.
Those seven empty years...
...are hitting us hard.

FAIRY TAIL

FAIRY TAIL

Name: **Romeo Conbolt**　Age: **13**

Magic:
Rainbow Fire

Likes: **The Guild**　Dislikes: **Twilight Ogre**

Chapter 257: Father's Seven Years

Remarks

Son of Macao, the fourth master of Fairy Tail.

He's always admired Natsu, calls him "big brother," and is very attached to him. Ever since a point seven years prior, it's been his dream to enter Fairy Tail. Soon after joining, he started taking lessons in Totomaru's magic class. He is now there learning Rainbow Fire, a magic that uses seven different colored flames that each have different properties.

After the disappearance of Sirius Island, he was never seen to smile in the presence of others, but after Natsu and the other members returned, so did his smile.

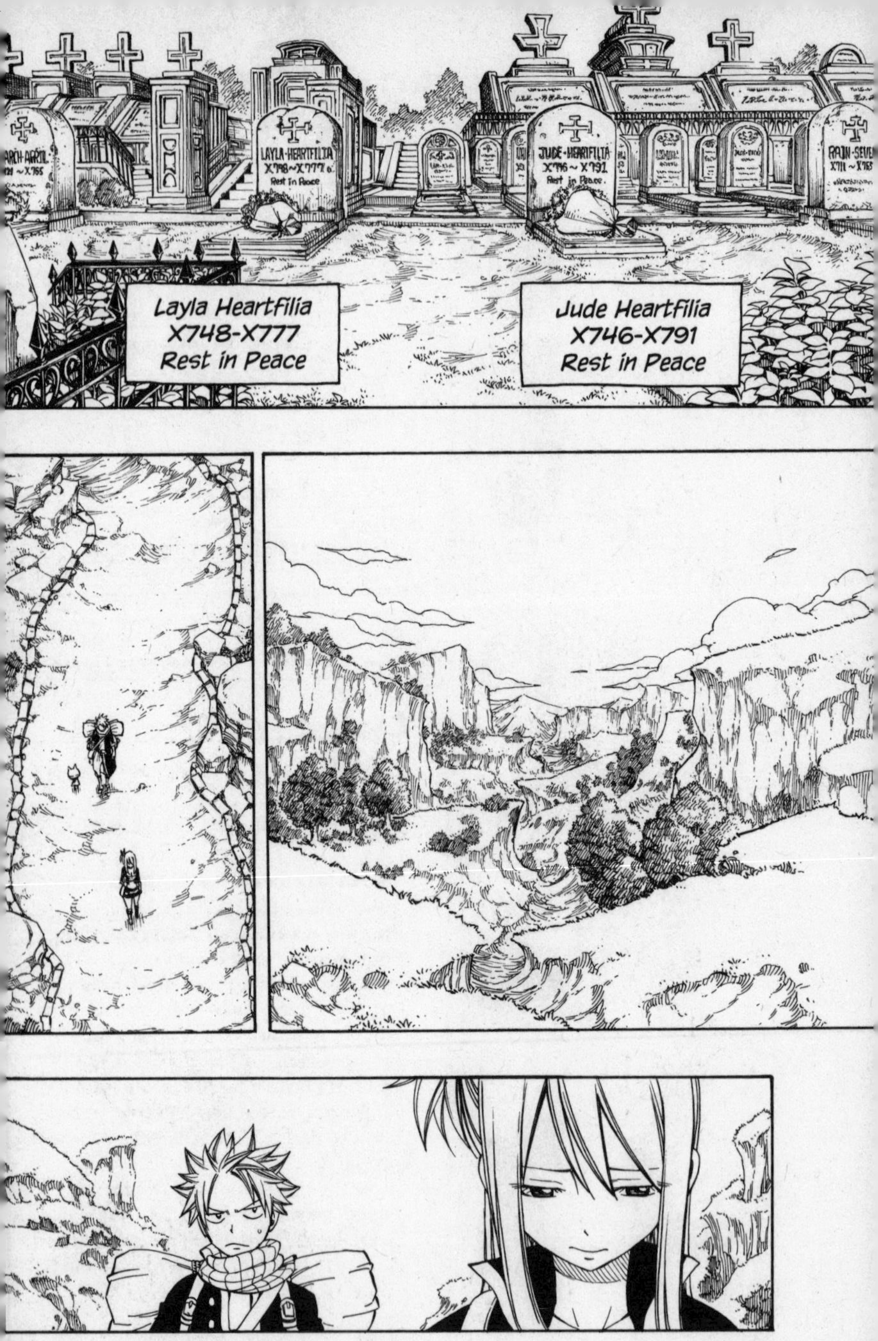
Jude Heartfilia X746-X791 Rest in Peace
Layla Heartfilia X748-X777 Rest in Peace

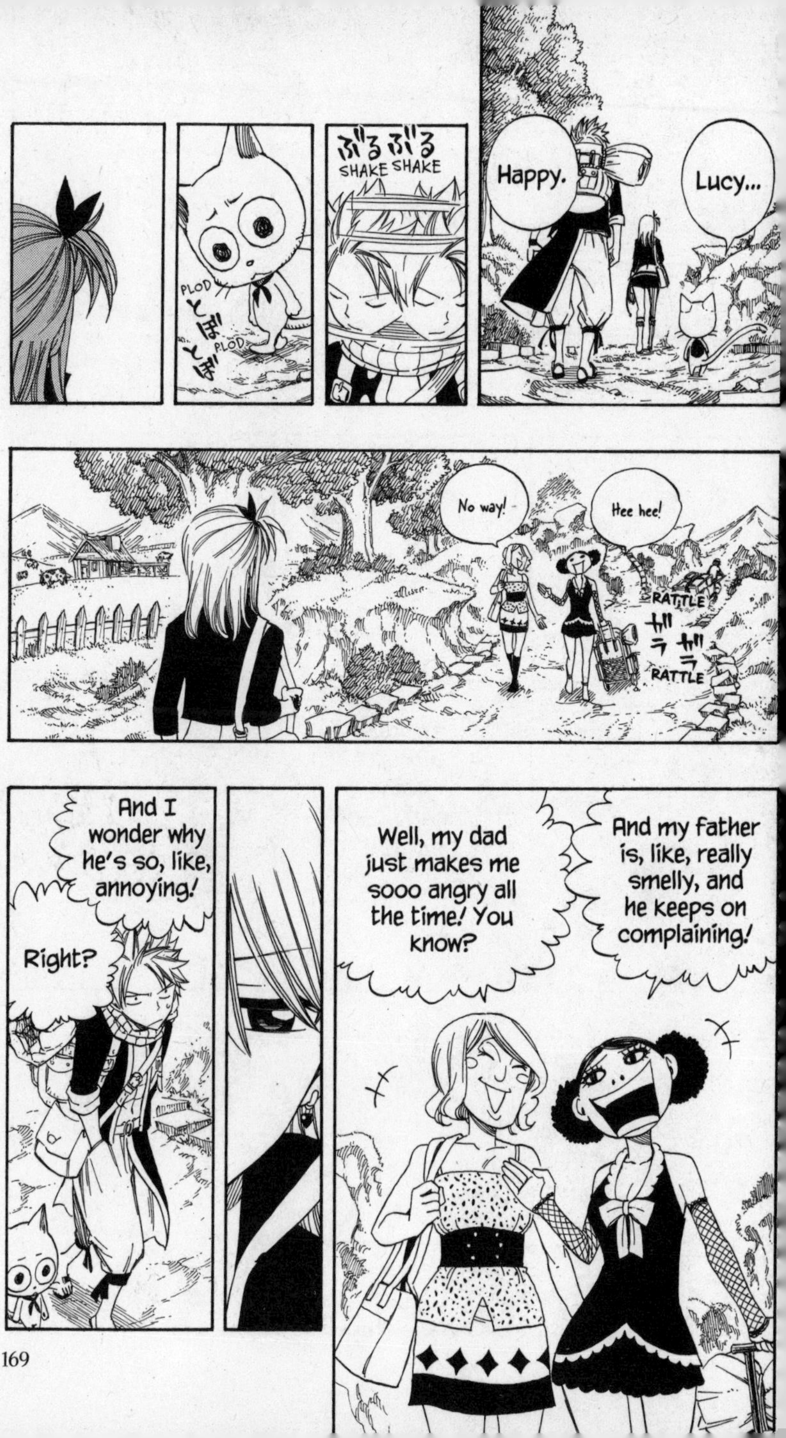
Lucy...
Happy.
ぶるぶる
SHAKE SHAKE
PLOD
とぼとぼ
PLOD
Hee hee!
No way!
RATTLE
ガラガラ
RATTLE
And my father is, like, really smelly, and he keeps on complaining!
Well, my dad just makes me sooo angry all the time! You know?
And I wonder why he's so, like, annoying!
Right?

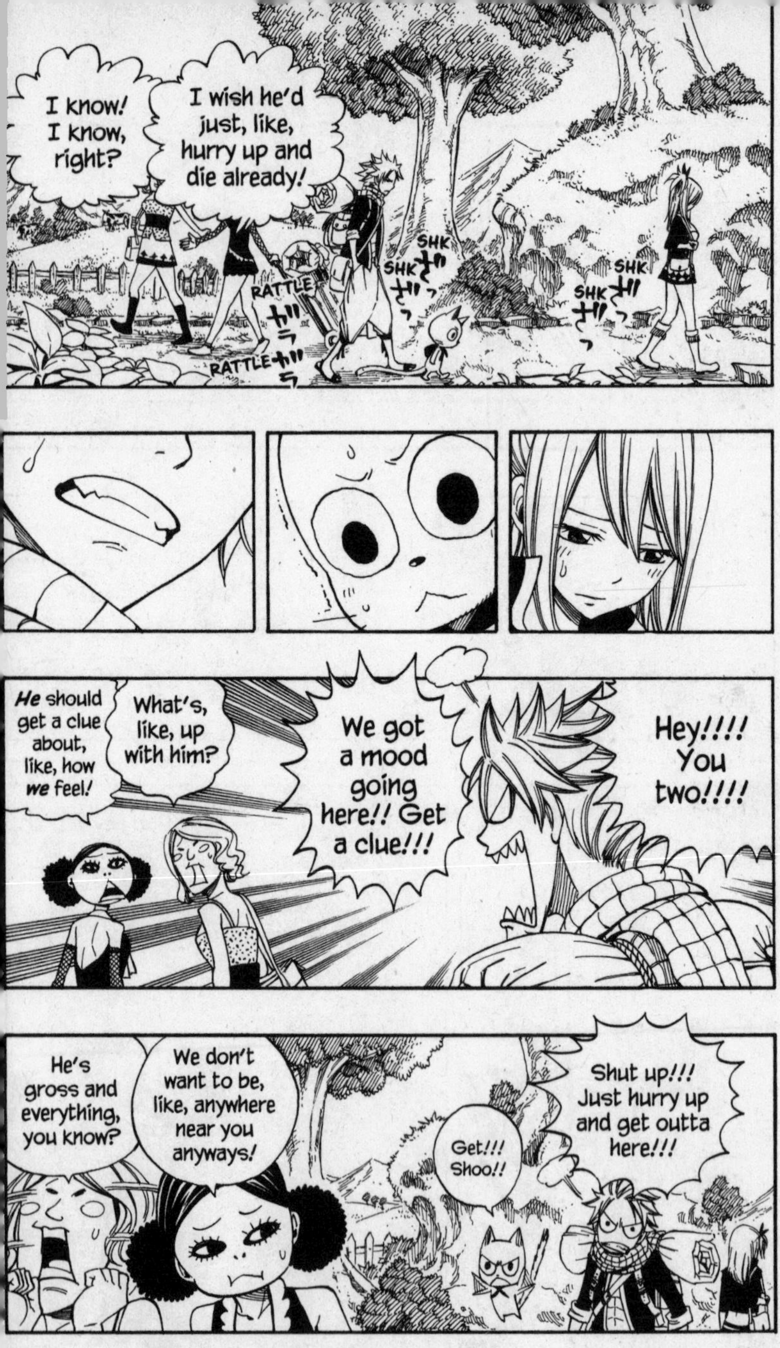
SHK SHK
SHK SHK
RATTLE RATTLE
I wish he'd just, like, hurry up and die already!
I know! I know, right?
Hey!!!! You two!!!!
We got a mood going here!! Get a clue!!!
What's, like, up with him?
He should get a clue about, like, how *we* feel!
Shut up!!! Just hurry up and get outta here!!!
Get!!! Shoo!!
We don't want to be, like, anywhere near you anyways!
He's gross and everything, you know?

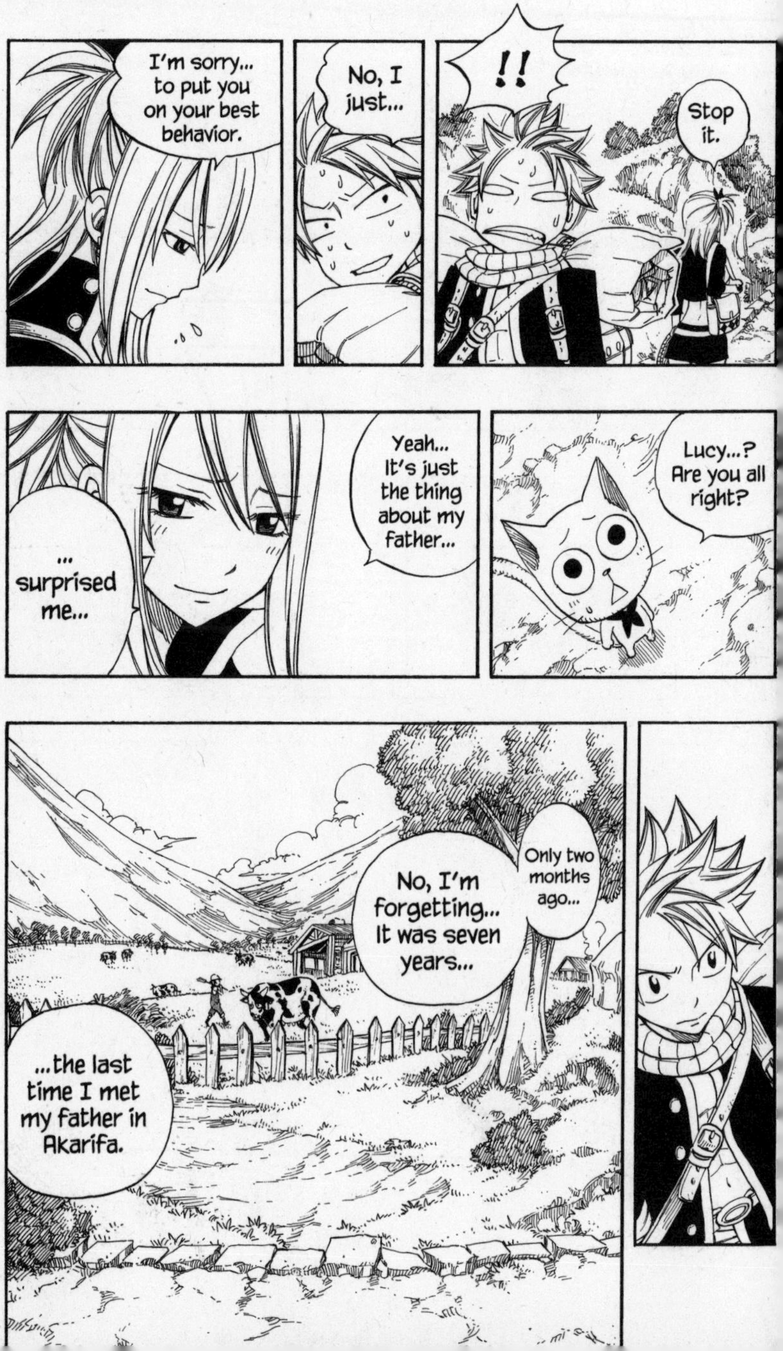
Stop it.
!!
No, I just...
I'm sorry... to put you on your best behavior.
Lucy...? Are you all right?
Yeah... It's just the thing about my father...
... surprised me...
Only two months ago...
No, I'm forgetting... It was seven years...
...the last time I met my father in Akarifa.

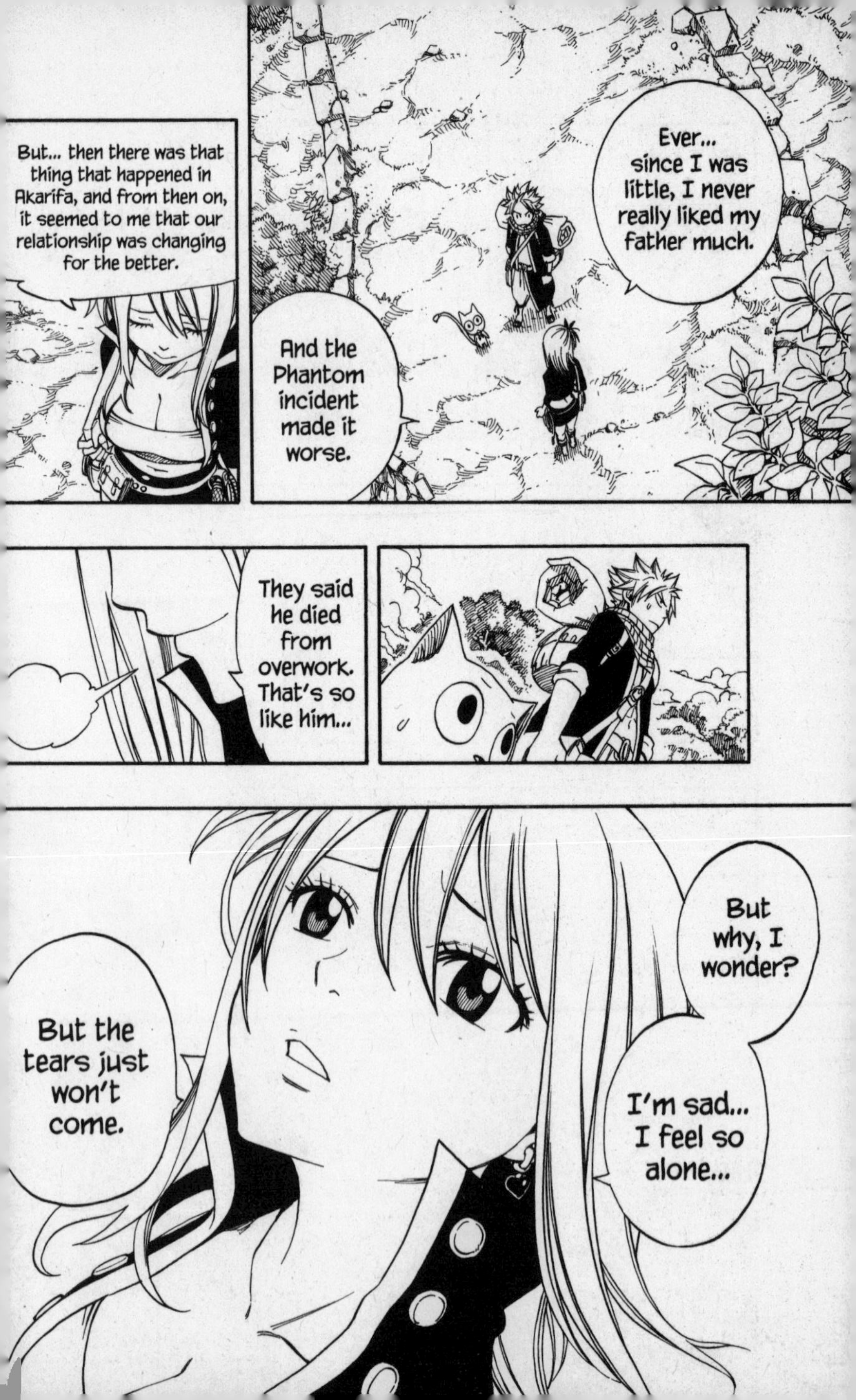

Ever... since I was little, I never really liked my father much.
And the Phantom incident made it worse.
But... then there was that thing that happened in Akarifa, and from then on, it seemed to me that our relationship was changing for the better.
They said he died from overwork. That's so like him...
But why, I wonder?
I'm sad... I feel so alone...
But the tears just won't come.

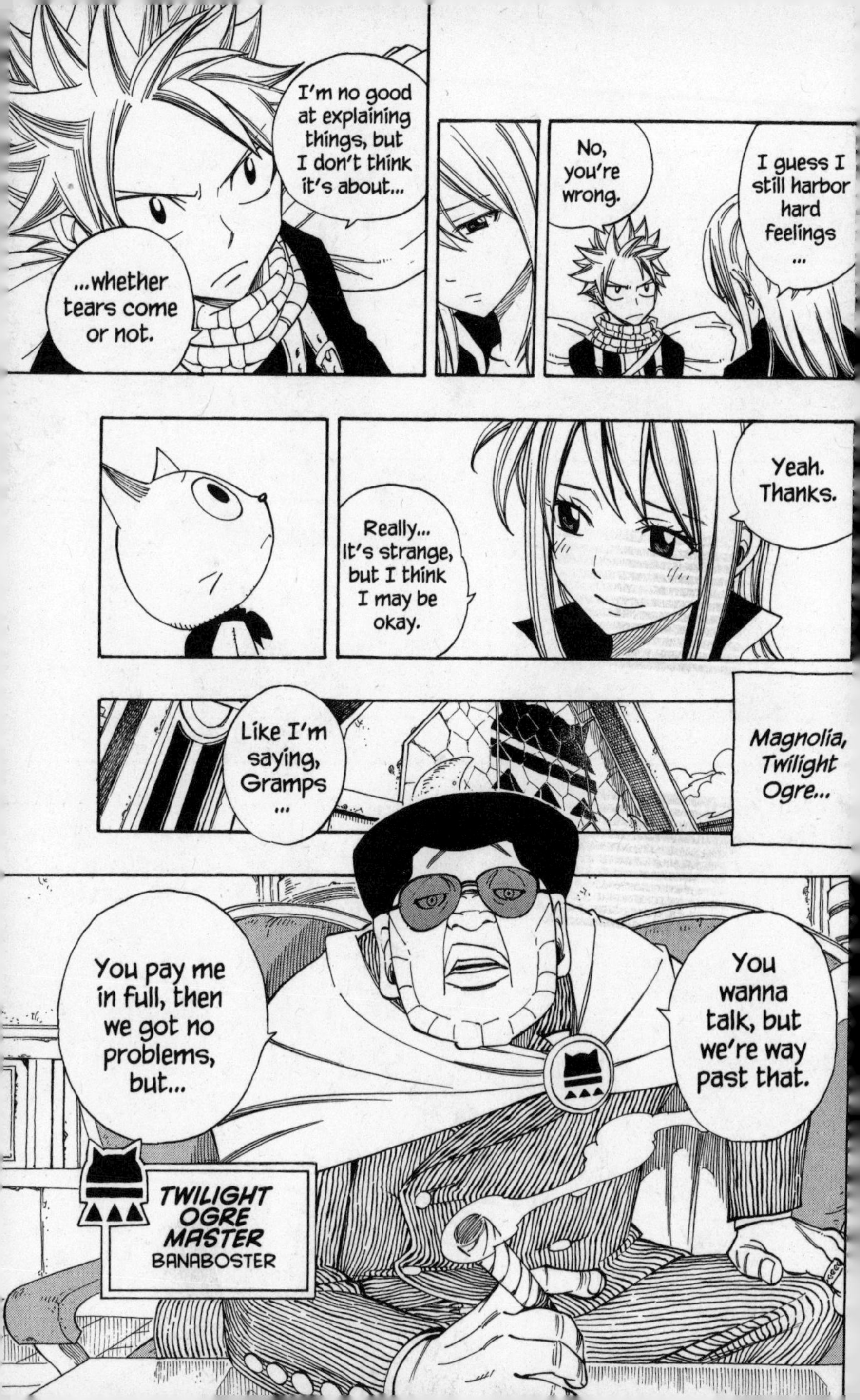
I guess I still harbor hard feelings ...
No, you're wrong.
I'm no good at explaining things, but I don't think it's about...
...whether tears come or not.
Yeah. Thanks.
Really... It's strange, but I think I may be okay.
Magnolia, Twilight Ogre...
Like I'm saying, Gramps ...
You wanna talk, but we're way past that.
You pay me in full, then we got no problems, but...
TWILIGHT OGRE MASTER
BANABOSTER

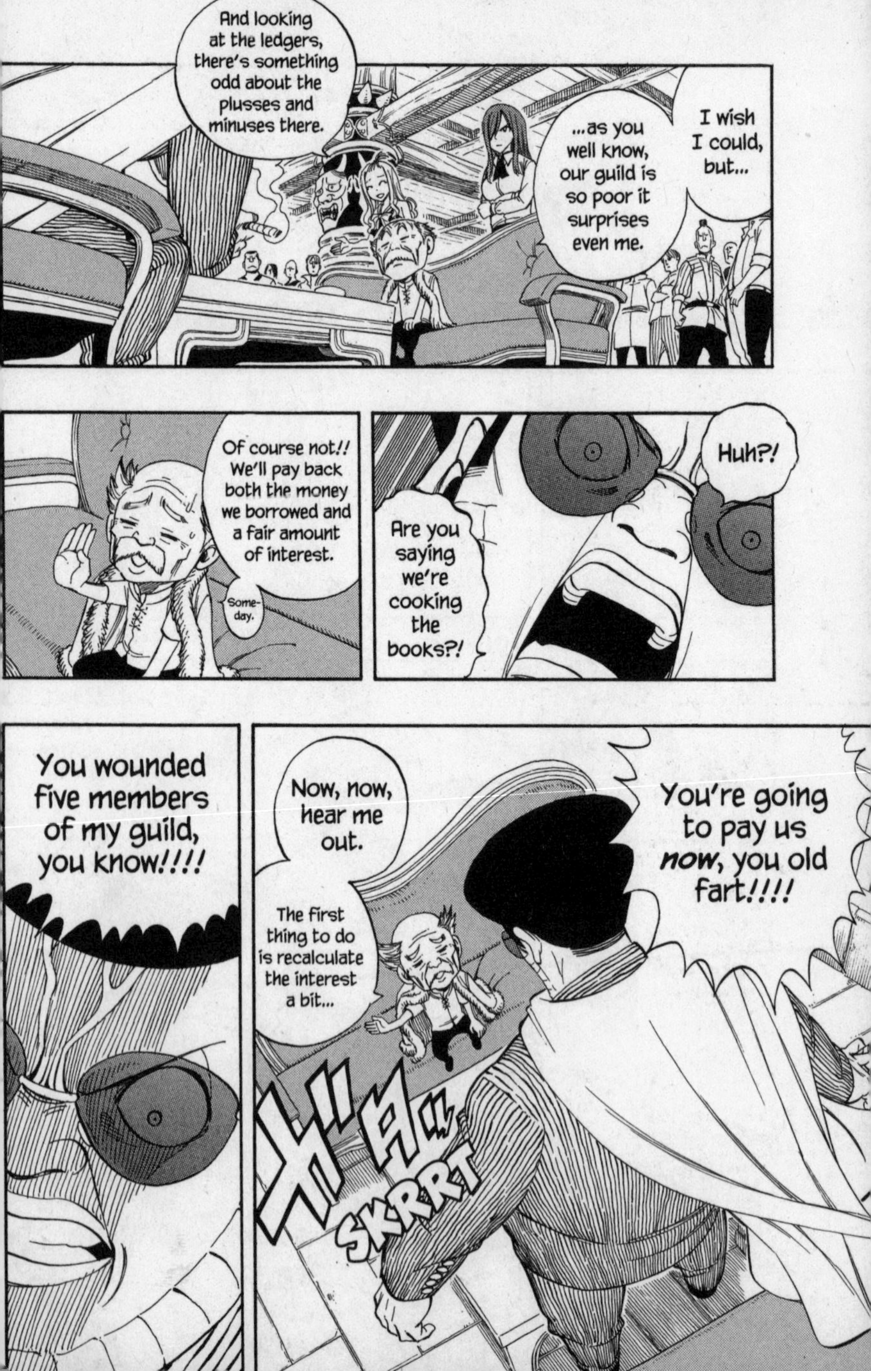

I wish I could, but...
...as you well know, our guild is so poor it surprises even me.
And looking at the ledgers, there's something odd about the plusses and minuses there.
Huh?!
Are you saying we're cooking the books?!
Of course not!! We'll pay back both the money we borrowed and a fair amount of interest.
Someday.
You're going to pay us *now*, you old fart!!!!
Now, now, hear me out.
The first thing to do is recalculate the interest a bit...
SKRRT
You wounded five members of my guild, you know!!!!

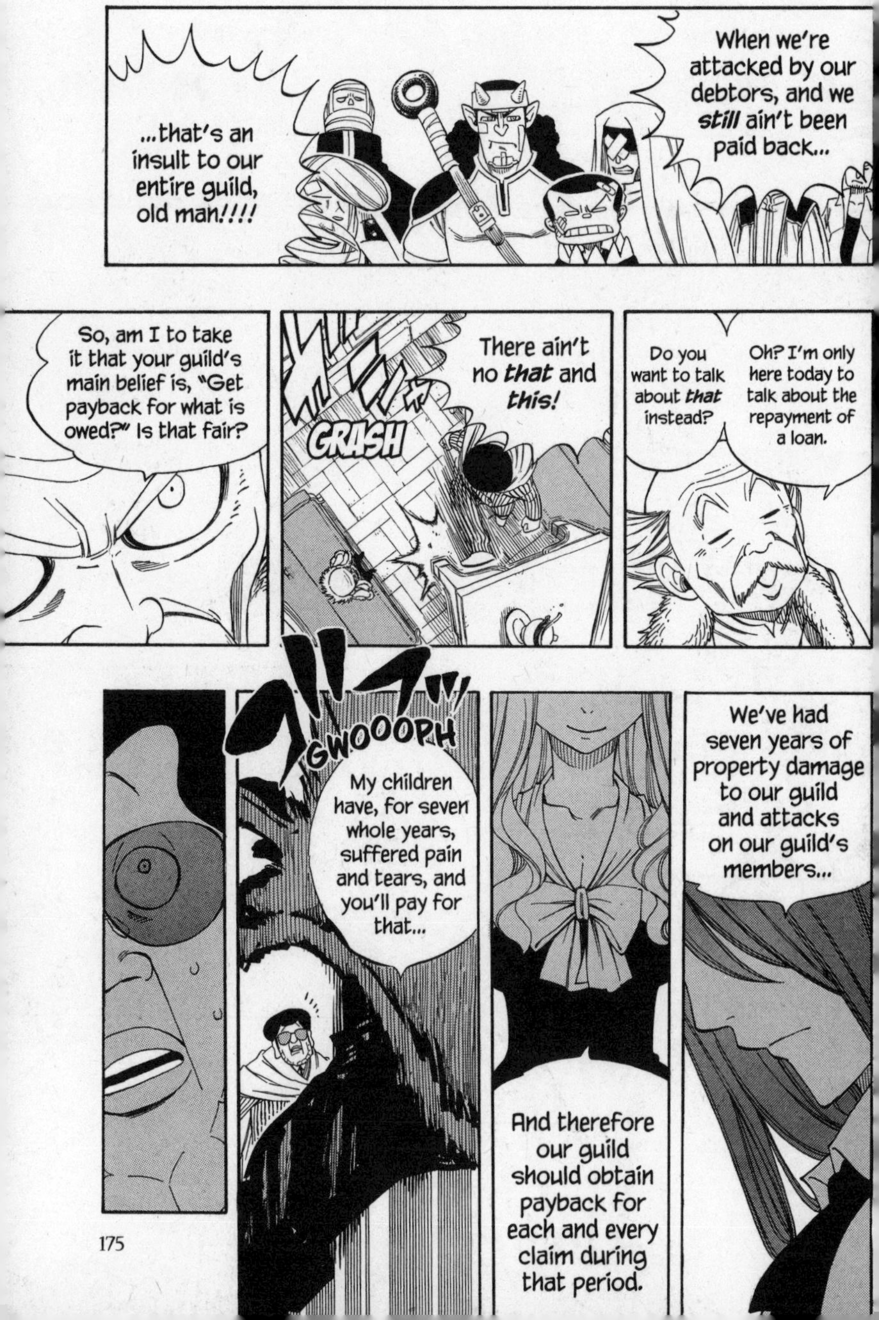

When we're attacked by our debtors, and we *still* ain't been paid back...
...that's an insult to our entire guild, old man!!!!
Oh? I'm only here today to talk about the repayment of a loan.
Do you want to talk about *that* instead?
There ain't no *that* and *this!*
GRASH
So, am I to take it that your guild's main belief is, "Get payback for what is owed?" Is that fair?
We've had seven years of property damage to our guild and attacks on our guild's members...
And therefore our guild should obtain payback for each and every claim during that period.
GWOOOPH
My children have, for seven whole years, suffered pain and tears, and you'll pay for that...

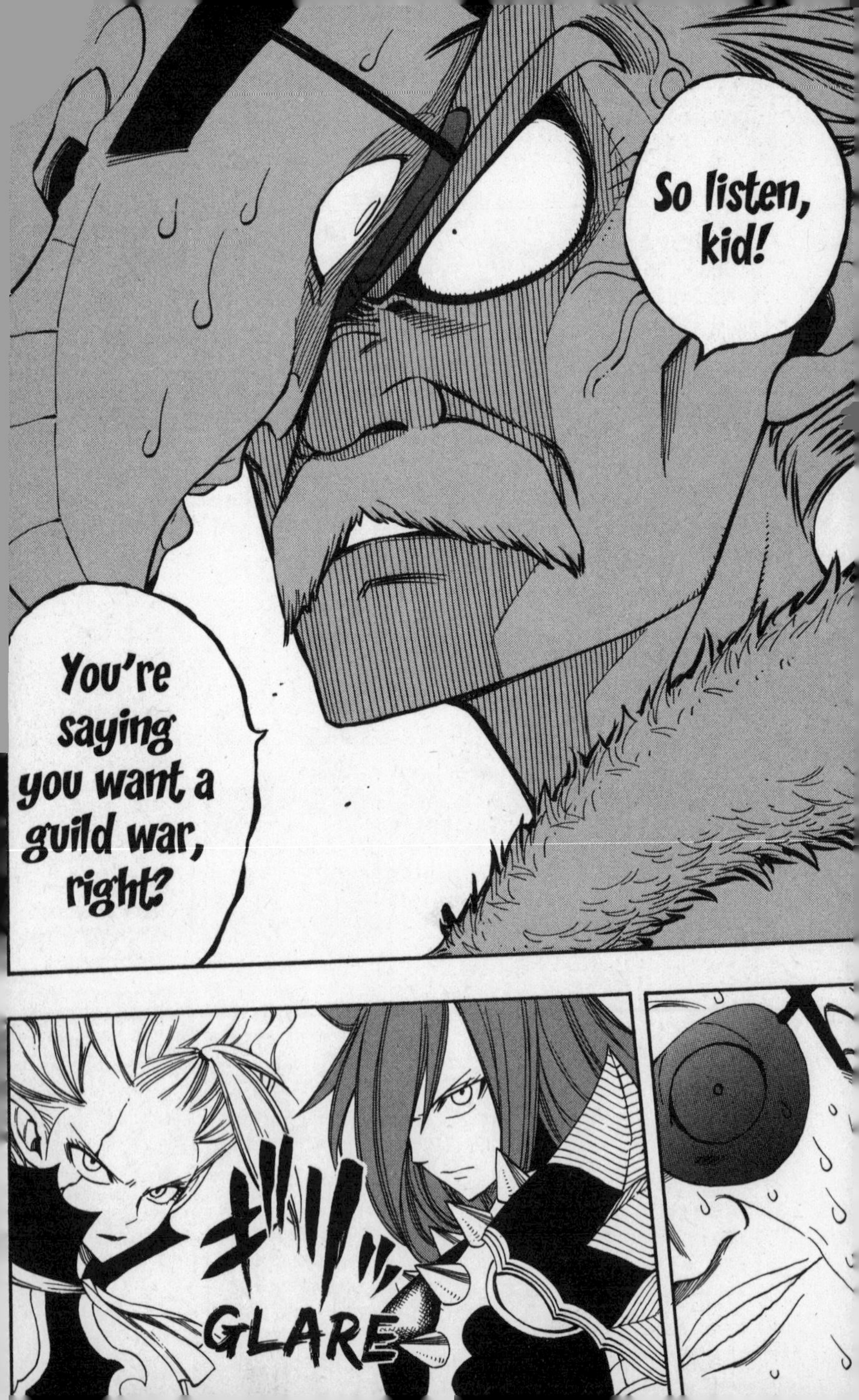
So listen, kid!
You're saying you want a guild war, right?
GLARE

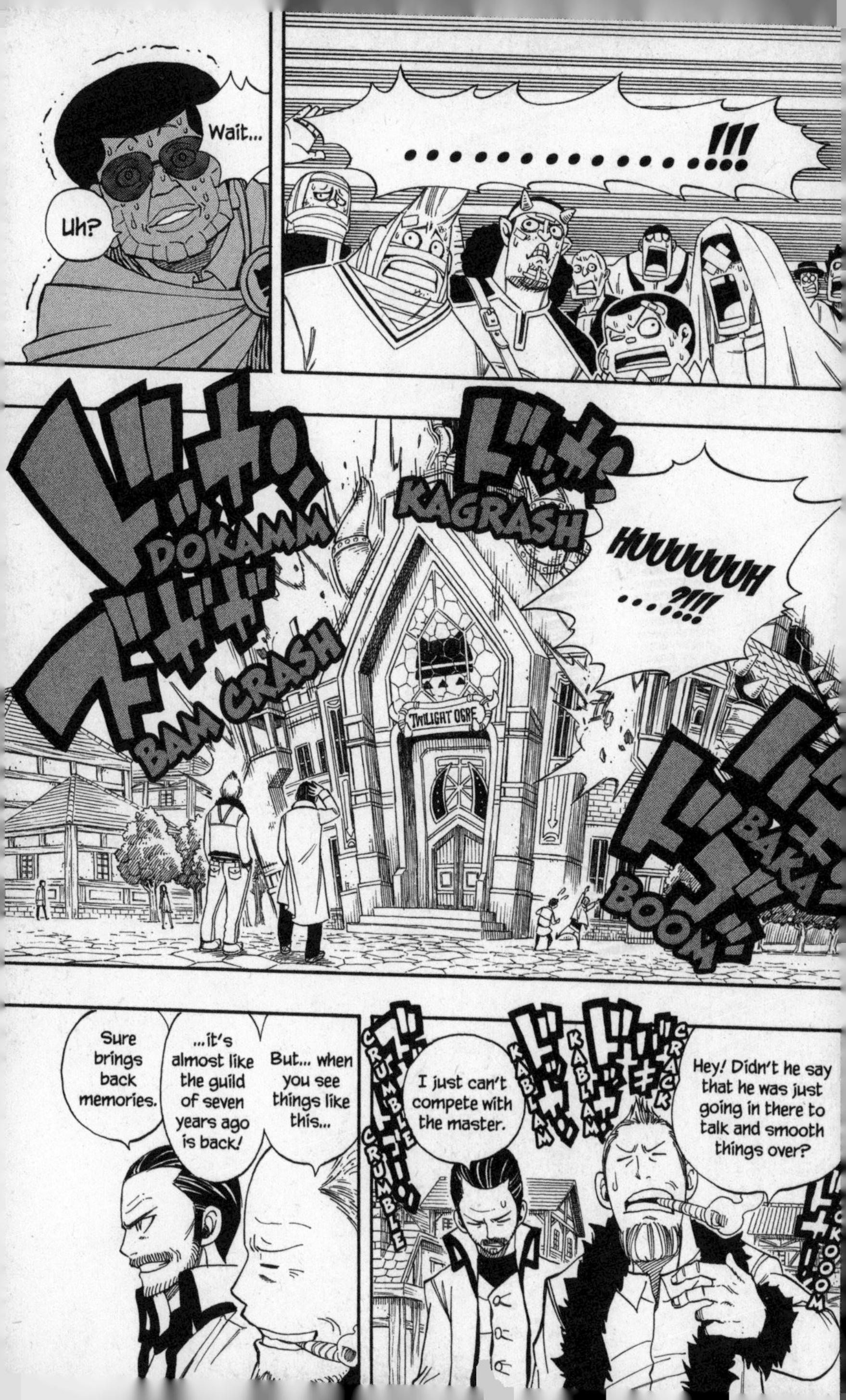
..............!!!
Wait...
Uh?
HUUUUUUH ...?!!!
KAGRASH
DOKAMM
BAM CRASH
BAKA BOOM
Hey! Didn't he say that he was just going in there to talk and smooth things over?
CRACK
KABLAM!
KABLAM
I just can't compete with the master.
CRUMBLE CRUMBLE
But... when you see things like this...
...it's almost like the guild of seven years ago is back!
Sure brings back memories.

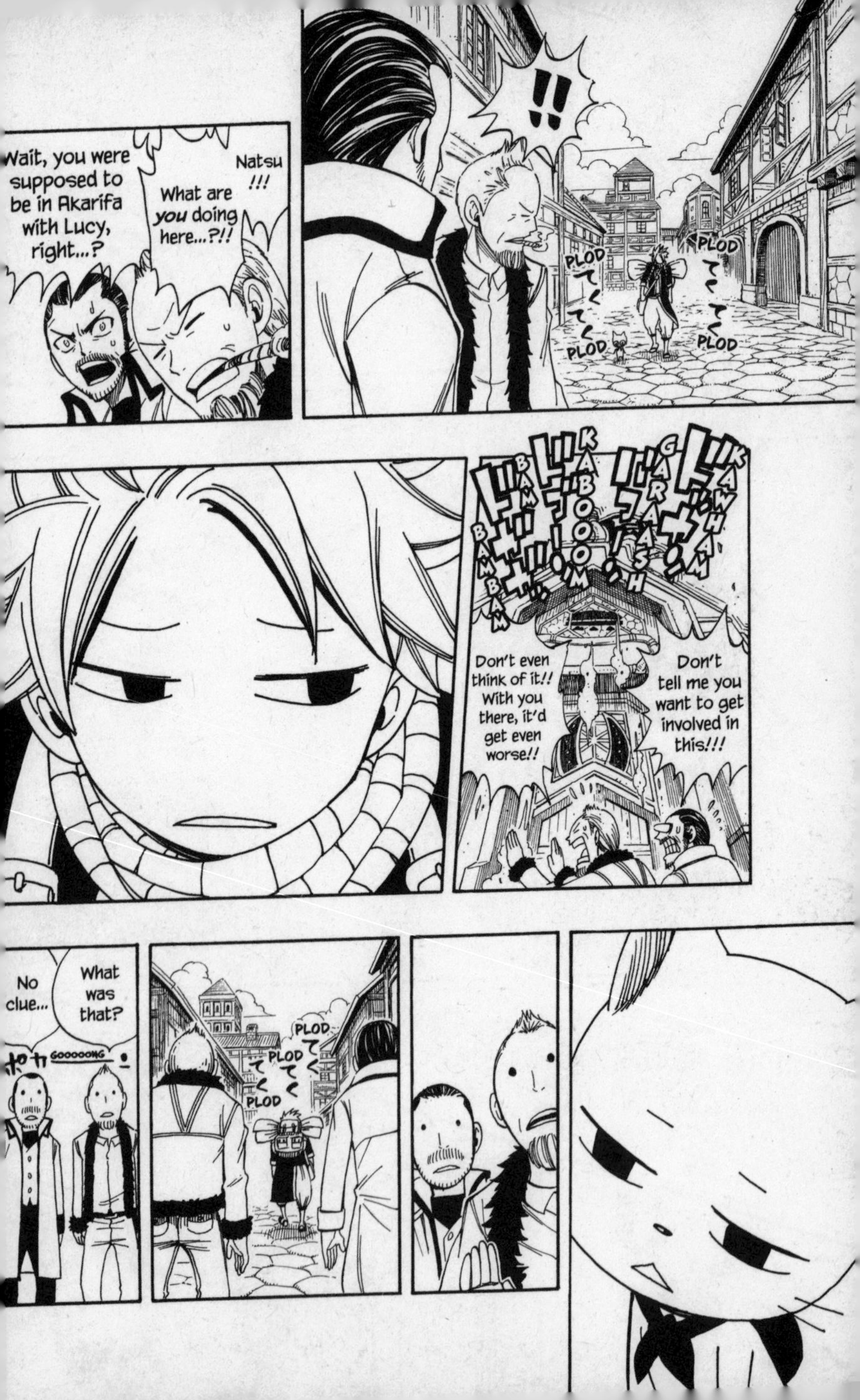

!!
PLOD
PLOD
PLOD
PLOD
Natsu!!!
What are *you* doing here...?!!
Wait, you were supposed to be in Akarifa with Lucy, right...?
KAWHAM
GARASH
KABOOOOM
BAMBAMBAM
Don't tell me you want to get involved in this!!!
Don't even think of it!! With you there, it'd get even worse!!
PLOD
PLOD
PLOD
What was that?
No clue...
GOOOOONG

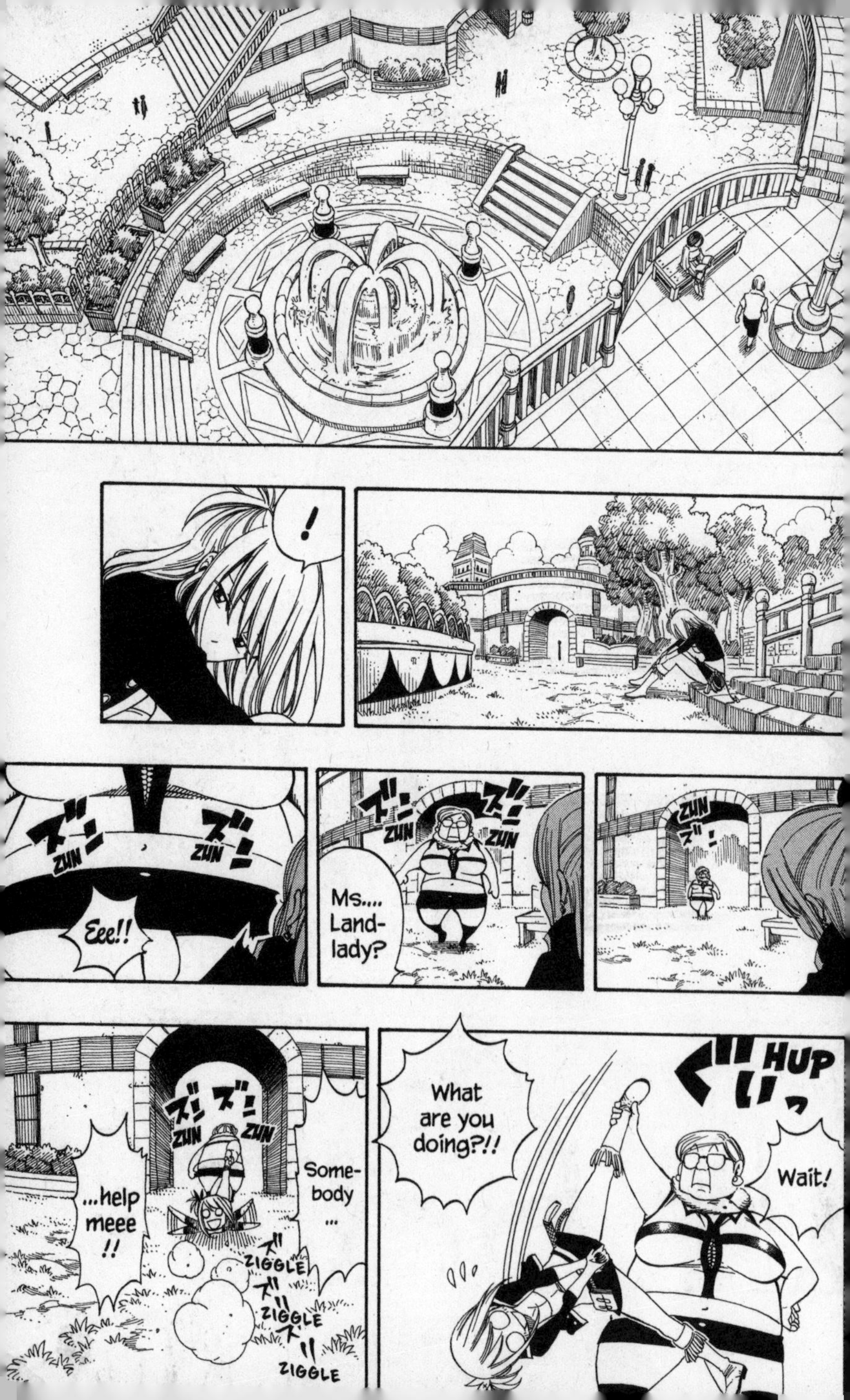
!
ZUN
ZUN
ZUN
ZUN
Ms.... Land-lady?
ZUN
ZUN
Eee!!
HUP
Wait!
What are you doing?!!
Some-body ...
ZUN
ZUN
...help meee !!
ZIGGLE
ZIGGLE
ZIGGLE

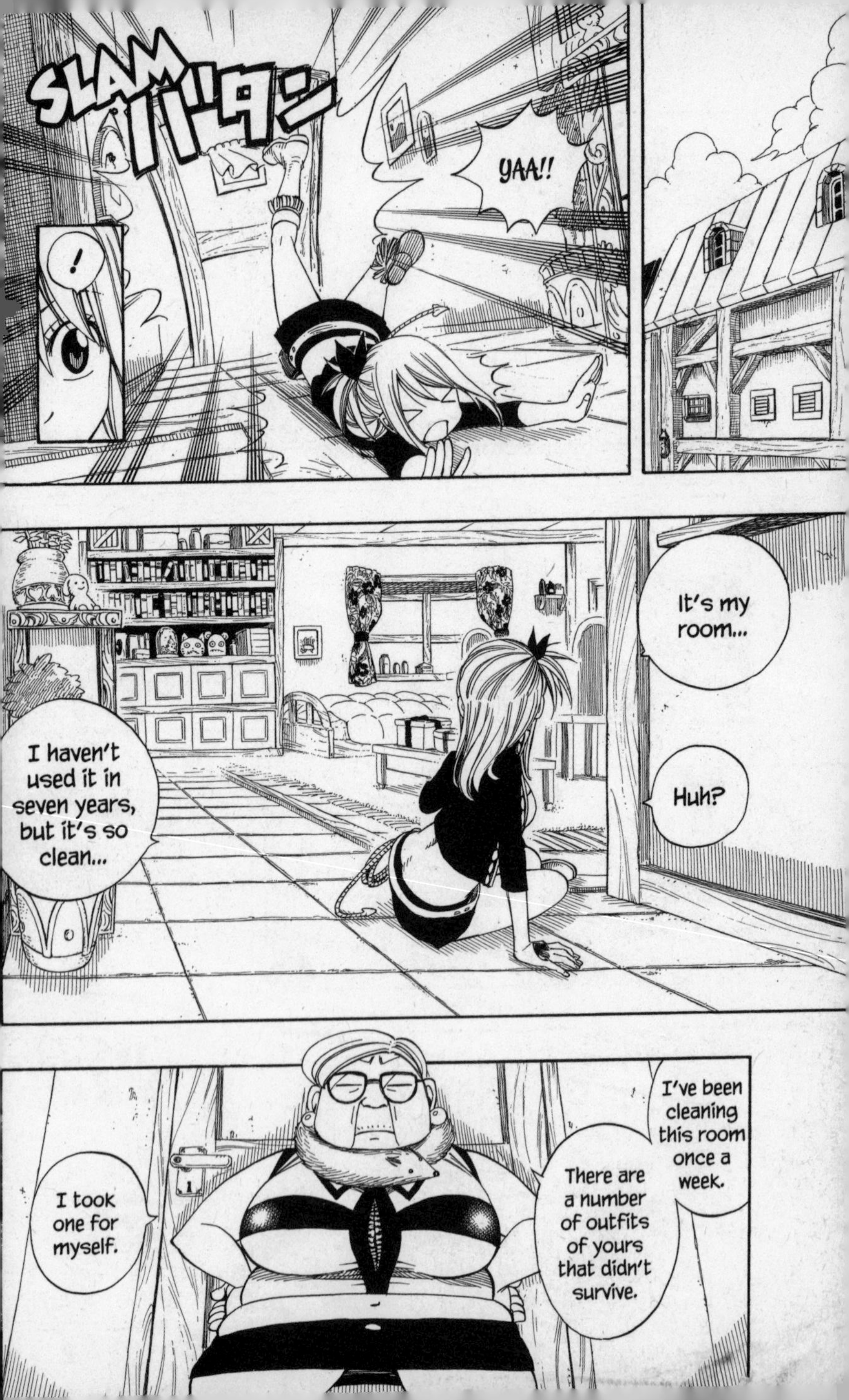
YAA!!
SLAM
!
It's my room...
Huh?
I haven't used it in seven years, but it's so clean...
I've been cleaning this room once a week.
There are a number of outfits of yours that didn't survive.
I took one for myself.

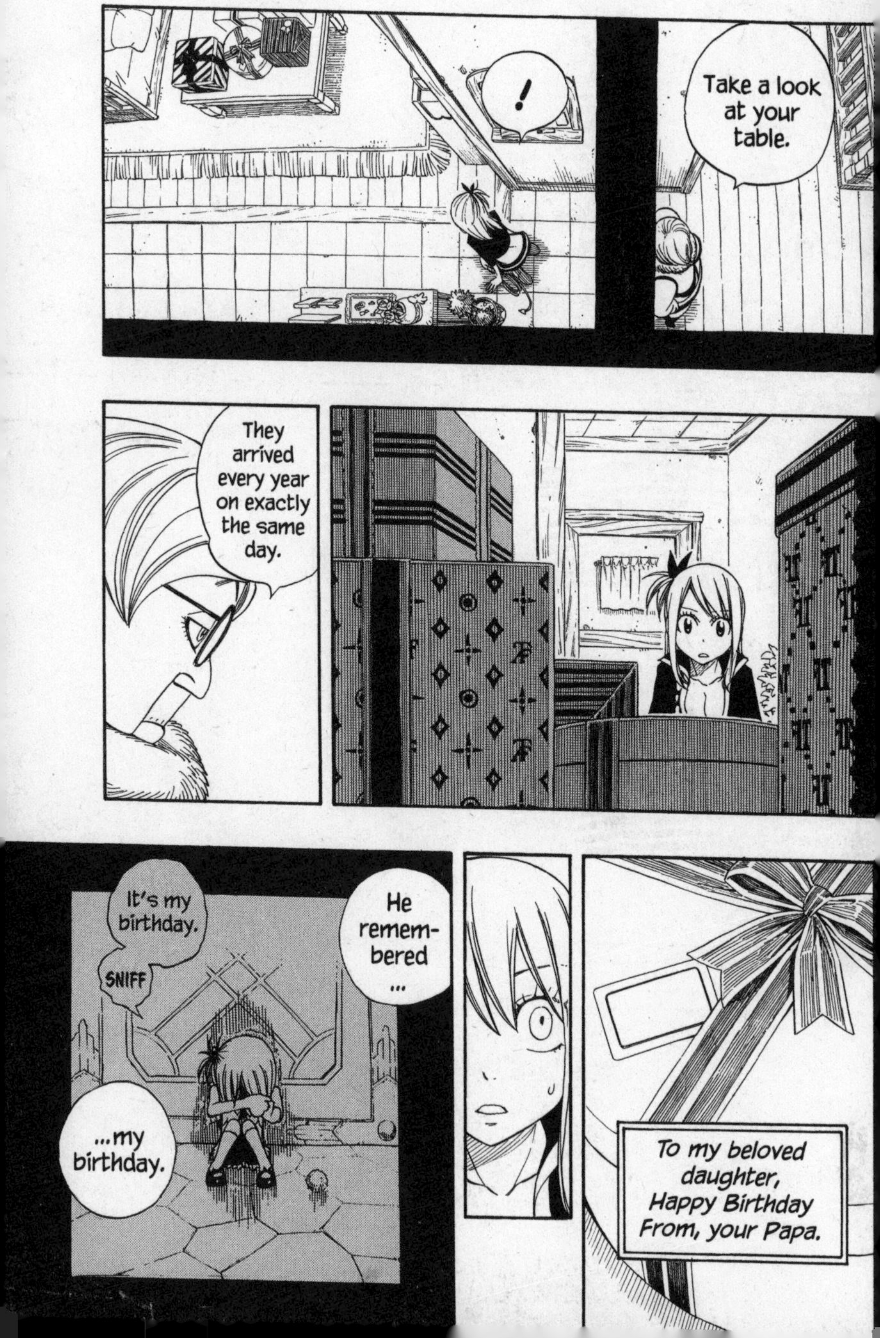
Take a look at your table.
!
They arrived every year on exactly the same day.
To my beloved daughter, Happy Birthday From, your Papa.
He remembered ...
It's my birthday.
SNIFF
...my birthday.

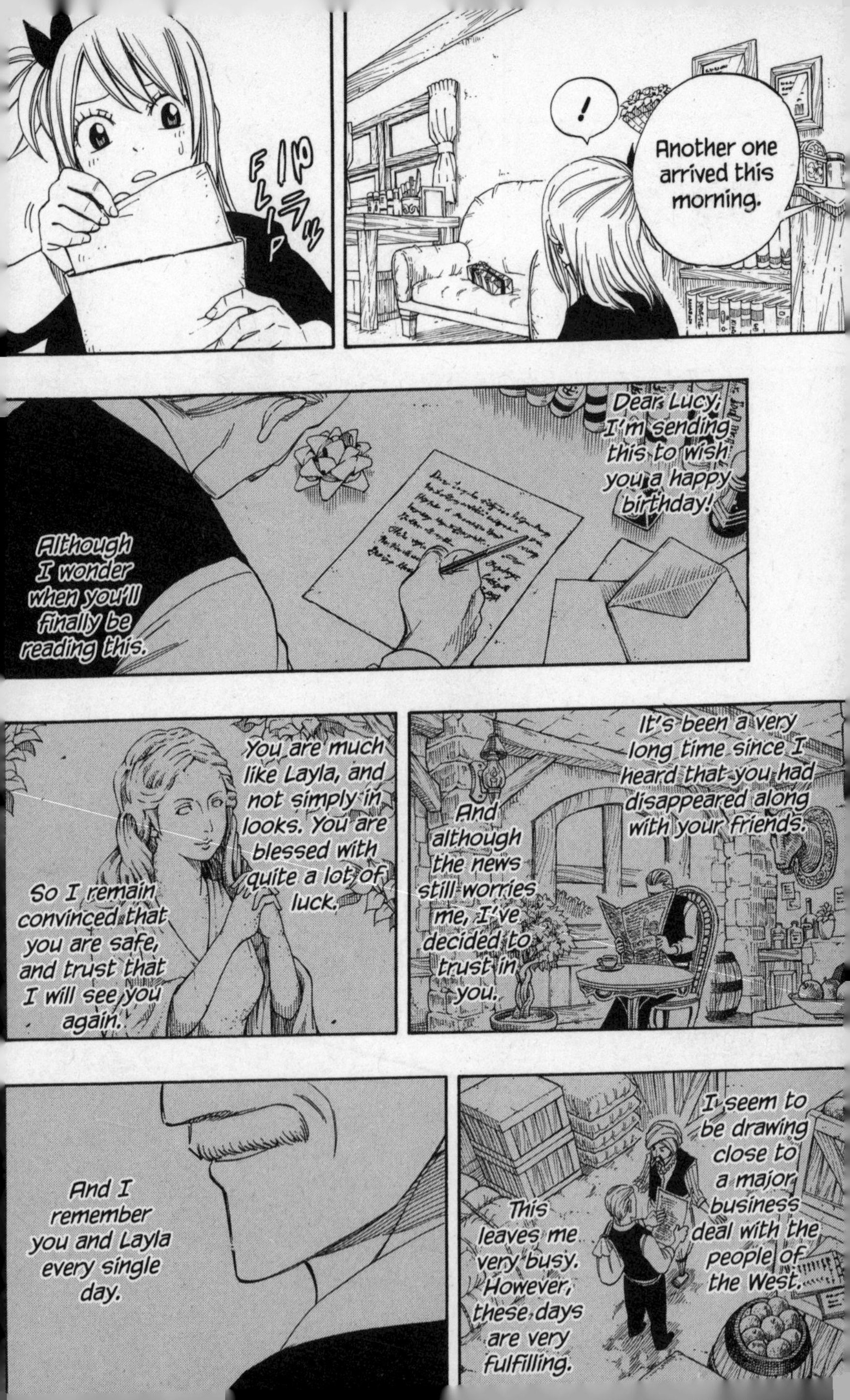
!
Another one arrived this morning.
FLIP
Dear Lucy, I'm sending this to wish you a happy birthday!
Although I wonder when you'll finally be reading this.
It's been a very long time since I heard that you had disappeared along with your friends.
And although the news still worries me, I've decided to trust in you.
You are much like Layla, and not simply in looks. You are blessed with quite a lot of luck.
So I remain convinced that you are safe, and trust that I will see you again.
I seem to be drawing close to a major business deal with the people of the West.
This leaves me very busy. However, these days are very fulfilling.
And I remember you and Layla every single day.

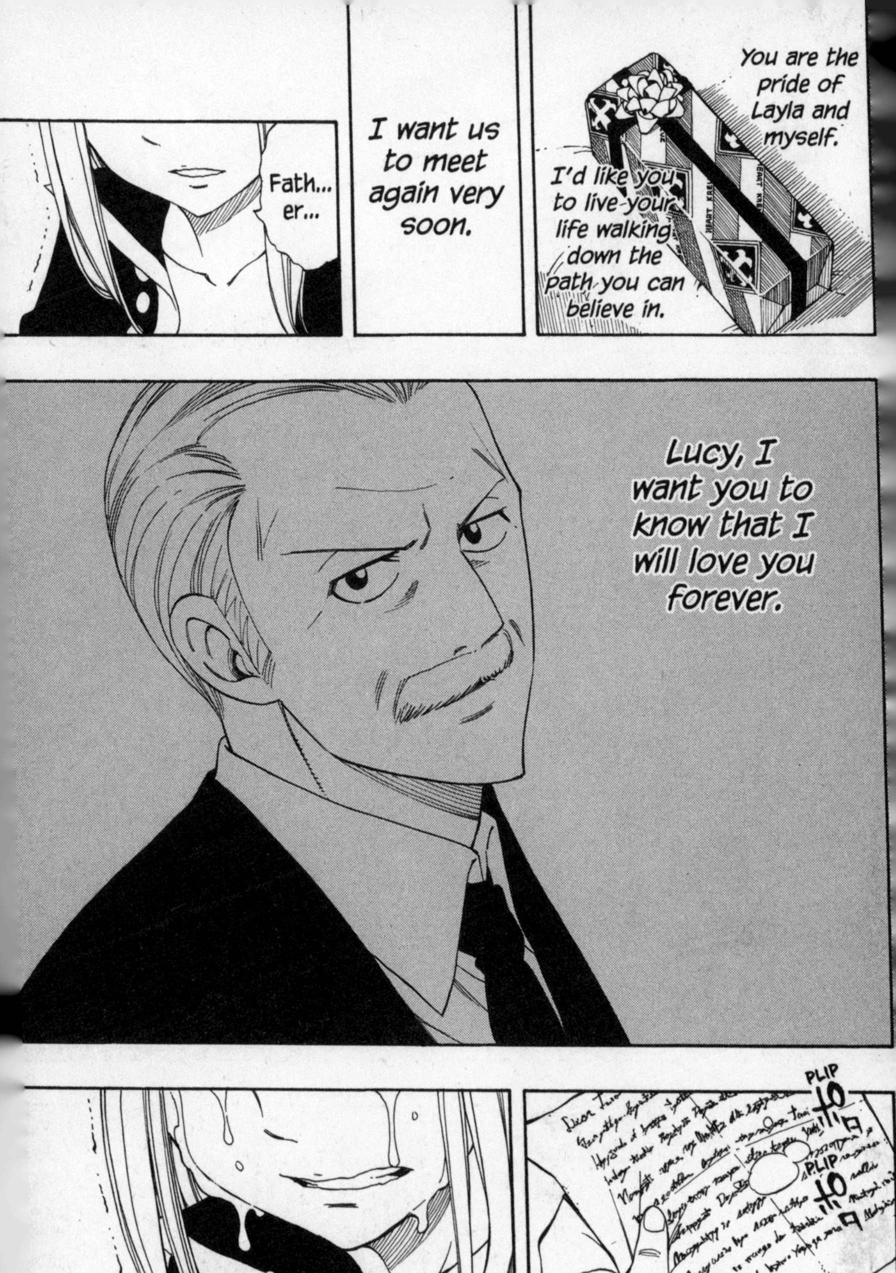
You are the pride of Layla and myself.
I'd like you to live your life walking down the path you can believe in.
I want us to meet again very soon.
Fath... er...
Lucy, I want you to know that I will love you forever.
PLIP
PLIP

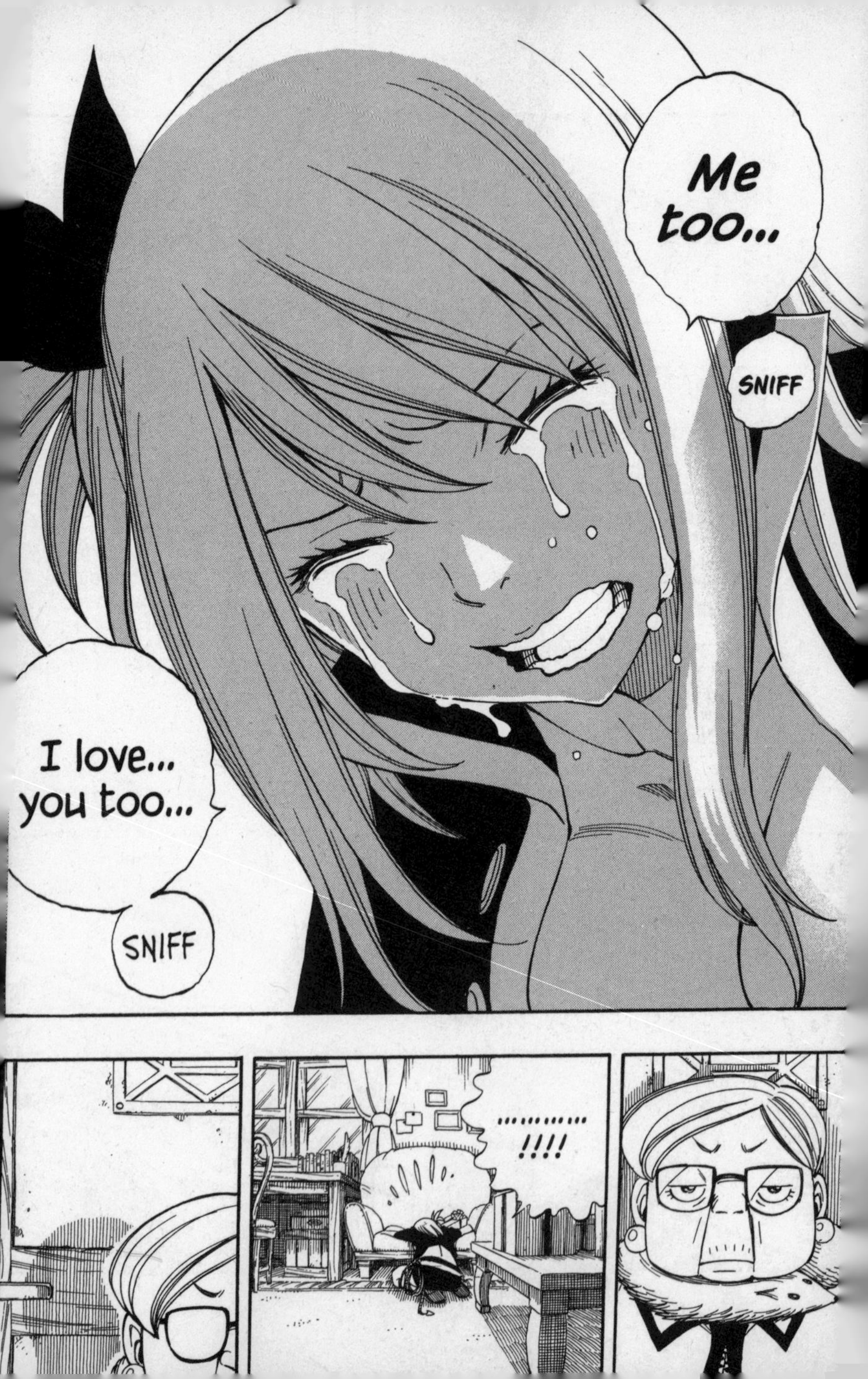
Me too...
SNIFF
I love... you too...
SNIFF
....
!!!!

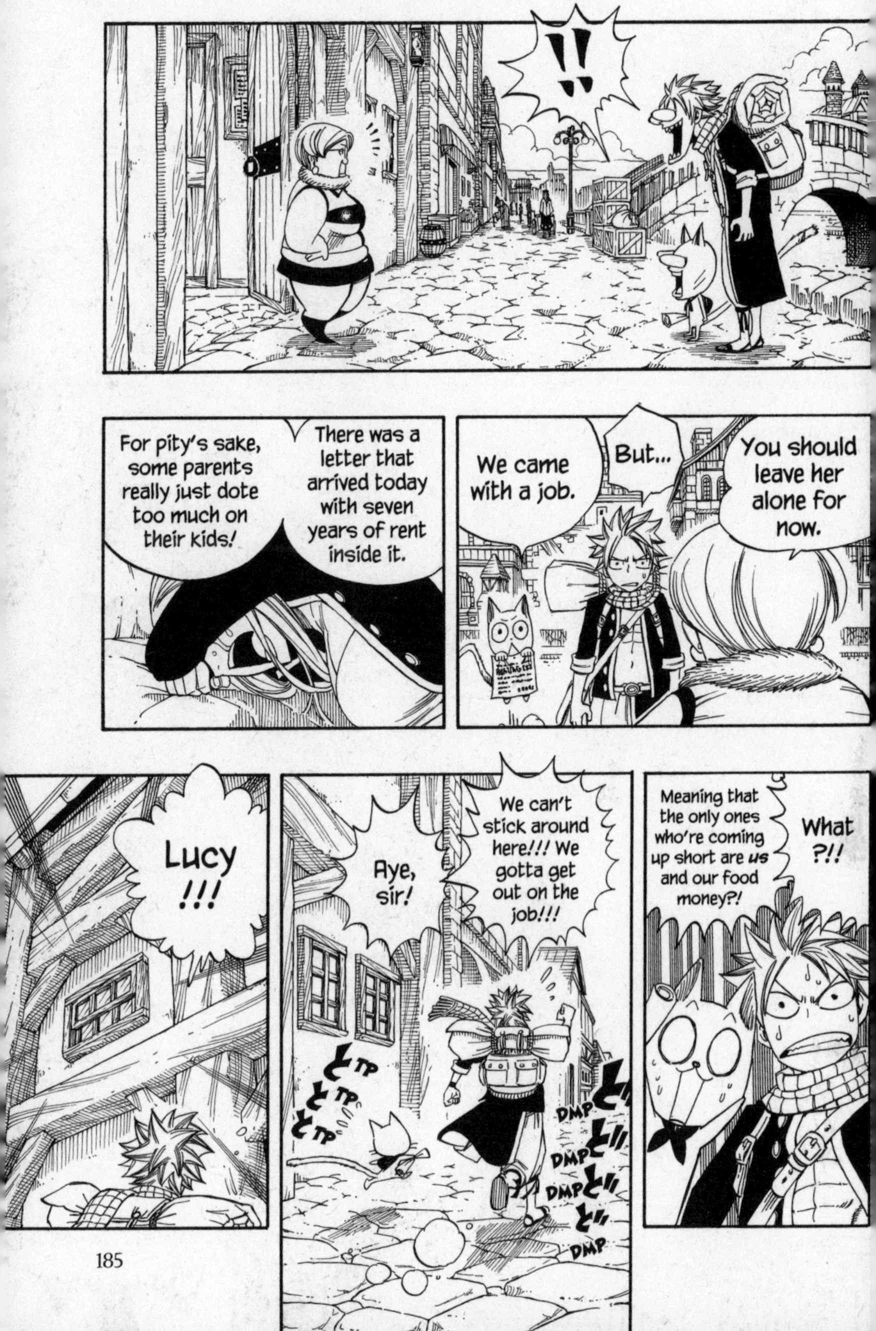
!!
You should leave her alone for now.
But...
We came with a job.
There was a letter that arrived today with seven years of rent inside it.
For pity's sake, some parents really just dote too much on their kids!
What ?!!
Meaning that the only ones who're coming up short are *us* and our food money?!
We can't stick around here!!! We gotta get out on the job!!!
Aye, sir!
DMP DMP DMP DMP
TP TP TP
Lucy !!!

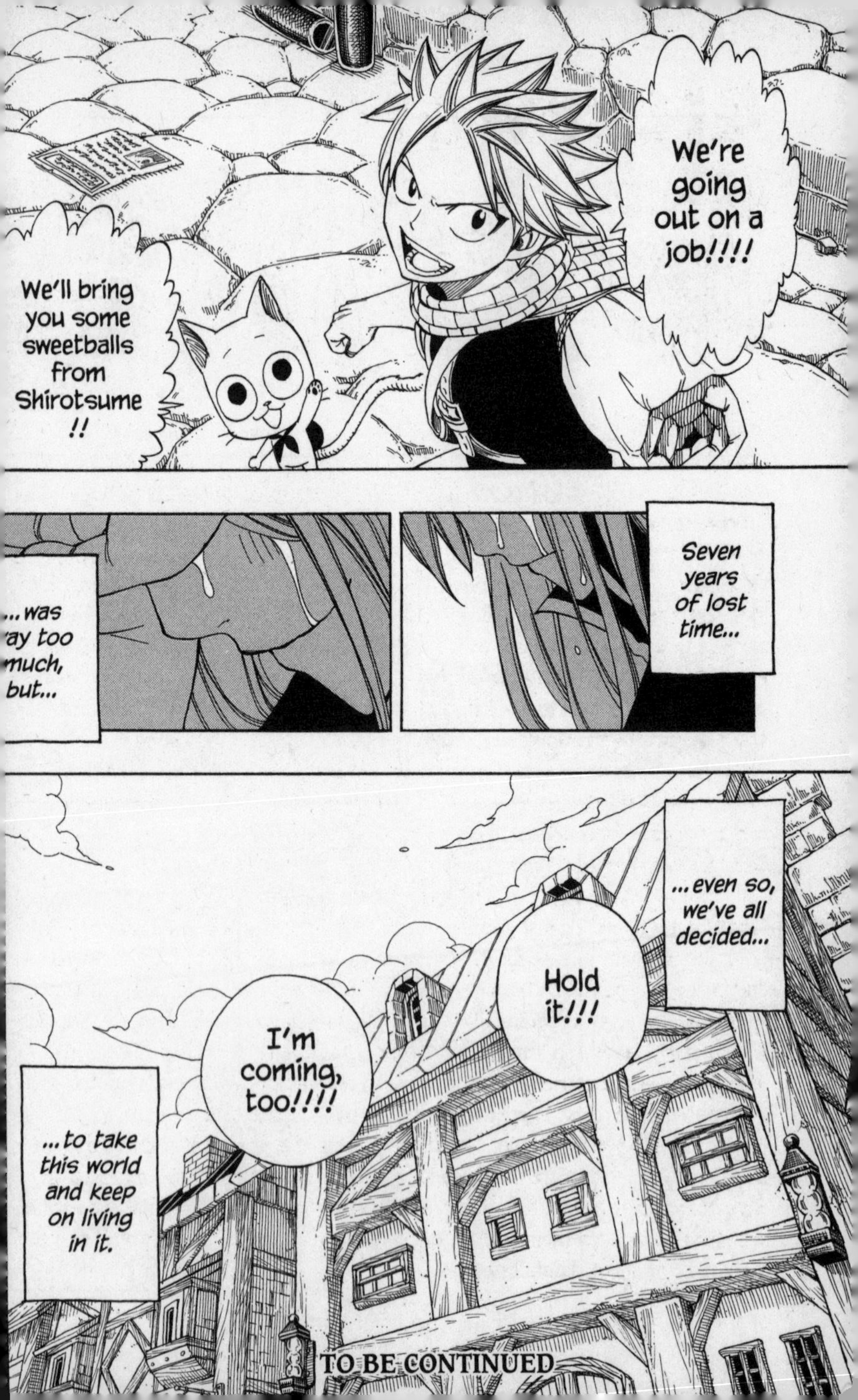
We're going out on a job!!!!
We'll bring you some sweetballs from Shirotsume!!
Seven years of lost time...
...was ay too much, but...
...even so, we've all decided...
Hold it!!!
I'm coming, too!!!!
...to take this world and keep on living in it.
TO BE CONTINUED

Afterword
あとがき

And finally the huge Sirius Island chapter comes to an end. It was long, huh? And there were lots of characters! (cries) The arc that follows on its heels is still just an idea, but it looks like it'll have **even more** characters featured in it that I'll have to draw! It's going to be rough! >_<

Now, the story has gone through a huge change, suddenly becoming a "seven years later" story. I'm sure there were a lot of you who were surprised, huh? When you're drawing a very long series, one way to add a fresh sense to the story is to have time advance within it. It's like a spice. It happens in so many stories that I thought I'd try to do it too, but with a slight difference. It's a pretty over-the-top plot twist to have time pass for everyone but twenty or so of the main characters. You don't see **that** in a whole lot of other stories now, do you? But it has its drawbacks, too. As time passes, the main characters usually get stronger and stronger (leveling up), which seems to be a standard for this genre, but in this case, that doesn't happen. (laughs) Everyone around them has gotten stronger, but they've stayed exactly the same. What's with that?!

And so, even though a lot of time has passed, this isn't really the beginning of Part 2 or anything. It's just going to carry on as the same Fairy Tail.

Now, the Japanese release for the next volume, Vol. 31, is going to have a special edition with an anime DVD included again, but in this one... wait for it... I drew the anime storyboards personally!! I draw the manga roughs all the time, but this was totally different, so it turned out harder than I imagined! Up until this last time, they were all stories based on my manga short stories, but this time, it was a wholly original story. There are all sorts of tricks and twists, so I don't want to give anything away via plot summary, but this is a story that answers a lot of questions, like, "What are those scars on Natsu's neck?" that I got in the early days of the series. Thankfully, the studio put in a lot of energy to take my terrible storyboards and turn them into a really high-quality anime! I think you'll find the story to be very fun! Look forward to it!

Continued from the left-hand page.

: That was an impressive way of running away from the problem.

Mira: Now, the next question is partly about me.

> ***Mira-chan, Elfman, and Lisanna are a sister-brother-sister combination, but when you write the kanji for kyôdai ("siblings"), how do you write it to capture the relationships?***

: In an age where a lot of authors are writing their manga with the foreign market in mind, this question is about as "domestic market" as you can get!

Mira: Let's explain this especially for the sake of those foreign editions!

Lucy: Okay, what this question is about is when the word for "siblings" is written in Japanese kanji, they use the term "kyôdai" which is made up of words for "older brother" and "younger brother." There's also shimai, which is "older sister" "younger sister." But in Mira-san's case...

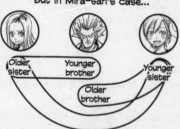

Older sister
Younger brother
Younger sister
Older brother

Th-That does complicate things, huh?

Mira: If we write it, shitei ("older sister" and "younger brother") then we leave out Lisanna, and if it's keimai ("older brother" and "younger sister") then I get left out.

Lucy: And if you just do shimai like we described above, then Elfman is left out. Hmm, that's a tough one...

Mira: I've done a bit of research on this, and it seems that when you have a mixed group like ours, you use all four kanji in the word, keitei-shimai.

: That seems kind of long and unwieldy, huh?

: We could also just not use kanji at all, using the hiragana, kyôdai. Maybe that's best.

Lucy: Finally, we have one more question that concerns Mira-san.

> ***Could you tell me Mirajane's and Elfman's family name?***

Mira: Huh? Haven't we ever mentioned it?

Lucy: Seems strange, but I don't think it's ever been officially revealed.

Mira: Our family name is "Strauss."

: Mirajane Strauss, Elfman Strauss, Lisanna Strauss... Really...? I never knew.

: Tswee!! Tswee!!

: And this little one shares the same family name too! Alexandria Strauss!

: So you've taken that weird-voiced dog... and officially made it your pet...

EXPLAIN THE MYSTERIES OF FAIRY TAIL!
EMERGENCY REQUEST!

At the broken-down guild...

: Seven years have gone by.

: Seven whole years, huh?

Lucy: Honestly!! What is this?! What a stupid plot twist!! I'm sure we're going to get a ton of mail with all the mistakes that the readers have caught!

Mira: No, a lot of them are here already.

Lucy: Aw, geez! >_<

Mira: Now, the first question.

What happened to the scene of Natsu crying that Carla foresaw in Volume 24?

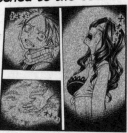

Lucy: We got this question a *lot!*

Mira: It's because the author is coming up with images without figuring out where to put them...

: Y-You're not supposed to say that...

Mira: The plan for this scene was to put it in when Natsu fights Gildarts. Toward the end, Natsu admits that he's been defeated and breaks down. That was where it was supposed to go.

Now go become an S-Class wizard, Natsu!!!

Lucy: Looking at the two of them together, they're completely different!

Mira: By the way, Cana's scene is from Vol. 28, page 42, and the scene with the hand was from Vol. 27, page 61.

Lucy: That was *my* hand, huh? But, come on!! Natsu's scene was just too awful! I can see why none of the readers understood it!

: Now, now... Remember that this was just a "premonition." The future doesn't always turn out exactly that way. We can leave it at that, right?

Continued on the right-hand page.

The Fairy Tail Guild is looking for illustrations! Please send in your art on a postcard or at postcard size, and do it in black pen, okay? Those chosen to be published will get a signed mini poster! ♪ Make sure you write your real name and address on the back of your illustration!

TAIL d'ART

Nagasaki Prefecture, YOU

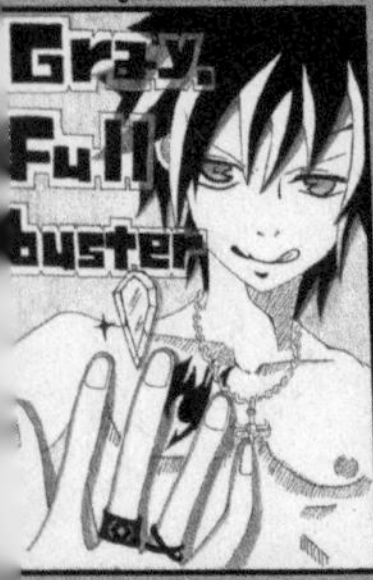
Gray.
Full
buster

▲Woow!! This drawing's really good!! Apparently Gray is really popular in America, too!!

Kyoto, Marina Murakami

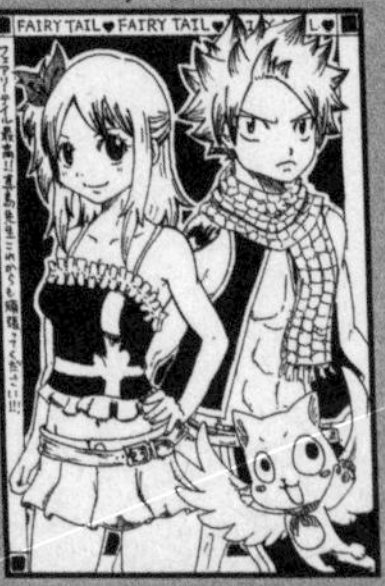
FAIRY TAIL♥FAIRY TAIL

▲As I thought, this team-up is the best!!

It's the three who are always together!! Oh? Plue is there too!! ▶

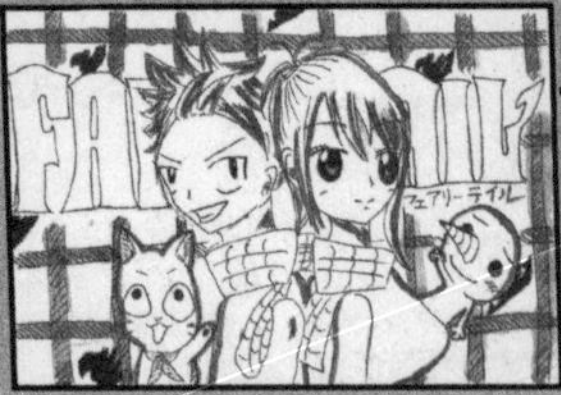
フェアリーテイル

Yamaguchi Prefecture, Fuku-chan

Yamaguchi Prefecture, Fuku-chan's Little Brother

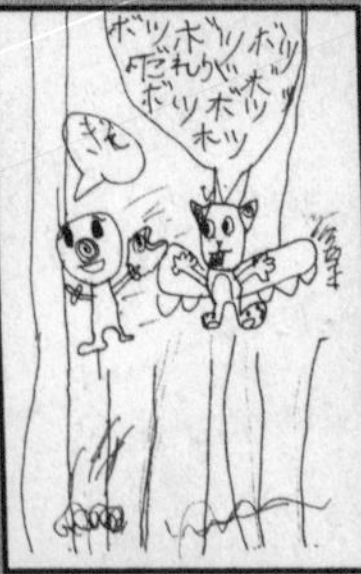

▲I don't know. Happy and Plue are both incredibly cute!

▼Mother and child both sent in their pictures! And Mom's great at drawing!!

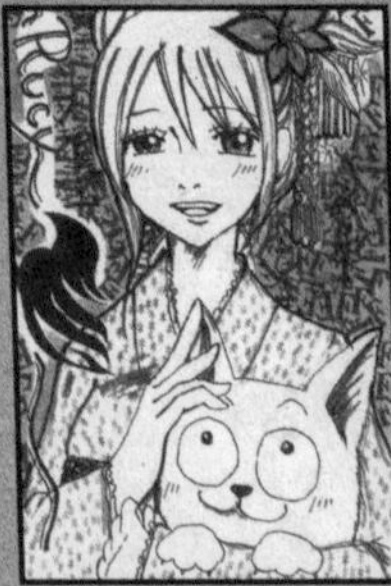

Yamaguchi Prefecture, Fuku-chan's Mom

Osaka, Macaroon

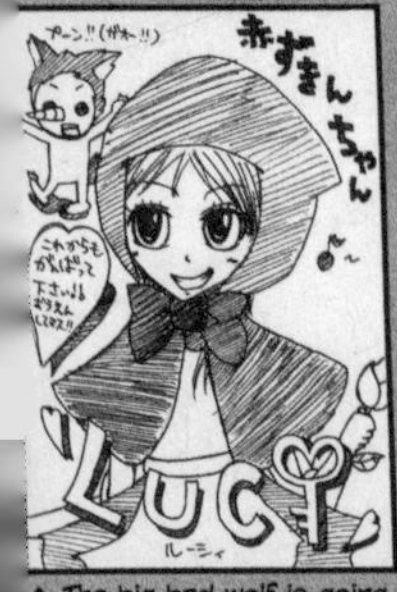
赤ずきんちゃん
LUCY
ルーシィ

▲The big bad wolf is going to eat you! But wait, the big bad wolf is Plue!

Gunma Prefecture, Alice

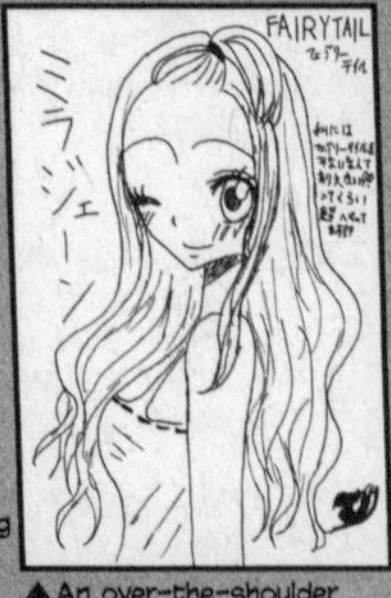
FAIRYTAIL
フェアリーテイル
ミラジェーン

▲An over-the-shoulder Mira-chan. The question corner this time was filled with Mira-chan's secrets!

Whoa, cute!! I'd like to see these come out as mascots! ▶

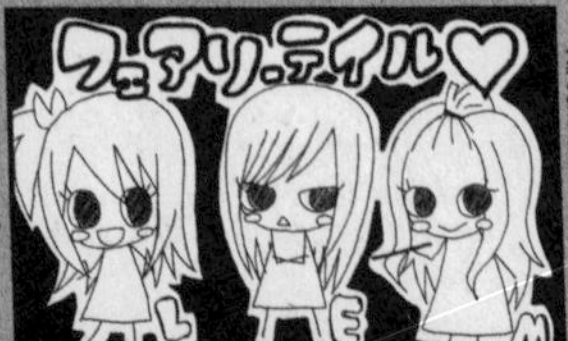
フェアリーテイル♥
L
E
M

Hiroshima Prefecture, Kuroneko

Send to Hiro Mashima, Kodansha Comics
451 Park Ave. South, 7th Floor New York, NY 10016

FAIRY GUILD

By sending in letters or postcards you give us permission to give your name, address, postal code and any other information you include to the author as is. Please keep that in mind.

Niigata Prefecture, Miyu Maruyama

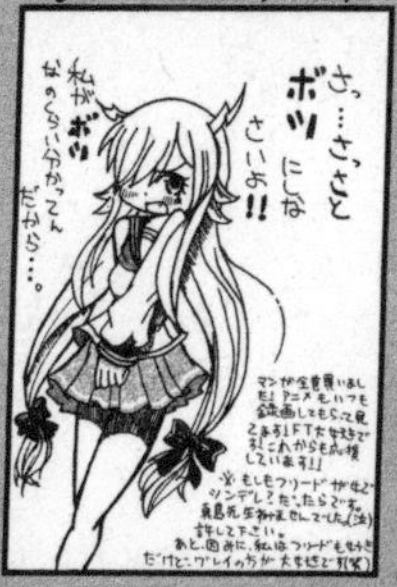
ボツ

▲Wow!! This is so moe! I don't know what to do! It's too cute!

Fukuoka Prefecture, Hiyoyokko

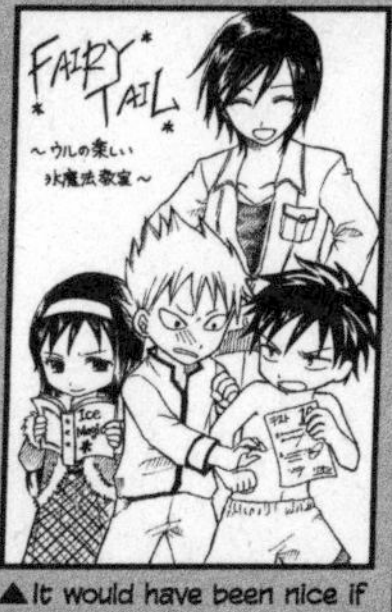
FAIRY TAIL

▲It would have been nice if they could all have had a fun childhood like that.

Fukushima Prefecture, Masami Kobayash

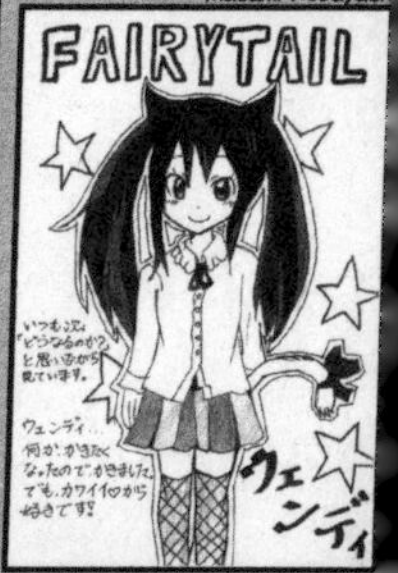
FAIRYTAIL
ウェンディ

▲This drawing is really cute! Wonderful!♡

REJECTION CORNER

Osaka, Wataru Tsuyuguchi

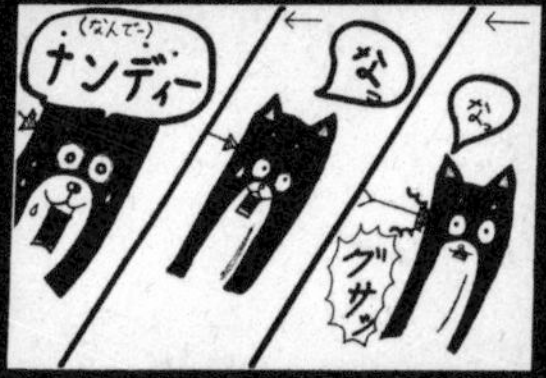
(なんでー)
ナンディー
グサッ

Gradually, gradually, the arrow hits. What is with how surreal this is?!◀

Kanagawa Prefecture, Akiteru

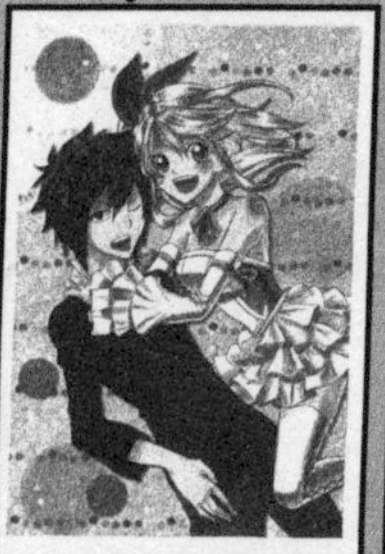

▲That's soo good! A two-shot with Gray and Lucy! That's actually pretty rare.

Saitama Prefecture, Aika Kubo

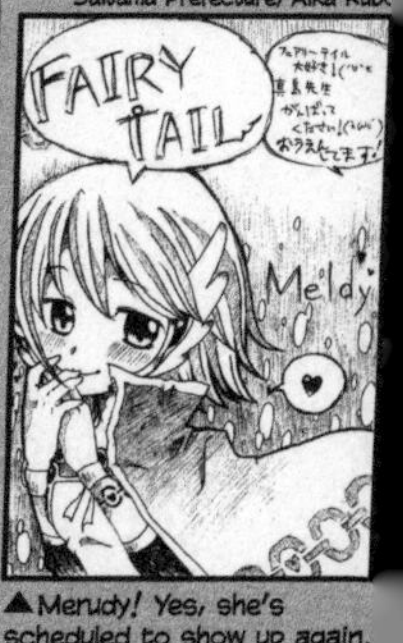
FAIRY TAIL
Meldy

▲Merudy! Yes, she's scheduled to show up again.

Shiga Prefecture, Yuka Takano

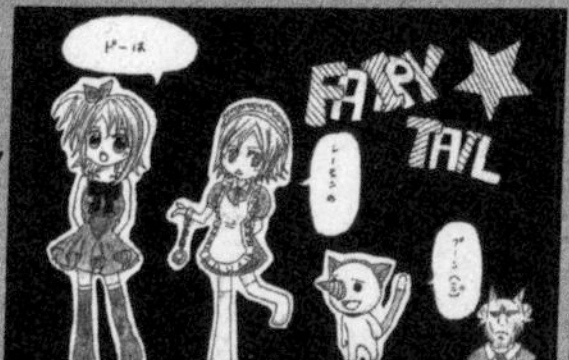
FAIRY TAIL

Don't know what everyone is saying, but they're all so cute!▶

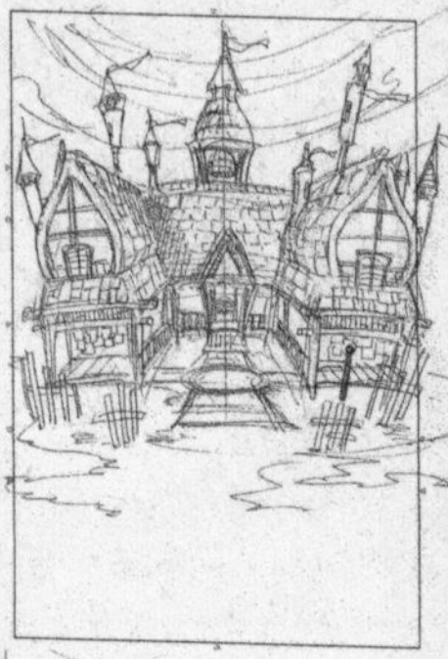

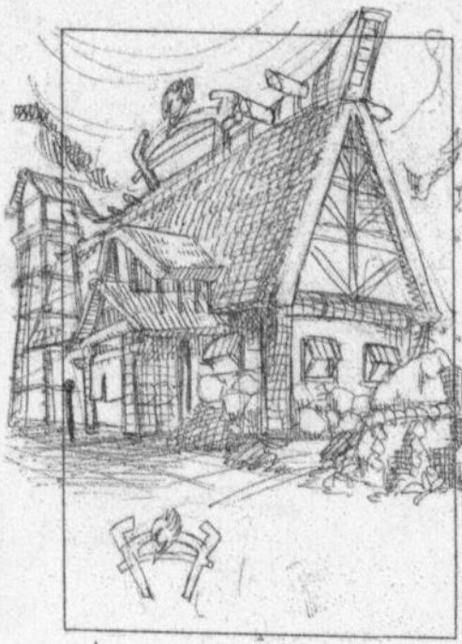

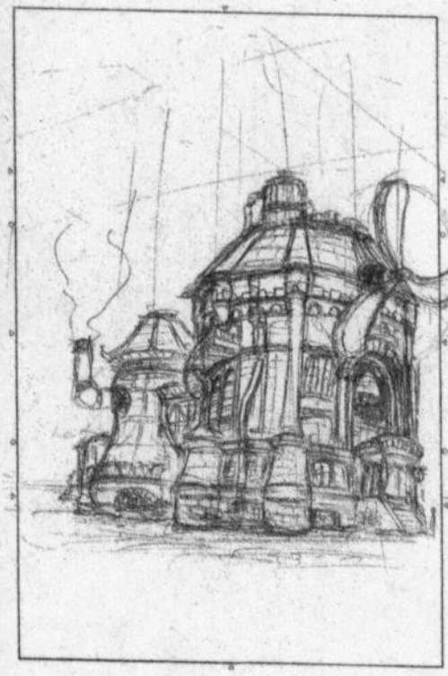

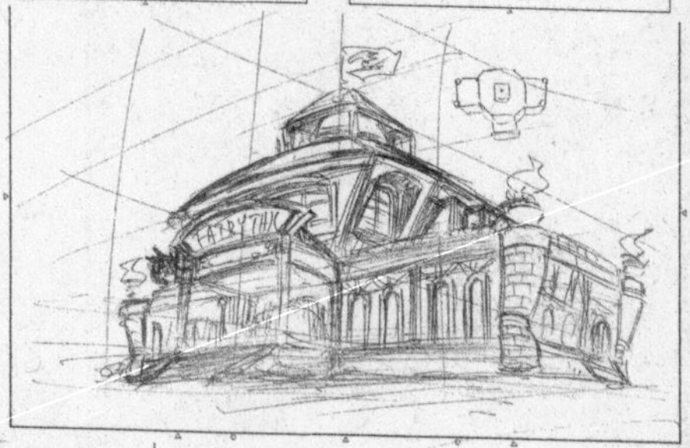
FAIRY TAIL

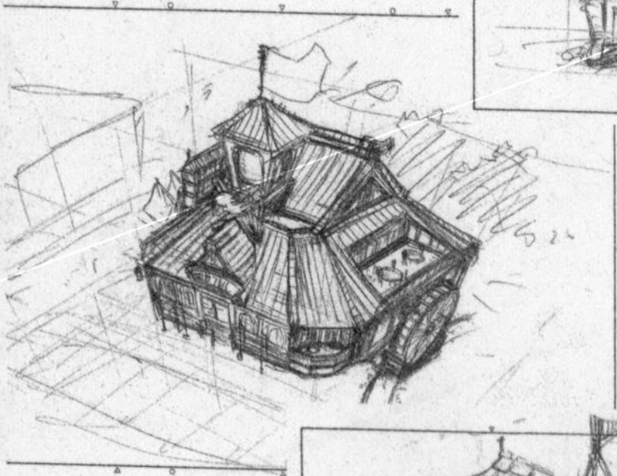

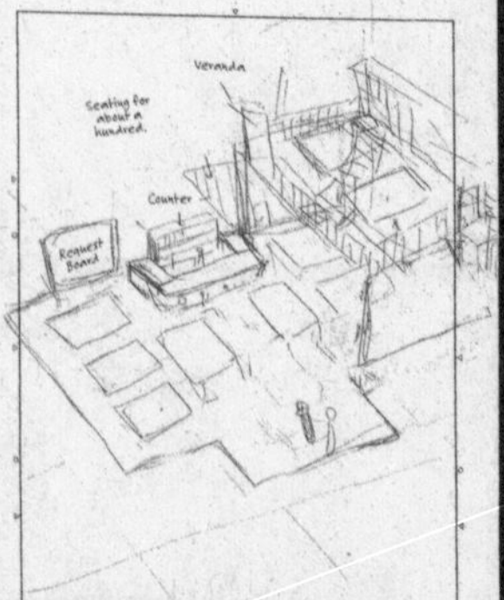
Veranda
Seating for about a hundred.
Counter
Request Board

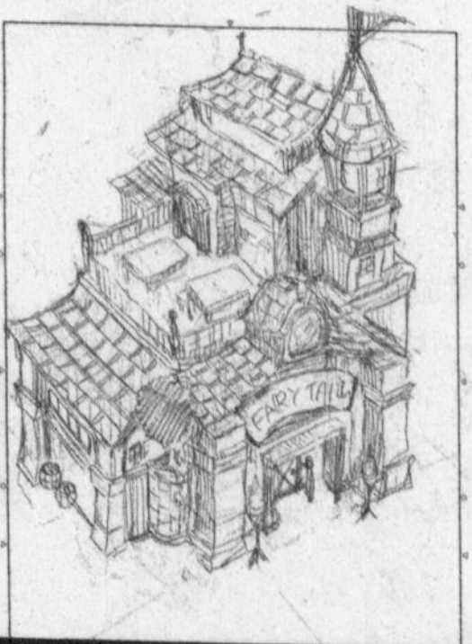
FAIRY TAIL

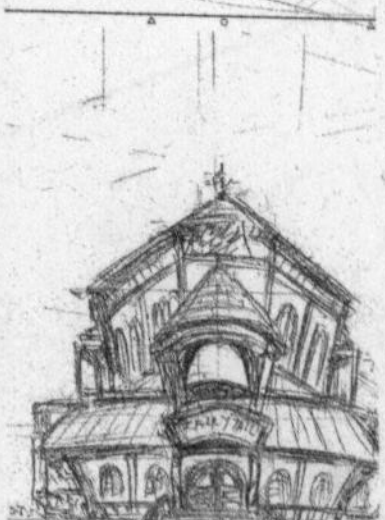

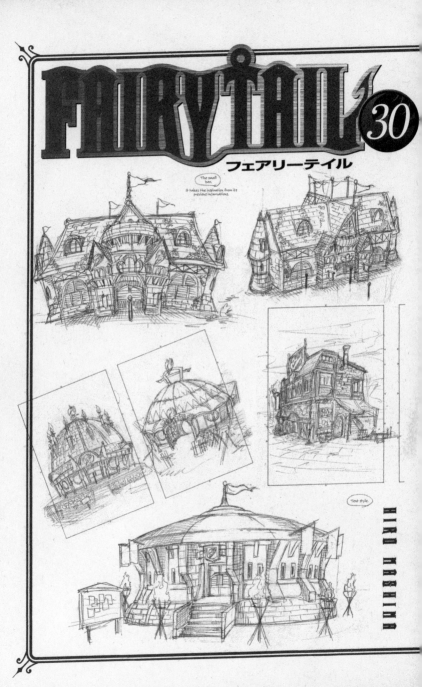

FAIRY TAIL 30

フェアリーテイル

The small bar.

It takes the inspiration from its previous incarnations.

Text style.

HIRO MASHIMA

FROM HIRO MASHIMA

I went to a signing in New York City, and these are a few of the Fairy Tail cosplayers who were nice enough to meet me there. There were plenty more! In fact, so many people came out to see me that words can't express my gratitude. I've gotten a renewed enthusiasm to make sure my stories are aimed at the whole world! Also, that Ichiya costume looked almost too good! (laughs). I'm so happy there are people in America who see how good that character is.

Original Jacket Design: Hisao Ogawa

Translation Notes:

Japanese is a tricky language for most Westerners, and translation is often more art than science. For your edification and reading pleasure, here are notes on some of the places where we could have gone in a different direction with our translation of the work, or where a Japanese cultural reference is used.

Page 159, 5,880,000 Jewels

As we mentioned back in the notes of Volume 1, the currency in Earth-land is based essentially on Japanese currency, and a quick way to get an approximate idea of how much they're talking about in dollars is to take off the final two digits (the final two zeros). Then, you would get the number "58,800," or something on the order of about $60,000. Not as bad as six million, but still way out of the range of a teenager like Lucy.

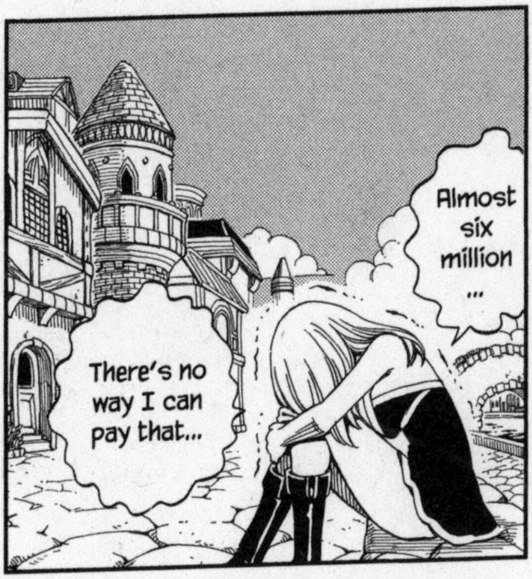
Almost six million ...
There's no way I can pay that...

Page 162, -dono

As mentioned in previous notes, *-dono* is an honorific much like *–sama*, one that indicates a lot of respect. But it is also somewhat archaic and is not used in everyday society. It gives off a sort of medieval feel.

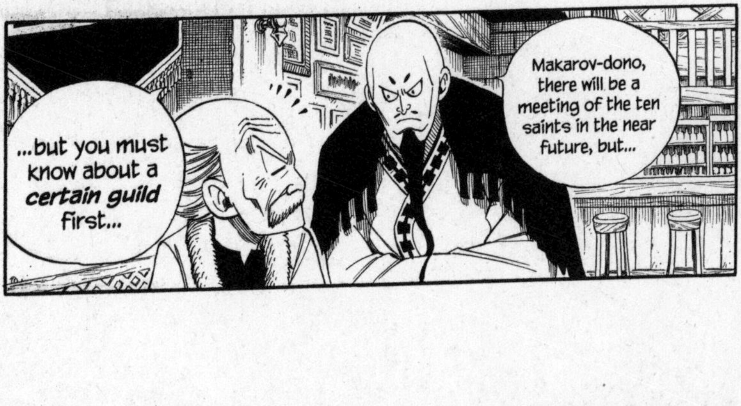
Makarov-dono, there will be a meeting of the ten saints in the near future, but...
...but you must know about a *certain guild* first...

Preview of *Fairy Tail*, volume 31

We're pleased to present you with a preview from Fairy Tail, volume 31, which will be released digitally in June 2013 and in print in September. See our Web site (www.kodanshacomics.com) for more details!

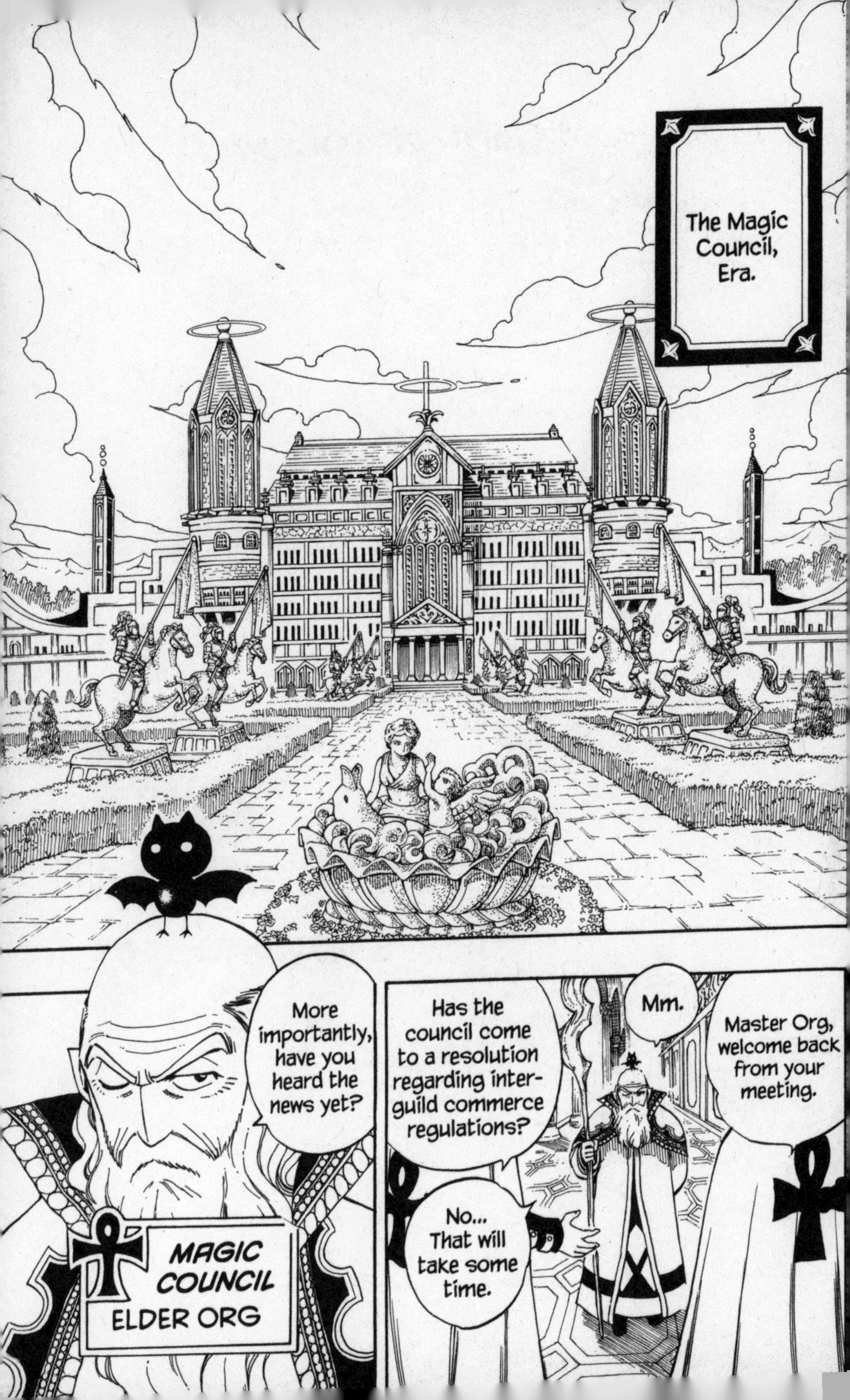
The Magic Council, Era.
Master Org, welcome back from your meeting.
Mm.
Has the council come to a resolution regarding inter-guild commerce regulations?
No... That will take some time.
More importantly, have you heard the news yet?
MAGIC COUNCIL ELDER ORG

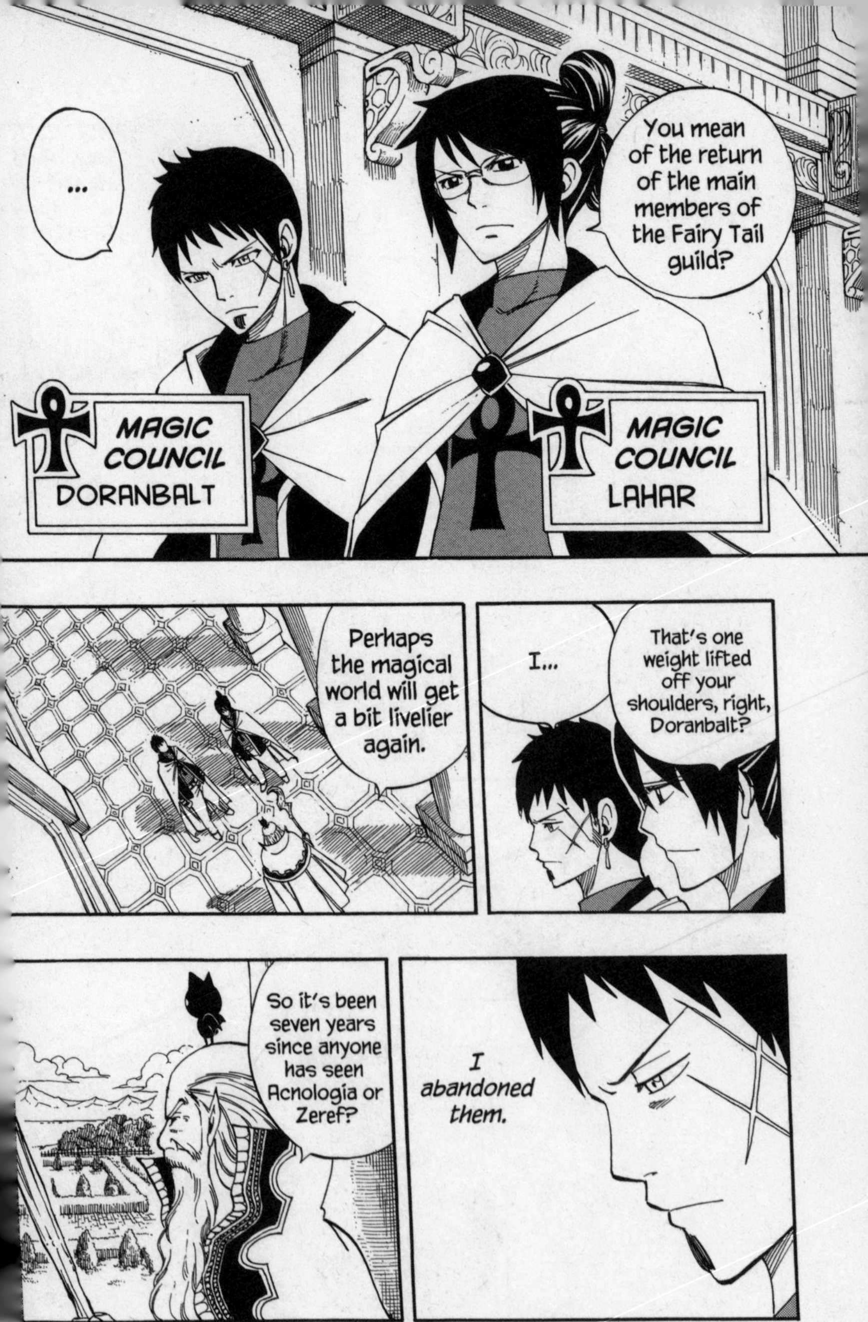
You mean of the return of the main members of the Fairy Tail guild?
...
MAGIC COUNCIL LAHAR
MAGIC COUNCIL DORANBALT
That's one weight lifted off your shoulders, right, Doranbalt?
I...
Perhaps the magical world will get a bit livelier again.
I abandoned them.
So it's been seven years since anyone has seen Acnologia or Zeref?

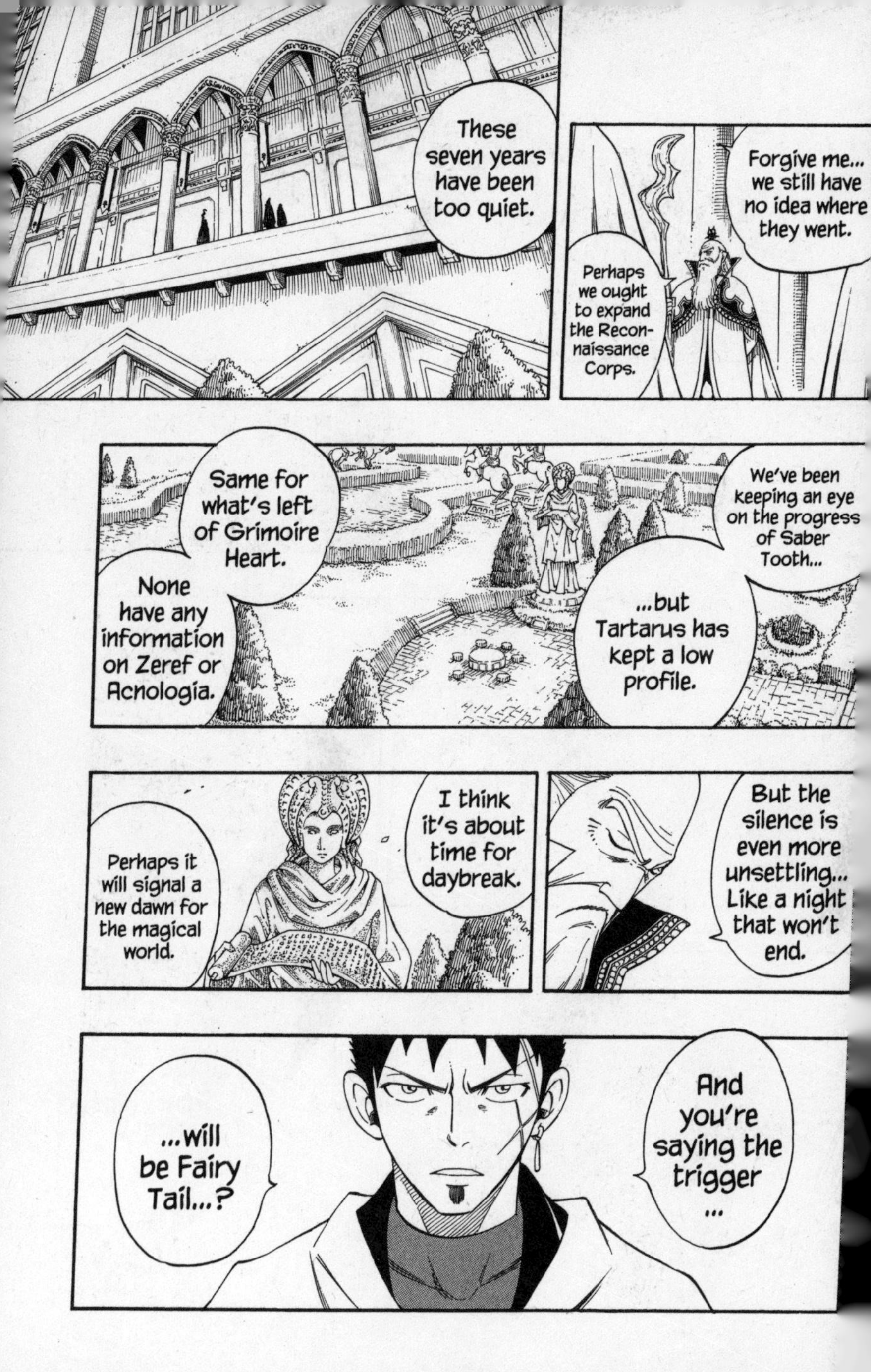
Forgive me... we still have no idea where they went.
Perhaps we ought to expand the Recon-naissance Corps.
These seven years have been too quiet.
We've been keeping an eye on the progress of Saber Tooth...
...but Tartarus has kept a low profile.
Same for what's left of Grimoire Heart.
None have any information on Zeref or Acnologia.
But the silence is even more unsettling... Like a night that won't end.
I think it's about time for daybreak.
Perhaps it will signal a new dawn for the magical world.
And you're saying the trigger ...
...will be Fairy Tail...?

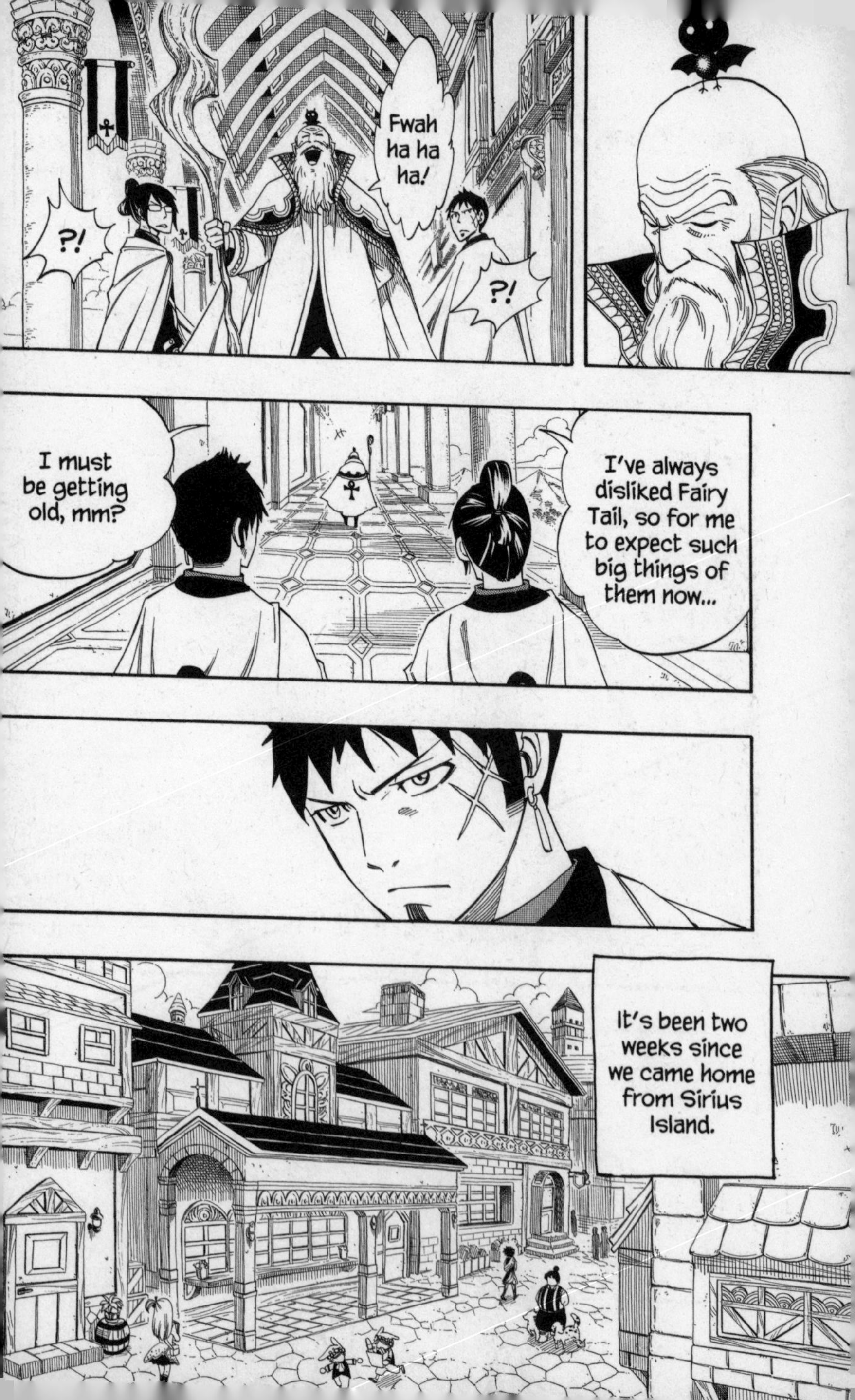
Fwah ha ha ha!
?!
?!
I've always disliked Fairy Tail, so for me to expect such big things of them now...
I must be getting old, mm?
It's been two weeks since we came home from Sirius Island.

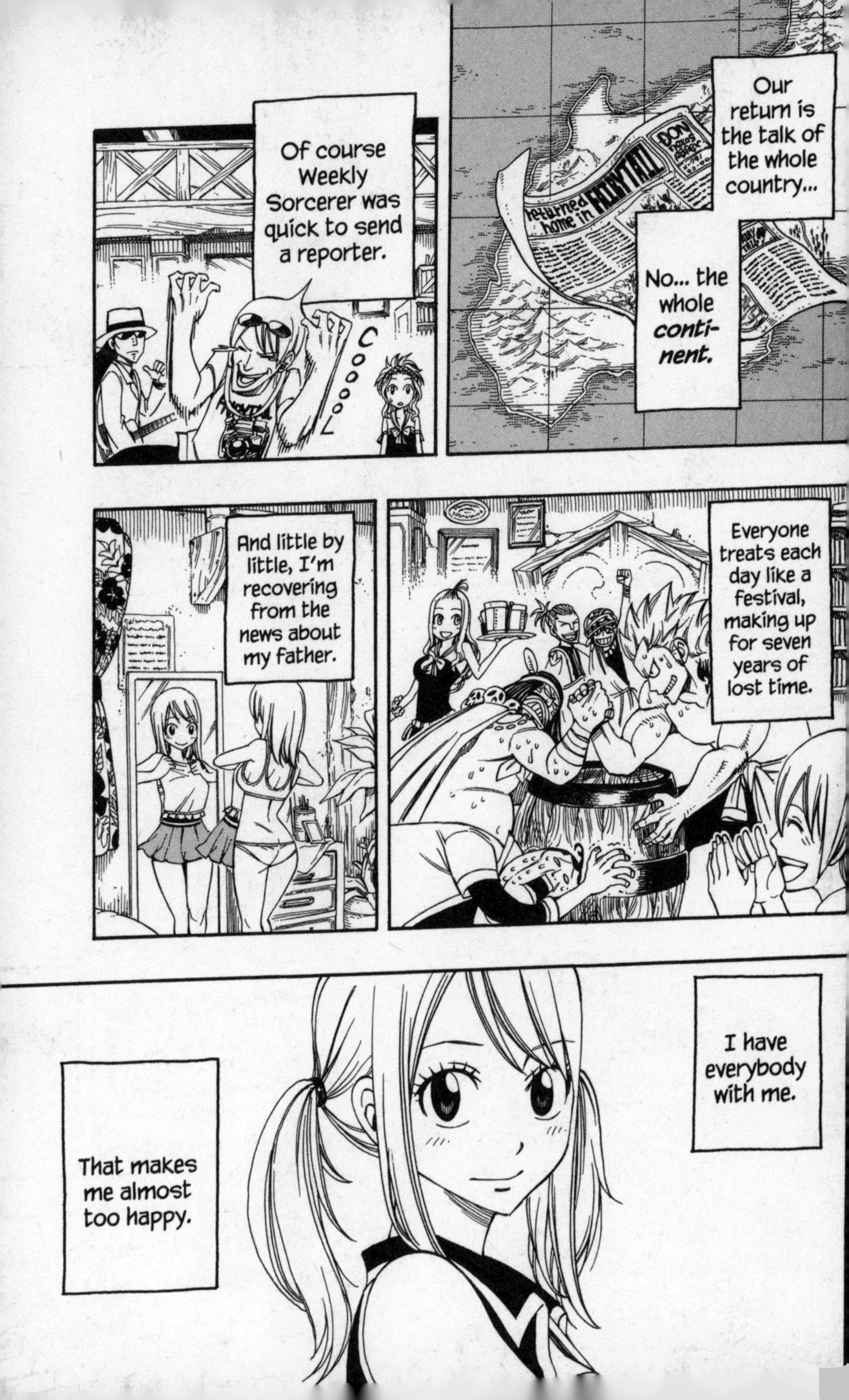
Our return is the talk of the whole country...
returned home in
FAIRY TAIL
No... the whole *conti-nent.*
Of course Weekly Sorcerer was quick to send a reporter.
COOOOOL
Everyone treats each day like a festival, making up for seven years of lost time.
And little by little, I'm recovering from the news about my father.
I have everybody with me.
That makes me almost too happy.

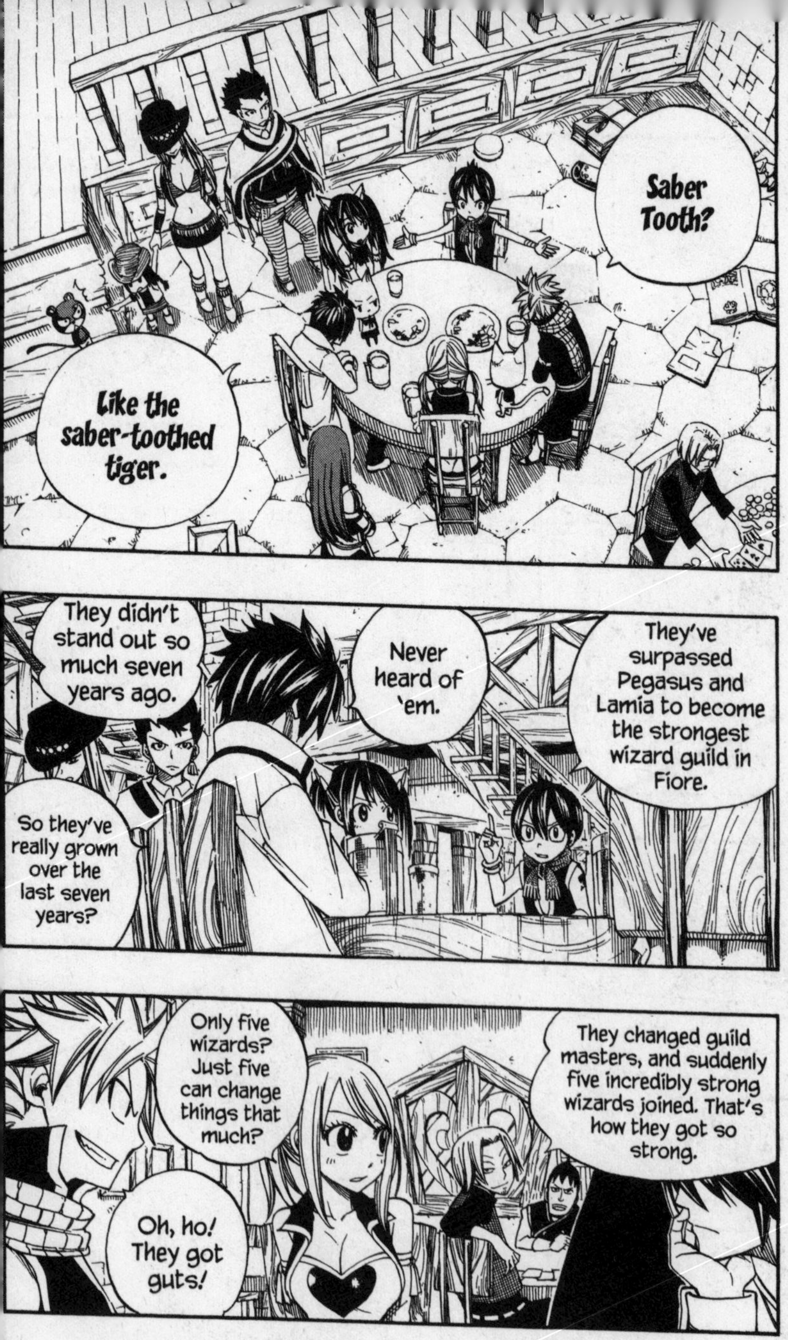
Saber Tooth?
Like the saber-toothed tiger.
They've surpassed Pegasus and Lamia to become the strongest wizard guild in Fiore.
Never heard of 'em.
They didn't stand out so much seven years ago.
So they've really grown over the last seven years?
They changed guild masters, and suddenly five incredibly strong wizards joined. That's how they got so strong.
Only five wizards? Just five can change things that much?
Oh, ho! They got guts!

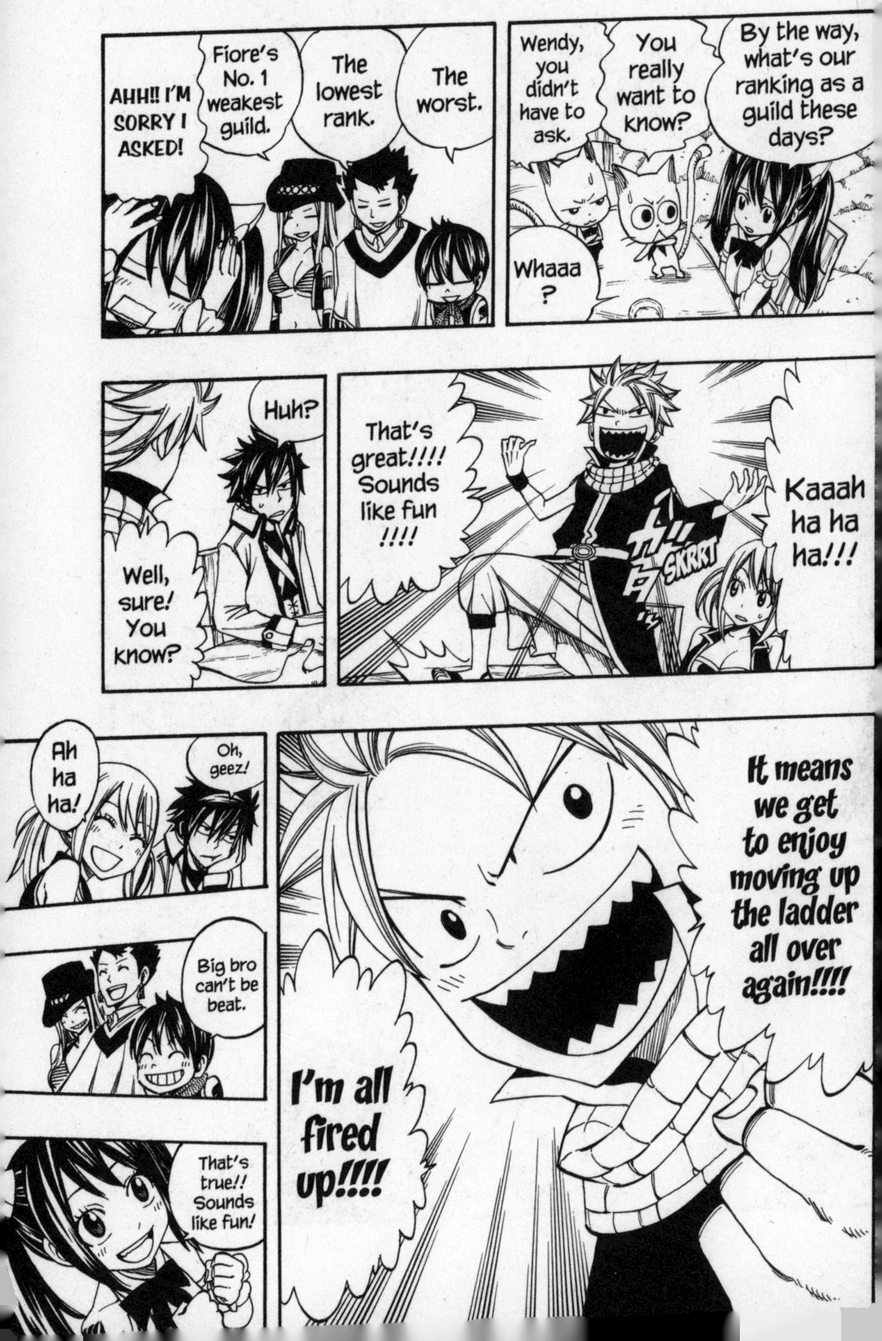
By the way, what's our ranking as a guild these days?
You really want to know?
Wendy, you didn't have to ask.
Whaaa?
The worst.
The lowest rank.
Fiore's No. 1 weakest guild.
AHH!! I'M SORRY I ASKED!
Kaaah ha ha ha!!!
That's great!!!! Sounds like fun !!!!
SKRRT
Huh?
Well, sure! You know?
It means we get to enjoy moving up the ladder all over again!!!!
I'm all fired up!!!!
Oh, geez!
Ah ha ha!
Big bro can't be beat.
That's true!! Sounds like fun!

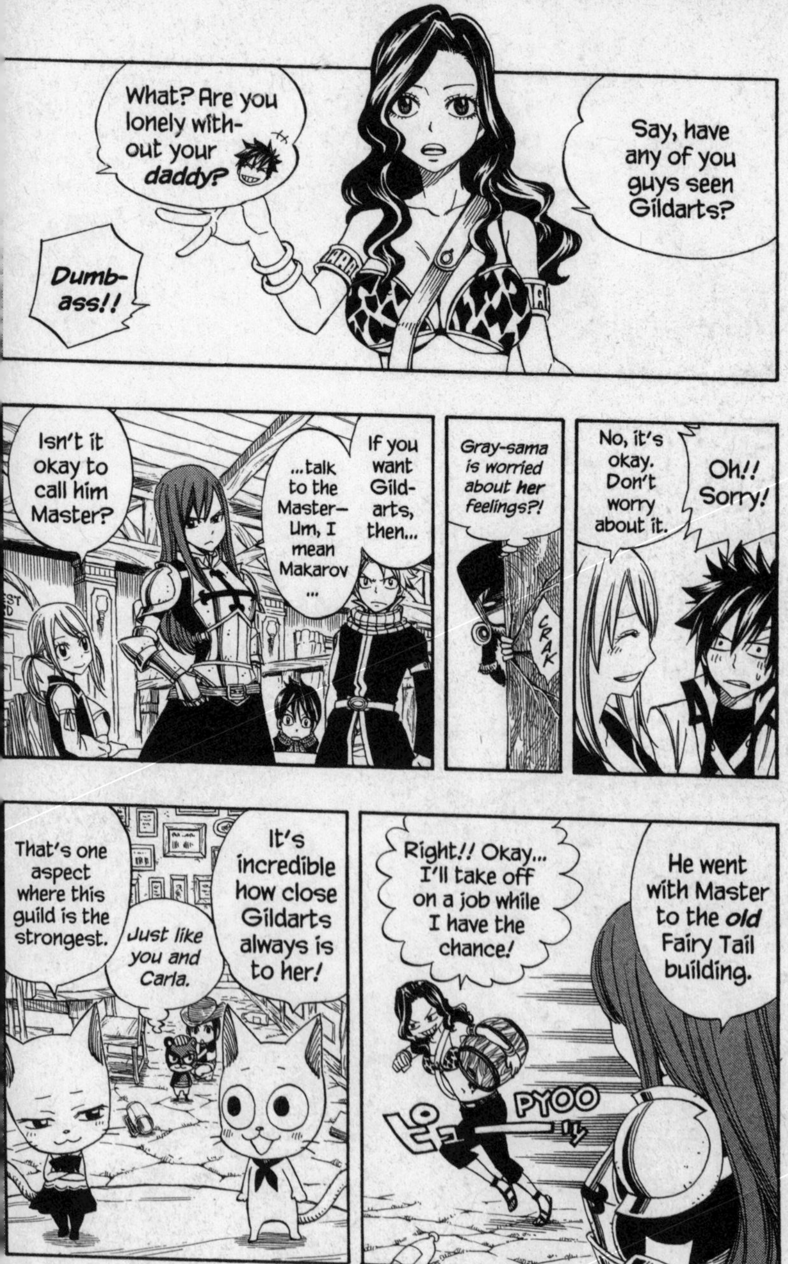
Say, have any of you guys seen Gildarts?
What? Are you lonely without your daddy?
Dumbass!!
Oh!! Sorry!
No, it's okay. Don't worry about it.
Gray-sama is worried about her feelings?!
CRAK
If you want Gildarts, then...
...talk to the Master— Um, I mean Makarov ...
Isn't it okay to call him Master?
He went with Master to the old Fairy Tail building.
Right!! Okay... I'll take off on a job while I have the chance!
PYOO
It's incredible how close Gildarts always is to her!
Just like you and Carla.
That's one aspect where this guild is the strongest.

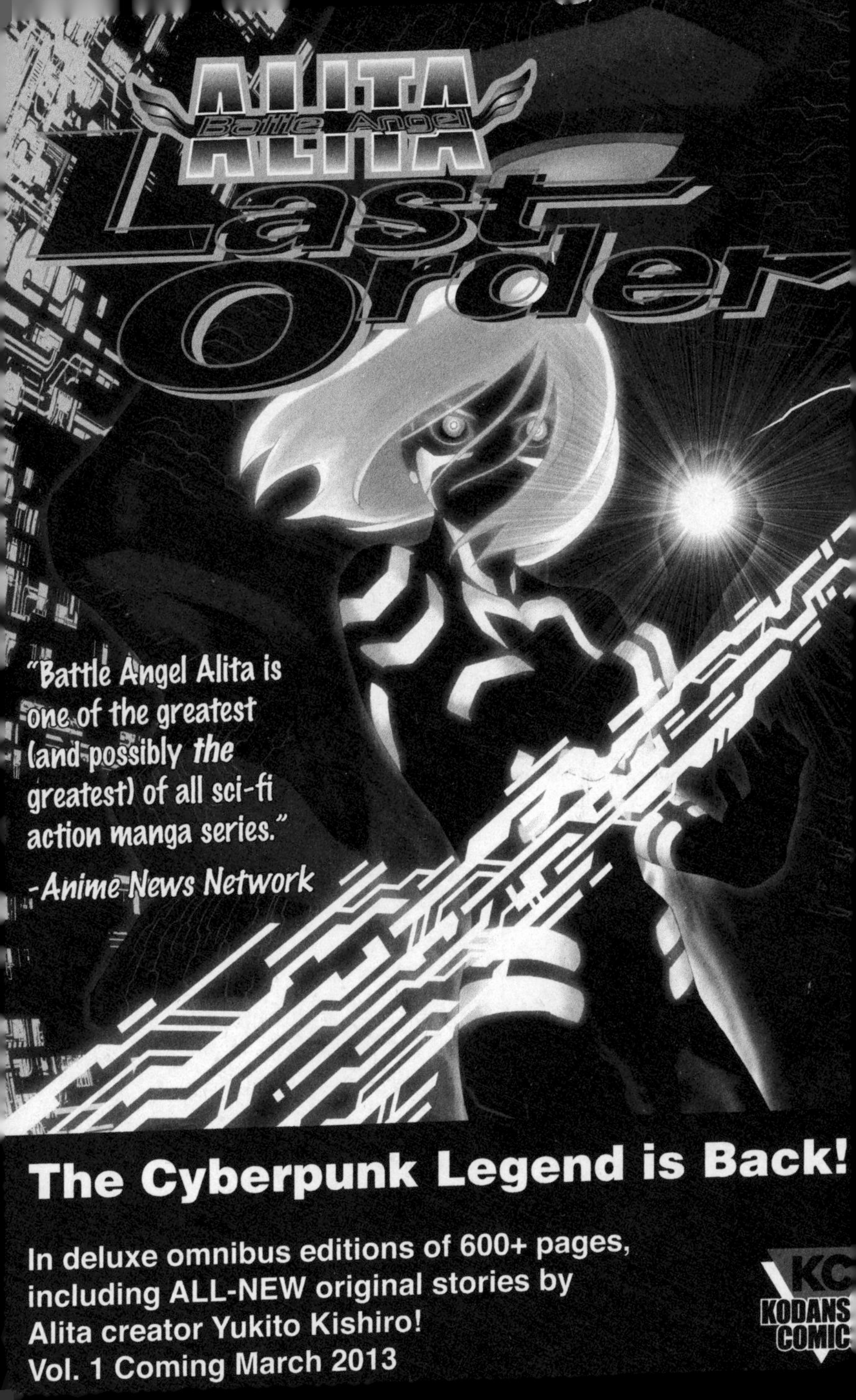
ALITA
Battle Angel
ALITA
Last Order
"Battle Angel Alita is one of the greatest (and possibly *the* greatest) of all sci-fi action manga series."
-Anime News Network

ATTACK ON TITAN

Humanity has been decimated!

A century ago, the bizarre creatures known as Titans devoured most of the world's population, driving the remainder into a walled stronghold. Now, the appearance of an immense new Titan threatens the few humans left, and one restless boy decides to seize the chance to fight for his freedom, and the survival of his species!

KC
KODANSHA COMICS

Fairy Tail volume 30 is a work of fiction. Names, characters, places, and incidents are the products of the author's imagination or are used fictitiously. Any resemblance to actual events, locales, or persons, living or dead, is entirely coincidental.

A Kodansha Comics Trade Paperback Original.

Published in the United States by Kodansha Comics, an imprint of Kodansha USA Publishing, LLC, New York.

Publication rights for this English edition arranged through Kodansha Ltd., Tokyo.

First published in Japan in 2011 by Kodansha Ltd., Tokyo
ISBN 978-1-61262-407-5

Printed in the United States of America.

www.kodanshacomics.com

9 8 7 6 5 4 3 2 1

Translator: William Flanagan
Lettering: AndWorld Design

TOMARE!

止まれ
[STOP!]

You're going the wrong way!

Manga is a completely different type of reading experience.

To start at the *beginning*, go to the *end!*

That's right! Authentic manga is read the traditional Japanese way—from right to left, exactly the *opposite* of how American books are read. It's easy to follow: Just go to the other end of the book and read each page—and each panel—from right side to left side, starting at the top right. Now you're experiencing manga as it was meant to be!